VOLUME 493                                          SEPTEMBER 1987

# THE ANNALS

*of* The American Academy *of* Political
*and* Social Science

RICHARD D. LAMBERT, *Editor*
ALAN W. HESTON, *Associate Editor*

## THE INFORMAL ECONOMY

*Special Editors of this Volume*

### LOUIS A. FERMAN

*Institute of Industrial and Labor Relations*
*University of Michigan*
*Ann Arbor*

### STUART HENRY

*Department of Sociology*
*Eastern Michigan University*
*Ypsilanti*

### MICHELE HOYMAN

*Department of Political Science*
*University of Missouri*
*Saint Louis*

§ SAGE PUBLICATIONS  *NEWBURY PARK  BEVERLY HILLS  LONDON  NEW DELHI*

# THE ANNALS

© 1987 *by* The American Academy *of* Political *and* Social Science

ERICA GINSBURG, *Assistant Editor*

*Editorial Office:* 3937 Chestnut Street, Philadelphia, Pennsylvania 19104.

*For information about membership\* (individuals only) and subscriptions (institutions), address:*

SAGE PUBLICATIONS, INC.

| | |
|---|---|
| 2111 West Hillcrest Drive | 275 South Beverly Drive |
| Newbury Park, CA 91320 | Beverly Hills, CA 90212 |

| *From India and South Asia,* | *From the UK, Europe, the Middle* |
|---|---|
| *write to:* | *East and Africa, write to:* |
| SAGE PUBLICATIONS INDIA Pvt. Ltd. | SAGE PUBLICATIONS LTD |
| P.O. Box 4215 | 28 Banner Street |
| New Delhi 110 048 | London EC1Y 8QE |
| INDIA | ENGLAND |

*SAGE Production Editors:* JANET BROWN and ASTRID VIRDING

*\* Please note that members of The Academy receive THE ANNALS with their membership.*

Library of Congress Catalog Card Number 86-061221
International Standard Serial Number ISSN 0002-7162
International Standard Book Number ISBN 0-8039-2936-6 (Vol. 493, 1987 paper)
International Standard Book Number ISBN 0-8039-2935-8 (Vol. 493, 1987 cloth)
Manufactured in the United States of America. First printing, September 1987.

The articles appearing in THE ANNALS are indexed in *Book Review Index; Public Affairs Information Service Bulletin; Social Sciences Index; Monthly Periodical Index; Current Contents; Behavioral, Social Management Sciences;* and *Combined Retrospective Index Sets.* They are also abstracted and indexed in *ABC Pol Sci, Historical Abstracts, Human Resources Abstracts, Social Sciences Citation Index, United States Political Science Documents, Social Work Research & Abstracts, Peace Research Reviews, Sage Urban Studies Abstracts, International Political Science Abstracts, America: History and Life,* and/or *Family Resources Database.*

Information about membership rates, institutional subscriptions, and back issue prices may be found on the facing page.

**Advertising.** Current rates and specifications may be obtained by writing to THE ANNALS Advertising and Promotion Manager at the Newbury Park office (address above).

**Claims.** Claims for undelivered copies must be made no later than three months following month of publication. The publisher will supply missing copies when losses have been sustained in transit and when the reserve stock will permit.

**Change of Address.** Six weeks' advance notice must be given when notifying of change of address to insure proper identification. Please specify name of journal. Send change of address to: THE ANNALS, c/o Sage Publications, Inc., 2111 West Hillcrest Drive, Newbury Park, CA 91320.

**Origin and Purpose.** The Academy was organized December 14, 1889, to promote the progress of political and social science, especially through publications and meetings. The Academy does not take sides in controverted questions, but seeks to gather and present reliable information to assist the public in forming an intelligent and accurate judgment.

**Meetings.** The Academy holds an annual meeting in the spring extending over two days.

**Publications.** THE ANNALS is the bimonthly publication of The Academy. Each issue contains articles on some prominent social or political problem, written at the invitation of the editors. Also, monographs are published from time to time, numbers of which are distributed to pertinent professional organizations. These volumes constitute important reference works on the topics with which they deal, and they are extensively cited by authorities throughout the United States and abroad. The papers presented at the meetings of The Academy are included in THE ANNALS.

**Membership.** Each member of The Academy receives THE ANNALS and may attend the meetings of The Academy. Membership is open only to individuals. Annual dues: $28.00 for the regular paperbound edition (clothbound, $42.00). Add $9.00 per year for membership outside the U.S.A. Members may also purchase single issues of THE ANNALS for $6.95 each (clothbound, $10.00).

**Subscriptions.** THE ANNALS (ISSN 0002-7162) is published six times annually—in January, March, May, July, September, and November. Institutions may subscribe to THE ANNALS at the annual rate: $60.00 (clothbound, $78.00). Add $9.00 per year for subscriptions outside the U.S.A. Institutional rates for single issues: $10.00 each (clothbound, $15.00).

Second class postage paid at Philadelphia, Pennsylvania, and at additional mailing offices.

Single issues of THE ANNALS may be obtained by individuals who are not members of The Academy for $7.95 each (clothbound, $15.00). Single issues of THE ANNALS have proven to be excellent supplementary texts for classroom use. Direct inquiries regarding adoptions to THE ANNALS c/o Sage Publications (address below).

All correspondence concerning membership in The Academy, dues renewals, inquiries about membership status, and/or purchase of single issues of THE ANNALS should be sent to THE ANNALS c/o Sage Publications, Inc., 2111 West Hillcrest Drive, Newbury Park, CA 91320. *Please note that orders under $25 must be prepaid.* Sage affiliates in London and India will assist institutional subscribers abroad with regard to orders, claims, and inquiries for both subscriptions and single issues.

# THE ANNALS

## *of* The American Academy *of* Political *and* Social Science

**RICHARD D. LAMBERT,** *Editor*
**ALAN W. HESTON,** *Associate Editor*

———————————— FORTHCOMING ————————————


### POLICIES TO PREVENT CRIME: NEIGHBORHOOD, FAMILY, AND EMPLOYMENT STRATEGIES
Special Editor: Lynn A. Curtis

Volume 494                                                  November 1987


### TELESCIENCE: SCIENTIFIC COMMUNICATION IN THE INFORMATION AGE
Special Editor: Murray Aborn

Volume 495                                                      January 1988


### STATE CONSTITUTIONS IN A FEDERAL SYSTEM
Special Editor: John Kincaid

Volume 496                                                        March 1988

See page 3 for information on Academy membership and
purchase of single volumes of **The Annals.**

# CONTENTS

# BOOK DEPARTMENT CONTENTS

## SOCIOLOGY

## ECONOMICS

## PREFACE

Any examination of social life is necessarily partial. We selectively and systematically omit in order to sharpen and differentiate. To focus on a special topic is both to eliminate and to enhance. The one begets the other. For many years discussions of economic activity have been silent on informality in order to enhance formality. Michel Foucault has reminded us that silences are strong tools in the construction of reality.[1] In recent years some scholars have begun to challenge that silence. In challenging silences the aim is to "interrupt the smooth passage of 'regimes of truth,' to disrupt those forms of knowledge which have assumed a self-evident quality, and to engender a state of uncertainty in those responsible for servicing the network of power-knowledge relations."[2]

Until the 1970s the silence on informal economic activity was part of the historical development of formal, rational, industrial economies, whether these were capitalist or socialist. In the early 1970s in the United States and Europe, scholars began to rediscover a long-ignored phenomenon. Goods and services did not have to be produced and consumed in officially recognized and registered enterprises. Instead they could be made, traded, swapped, and bartered among members of informal networks. Anthropologists of nonindustrial society were not surprised at this realization. They had recognized such activity as a universal form of exchange,[3] but some now began applying this insight to aspects of industrial society.[4] Others documented "informal income opportunities" in global capitalism.[5] Yet others were exposing the second or parallel economies of socialist planned economies.[6]

However, it was the identification of informal economic exchange as a means of survival among the urban poor of American cities that was to serve as a major corrective to our perception of the hegemony of modern industrial and commercial rationalism. The paper by Ferman and Ferman in 1973 set the scene and was supplemented with the ethnographies by Stack, Lowenthal, and Dow[7] and in Europe by the comparable works of Henry, Mars, Gershuny, and Pahl.[8] In 1978

1. Michel Foucault, *The History of Sexuality: An Introduction* (New York: Penguin, 1978).

2. Barry Smart, *Foucault, Marxism and Critique* (Boston: Routledge & Kegan Paul, 1983), p. 135.

3. Marshall Sahlins, *Stone Age Economics* (Chicago: Aldine-Atherton, 1972).

4. John Davis, "Gifts and the UK Economy," *Man*, 7:408-29 (1972); idem, "Forms and Norms: The Economy of Social Relations," ibid., 8:159-76 (1973).

5. Keith Hart, "Informal Income Opportunities and Urban Employment in Ghana," *Journal of Modern African Studies*, 11:61-89 (1973).

6. D. K. Simes, "The Soviet Parallel Market," *Survey*, 21:42-52 (1975); A. Katzenelinboigen, "Coloured Markets in the Soviet Union," *Soviet Studies*, 29:62-85 (1977).

7. Patricia R. Ferman and Louis A. Ferman, "The Structural Underpinning of the Irregular Economy," *Poverty and Human Resources Abstracts*, 8:3-17 (1973); Carol B. Stack, *All Our Kin: Strategies for Survival in a Black Community* (New York: Harper & Row, 1974); Martin Lowenthal, "The Social Economy in Urban Working Class Communities," in *The Social Economy of Cities*, ed. G. Gappert and H. Ross (Newbury Park, CA: Sage, 1975); Leslie M. Dow, "High Weeds in Detroit," *Urban Anthropology*, 6:111-28 (1977).

8. Stuart Henry, *The Hidden Economy* (Oxford: Martin Robertson, 1978); Stuart Henry and Gerald Mars, "Crime at Work: The Social Construction of Amateur Property Theft," *Sociology*,

Louis Ferman began reporting the results from his innovative Detroit study, which combined anthropological ethnography with survey techniques[9] and became a standard methodological approach for similar local-area studies.[10]

By the late 1970s social science interest had been stimulated, but disciplinary colonization had also taken root. Economists and tax specialists such as Gutmann, Feige, Simon, and Witte began measuring the size of what was now being labeled variously as irregular, underground, and hidden economies. Their measures produced estimates of between 5 and 33 percent of gross national product.[11]

The existence of a significant level of informal economic activity clearly had a number of implications. What it meant depended very much on who was looking at it. Government officials and tax collectors became very concerned that there may exist substantial areas outside of conventional administrative categories that were escaping the formal record. The activity evidently signals a loss of tax revenue, but it also indicates a safety net for the poor. It was illegal, although the term "criminal" seemed inappropriate for much of what was being discussed. How could growing one's own fruit and vegetables for exchange with a neighbor, who might fix a car or decorate a house in return, be called criminal? Less easy was to classify working off-the-books, but this was certainly not as criminal as prostitution or drug dealing even if they all may be described as informal economies. And were the social economies of self-help and mutual-aid networks also informal economies?

The same ambiguity surrounded other dimensions of the phenomenon. Legitimate businesses could be undercut by informal economies, but other businesses were only able to begin because of them. Money was made, but love, status, friendship, and reciprocity all had a place in the motivational matrix that led people to trade informally. If activity in the formal economy was white, informal economic activity was black, but it was colored, too, and, most important, it was gray. It straddled boundaries between the legal recorded and the illegal recorded, between the autonomous and the dependent. Perhaps it even penetrated the formal economy or provided its foundation, as was implied by the numerous speculations that some national economies would collapse without it. Indeed, it is not insignificant that the first world conference on informal economies in industrial society was held in Rome in 1982, nor surprising that the Hungarian and Yugoslavian delegates were able to find both similarities and differences between their second economies and those

12:245-63 (1978); J. I. Gershuny, "The Informal Economy: Its Role in Post Industrial Society," *Futures*, 11:3-15 (1979); Jay I. Gershuny and Ray E. Pahl, "Work outside Employment: Some Preliminary Speculations," *New Universities Quarterly*, 34:120-35 (1979); Jay I. Gershuny and R. E. Pahl, "Britain in the Decade of the Three Economies," *New Society*, pp. 7-9 (Jan. 1980).

9. Louis A. Ferman, Louise E. Berndt, and Elaine Selo, "Analysis of the Irregular Economy: Cash Flow in the Informal Sector," mimeographed (Ann Arbor: University of Michigan; Detroit, MI: Wayne State University, 1978).

10. R. E. Pahl, *Divisions of Labour* (New York: Basil Blackwell, 1984).

11. Peter M. Gutmann, "The Subterranean Economy," *Financial Analysts Journal*, vol. 34 (1977); Edgar L. Feige, "How Big Is the Irregular Economy?" *Challenge*, pp. 5-17 (Nov.-Dec. 1979); Carl P. Simon and Ann D. Witte, "The Underground Economy: Estimates of Size, Structure and Trends," mimeographed (Washington, DC: U.S. Congress, Joint Economic Committee, 1979), also published as *Beating the System: The Underground Economy* (Boston: Auburn House, 1982); Michael O'Higgins, *Measuring the Hidden Economy: A Review of the Evidence* (London: Outer Circle Policy Unit, 1979).

reported by the French, German, British, Spanish, and U.S. delegates.[12]

Some of those writing on informal economies suggested that, at a time of world inflation, energy crisis, limits to state growth, and an ideological shift away from bureaucratic rationalism and collective provision, such economies could have a positive functional role in industrial society.[13] Others were not so sure.[14] This doubt came not only from those belaboring the potential negative effects of off-the-books work but also from those who were conscious of the debilitating conditions of Third World sweatshops and women's domestic labor.[15] Among radicals, informal economies were either depicted as another example of capitalist exploitation[16] or, by those acknowledging the dearth of mass labor movements, as effective forces for social change, as a pathway to paradise.[17] Indeed, as James Cornford has astutely observed,

Twenty years ago social scientists (and social democrats) would have been inclined to dismiss these informal and irregular arrangements as peripheral, transitional or marginal to the development of an orderly, planned society. Today informal institutions are interpreted as evidence of a latent capacity to make good the inevitable deficiencies of the planned society; or even for an odd coalition of neo-classical liberals and anarchists as the basis of replacing it altogether.[18]

Recently there has been an explosion of diverse works on the informal economy from new area studies[19] and international reviews of the measurement issue[20] to

12. The First World Conference on the Informal Economy was entitled "The Informal Economy: Social Conflicts and the Future of Industrial Societies" and was held by the Consiglio Italiano per le Scienze Sociali.

13. Graeme Shankland, *Our Secret Economy* (London: Anglo German Foundation, 1980); Joseph Huber, "Social Ecology and Dual Economy," *IFDA-Dossier*, vol. 18 (1980); James Robertson, *The Sane Alternative: Signposts to a Self-Fulfilling Future* (London: James Robertson, 1975).

14. For instance, R. E. Pahl, "Employment, Work and the Domestic Division of Labour," *International Journal of Urban and Regional Research,* 4:1-20 (1980).

15. Ivan Illich, "Vernacular Gender," *Coevolution*, pp. 4-23 (Spring 1982); idem, *Shadow Work* (London: Marion Boyars, 1981); Nanneke Redclift and Enzo Mingione, eds., *Beyond Employment: Household, Gender and Subsistence* (New York: Basil Blackwell, 1985).

16. J. Bremen, "A Dualistic Labour System: A Critique of the Informal Sector Concept," *Economic and Political Weekly*, 11:1870-76 (1976); R. Davies, "Informal Sector or Subordinate Mode of Production? A Model," in *Casual Work and Poverty in Third World Cities*, ed. Ray Bromley and Chris Gerry (New York: John Wiley, 1979); Jason Ditton and Richard Brown, "Why Don't They Revolt? Invisible Income as a Neglected Dimension of Runciman's Relative Deprivation Thesis," *British Journal of Sociology,* 32:521-30 (1981); Phil Scraton and Nigel South, "The Ideological Construction of the Hidden Economy: Private Justice and Work Related Crime," *Contemporary Crisis*, vol. 8 (1984); Redclift and Mingione, eds., *Beyond Employment*.

17. Andre Gorz, *Paths to Paradise: On the Liberation from Work* (London: Pluto Press, 1985). See also A. Gorz, *Farewell to the Working Class: An Essay on Post-Industrial Socialism* (London: Pluto Press, 1982); Rolf G. Heinze and Thomas Olk, "Development of the Informal Economy: A Strategy for Resolving the Crisis of the Welfare State," *Futures*, pp. 189-204 (June 1982); I. Szelenyi, "Structural Changes of and Alternatives to Capitalist Development in the Contemporary Urban and Regional System," *International Journal of Urban and Regional Research*, 5:1-14 (1981).

18. James Cornford, "The Revival of Self-Help?" in *Informal Institutions*, ed. Stuart Henry (New York: St. Martin's Press, 1981).

19. Pahl, *Divisions of Labour*.

20. Vito Tanzi, *The Underground Economy in the United States and Abroad* (New York: Basil Blackwell, 1982); Bruno S. Frey and Hannelore Weck, "Estimating the Shadow Economy: A 'Naive'

radical critique,[21] and challenges to found a new economics,[22] let alone a rethinking of social science.[23] In this volume we have gathered together a number of contributors, some of whom were first on the scene, others who are relatively new to it. While they disagree about various aspects of the phenomenon, all share the view that it is important and that any serious discussion of the economic life of a society must take account of informal economies in their relationship to the wider and apparently all-pervasive political system in which they are set. Taking account means more than counting. For this reason our volume focuses more on the structure, context, and dynamics of informal economies than on their size. The size issue and the competing ways of measuring it have been covered thoroughly elsewhere,[24] and, for our part, rather than re-creating that debate, we have chosen to concentrate on the sociopolitical dimensions of the phenomenon.

In the first article, Joseph Gaughan and Louis Ferman cast the informal economy in a sociological and anthropological framework and assert that informal trading and exchange patterns arise from fundamental processes of human life and social organization. The informal economy in many cases is viewed as an adaptation to social rather than economic needs.

S. M. Miller sees the informal economy not as a unitary concept but as an umbrella term under which a number of informal exchanges are grouped together. He prefers the term "informal economies" rather than "informal economy." He suggests a number of policy perspectives under which the irregular economy might be analyzed.

Ray Pahl is concerned with the relationship between unemployment and informal work activities. In both unemployment and informal work, there is an absence from work in the mainstream economy. How do these relate to each other?

The impact of technological change on the relationship between the formal and informal economies is discussed by Jonathan Gershuny. He argues that a major effect of new technology is to increase the extent of informal production through the development of new productive equipment for private households.

Michele Hoyman's article deals with a long-neglected topic: female participation in the informal economy. She shows that, contrary to stereotypes, females do participate in selected ways in the informal economy.

Approach," *Oxford Economic Papers*, 35:23-44 (1983); Carol S. Carson, "The Underground Economy: An Introduction," *Survey of Current Business*, 64:21-37 (1984); Michael Carter, "Issues in the Hidden Economy—A Survey," *Economic Record,* 60:209-21 (1984).

21. Enzo Mingione, "Informalization, Restructuring and the Survival Strategies of the Working Class," *International Journal of Urban and Regional Research*, 7:311-39 (1983); Redclift and Mingione, eds., *Beyond Employment*.

22. Bryan Roberts et al., *New Approaches to Economic Life* (Manchester: Manchester University Press, 1985).

23. Henry, ed., *Informal Institutions*. Numerous bibliographies also exist, three of the most notable being R. E. Pahl and Julian Laite, *Bibliographies on Local Labour Markets and the Informal Economy* (London: Social and Economic Research Council, 1982); Canadian Network on the Informal Economy, *A Bibliography on Material Pertinent to the Informal Economy* (Ottawa: Vanier Institute, 1982); Michel Schiray, *L'économie cache: Bibliographie française elargie* [The cash economy: French enlarged bibliography] (Paris: Centre international de recherche sur l'environnement et le développement, 1983).

24. Carson, "Underground Economy."

James Smith's article reviews empirical findings on a national study of participants—vendors and consumers—in the informal economy in the United States. He also identifies a number of perceptions and motivations of consumers who do business in the informal economy.

Chris Gerry adds a historical dimension to the collection by analyzing the role of small businesses and enterprises in the economic development of a nation-state. He asserts that such small-scale work systems, largely informal, have been a crucial element in the development of the economy in nation-states.

The informal economy is not a concept restricted to an understanding of the economies of the Western world. Steven Sampson contends that informal work systems are found behind the Iron Curtain, suggesting that informal economies are generic to any nation-state—capitalist or socialist—although they may perform different functions and fulfill different needs in the two systems.

Stuart Henry asserts that the informal economy does not exist or operate in a vacuum. There is a political economy environment where the operation of diverse interest groups helps to shape or govern the growth or contraction of informal exchanges.

Ferman, Henry, and Hoyman conclude the volume by reviewing and analyzing a number of conceptual, research, and policy issues that are associated with the informal economy.

As a collection, we feel that these articles are another stepping stone to an understanding of the structure and processes of this important phenomenon, the informal economy.

LOUIS A. FERMAN
STUART HENRY
MICHELE HOYMAN

ANNALS, *AAPSS*, **493,** September 1987

# Toward an Understanding of the
# Informal Economy

*By* JOSEPH P. GAUGHAN and LOUIS A. FERMAN

ABSTRACT: After surveying some of the typical content of the informal economy, the authors argue that the most substantial amount of activity in this sector is based on family and community and may not involve an immediate expectation of financial return. It would include local barter, mutual aid and self-help networks as well as other activities such as light construction and repair work. Reliance on such networks, common in preindustrial economies, continues to serve specific needs in industrial and postindustrial societies, filling in where the conventional economy falls short or fails. By its very definition, informal activity is difficult to investigate and monitor and raises questions about the legitimate concerns of government.

---

*Joseph P. Gaughan received his Ph.D. in cultural anthropology (Columbia University). At the Institute of Labor and Industrial Relations, University of Michigan, he has researched the informal economy, industrial development, and recession in the automobile industry. In 1986-87 he was a research fellow at the University of Paris, Nanterre.*

*Louis A. Ferman received his Ph.D. in sociology and industrial relations (Cornell University). His books and articles include the topics of unemployment and the informal economy. He is professor of social work and research director of the Institute of Labor and Industrial Relations, University of Michigan.*

A preliminary inventory of the informal economy might list among its components the following activities: barter, or trade in goods not involving cash; moonlighting or off-the-books employment—work performed for wages that are not reported; volunteer work; household-based work activities; deviant or criminal work activities; and the social exchange of services, such as neighborhood self-help networks. Activities in this sector may vary according to their capital and labor intensiveness, the presence or absence of monetary exchange, and their scale of operations. They will also display differing degrees of reliance on family and community-based resources and networks. Informal activity that takes place largely in personal and intimate social domains will often offer gratifications different from any material rewards that may also be obtained and these gratifications will be of equal or greater importance. Depending on the type of social milieu, informal economic activities will employ different modalities of exchange, each with different motivations and different expectations of return. These modalities will reflect the nature of the personal ties between participants, defined by norms and institutions that are in essence noneconomic.

An examination of the informal economy will take us into domains quite different from that large-scale arena where most conventional economic activity is assumed to take place. Difficult as this makes our endeavor, we are further hampered by the vagueness of the boundaries separating the personal and intimate spheres of family and community from the conventional economic sphere. Household and family are often regarded as playing an economic role only in the secondary capacities of consumption or biological reproduction. Of course, ethnographers have repeatedly stressed that the "domestic mode of production," a low-intensity, kin-based, and reciprocity-linked system, is the chief form of economic organization in primitive and traditional societies.[1] But sociologists and economists, of both the classical and Marxist schools, have maintained that the economic role of the family and household has been progressively reduced by the advances of industrial capitalism.

Capitalism has certainly substituted a different set of organizing principles in the large-scale operations that constitute the economic core of industrial society. Yet the old kinship structures have proved more durable than has been frequently assumed. In her study of New Hampshire textile workers in the nineteenth and early twentieth centuries, Tamara K. Hareven shows the persistence of traditional kinship networks throughout the process of "proletarianization."[2] As we shall argue, these

1. Classical ethnological work on the problem of reciprocity begins with Marcel Mauss, *Essai sur le don* [The gift] (London: Cohen and West, 1954). Others include Bronislaw Malinowski, *Argonauts of the Western Pacific* (Boston: Routledge & Kegan Paul, 1922); Raymond Firth, *Elements of Social Organization* (London: Watts, 1951); and Claude Lévi-Strauss, *The Elementary Structures of Kinship* (Boston: Beacon Press, 1969). A more recent and very important discussion is by Marshall Sahlins, *Stone Age Economics* (Chicago: Aldine-Atherton, 1972), from which we have taken the expression "domestic mode of production." Ibid., p. 74. From a sociological standpoint, a valuable contribution has come from Alvin W. Gouldner, "The Norm of Reciprocity: A Preliminary Statement," *American Sociological Review*, 25:161-78 (1960). See also the article by J. Davis, "Forms and Norms: The Economy of Social Relations," *Man*, 8(2):159-76 (June 1973).

2. Tamara K. Hareven, *Family Time and Industrial Time* (New York: Columbia University Press, 1982).

informal networks continue to serve a variety of functions, both within the world of work and outside of it. Moreover, the economic significance of kin ties may not be eroded by the introduction of capitalist relations of production. Kinship relations maintain their connection with traditional cultural values and continue to embody personal gratification for many people.

## INFORMAL EXCHANGES IN PRE- AND POSTINDUSTRIAL SOCIETY

Kinship-based economic strategies may be considered a preindustrial phenomenon, a vestigial of traditional society, when found in populations recently displaced from the traditional agricultural mode of production. This displacement, however, will vary greatly according to local economic circumstances. Populations are displaced from agriculture through pressure resulting from economic and demographic changes in the countryside. This pressure may be due to processes such as turning cropland into grazing land, mechanization, or intensification of the economic burden on the peasantry through higher rents or taxes. Increased fertility of the population due to improved health conditions will also contribute to this pressure.

The transfer of labor to other sectors of the economy is achieved most smoothly when industrial growth is sufficient to employ a large portion of the population displaced.[3] This is the case when large-scale labor-intensive manufacturing is on the increase. But when industrial development is largely capital and technology intensive, as in much of the world today, the transfer is not so readily accomplished and large groups are often left in marginal economic circumstances. Within these groups, kin relations of the preindustrial variety can be crucial to survival. This is most visible today in the barrio and shantytown populations of many Third World cities.[4] Clearly, when industrial growth in the Third World does not match economic and demographic pressures in the agricultural sector, developmental models drawn from the history of Western Europe and North America do not apply. Much of the Third World today suffers from this critical impasse, and the growth of informal economic activity is one result. Of course, this varies with the pace and direction of industrial development, a process that will display distinctly different features from one locale to another. As Keith Hart observes for western Africa:

Old cities like Acrra, lacking significant industrial development, may be contrasted with newer urban complexes such as the Gambian Copperbelt in the scope and relative attractiveness of informal opportunities—a contrast which is sustainable for western cities in the industrial revolution, for example between London and Manchester in the nineteenth century.[5]

---

3. The labor transfer theory of economic development is set forth in W. Arthur Lewis, "Economic Development with Unlimited Supplies of Labour," in *The Economics of Underdevelopment*, ed. A. N. Agarwala and S. P. Singh (New York: Oxford University Press, 1958), pp. 400-409. See also John C. H. Fei and Gustav Ranis, *Development of the Labor-Surplus Economy: Theory and Policy* (Homewood, IL: R. D. Irwin,

1964). An excellent discussion of this theory and its implications can be found in an article by John Weeks, "The Political Economy of Labor Transfer," *Science and Society*, 35(4):463-80 (Winter 1971).

4. Lisa R. Peattie, "Tertiarization and Urban Poverty in Latin America," *Latin American Urban Research*, 6:109-23 (1976).

5. Keith Hart, "Informal Economic Opportunities and Urban Employment in Ghana," *Journal of Modern African Studies*, 11(1):89 (1973).

An adequate understanding of such situations requires a case-by-case approach. It is hoped that such considerations will dispel the notion that development is unilinear and will help contribute to an appreciation of those problems particular to each locale.

Investigations of informal economic activity will show results that vary according to where or with whom the activity is carried out. Hence the term "informal economy" will mean different things in advanced industrial nations from what it does in developing countries. Similarly, it will display different features in poor communities as opposed to middle-class communities, or in an urban as opposed to a rural setting. The modalities of local kinship-based and community-based exchange, founded on the principle of reciprocity, may be considered as characterizing phases in the evolution and history of economic behavior, but they must also be seen as coexisting with other types of economic activity in any given period or locality. These modalities are one of several possibilities for economic organization in any society, whatever the dominant mode may be. Ethnography has contributed to our understanding of the convergence of types of economic activity since it is steeped in the experience of small-scale societies with multiplex relations and very intimate domains of social interaction.

## RECIPROCITY AND INFORMAL ECONOMIC EXCHANGES

The work of anthropologists may be relevant here as many of them seek their research subjects in those small and remote societies considered primitive or traditional. Understanding exchange between these subjects involves considera-

tion of very personal social domains and social-network relationships, contrasting sharply with classical economics, which focuses on the impersonal marketplace and the atomized individual. Exchange in the face-to-face world of small populations is often observed to be based in some notion of reciprocity, where expectation of return depends on local cultural norms. It is possible that Marshall Sahlins's typology of reciprocities, based upon "immediacy of returns, equivalence of returns, and like material and mechanical dimension of exchange," may be useful in examining the informal economy[6] in its relation to the wider society.

At one extreme, reciprocity may be characterized as "generalized reciprocity," referring to "transactions that are putatively altruistic," where the obligation to return is vague and at best implicit. Sahlins elaborates:

At the extreme, say voluntary food-sharing among near kinsmen—or for its logical value, one might think of the suckling of children in this context—the expectation of a direct material return is unseemly. . . . The material side of the transaction is repressed by the social: reckoning of debts outstanding cannot be overt and is typically let out of account.[7]

The midpoint of this typology Sahlins calls "balanced reciprocity," referring to "direct exchange." "In precise balance, the reciprocation is the customary equivalent of the thing received and is without delay."[8] This type of reciprocity is less personal than the first, and the participants confront each other as economic subjects acting in their own interests. At the other extreme, Sahlins proposes the term "negative reciprocity," referring to

6. Sahlins, *Stone Age Economics*, p. 191.
7. Ibid., p. 194
8. Ibid.

"the attempt to get something for nothing with impunity, the several forms of appropriation, transactions opened and conducted toward net utilitarian advantage."[9] This may range from outright theft to the various kinds of bartering aimed at individual maximization.

Sahlins goes on to show how these three reciprocity types characterize exchange relations in primitive and traditional societies. He found that the particular reciprocal arrangement will vary according to the crucial variable of kinship distance. Generalized reciprocity will characterize exchange within the most intimate of kinship domains, the family and domestic units, residential groups, and lineages. Balanced reciprocity will dominate at the level of wider social networks involving the village, tribe, or larger social groups. Finally, negative reciprocity will dominate outside the kin group as such, where participants confront each other as strangers not immediately bound by social ties. Complementing Sahlins's typology is Karl Polyani's nonlinear model of economic evolution. He illustrates how a stratified system of redistribution dominated by negative reciprocity and controlled from the top can emerge from traditional reciprocity networks. Through a similar dynamic redistribution, systems may ultimately yield to a market economy under the right historical circumstances.[10] So again we see that modalities of exchange coexisting at a given moment may become stages in historical development, each dominating in a particular period.

Such reciprocity types, always coexisting but with certain types dominating in specific social formations, represent one possible variation in the principles that govern exchange in human groups. They depend on the degree to which participants in an exchange are bound by noneconomic social ties, particularly those of kinship.

Reciprocity may be a universal human norm, but it varies widely in social practice.[11] In certain patterns of development, the flow of goods in traditional reciprocity networks becomes subject to arrest and diversion, making possible surplus accumulation and facilitating the appearance of an economic domain outside of the circle of kinship. This is the historically observable process whereby redistribution systems yield to the market and to the utilitarian calculus of capitalism. As has been frequently pointed out, it should be remembered that a strong economic and emotional infrastructure in the family is necessary for the entrepreneurial class of classical capitalism to emerge. Christopher Lasch has described the ideology of the nineteenth-century family as "a haven in a heartless world" in this context:

The new style of domestic life created psychological conditions favorable to the emergence of a new type of inner-directed, self-reliant personality—the family's deepest contribution to the needs of a market society based on competition, individualism, postponement of gratification, rational foresight, and the accumulation of worldly goods.[12]

9. Ibid., p. 195.

10. The classic statement of the substantivist approach to economic development comes from Karl Polyani, *The Great Transformation* (New York: Rinehart, 1944). See also Karl Polyani, Conrad Arensberg, and Harry W. Pearson, eds., *Trade and Market in the Early Empires* (New York: Free Press, 1957).

11. See Gouldner, "Norm of Reciprocity."

12. Christopher Lasch, *Haven in a Heartless World: The Family Besieged* (New York: Basic Books, 1977), p. 4.

In similar terms Alvin Gouldner has stressed the necessity of a firm familial infrastructure for participation in all types of public life—economic, political, or intellectual:

In both bourgeois society and in classical antiquity, public rationality was grounded in class privilege and in unchallenged male domination of the family. Both provided that indispensable requisite for rational discourse: leisure, free from time-consuming work in the household and in the work place, and the freedom to allocate one's own "free time" without the control or permission of another. Patriarchal subjugation of women and private property, then, were the unmistakable conditions and limits of the post-enlightenment development of public rationality in bourgeois society.[13]

## SOCIAL COHESION AND THE INFORMAL ECONOMY

It would appear that some form of kin-based informal economy is necessary to any type of social formation. However eroded and attacked in modern industrial society, a familial infrastructure still serves as a support for all other sorts of economic activity. To reach a satisfactory understanding of this central economic domain requires a penetration into what is most personal and intimate in human life. It challenges our very definitions of what is economic and demands a new understanding of what constitutes work. The values produced and exchanged in the domestic and community realms are often subtle and nonmaterial and consistently elude quantification.

The continuing importance of informal social links involving kinship,

neighborhood, and friendship remains a crucial factor in understanding the informal economy as well as a major obstacle to conventional methods of measurement and analysis. The social history of industrial development shows that traditional community and kin-based institutions have often resisted the introduction of the wage-price system and have been blamed for maintaining backwardness. Such institutions have persisted within capitalist economies, just as tribal social organization persisted at the interstices of feudal society. These kinship and quasi-kinship exchange systems become the building blocks for a more complex, varied system of informal economic trade.

In today's industrial world, informal economic activity takes place in a society where the impersonal marketplace has come to dominate most economic life. Yet the same wide variations in exchange modalities persist.

Any of Sahlins's reciprocity types may operate in the informal economy, and thus expectations of return will differ greatly from one activity to another. Work performed in the household is usually done with no specific promise of compensation and little or no contractual stipulation of expectations or duties. This corresponds to Sahlins's most personal category of generalized reciprocity. Yet such exchange relations commonly extend beyond the household to cooperative efforts between households involving the exchange of services and goods among relatives, neighbors, and friends.

Indeed, a large share of economic activity in the informal sector involves no exchange of cash at all. Following Lowenthal,[14] we have called this sector

13. Alvin W. Gouldner, *The Dialectic of Ideology and Technology: The Origins, Grammar, and Future of Ideology* (New York: Oxford University Press, 1976), p. 99.

14. Martin D. Lowenthal, "The Social Econ-

the social economy. This category includes much domestic labor exchanged within and between families, such as housework, child care, and yard work. It can be expanded to include wider mutual-aid networks, such as the traditional country barn raising, barter, and unofficial payment-in-kind. The social economy is more likely to maintain its activities within local limits and is usually more family and community based and less intensive than informal activities that involve cash.

Thus we can see informal activities as providing a necessary part of the force of social cohesion, important in the definitions of kin and community. Within such networks a social ethic often operates whereby members are protected from total and abject economic failure. A well-integrated community resists allowing one of its own to fall into truly intolerable economic circumstances and will often send forth its own informal safety net. This is particularly observable in disadvantaged communities where very scarce resources must be shared in order to ensure the survival of the network. Carol B. Stack has described this for poverty-level communities in an urban American black ghetto,[15] but such networks exist among all social classes and are ready to extend their supportive functions with any change in the economic circumstances.

## CATEGORIES OF INFORMAL ECONOMIC ACTIVITIES

There is no distinct boundary between the social economy, which does not involve cash, and that category of informal economic activity that does involve cash. Cash-based exchanges we call, following Ferman, the irregular economy.[16] This category contains a large amount of varied economic activity that may be family and community based, but that can be to some degree independent of the traditional kin framework. Irregular economic exchanges tend to have a higher capital investment than the other, more kin-based operations; may employ more people; and are generally more profit motivated. Ric Thompson, in a study of a white working-class neighborhood in Detroit, chose as the label for this type of irregular economic exchange entrepreneurial activity. The activities that were low in capital investment and high in kin-based inputs were labeled associational. Associational activities are tightly linked to the social economy and can be seen as essentially a cash-based extension of it. Here again it must be stressed that the rewards in the irregular economy are not exclusively material.

Thompson lists some major features that characterize the two types of irregular economic activity. Associational activity is likely to be low in capital investment, part-time, and based on informal contacts, while the entrepreneurial type is more likely to be capital intensive, full-time, and based on formal contacts. Participants in the entrepreneurial type are generally of higher income than those in the associational type. Of course, here again the distinction is not too definite, since the passing from one type to the other may happen imperceptibly, particularly for the indi-

omy in Urban Working Class Communities," in *The Social Economy of Cities*, ed. G. Gappert and H. M. Ross (Newbury Park, CA: Sage, 1975).

15. Carol B. Stack, *All Our Kin: Strategies for Survival in a Black Community* (New York: Harper & Row, 1974).

16. Louis A. Ferman, "The Irregular Economy," mimeographed (Ann Arbor: University of Michigan, Institute of Labor and Industrial Relations, 1969).

vidual or individuals involved. Such endeavors as light construction, machine repair, and junk dealing, among others, occur along a continuum between these two poles. Associational activity tends to be closer to the social economy, while entrepreneurial irregular activity more closely resembles activity in the formal sector and is more likely to be governed by the wage-price system of the larger economy.[17] The point at which such social economy activities become entrepreneurial, calculated toward economic gain—in Sahlins's terms, negative reciprocity—is always indeterminate. The difference again depends on factors such as kinship distance and the extent to which economic relations dominate social relations.

At its extreme, negative reciprocity is seen as that form of informal activity, involving considerable cash flow and often taking place between strangers, that we know as the criminal economy. This involves traffic in goods and services forbidden by law, such as drugs, prostitution, gambling, loan-sharking, dealing in stolen goods, and so forth. Though much of the irregular economy may be considered outside the law because it avoids government regulation and taxation requirements, it is not explicitly illegal as are the activities of the criminal economy. Once again there is a class of ambiguous, borderline, relationship-based activities, such as perks, pilferage, and fiddles.[18] These sorts of activities are often tacitly tolerated or even encouraged, so their status with respect to the law may vary. They occupy a hazy territory between the criminal economy and the social and irregular economies.

The dubious legality of much informal economic activity is one factor that makes it difficult to investigate. Participants are frequently motivated to conceal such activities when they involve either avoidance of taxes or regulation, or outright criminal activity. Income may also be concealed to avoid specific taxes or the denial of welfare benefits. Efforts by the government to deal with the informal economy, whether to tax it, regulate it, suppress it, or even encourage it, are likely to encounter barriers to governmental scrutiny for a variety of reasons.

The categories of the informal economy we have enumerated here are far from exhaustive. Indeed, it is far easier to demonstrate the existence of specific kinds of informal activity than to demonstrate that one category exists or that another does not. Moreover, none of these categories is totally exclusive of any other, and a considerable degree of interdependence and overlap is evident. Like many criminal activities, the more capital-intensive or entrepreneurial activities in the informal sector may be relatively independent of the social economy and its household-based activities, but the distinction is never without ambiguity. What is essential, however, is the degree to which informal economic activity varies in its modality of exchange.

### UNDERSTANDING THE NEED FOR AND PERSISTENCE OF IRREGULAR ECONOMIC ACTIVITY

The persistence of kin-based and community-based economic networks is observable historically and cross-culturally

17. Ric Thompson, "Brightmoor: A Study of Community and Economy in an Urban Neighborhood," mimeographed (Ann Arbor: University of Michigan, Institute of Labor and Industrial Relations, 1975).

18. Jason Ditton, "Perks, Pilferage and the Fiddle," *Theory and Society*, 4:39-71 (1977). See also Stuart Henry, *The Hidden Economy: The Context and Control of Borderline Crime* (Oxford: Martin Robertson, 1978).

in many different types of social formation. Perhaps it is reasonable to see this
persistence as not simply a vestige of
earlier modes, but rather as manifesting
a spontaneous human disposition toward
reciprocity and cooperation founded
upon the means of biological and social
reproduction. But this should not lead
us to ignore the way particular social
structures shape and foster informal
economies.

In advanced industrial nations the
manufacturing sector displays structural
inadequacies with serious consequences
for some sectors of the labor force. A
number of case studies have shown that
low-income communities rely on informal economic resources.[19] The importance of hustling in the black ghetto, the
persistence of tight kinship networks in
working-class urban communities, and
the increasing visibility of street peddlers
and entertainers testify to this. One
explanation offered for this movement
toward informal work sees informal
employment and markets as alternatives
adopted by people restricted to marginal
jobs in low-paying, labor-intensive, non-
unionized industries.[20] For people restricted to this peripheral labor force and
thus denied an adequate and secure
income, informal economic activity
holds a powerful attraction. Economic
deprivation is always relative, however,
and can only be measured according to
the standards of the participants. These

standards will reflect cultural norms as
well as established habits and desires.
Not all participation in the informal
economy can be ascribed solely to the
dispossessed, and much documentation
and analysis demonstrate that the informal economy is used by many middle-
income and upper-income people. Therefore one must consider that low-income
groups use informal exchange systems
to meet different needs from those of
middle-class groups—for example, survival versus stretching a dollar, respectively.

In particular, analysts concerned with
the shift to postindustrial society have
called attention to a significant growth
in the informal sector among relatively
affluent populations in the modern welfare state in North America and Western Europe. These analysts argue that
when manufacturing fails to create jobs
commensurate with the demand for
them, resources may be more fruitfully
reinvested in family and domestic production.[21] Hence the growth in modern
cottage industries ranging from traditional canning or sausage making to the
manufacture of small electric components. High unemployment appears
with increasing evidence to be a permanent and structural consequence of the
shift from the older smokestack industries to the new microchip industries.
Employment in the tertiary or service
sector, popularly proposed as the solution to this postindustrial employment
crunch, has often proved to be unattrac-

19. Stack, *All Our Kin*; Leslie M. Dow, Jr.,
"High Weeds in Detroit: The Irregular Economy
among a Network of Appalachian Migrants,"
*Urban Anthropology*, 6(2):111-28 (1977); Gretchen
Chesley Lang, "Making a Living a Hard Way:
Urban Chippewa Drinkers," *Central Issues in
Anthropology*, 1(2):19-40 (Nov. 1979).

20. Barry Bluestone, "Lower-Income Workers
and Marginal Industries," in *Poverty in America*,
ed. L.A. Ferman et al. (Ann Arbor: University of
Michigan Press, 1976).

21. Analyses stressing the importance of informal economic activity in postindustrial society can
be found in J. I. Gershuny, "The Informal Economy: Its Role in Post-Industrial Society," *Futures*,
pp. 3-15 (Feb. 1979); R. E. Pahl, "Employment,
Work and the Domestic Division of Labour,"
*International Journal of Urban and Regional
Research*, 4(1):1-20 (Mar. 1980).

tive due to its low wage scale and its lack of security and opportunity for advancement. Income earned in the service sector proves increasingly to be intermittent, derived from part-time and/or temporary work. It is thus commonly supplemented by informal economic activity, with a household and community base, which maintains the importance of kin ties and is more consistent with traditional cultural values. In such cases it appears that individuals relying exclusively on conventional employment in low-paying jobs might more accurately be labeled dispossessed.

The economic shocks of the 1970s, which combined growing unemployment with escalating inflation, led to an aggravated recession cycle and fiscal austerity. These factors may have contributed to this growth of informal economic activity, as Gershuny and Pahl argue.[22] Thus in addition to being a preindustrial phenomenon, economic strategies based on kinship and community must also be recognized as postindustrial alternatives, serving the needs of an increasing number excluded by or dropping out of advanced industrial economies.

### SUMMING UP

Bringing the informal economy into the wider picture of economic activity thus challenges our accepted categories of economic behavior. Dealing with the domestic and kin-based sectors of the irregular economy involves the consideration of realms of human behavior generally left aside in economic investigations. Once we leave the macroeconomic sphere with its profit motivation and self-interest strategies, we must look more closely at the subjective domain and the range

of human emotion and intimacy. But again we must stress that these categories do not distinguish themselves easily, but rather constitute poles of a continuum that is exceedingly difficult to subdivide. No absolute demarcation of what is motivated by material gain against what is motivated by subjective and personal factors is possible. Thus the questions of monitoring and measuring the informal sector become very difficult to answer. As one domain is brought into better focus, others often blur and fade. The goal of a total economy brought into public light and transparent to the gaze of policymakers is an abject delusion, and quite possibly a dangerous one.

The prevailing contention that informal economic activity is rapidly growing in the advanced industrial nations has led to a variety of explanations. Of these the one that has most attracted the attention of political leaders and government officials is the explanation that attributes underground activity to evasion of burdensome government regulation and taxation. Estimates of informal cash flow generally rely on banking data about money supply, demand deposits, and checking transactions.[23] Elsewhere such estimates have been challenged on the basis of Census Bureau survey data.[24] This debate points to the essential question of what is being measured. What constitutes economic activity? What constitutes work? Clearly, if efforts at understanding these problems are undertaken with a view toward further taxation and regulation, they will embody certain attitudes and presuppositions about what work and economic activity are.

Certainly, the informal economy comprises activities that resemble much of

22. Gershuny, "Informal Economy"; Pahl, "Employment, Work and the Domestic Division of Labour."

23. Peter Gutmann, "The Subterranean Economy," *Financial Analysts Journal,* pp. 26, 27, 34 (Nov.-Dec. 1977).

24. *Employment and Earnings* (Jan. 1978).

what we commonly consider conventional economic activity. Entrepreneurial informal activity, moonlighting, and what is known as sweatshop manufacturing constitute informal activities of this type. Also much criminal activity must be considered of sufficient scale to be classified within this group. Nonetheless, as we have argued, a very wide range of informal economic activity is of the social variety, part of the cohesive force uniting people in all societies founded upon kinship and community. This type of informal activity we consider to be the most pervasive and most crucially linked to our definitions of economic activity. In this perspective, then, we can postulate a very different question about the informal economy: at what point does the exchange of goods and services attain a character whereby it requires monitoring and regulation by the state? This is a political as well as sociological question. It raises a problem of legitimacy. How is state intervention justified? Since economic activity cannot be entirely distinguished from the complex array of other social activities, limits to the legitimate interests of government must be established. At this point in history, political institutions are required to develop means of responsiveness to their citizenry while leaving them sufficient room for the personal and intimate activities so critical for social life.

As we have seen in considering the historical vicissitudes of the household economy and local informal networks, much work in the informal economy may appear to be marginal to the conventional economy but may become more significantly productive with historical developments. New demands and new markets may be created as old minorities become new elites and countercultures become dominant life-styles. The personal and community domains of reciprocal exchange are often areas of innovation for the emergence of new kinds of production that may prove to be of crucial importance in the evolution of the economy as a whole. Developing new markets around new—or old—cultural modes is a critical part of economic adjustment to historical change. This creative potential of the informal sector rests upon its grounding reciprocity and its social motivation rather than its profit orientation. Personal and informal economic networks are areas where people can explore their own needs and seek to meet them in their own way. In this respect the informal economy might be understood as containing the very foundation of all other economic activity and as necessary to the functioning of any social arrangement. In its most pervasive social component, the informal economy comprises the supportive and sustaining functions of the personal sphere, without which all public activity—whether economic or political, intellectual or artistic—could not take place.

In summary, then, the informal economy cannot and should not be conceptualized as merely a substitute for or complement of traditional market exchanges. The informal economy has not developed simply because there is a failure in traditional economic systems of distribution. A good part of the informal economy, with its emphasis on mutual obligation and reciprocity, forms a nexus of social glue that makes the formation and maintenance of social life possible. The failure to understand this social basis of informal economic exchanges, and indeed of all economic behavior, leads us to an inadequate picture of economic life in both traditional and postindustrial societies.

ANNALS, *AAPSS*, **493,** September 1987

# The Pursuit of
# Informal Economies

*By* S. M. MILLER

ABSTRACT: Considerable differences exist between informal economies. Consequently, a wide range of interests and frames of analysis influence the way they are thought about. Four main approaches are discussed: economic, social, fiscal and regulatory, and living conditions. In turn, four policy choices dealing with informal economies compete: drive them out, make them pay up, improve them, and expand them. The future of informal economies is uncertain, but the concern with them is likely to continue and will challenge the hegemonic role of neoclassical economic theory and the concern with the large corporation.

---

*S. M. Miller is professor of sociology and economics at Boston University. His interests are in the interactions of economic and social policy, community organizing, and strategies for political and social change. He is a contributing editor of* Social Policy Magazine, *was the cofounder and first president of the Research Committee on Poverty and Social Welfare of the International Sociological Association, and was a long-time member of the National Committee on Employment Policy. Recently he coauthored* Recapitalizing America *and is the coeditor of* Dynamics of Deprivation.

NOTE: I am grateful to Louis Ferman for yeoman editorial services.

26

SOCIAL scientists lack an understanding of what has been called the postindustrial society, says Krishan Kumar, because we lack an understanding of industrial society.[1] Distorted views about the past and present confuse our views of what we think is emerging. Similarly, our view of the informal economy is blurry because our understanding of the formal economy is inadequate. The theoretical approach to formal economics is so abstracted that it pays almost no attention to human interaction, social associations, or institutional life. The empirical approach to the study of economy largely involves aggregated numbers, frequently mixing horses and apples so that a single number or average may hide more than it reveals.

A major difficulty in understanding the capitalist economy, found in analyses of both the political Right and Left, is to focus on the modern large corporation as the exemplar of contemporary capitalism. Yet *Fortune Magazine*'s famous listing of the largest 500 and 1000 nonfinancial corporations covers less than one-half of the employment in the United States.[2] Similarly, we think of advanced industrial nations as heavily involved in manufacturing, but only West Germany of the nations of the Organization for Economic Cooperation and Development in the post-World War II period has had a majority of its labor force in manufacturing. The United States, except for World War II, has never had a majority of its labor force in manufacturing.

The confusion about past and present deepens when the corporate economy—the on-the-books economy—is taken as the exclusive locus of economic activities. When we do this, we perceive other forms of economic activity as deviants and aberrations, not as important parts of the economic sustenance of many people. We overlook the fact that people provision themselves from a wide and diverse range of economic exchanges and transactions, with corporate-derived goods and services only fulfilling a small part of any person's needs.

The concept of informal economy attempts to rescue economic activity from the grasp of the economist. In doing so, it, too, narrows the world. When we contrast the informal with the formal economy, we ignore the vast differentiation that exists within this latter category—corporations of varied sizes, partnerships, single entrepreneurs, unincorporated activities, the government as economic actor. But it is convenient to have a contrast, and in this article the term that is used in opposition to "informal" is "mainstream economy," despite the terrible simplification involved. In a similar fashion, the concept of informal economy covers an enormously diverse territory, as the articles in this volume demonstrate. To pay heed to that differentiation, the term that is employed is "informal economies," but it is one thing to flay the importance of differentiation, quite another actually to deal with it.

## COMPETING PERSPECTIVES ON INFORMAL ECONOMIES

Heisenberg's principle of uncertainty—that the process of measurement changes the object that is measured—applies to conceptualization. The act of conceptualizing changes the phenomena

1. Krishan Kumar, *Prophecy and Progress: The Sociology of Industrial and Post-Industrial Society* (New York: Penguin Books, 1978), p. 8.

2. S. M. Miller, "Notes on Neo-Capitalism," *Theory and Society*, 2(1):1-35 (Spring 1975).

that are conceptualized. The conceptualizing draws attention to one or another aspect of the phenomena. As Max Weber said of his ideal-type approach, it one-sidedly emphasizes particular elements of a phenomenon in order to stress them, rather than others, as central. In an important sense, then, conceptualizing is a political act since it focuses attention on some dimensions and diverts interest from what some might consider the more significant.

With informal economies the principle of attention is particularly appropriate. Investigators of informal economies compete in what they choose to bring to our attention. They offer different frames for thinking about these economies, which are grouped together under the single label of "informal economy." The investigators' frames depend on their discipline, occupation, or ideology. The choice of frame is fateful for what we think about when we study—or act on—informal economies, especially when we regard them as a unitary phenomenon, called the informal economy. The implication of this variance and diversity in focus among scholars is that it is almost impossible to integrate the conclusions of a number of articles, such as in this collection, into a new synthesis on informal economy. We must be careful to treat this collection not as a single, exhaustive whole but as separate pieces of a complex jigsaw puzzle where most of the pieces are still missing.

Informal economies can be analyzed from a number of perspectives, each of them at a low level of abstraction. Four major perspectives and a number of variations within each are readily discernible. The four perspectives are economic, social, fiscal and regulatory, and conditions of insufficiency.

*Economic perspectives*

One school of investigation of irregular economies focuses on questions about the organization of the economic system and how it functions. Such studies might focus on questions of economic measurement, human resource development, or labor market operation. In each case, the objective is to learn more about economic behavior and how it relates to processes of allocation and distribution.

*Economic measurements.* As discussed in this issue of *The Annals*, the many indicators used to judge the structure and state of the economy are deeply flawed by their neglect or faulty measuring of the activities in informal economies. Sizable segments of economic activities, such as household production for family consumption, are ruled out of the economic accounts; governmental activity is undervalued and voluntary contributions of time and effort for the well-being of others are uncounted for they do not have a market and therefore are unpriced, though not necessarily unpriceable. The existence of informal economies requires new ways of thinking about conventional economic indicators such as gross national product, productivity, and income distribution.

*Economic functioning.* One currently popular dimension of economic policy is the emphasis on entrepreneurialism in Thatcher's Britain and Reagan's America. The goal is to expand small-scale entrepreneurs so that they can become mainstream entrepreneurs. A broader question is, To what extent are informal economies shaped by the mainstream economy and to what extent do they contribute to it or act against it? The answer obviously depends on what informal economy in what economic sector is studied. Does the informal sector bring down consumption costs and thereby lower the wages that employers are forced to pay? The perspective raised by that question is contemplated by those who have approached informal economies from a Marxian framework.

Neoclassical economists focus on the possibility that those officially labeled as unemployed may actually have earnings in the informal economies. The official unemployment rates are thereby inflated, and macro policies to stimulate the economy may therefore be followed inappropriately. The tendency, then, is to show involvement in informal economies in order to promote reductions in governmental interference with mainstream economies.

*Enterprise functioning.* In the Soviet Union and Eastern Europe, informal economies grow up to make it possible for the mainstream socialist firms to appear to perform more effectively. These informal economies are supplementary and complementary rather than substitutive. Informal trading and exchange systems frequently operate to ease the pressures of meeting enterprise quotas and of securing resources and supplies that may not be available in the mainstream economy.

*Alternative economic systems.* A contrasting approach is taken by those of a more "green" mentality who see informal economies as the likely or, at least, desirable wave of the future. Informal economies offer a community-based, solidaristic, cooperative, smaller-scale, more personal, less market-valued way of economic production. Sometimes the

argument is that mainstream economies are in enduring crises: full employment will not recur in Western Europe. Inevitably, new forms of economic institutions, especially informal economies, will have to emerge. This instrumental or necessitarian approach may not be the main argument, and the superior moral and community quality of an alternative, more informal economy may be stressed.

*Labor process.* Some see informal economies as ways of training people who will later move into the mainstream economy. Others see them as a way of focusing attention on the enormous amount of unpaid, unmarketed work that should make us analyze differently the mainstream economy. Others extend the concept of the internal labor markets of the mainstream economy and see informal economies as irregular internal labor markets offering little hope of improvement and advancement to those in them.

A contrasting perspective concentrates on pilfering as part of the wage system, at least as seen by workers. They steal from the employer or the customer as a regular or irregular way of increasing their incomes. Since crime is glamorous, this view receives a great deal of attention.

*Income production.* Here the concern is with the contribution that informal economies make to the economic well-being of households. Informal economies may operate as income supplementation or as the main source of income. The interest may be in the overlap of work in both formal and informal economies, or in time allocations, or in the economic—if usually unmeasured—roles of various members of a household.

*Social perspectives*

Another set of perspectives focuses on the social organization of the society and how irregular economies operate to permit social functioning and role fulfillment for different groups. The emphasis here is on sociological aspects rather than economic.

*Gender.* The importance of unpaid labor by women in household tasks is the locus of interest for many students of informal economies. Sometimes the concern is with women's contributions to the reproduction of labor force activities. For others, the relative time and effort of activities of men and women in household tasks may frame the gender issue. The dual burdens of women as homemakers and as workers in paid or unpaid employment compel the attention of many analysts.

*Marginality.* Many of those who work in informal economies are marginalized by ethnicity and race, immigrant status, or geographic isolation. The perspective here, as with gender, is to concentrate on the characteristics of those who supply the labor in informal economies. The notion is that some informal economies are generated by marginalized people who have no economic alternative, or that particular informal economies are carried through by specific marginalized populations, as with gypsies and knife-sharpening.

*Family.* The perspective here is to move away from economic analysis that examines individual economic actors to study the family as an economic unit that shapes the labor market participation of its members. Among the important issues that surface are who works at what, when, and how the income is utilized. It treats the family as a production unit from the viewpoint of gaining command over resources rather than only as a consuming unit. The mix of household production, outside informal economic activities, and mainstream economic participation is often the focus. Reciprocal economic activities of kin that do not involve monetary exchanges are of special interest to many analysts.

*Community.* Similarly, a neighborhood or community perspective fastens on nonmonetary exchanges between residents based on generalized notions of reciprocity and mutuality. If money is involved in such exchanges, it is much less than would be required in a mainstream economic transaction. A gender concern distinguishes between the nature of male and female services and products that are exchanged.

Voluntary activities that do not involve expectations of reciprocity, as in aid to elderly members of the community, provide a somewhat different perspective. These activities are contributions to community solidarity and do not create obligations for those helped.

*Service provision.* Many low-income neighborhoods lack important services and stores. Informal, itinerant entrepreneurs often meet these needs. Frequently, they offer lower prices than those demanded in established outlets. The social network embedded in these kinds of entrepreneurial activities is at the center of a distinctive perspective.

The social relations of production and consumption in informal economies furnish, then, a variety of ways of thinking about these activities that differ from the usual style of economic thinking that abstracts market behavior from social connections and contexts.

*Fiscal and
regulatory perspectives*

Still another set of perspectives focuses on the flow of money through irregular economies and the issues posed by untaxed income and unmonitored work.

*Fiscal.* The outlook here is to focus on the enormous loss in tax revenues because of the nonpayment of required taxes by informal economic structures. The estimates of tax loss vary enormously, though Susan Long's study suggests that many tend to be exaggerated.[3] Nonetheless, some economists contend that the hidden income-tax loss estimates demonstrate the disincentive effects of taxation and wage and other labor regulations. An overintrusive and expensive government produces an off-the-books defense; the remedy, in this view, is to reduce governmental activity, scope, and impact.

One need not adhere to this ideological assessment of the sources of informal economies to assert the need for more vigorous enforcement of tax laws so as to recoup the lost taxes. The argument can shift to a class analysis of tax loss: are low-income people in informal economies the chief source of tax losses, or is the tax loss primarily due to the engagement of formal enterprises and well-to-do persons in activities that are camouflaged and bar the scrutiny of the Internal Revenue Service? Progressives see the latter as the problem; conservatives fasten on the low-income as the main culprits and see confiscatory tax rates as the cause of tax evasion by the well-to-do.

3. Susan Long, "Growth in the Underground Economy: An Empirical Issue" (Manuscript, Bureau of Social Science Research, 1980).

Some believe that the major issue of off-the-books activity is that it inflates governmental outlays for social programs. Many receiving public welfare, housing assistance, food stamps, and Medicaid have incomes, it is asserted, above the eligibility lines for these programs but do not report their receipts from informal economies. The consequences are that heavy social spending occurs, leading to higher taxes, and macroeconomic policies are mistakenly oriented toward reducing unemployment.

*Justice system.* The other side of this concern for illegitimate receipt of public assistance is that ineligibles who receive it should be punished. More generally, tax evaders, whether poor or wealthy, should be brought to justice. The policing and prosecution of informal economies form an important perspective that dominates much of the discussion of informal economies. When the political attention cycle shifts back to welfare change, punishing low-income ineligibles receiving public assistance becomes a focus.

*Crime.* Organized crime is regarded by some as the major force in informal economies. Here, illegality is not seen in avoiding taxation but in the basic activity itself. How to reduce, eliminate, or punish organized crime, which is often calculated to be enormous in its take, is the major question.

Petty crime is also an issue, especially in certain neighborhoods. It is of special concern where it involves young people who may adopt the criminal road as their major economic activity and where it disrupts community life. Hustling, interpreted as gaining money from illicit and near-illicit activities, is regarded as offering an economic way of life that competes successfully against the settling-down processes of mainstream economies.

*Regulation.* This orientation is concerned with the informal economies' violation of laws regulating labor practices: violation of the minimum-wage provisions; hazardous working conditions; child labor. How to enforce the codes protecting those involved in employment is the governing question, quite different from that posed by those concerned with social expenditures.

## Conditions of insufficiency

This perspective focuses on the reality that some groups are coerced into irregular work and are exploited by it. The perspective, which starts from the same concerns as the regulatory perspective, emphasizes the exploitation experienced by many in the informal economies. The general theme is the low income received by many, the insecurity suffered. Work in the informal economy is not seen as a road to economic advance but as a dead end. Improving the conditions of those caught in informal economies is the issue. The concern with exploitation is a class perspective, focused on one of the groups worst off in society.

Some ethnic groups have limited economic chances and are forced into the informal economies. At the present time, this pressure is particularly evident in the so-called new immigration of Hispanics and Asians. Even those fully equipped with legal papers are often forced into off-the-books economic activities with high degrees of exploitation.

More generally, the issue is the low incomes received by those in informal economies. Often their incomes may not provide even bare subsistence. Children may have to work to augment family income. The conditions of work may be insanitary, harsh, and oppressive. Frequently workers have no protection or recourse. In short, informal economies can be bad places to work both economically and environmentally.

The multiple perspectives from which informal economies are viewed point not only to the limitations of focusing on the mainstream economy but also to the important variety of forces affecting nonmainstream activities. Where many forces are at work, differentiation of forms and processes, interests and ideologies, appears. An informal economy is not a simple production or consumption mode but a complex interweaving of these and other influences. There is value in lumping together the variety of nonmainstream activities to highlight the limitations of conventional economic activity; there is also value in delineating the different types, sources, and consequences of informal economies. Their multiple roles, their pervasiveness, their durability mean that they have not only a past and a present but a future as well. What that future will be or should be is in doubt and will be only partly influenced by developments in the mainstream economy. Informal economies are not only responses to the latter.

## COMPETING POLICIES FOR INFORMAL ECONOMIES

What policies should be adopted to deal with informal economies? Obviously, the answer depends on perspective and interest. The basic choices are to drive out, pay up, improve, or expand.

### Drive out

The drive-out choice seems largely unworkable except for a major onslaught on organized crime and tax evasion. Despite much rhetoric, not much success has been achieved in reducing organized crime or corporate and high-income recipients' evasions. Presumably, the lower tax rates in the 1986 tax legislation would lower the incentive to evade by well-to-do and low-income populations. Perhaps.

The omnipresence and persistence of informal economies strongly suggest that stamping them out has little possibility. Some forms are curtailed but others, especially small-scale activities, are hardy and recurring growths.

## Pay up

The pay-up choice requires much more stringent policing. Whether it can be achieved is largely a political decision about the degree of obtrusiveness, harshness of penalties, and expenditures on policing that are possible. Past history suggests that—with the exception of policing of welfare recipients—too little would be done to be deeply effective. But some advances in taxing participants in informal economies—or excluding them from social payments—could be achieved.

## Improve

Governmental concern about informal economies could follow the path of more governmental intervention. One step would involve extending present programs of Medicaid and Supplementary Social Insurance so that workers in informal economies who usually lack fringe benefits have a basic package of services and income that is not dependent on employment in the mainstream economy. A higher and more stringently enforced minimum-wage law would improve the income flow from work in informal economies. The counterargument is that it would reduce the number of jobs because labor costs would rise.

A family-allowance scheme not connected to employment could significantly supplement the income of low-income workers without requiring paperwork and identification of employments, which some would be reluctant to do. Stronger enforcement of occupational safety and health rules would require a resolute and larger regulatory staff; therefore, it is not likely to be acceptable. Unionization of informal work settings would make an enormous difference, but unions, as presently constituted, do not find such endeavors worthwhile; certainly, organization of low-income workers is hard to carry through successfully. Perhaps new forms of economic association, connected to ethnicity or gender, might be more effective. The effect of strong wage pressure might, however, decrease employments in the informal economies.

## Expand

Would governmental efforts to aid and expand informal economies automatically make them into mainstream activities? Assuming that this is not the case, low-cost loans directly provided by government or insured by it could facilitate the starting up and continuity of informal jobs. Another way is increasing the flexibility of social programs so that groups of citizens could provide services in their communities and receive financial support for them from government. The emerging pattern of treating welfare as an employment program is likely to increase involvements in informal economies as welfare payments are treated increasingly as short- or long-term wage supplementation. The relatively low wages and part-time work in informal economies would become more attractive if additional income were available from public funds. The Hungarian legitimation and extension of informal factory production arrangements suggest that many ways could be found to energize informal economies in both capitalist and socialist societies.

In a different view, government policies that lead to various patterns of income and wealth distribution could affect the demand for and supply of informal economic arrangements. At this point it is not clear what pattern is most conducive or resistant to informal economic operations. More important, shaping income flows to increase informal economic activity would have little political support. On the other hand, austerity—lower wages, reduced labor force, less public spending—as government and corporate policy to adjust the mainstream economy to new international competitive conditions is likely to generate informal economic activities to overcome the decline in employment in mainstream sectors. Austerity promotes informal economies.

Training is often proposed as a transitional effort, a way of moving people from low-wage, informal sectors to better-paid, more stable mainstream employments. Government training programs have been severely, often unfairly, criticized. They tend to suffer from poor quality, poor choice of skills to develop, short-term periods, creaming, pushing people into poor jobs to show a placement record, inadequate support systems, and so on. On the other hand, minorities who have been excluded from mainstream construction jobs and have had, as a result, to work in informal settings have been aided by some training programs. Since sizable public spending

on these programs occurs, improving them would seem a political possibility.

## THE FUTURE OF INFORMAL ECONOMIES

What can be confidently said about informal economies is that they are durable, pervasive, and flexible. As a consequence, all types of national economies will experience phenomena that resemble informal economies in their nonofficialness.

The political advantage of bringing together a great variety of economic-type activities under one label has to be accompanied by a detailed analysis of each of the different forms. If not, analysts are in a conceptual swamp where we are not helping one another but are pushing each other deeper into its murky depths. Which part of informal economies is under discussion should always be specified.

The scale of each form or type of informal economy is one of the key issues. Are we dealing with a major activity or a minor one in this or that case? Size makes a difference.

Linkage is another important issue. To what extent and in what ways is an informal economy activity intermeshed with the mainstream economy? How does it connect to social patterns? We should not assume linkages and connections—that informal economies are instrumental or functional imperatives—but we should search to see whether they are. Sometimes informal economies are relatively freestanding forms not deeply enmeshed with economic or social patterns.

Informal economies have contingent consequences. How they work out depends on a number of other economic and social influences. Consequently, we should not praise them as the wave of a more flexible future or condemn them as the remnant of a dying world. It all depends. These contingent influences need close examination if we are to understand how and why informal economies have the impacts that they do.

Like most things, informal economies exhibit a duality. They have positive features; they have negative features. Recognizing both is important. Efforts to reshape informal economies also can have such mixed effects—for example, improving informal jobs may decrease their numbers.

The adequacy of the concept of informal economies is not the issue. The basic question is how we should think about nonmainstream economic activities in three relations: their connections to the mainstream economy, to social institutions, and to the conditions of those involved in them. This issue of *The Annals* shows that we are making headway in all three respects.

It is likely that informal economies will have a renewed resurgence. In socialist societies, the widened legitimation of market, nonsocialist production will lead, if it is continued, to more activities regarded as in the informal economic spheres. In the United States and perhaps some other capitalist nations, new immigrants are likely to swell informal economic activities. Austerity, as I have noted, will also have that effect. The slowing down of economic growth could mean that informal economies will become more important even if they do not expand mightily. Their relative significance may become greater because of the difficulties of the mainstream economy.

From a policy point of view as well as from that of alternative economics, the major question is: Under what conditions can quality informal economies flourish? Diverse circumstances are likely to lead to expansion of some informal economies but growth is not necessarily a qualitative improvement.

A second policy question is to what extent the focus should be on improving and hastening transitions from informal economies to mainstream ones or on qualitative improvement of informal sectors. Concentrating exclusively on either may work to the detriment of the other.

As mentioned at the beginning, the existence of informal economies questions the accuracy and usefulness of formulations about mainstream economies and neoclassical economic analysis. A fundamental issue of the politics of intellectual analysis underlies this doubt.

To a large extent, the enormous amount of attention to informal economies in recent years is an effort to undermine or weaken the hegemonic role of mainstream economic thinking, which is largely neoclassical in its bases. Attention to informal economies reconnects economics to society, to concrete individuals in specific settings trying out actions to improve their lives. The informal economic viewpoint threatens the neoclassical perspective that universally useful concepts that divorce economic functioning from social structures are adequate in analyzing activities that are termed economic. Whatever the present limitations of the concepts and empirical work of informal economies, the search for a fuller understanding of the wide range of activities that are somewhat economic is necessary for realistic economic policies and for overcoming the damage resulting from the artificial separation of economy from society.

ANNALS, *AAPSS*, **493,** September 1987

# Does Jobless Mean Workless?
# Unemployment and Informal Work

## *By* RAYMOND E. PAHL

ABSTRACT: The spate of interest in informal work in recent years may be related to the hope that such work provides a safety net or survival strategy for those who would otherwise be seriously disadvantaged. Closer examination of this notion requires the disaggregation of informal work into its different forms and also the disaggregation of the unemployed into distinctive categories. The so-called new unemployed people, produced by the economic circumstances of the last decade, have no tradition of working informally to get by. Indeed, most evidence suggests that those in employment are best placed to do other forms of work as well. A detailed sociological study of the Isle of Sheppey in Kent, England, illustrates both divisions in participation in forms of work between men and women and also a process of polarization between work-rich households, with multiple earners engaging in all forms of work, and work-poor households, typically headed by elderly people, single parents, or unemployed people. The social polarization is likely to increase. The article concludes that jobless indeed means workless.

*Raymond E. Pahl is a graduate of St. Catharine's College, Cambridge, and took his doctorate at the London School of Economics. He joined the University of Kent at Canterbury on its foundation in 1965 and was appointed to a personal chair in sociology in 1972. He is now a part-time research professor in sociology at Kent and also a visiting professor at the University of Essex. His latest book,* Divisions of Labour, *was published in 1984.*

ANY society that has to sustain high levels of unemployment for long periods of time has a problem with its conscience. All Western industrial countries have the problem to a greater or lesser extent. In many countries the unemployment rate is more likely to be steady or increasing rather than declining. The proportion of those unemployed for over a year is also increasing. Manifestly, the problem is showing no sign of going away.[1]

Faced with this troublesome burden on their collective consciences, nations resort to various strategies to numb the pain for those in employment—if not for the unemployed themselves. The problem will, it is hoped, be solved "in time" or "when we get the economy right." The statistics, it is claimed, are inflated by those who "do not really want a job," or they include many who are passing through a period of unemployment before finding a new job, albeit at a lower rate of pay, elsewhere. These various notions rest on the idea that the present high levels of unemployment are the product of a necessary and ultimately beneficial period of transition, as the first industrial nations readjust to an industrial restructuring involving the decline of the old smokestack industries and the growth of new high-technology and service industries.[2]

However, these conscience-numbing devices are not as effective as they might be. Government statistics give no indica-

tion of any return to full employment in the short term; long-term unemployment continues its proportionate increase and the U.S. Bureau of Labor Statistics provides regular reports on the inadequacy of high-tech industries as the source for new jobs.[3]

SURVIVAL STRATEGIES
OF THE POOR:
AN INFORMAL SAFETY NET?

Faced with such setbacks, and recognizing the extreme difficulty of getting by without the benefit of earned income for those who do not have access to unearned income, an assumption has gained ground in recent years that the unemployed must have some survival strategies that have hitherto been overlooked.[4] The possibility that unemployed people are engaged in other forms of work is, of course, a mixed blessing. It is certainly agreeable for those responsible

1. Organization for Economic Cooperation and Development (OECD), *Employment Outlook* (Paris: OECD, 1986).

2. For contrasting views on the consequences of this for Britain, see, for the optimistic version, Great Britain, Department of Employment, *Employment: The Challenge for the Nation*, Cmnd. 9474, 1985; and for a much gloomier version, *Report from the Select Committee on Overseas Trade*, HL 1984/5, 238, vols. 1, 2 (*Aldington Report*), 1985.

3. Richard W. Riche, Daniel E. Hecker, and John U. Burgan, "High Technology Today and Tomorrow: A Small Slice of the Employment Pie," *Monthly Labor Review*, 106(11):50-58 (Nov. 1983); John A. Alic and Martha Caldwell Harris, "Employment Lessons from the Electronics Industry," ibid., 109(2):27-36 (Feb. 1986).

4. Some representative examples from a larger literature include Jason Ditton and Richard Brown, "Why Don't They Revolt?" *British Journal of Sociology*, 32(2):521-30 (1981); Kent Mathews, "National Income and the Black Economy," *Journal of Economic Affairs*, 3(4):261-67 (1983); P. Gutmann, "Are the Unemployed, Unemployed?" *Financial Analysts Journal*, pp. 26-29 (Sept. 1978); Rolf G. Heinze and Thomas Olk, "Development of the Informal Economy: A Strategy for Resolving the Crisis of the Welfare State," *Futures*, pp. 189-204 (June 1982); Richard Rose, *Getting by in Three Economies: The Resources of the Official, Unofficial and Domestic Economies* (Glasgow: University of Strathclyde, Centre for the Study of Public Policy, 1983); Wulf Gaertner and Alois Wenig, eds., *The Economics of the Shadow Economy* (New York: Springer-Verlag, Heidelberg, 1985).

for running the economy to think that those not earning wages are not having too bad a time. However, it is less acceptable to face the possibility that there are alternative and, possibly, more congenial ways of surviving in contemporary industrial society. If a component of contemporary economic strategy is the belief that high unemployment benefits employers by ultimately reducing the overall wage level, then such a strategy would be undermined if the unemployed were busily engaged in various forms of hidden work. So what may be good for placating the conscience may be bad for monetarist economic doctrines.[5]

This, then, is the part of the context in which work outside employment has been discussed. Much of the scholarly activity both in the United States and in Europe has been devoted to a debate about defining and measuring an economy described as hidden, submerged, irregular, informal, or whatever. This economy comprises the work that governments found difficult to tax effectively and that eluded economists' capacity to measure and analyze. Since relatively little was known about this work a decade or so ago, it was not surprising that it was defined in terms of its elusiveness.[6]

### THE NEED TO DISAGGREGATE INFORMAL WORK

Unfortunately, the more that was discovered about irregular or hidden

work outside employment, the more it became doubtful whether this work was disproportionately benefiting poor and unemployed people.[7] First, and most obvious, much hidden or irregular work is associated with being employed. Receiving extra goods, services, or income from an employer that is not declared to the tax authorities, using the workplace to produce goods, provide tools, or as a locus of pilfering are all ways of adding to one's informal income that are not available to those who are unemployed. Second, British tax authorities have repeatedly emphasized that one of the main sources for the loss of tax revenue is among the self-employed and small companies, particularly family companies. Some British evidence shows that in 1981, 87 percent of a sample of smaller cases investigated by the revenue authorities yielded additional tax income. The encouragement of small businesses and self-employment will almost certainly lead to a growth in the hidden economy and the loss of tax revenue.[8] However, even large companies can be guilty of fraudulent activity adding substantially to the loss of tax revenue:

The fraud may take the form of the omission of takings, the overstatement of business expenses or the charging to the business of private expenditure on behalf of the main shareholder or shareholders (as with the unincorporated trades), or of more sophisti-

5. For a lively and informed introduction to these issues, see Philip Mattera, *Off the Books* (London: Pluto Press, 1985); see in this context chap. 6, "The Government's Dilemma."

6. Edgar L. Feige, "How Big Is the Irregular Economy?" *Challenge,* pp. 5-13 (Nov.-Dec. 1979); OECD, *Employment Outlook,* chap. 3, "Concealed Employment."

7. Stuart Henry, "The Working Unemployed," *Sociological Review,* 30(3):460-77 (1982); Ian Miles, "Adaptation to Unemployment" (SPRU Occasional Paper no. 20, University of Sussex, England, 1983); Claire D. Wallace and Raymond E. Pahl, "Polarisation, Unemployment and All Forms of Work," in *The Experience of Unemployment,* ed. S. Allen et al. (New York: Macmillan, 1986).

8. *Committee on Enforcement Powers of the Inland Revenue Report* (hereafter cited as *Keith Report*), Cmnd. 8822, Mar. 1983, tab. 21, p. 270.

cated devices which seek to shift profits from one accounting period to another or to conceal them altogether. Some cases involve the fabrication of invoices or other documentary evidence; others involve the illegal transfer of profits to a tax haven outside the UK.[9]

Similarly, in the United States, James D. Smith has categorically asserted that "it would be incorrect . . . to assume that the underground economy is predominantly a force for more egalitarian distribution of income or a more equitable tax system."[10] In this case Smith is referring to all market activity, legal or illegal, that escapes the eye of the national income accountants. From this point of view, drug trafficking, illegal gambling, and prostitution are part of the underground economy activities, which Smith laconically notes "are no strangers to the richest decile of the population."[11] There is a substantial literature on the vexed question of whether the poor and unemployed are more likely to commit crimes than the rich and the employed.[12] On the face of it, it would seem inherently implausible that a newly redundant steelworker or clerical worker either is equipped for or desires a life of crime. A distinction must clearly be made between, on the one hand, traditional unemployment among unskilled, casual workers in particular cities and regions and, on the other, the new unemployment resulting from the industrial restructuring of the last decade. We may conclude, third, that it would be most unwise to label unemployed people as members of a new criminal class. Politicians of the Right are particularly anxious to avoid accepting such a conclusion, in order to avoid simpleminded public correlations of monetarist economic doctrines and increasing crime.

A fourth area of informal work involves a range of goods and services related to the maintenance of the domestic dwelling and private cars, together with a whole range of domestic tasks and child care. Carpenters, plumbers, electricians, hairdressers, window cleaners, child minders, gardeners, and a host of others are paid directly in cash or, perhaps, indirectly by reciprocal exchange of other goods or services. Here, it might be confidently assumed that those not in formal employment have the advantage. For those who lack economic resources there is said to be a kind of social capital in long-established neighborhoods and communities, such that those who encounter misfortune are aided by those have more resources, whether of time, money, or goods and services. This approach, which has long antecedents, is based on assumptions about mutual aid among both kin and nonkin, brought about by long-standing social relationships cemented through propinquity. While there may be some discussion about how far such community supports have been eroded by urban renewal and consumerism, many commentators still emphasize this response to adversity. Thus, for example, Lowenthal has said that "although needs may go unmet and thus give rise to problems such as poor health and sub-standard housing . . . many needs are provided for not through money income, but by the social networks and mutual aid systems that people participate in."[13]

9. "The Black Economy: Note by the Inland Revenue and Customs and Excise," note 41, *Keith Report*, p. 771.

10. James D. Smith, "The Invisible Other Hand: The Informal Economy of the United States," mimeographed (Ann Arbor: University of Michigan, Survey Research Center, 1982), p. 1.

11. Smith, "Invisible Other Hand," p. 2.

12. Mattera, *Off the Books*, chap. 5.

13. M. Lowenthal, "Non-Market Transactions in an Urban Community," in *Informal Institu-*

Certainly, such arguments have force in the long-established centers of deprivation, but it is hard to see how they could apply to, say, displaced workers in an area without any strong tradition of poverty or unemployment. The survival strategies of the poor cannot be assumed to be a readily available alternative lifestyle for displaced steelworkers. On the contrary, evidence from detailed empirical research in South Wales suggests that informal patterns of work based on reciprocity and cash transactions arose out of the common experience of meeting daily in the steelworks. The collapse of the industrial basis of employment carries with it a collapse of the social and material base for informal work as well.[14] Much work outside employment involves access to tools, transport, and markets—all of which require money. You need money to make money. Newly impoverished and unemployed people may have the time and, indeed, the skills to work informally for themselves. However, if the experience is novel and unexpected, it may be difficult to break into already established patterns of informal work.

Evidence from surveys in Europe and the United States shows that the unemployed in general are not likely to be involved in gaining much extra money from informal work, despite such activity being relatively widespread. A national representative sample of unemployed people, commissioned by the Economist Intelligence Unit in Britain in 1982, showed that while 23 percent

had done jobs for other people, only 4 percent of these had received payment in cash, most of these being in groups that had received further education.[15]

Evidence from a national sample of the U.S. population carried out in 1981 by the Institute for Social Research at the University of Michigan asked about the opportunities people have to buy goods and services from persons who sell them on the side. The conclusions certainly did not support the assumption that this kind of informal activity is limited to the poor and less privileged. The author of this study concluded that the "mean amount spent in the informal economy increases rather systematically with level of income. In general there are no surprises in the characteristics of buyers doing business in informal markets; they are pretty much a cross-section of the US population."[16] Similar conclusions have been adduced for other countries of the Organization for Economic Cooperation and Development.[17]

From the discussion so far, it is clear that there are many components of the underground economy and irregular work. One of the most important distinctions is whether the work is paid or unpaid. Much of the unpaid work outside employment is done by women making it, in a sense, doubly invisible. The essential point, central to a discussion of the question of whether jobless does indeed mean workless, is that both the forms of work and the jobless have to be disaggregated in order for the discussion to be meaningful.[18]

*tions,* ed. S. Henry (New York: St. Martin's Press, 1981), p. 91.

14. Lydia D. Morris, "Patterns of Social Activity and Post-Redundancy Labour-Market Experience," *Sociology,* 18(3):339-52 (1984). Further papers relating to this research are available from the Department of Sociology and Social Anthropology, University College of Swansea, Wales.

15. Economist Intelligence Unit, *Coping with Unemployment: The Effects on the Unemployed Themselves* (London: Economist Intelligence Unit, 1982).

16. Smith, "Invisible Other Hand," p. 14.

17. OECD, "Concealed Employment."

18. Jonathan I. Gershuny, "Prospects and Policies for the Informal Economy," mimeographed (Bath: University of Bath, 1986); Jan G.

## THE NEED TO DISAGGREGATE
## THE UNEMPLOYED

The survival strategies and options for informal work inevitably vary between, say, an unemployed female clerical worker obliged to support two dependent children on her own and an unemployed plumber, with his wife still in employment. There is a danger that use of a generic label such as "the unemployed" will bring to mind an image of adult, probably unshaven, men. Clearly, this stereotype has to be modified. Nearly half of all those unemployed in North America in 1979 were aged between 16 and 24, and in Australia it was as high as 56 percent. These proportions had declined by about 10 percentage points by 1985, partly due to a modest economic recovery, partly due to changes in the demographic structure, and partly due to the expansion of social measures that have taken many young people out of the labor force,[19] such as the youth training scheme and other programs financed by the U.K. government's Manpower Services Commission. However, it is important to recognize that for most of the countries of the Organization for Economic Cooperation and Development, out of every 10 people unemployed 3 or 4 will be aged 24 or younger.[20] The proportion in Europe has grown to 46 percent for those who have been unemployed for one year or longer. It seems likely that it will not be long before half of all unemployed people in Europe will have been out of work for a year or more. In Sweden in 1985 half of all the long-term unemployed were women; in France, 57 percent and in Germany, 65 percent. The proportion in the United Kingdom in that category was 23 percent, and in the United States, 33 percent.[21] Clearly, any attempt to tie patterns of work outside employment to an undifferentiated category of the unemployed is fraught with difficulties, although this has not deterred some observers from making the attempt.[22] More recent work, however, has thrown into question such attempts at classification.[23]

It might be prudent to pause at this point in the discussion. There is substantial historical and anthropological evidence that the poor do, indeed, have distinctive survival strategies in a variety of periods and contexts. A shrewd observer might adduce apparently contradictory evidence and I have even reported such evidence myself.[24] It was precisely because I considered that "shadow wage labour" or unrecorded economic activity might provide some kind of solution to the problems of deindustrialization and high levels of unemployment that I established a relatively large-scale research project to clarify in detail who did what work for whom and whether or not it was paid.[25]

Lambooy and Piet H. Renooy, "Informal Economy and the Labour Market: Relations with the Economic Order," mimeographed (Amsterdam: University of Amsterdam, Institute of Economic Geography, 1986); OECD, "Concealed Employment."

19. OECD, *Employment Outlook*, p. 33.
20. Ibid.

21. Ibid., p. 34.
22. See fn. 4.
23. Mattera, *Off the Books*; Wallace and Pahl, "Polarisation, Unemployment"; Raymond E. Pahl, "The Politics of Work," *Political Quarterly*, 56(4):331-45 (Oct.-Dec. 1985).
24. Jason Ditton, "Perks, Pilferage and the Fiddle: The Historical Structure of Invisible Wages," *Theory and Society*, 4:1-38 (1977); Carol B. Stack, *All Our Kin: Strategies for Survival in a Black Community* (New York: Harper & Row, 1974); Raymond E. Pahl, "Employment, Work and the Domestic Division of Labour," *International Journal of Urban and Regional Research*, 4(1):1-20 (1980); Enzo Mingione, "Informalization, Restructuring and the Survival Strategies of the Working Class," ibid., 7(3):311-39 (1983).
25. The research focused on the Isle of Shep-

## THE ISLE OF SHEPPEY:
## A DETAILED CASE STUDY

The study site was chosen because, following preliminary fieldwork in other areas, I was constantly assured that if I was looking for somewhere where people were engaged in irregular work I would be hard-pressed to find a more suitable locale. My intention was to find a place where there was a substantial amount of unemployment—by the end of the study the proportion had reached 20 percent—and there were apparently good opportunities for work outside employment. If those who were unemployed were less likely to be engaged in informal work in such a context, they were unlikely to be doing it where conditions were less favorable. The Isle of Sheppey was an extremely good choice for my purpose and while it is true that no one locale can be said to be typical of the aggregation of locales that makes up a society, nevertheless the processes at work are certainly likely to apply universally and are, therefore, generalizable. I began by making a detailed historical study of the island. There had been an industrial work force on the island since the early eighteenth century, based on the Admiralty Dockyard at Sheerness.

The dockyard fitted out and repaired ships but did not construct them and hence was not what we might call a shipyard. It had dry and wet docks into which ships went for repair. There was a long tradition of doing personal jobs at work, using the equipment and tools of the dockyard workshops. There was also a tradition of occupational theft, as houses were improved or largely built using Admiralty paint and timber. More recently there was a tradition of building or extending homes: both building land and property were substantially cheaper than on the mainland. Finally, the dockyard was closed and was replaced by a port importing a variety of goods including, initially, New Zealand lamb, bananas, oranges, and wine but later, more typically, cars and containers. The opportunities for pilferage in the years before the main fieldwork commenced were substantial.[26]

The dockyard had developed a tradition of craft skills in the community and yet Sheppey is still largely rural in character with opportunities for shooting duck, trapping rabbits, as well as fishing.

The research strategy undertaken by Claire Wallace and myself followed that pioneered by Ferman and his colleagues at the University of Michigan.[27] Initial fieldwork over a period of two years before the survey was carried out helped to establish a list of tasks in and around the home that might be done by friends or neighbors for payment or for recipro-

pey, the site of a port and much heavy industry, which is situated in the Thames Estuary off the coast of Kent, England. A 1-in-9 sample of households was interviewed in the summer of 1981, yielding 730 cases, a response rate of 79 percent. The research was funded by the British Social Sciences Research Council from 1980 to 1983. A full report appears in Raymond E. Pahl, *Divisons of Labour* (New York: Basil Blackwell, 1984).

26. Raymond E. Pahl, "The Restructuring of Capital: The Local Political Economy and Household Work Strategies," in *Social Relations and Spatial Structures,* ed. Derek Gregory and John Urry (New York: Macmillan, 1985).

27. Louis A. Ferman, Louise Berndt, and Elaine Selo, "Analysis of the Irregular Economy: Cash Flow in the Informal Sector," Report to the Bureau of Employment and Training, Michigan Department of Labor, mimeographed (Ann Arbor: University of Michigan, Institute of Labor and Industrial Relations; Detroit, MI: Wayne State University, 1978).

cal services. In addition, information was gathered on extra work done for the main or another employer or for anyone else who might provide income. Hence it was possible to provide a matrix of all the forms of work in which members of the household engaged, together with a fairly accurate measure of the sources of labor on which they drew to get work done in and around the household. Four types of work were distinguished:

— work done by members of a household with their own tools and in their own time for themselves. This provides a range of goods and services—from homegrown vegetables to the repair of car brakes—and has been referred to by others as the "domestic" or "household economy." We prefer the term "self-provisioning."
— work outside formal employment for others, outside the household, which is remunerated. This is generally known as "working on the side."
— work done for others outside the home that is not paid for in money but is repaid in favors or in kind. This may or may not be calculative—as when reciprocities are, as it were, converted into cash terms. Sometimes such work is simply part of an affective involvement with others.
— work outside the household to obtain food or materials without involving anyone else or without it necessarily being illegal. Such activity would include fishing, ferreting, "totting," and scavenging-type activities.

Information was gathered about the present occupation of all members of the household and the job histories of respondents. A main concern of the study was to explore the relatively unresearched area of the divisions of labor by gender in the four forms of work that were distinguished.

Self-provisioning, the most substantial form of informal work, cannot be understood in relation to one partner's activity alone. While men and women have their distinctive spheres—men fix cars, women knit and sew—there was an increasing tendency for certain decorating and home-improvement tasks to be shared by both partners, who may be heavily involved in this kind of work. Work on the side, which may or may not be illegal, was also undertaken by both men and women. Men may fix cars for cash; women scrub pub floors or work in the fields picking fruit and vegetables. As a parallel to the formal labor market there appeared to be an informal labor market segmented between men and women—and indeed between young and old. Little research has been done on the relative monetary rewards of men's informal work and women's informal work, but we do know that much of the formal work women do is very poorly paid. In the third category—unremunerated supportive reciprocity—there was again a division of labor by gender. Women were more likely to provide emotional and social support—caring for other children, shopping for the elderly, lending food, and similar assistance in resolving day-to-day crises in the community. For men, on the other hand, favors were provided on an occasional basis and included such things as lending tools or helping to mend a fence or lay a path. In short, as in the formal economy, women were more likely to do caring work and men to do practical, manual work. Finally, the work we termed scavenging was almost entirely done by men.

In order to more thoroughly explore the socioeconomic characteristics of the households most likely to use this form of labor we devised a scale to measure the amount of informal work engaged in by the household. The conclusions were somewhat paradoxical. Those who used the most informal unpaid labor were either those who could not afford to pay but needed to complete tasks—most likely single-parent families and retired single people—or those who were well placed to reciprocate informal work—namely, women under 35 with growing children. Clearly, reciprocal child-care arrangements fall into this category. These conclusions demonstrate that the range of domestic tasks that most households need to have done depends on the division of labor by gender in the home. Where one partner is missing, the necessary labor has to come from outside the household.

Turning to the supply side of this form of work, the data are much richer. Table 1 shows unpaid informal work done for others by the separate male and female respondents and their economic activity.

From this will be seen that the unemployed men are the least likely to engage in such work and the unemployed women are the most likely. One possible explanation for this finding has already been mentioned, namely, the nature of the gender-linked tasks that are done for others. Table 2 shows the types of work that are done by respondents. It will be seen that men are more likely to do home improvements such as minor repairs, carpentry, decorating, and gardening—all fixed tasks that could have a price and could, therefore, be interpreted as illegal work that could be reported.

## SOCIAL POLARIZATION

Taking all these forms of work together, and including engagement in the formal economy, it was found that rather than one form of work being a substitute for another—for example, work on the side substituting for formal employment—there appeared to be a process of polarization. This resulted in those in formal employment being more likely to do more self-provisioning and informal, irregular work as well. The cumulative effect of the process was that there were some very busy productive households at one pole and at the other pole there were households unable to engage in little more than communal reciprocity and scavenging—indeed, some households could not even engage in these forms of work.[28]

Previous publications reporting the main findings of our research have not given particular prominence to the unemployed. Rather, they have focused on the way all forms of work have become concentrated in the more affluent households with multiple earners. For instance, a high proportion of working-class households with multiple earners earn more than those middle-class households with only one earner. These are the working-class households most likely to be engaged in buying their own dwelling from the local authority or in making all kinds of interior improvements if they already own it.[29] This increasing divergence between households with multiple earners—and hence high income—undertaking many forms of work and those households with no

28. Raymond E. Pahl and Claire Wallace, "Household Work Strategies in Economic Recession," in *Beyond Employment,* ed. Nanneke Redclift and Enzo Mingione (New York: Basil Blackwell, 1985).

29. Pahl, *Divisions of Labour.*

## TABLE 1
### ECONOMIC ACTIVITY OF RESPONDENT, BY WHETHER HE OR SHE ENGAGES IN UNPAID INFORMAL WORK OUTSIDE THE HOUSEHOLD

| Formal Economic Activity of Respondent | Does Respondent Engage in Informal Activity Outside the Household? | | | | | | Total |
|---|---|---|---|---|---|---|---|
| | Men | | | Women | | | |
| | Yes (%) | No (%) | Total (N) | Yes (%) | No (%) | Total (N) | (N) |
| Full-time work | 31 | 69 | 206 | 21 | 79 | 81 | 287 |
| Part-time work | 40 | 60 | 5 | 21 | 79 | 76 | 81 |
| Unemployed | 19 | 81 | 26 | 37 | 63 | 16 | 42 |
| Retired | 21 | 79 | 63 | 22 | 78 | 85 | 148 |
| Full-time housework | 0 | 100 | 1 | 23 | 77 | 168 | 169 |
| Other/Did not answer | — | — | 1 | — | — | — | 1 |
| All % | 28 | 72 | | 23 | 77 | | |
| N | 84 | 218 | 302 | 96 | 330 | 426 | 728* |

SOURCE: Author's tabulations from the Sheppey Survey, 1981. For details of this survey, see Gill Courtenay, *Isle of Sheppey Study: Technical Report*, report no. P. 631 (London: Social and Community Planning Research, 1982).

NOTE: The question on the interview schedule was, "Are there any jobs that you do *outside* your home, for other people?"

*Two respondents failed to give information.

## TABLE 2
### TYPE OF INFORMAL WORK FOR OTHERS BY GENDER

| Type of Informal Work | Men | | Women | | Total | |
|---|---|---|---|---|---|---|
| | N | % | N | % | N | % |
| Routine domestic work | 11 | 18 | 49 | 82 | 60 | 22 |
| Social support | 6 | 18 | 28 | 82 | 34 | 13 |
| Personal services | 1 | 8 | 11 | 92 | 12 | 13 |
| Home improvement | 72 | 87 | 11 | 13 | 83 | 31 |
| Formal community work | 11 | 35 | 20 | 65 | 31 | 12 |
| Transport | 4 | 44 | 5 | 56 | 9 | 3 |
| Other help | 19 | 48 | 21 | 53 | 40 | 15 |
| Total | 124 | 46 | 145 | 54 | 269 | 100 |

SOURCE: Author's tabulations from the Sheppey Survey. For details of this survey, see Courtenay, *Isle of Sheppey Study*.

earners and with low income we have termed social polarization.

In this process of polarization, it appears that the loss of employment has implications for the degree of involvement of household members in other forms of work. It is now clear that there is no direct substitution of various forms of informal work for the loss of employment. Indeed, as O'Higgins has demonstrated, there is a positive relationship between the hidden economy and the strength of the formal economy and not the other way round.[30]

As a result of surveying a number of studies, including the research previously referred to in this article, the Organization for Economic Cooperation and Development's *Employment Outlook* for 1986 concluded:

The inequalities of declared income are very often carried over into concealed employment. The small-scale jobs common in concealed employment tend to go to families whose heads already have full-time work. The unemployed, and especially the long-term unemployed, have relatively low levels of skill or training and impaired social contacts. They would seem to be particularly badly placed in any attempt to find concealed employment.[31]

### EXPROPRIATION OF THE POOR BY THE MIDDLE MASS

The reasons for this social polarization—the so-called Matthew Effect: to them that hath more is given abundantly while even that which the poor hath is taken away—are complex. Part of the answer is the democratization of skills through technological advances in the do-it-yourself industry. Jobs that in the past would require hiring a skilled craftsman can be done by a much wider range of people, using their own tools in their own time. Earlier research on this topic emphasized the need for time but neglected to consider the cost of tools, trans-port, and materials. I have interviewed unemployed men in homes where much work needed doing, but they did not have the resources to buy materials. People with their own tools and materials owning their own dwellings and cars and having spare time, perhaps as a result of longer holidays or shift work, have the resources to do more self-provisioning. They are also more likely, as my Sheppey Survey demonstrates, to do more work for other households and also perhaps to take a second job as a moonlighter. Those in employment are best placed to find more work, both formal and informal. Those who are unemployed find opportunities taken away from them, and they are often afraid to risk taking unemployment benefits while doing extra work.[32]

Work outside employment, particularly if it is potentially income generating, has been expropriated by the work-rich households. To be sure, the low-paid and sweated twilight employment is left for the jobless as, too, is the unpaid work of caring and support carried out almost entirely by women. Those who wish to encourage all forms of work, particularly for the long-term unemployed, need to recognize that most informal or irregular work is dependent on having the money to supply tools, transport, materials, and social contacts. Without a basic income support the polarization between work-rich and work-poor households is likely to continue to increase.

30. Michael O'Higgins, "The Relationship between the Formal and Hidden Economies: An Exploratory Analysis for Four Countries," in *Economics of the Shadow Economy,* ed. Gaertner and Wenig.

31. OECD, *Employment Outlook,* p. 77.

32. Rachid Foudi, François Stankiewicz, and Nicolas Vaneecloo, "Les chomeurs et l'economie informelle," in *Travail noir* (Lille: University of Lille, Laboratoire d'analyse des systemèmes et du travail, 1982), pp. 11-124.

ANNALS, *AAPSS*, **493**, September 1987

# Technology, Social Innovation, and the Informal Economy

## By JONATHAN GERSHUNY

ABSTRACT: Unpaid work in the home is an important contributor to national wealth: very nearly half of all work in a modern economy takes place outside the formal economy. A major effect of new technology is to increase the extent of informal production through the development of new productive equipment for installation in private households. Domestic production becomes more efficient, and the pattern of demand for commodities from the formal economy is changed: we buy goods rather than services. This article uses evidence about historical changes in the patterns of use of time, from a number of different developed countries, to investigate the effect of technical change on the relationship between the formal and informal economies.

*Jonathan Gershuny has bachelor's and master's degrees in economics and political science and a doctorate from the University of Sussex in the United Kingdom. From 1974, he was successively fellow and senior fellow of the Science Policy Research Unit at Sussex University. He held a German Marshall Fund Fellowship during 1981 and 1982. In 1984 he was appointed professor of sociology and head of the Sociology and Social Policy Group at the University of Bath, United Kingdom. His books include* After Industrial Society? *and* Social Innovation and the Division of Labour.

CONVENTIONAL economics is concerned to an overwhelming extent with the formal economy—with those human activities that are mediated through monetary exchanges. The yearly published government figures on economic activity describe economic behavior through such concepts as value added through employment, capital investment, final expenditure, government transfer payments, imports, exports, and so on. These sorts of concepts and the changing relationships between them constitute the reality to which economists normally address their theories.

The significance of the informal economy perspective lies in its assertion that economic processes, of great importance to the development of the society, take place outside the formally accounted economy. Some of these extra-economic processes involve monetary transactions that only take place outside the formal economy because of inadequacies of the system for collection of national accounting statistics, or because of individuals' determination to evade registration of their activities in order to avoid tax or some other statutory duty. This article is not, however, concerned with these so-called "hidden"[1] or "irregular"[2] aspects of the informal economy. Instead it concentrates on the nonmonetized part of the informal economy. In this I include the set of processes in which, to produce final services, unpaid labor is combined with materials and capital equipment installed in private homes. This part of the informal economy is a sphere of economic activity not covered by the national accounting definitions

and is described variously as the "household"[3] or "domestic" economy[4]—though neither of these terms is really adequate insofar as they both overlook nonmonetized production activities undertaken by civic, church, or other community organizations.[5]

I have argued elsewhere that the European economies in the last fifty years have seen technical and organizational changes in household production that have had profound consequences for the structure of the formal economy. Instead of an emerging service economy, the rising price of at least some final services relative to the general trend of prices, together with the falling relative price and greatly improving performance of some sorts of domestic equipment, has meant, quite contrary to the conventional perception, a shift away from many areas of service employment. For example, there are fewer laundry or transport workers, but more people are employed in manufacturing and also in maintaining washing machines and cars.

Europe's historical growth in service employment has been explained by two major developments outside the private household: the increase in educational and medical services funded from government or publicly regulated and subsidized insurance sources; and the growth of provision of intermediate, or producer, services[6]—services provided to other firms rather than to final consumers.[7] A

1. Stuart Henry, *The Hidden Economy* (Oxford: Martin Robertson, 1978).

2. Louis A. Ferman and Louise E. Berndt, "The Irregular Economy," in *Can I Have It in Cash?* ed. S. Henry (London: Astragal, 1981).

3. Scott Burns, *The Household Economy* (Boston: Beacon Press, 1977).

4. Jonathan I. Gershuny, *After Industrial Society?* (New York: Macmillan; Atlantic Highlands, NJ: Humanities Press, 1978).

5. Jonathan I. Gershuny, "The Informal Economy," *Futures*, 11:1 (Feb. 1979).

6. Jonathan I. Gershuny, *Social Innovation and the Division of Labour* (New York: Oxford University Press, 1983).

7. The latter term is from Herbert C. Green-

third element of particular importance for the United States that does result from a growth of private spending on services is a growth of mainly low-wage employment in such areas as fast food, restaurants, and related service industries. However, the recent decline in final household expenditures on services as a fraction of all household expenditures[8] has been explained by changes taking place in the informal economy. Self-servicing—unpaid work in the household sector, using manufactured goods and materials—substitutes for what might previously have been paid service employment. New equipment in the home enables new patterns of self-provisioning and leads to a changed relationship between the formal and informal economies.

But all the evidence previously used to demonstrate the argument was drawn from conventional economic statistics. It has been shown, for instance, how the balance of household expenditure on transport has shifted proportionately away from purchased entertainment services—for example, going to the movies or theater—toward expenditure on entertainment goods such as compact-disc players, televisions, and videos. From this we may infer that an increasing proportion of all final entertainment occurs within the household economy rather than in the formal economy.

One conclusion from this line of argument is that if we are to understand the processes of structural change in the formal economy, we need to consider evidence about behavior outside it. We

need to know more about the details of daily life. To understand the operations and historical dynamics of the household economy, we need evidence of how people spend their time and what they do with the goods and services that they buy. Economic statistics tell us little about people's use of time. But there is a technique for collecting quantitative statistical evidence about the household economy: the time budget survey.[9] This article outlines one way that time budget data can be used to extend our understanding of the relationship between the formal and informal economies. It suggests a new way of organizing socioeconomic accounts, using time rather than money as a *numéraire*. And it very briefly summarizes the intermediate results of a study that yields some clues about how current new technologies may be expected to affect the informal economy over the coming decades.

### TIME USE AND CHAINS OF PROVISION

The conventional time budget shows the individual's allocation of his or her own time to a range of activities that may include paid work, unpaid work in the home, leisure activities, sleep, and personal care. In addition, the individual uses other people's time. All the goods and services used by one individual derive from the work time of others. An alternative way of organizing time-use accounts, therefore, is to consider how individuals use their own or other people's time for their own purposes. Consider, for example, food. We spend some of our time in consuming it, some

field, *Manpower and the Growth of Producer Service* (New York: Columbia University Press, 1966).

8. Jonathan I. Gershuny and Ian D. Miles, *The New Service Economy* (London: Francis Pinter; New York: Praeger, 1983).

9. John P. Robinson, *How Americans Use Time* (New York: Praeger Scientific, 1977), provides a concise description of time budget techniques and their application in the United States.

more of our own time preparing it for eating—cooking—and we spend money to buy the raw materials and equipment and utensils that we use in the course of preparing and eating it. Embodied in the materials and commodities we buy is the paid work time of other people and perhaps a very small part of our own paid work time. The individual's level of nutrition results from the combination of his or her own consumption and unpaid work time—eating and cooking—with the paid work time of those workers in the farming, fishing, transport, manufacturing, retail, and other service industries.

We might think of three distinct, broad categories of time: paid work time, unpaid work time, and leisure or consumption time. Each individual's state of material well-being results from the combination of these. There is a chain of provision—or perhaps a better metaphor might be a complex interwoven net of threads of provision—passing from the farmer—and before the farmer, from the workers in the agrochemical industry, farm vehicle manufacturing, and so on—through manufacturing process workers who prepare and package the food, truck drivers who transport it, workers in retail industry who sell to households, and then the unpaid work in households, preparing the food to be eaten, and finally the consumption of the food. Each link in the chain can be accounted for in terms of one of the three sorts of time use. Add together each link in the chain and we have the total time that the society devotes to nutrition. Similarly, we can think of other purposes—shelter, entertainment, education, and so on—each of which has its own chain of provision, its own thread of paid work, unpaid work, and consumption. Every activity in the soci-

ety may be defined as having a place in one such chain of provision. In this conceputalization, the nonmonetized sector of the informal economy is not some freestanding, alternative locus of production, competing with the formal economy. It is merely a phase of production, complementary to the formal production process, a link in the chains of provision for needs.

This way of looking at economic activity demands a new form of accounts, organized around a classification of the day-by-day purposes of economic activity, such as the acquisition of food or entertainment or medical services. Any classification of such purposes will inevitably give rise to arguments about means and ends. One might ask, "Are not housing and clothing both means to the same ends?" In this case, however, the classification is simply a way of linking together the chain of provision, of associating particular sorts of paid work with particular sorts of unpaid work and consumption. The paid work time of the farmers is clearly linked with the time spent cooking food and washing dishes and the time spent in eating; we need a system of accounts that registers these connections.

### HISTORICAL CHANGE IN CHAINS OF PROVISION

It may be helpful at this point to outline some of the sorts of changes in chains of provision that we may expect to find over a historical period. We might divide these changes into three classes, of which the third is of particular importance to the evolution of the informal economy.

First, there are changes in the organization of production in the formal economy, such as occupational specialization, whereby jobs are subdivided and demand for the more skilled classes of labor is increased. There is also industrial special-ization: industries subcontract elements of their production processes to other specialist firms, so that the extent of vertical integration in the economy is reduced.

Second, there are changes in the distribution of time between the various categories of day-to-day purposes, or, we might alternatively term them, needs. As the level of satisfaction with these particular purposes rises, so individuals and societies will wish to transfer their production and consumption time to the satisfaction of other purposes. Part of the explanation of change in economic structure comes from this sort of develop-ment.

Third, there are changes involving radical innovation in chains of provi-sion—changes in the mode of provision for particular needs or purposes.

Consider, for instance, the provision of domestic services in the 1930s. We can see what are in fact two quite distinct ways of satisfying requirements for the maintenance of the domestic environment. One involved a good deal of paid work time—the work of domestic servants. Middle-class and upper-class households might have to contribute a certain amount of unpaid work in the form of supervision, and perhaps house-hold marketing, but as we shall see later in this article, the greater part of the domestic services in such households was purchased from the formal econ-omy. The result of the purchase of this skilled service labor was a high level of domestic comfort for the household members, if not necessarily for the ser-vants. This high-income mode of provi-sion of domestic services very adequately satisfied this particular purpose—for a minority of the population.

By contrast, the other mode of provi-sion involved much less paid work. The majority of households could not afford to employ servants but acquired domes-tic services largely through their own unpaid labor. Some paid work was still involved. Such households would still have to acquire materials from the money economy, but this would be a different sort of paid labor and on a much smaller scale than that used in the high income chain of provision. And accordingly, the low-income modes of provision involved very much more unpaid work, heavy, largely unmechanized drudgery that pro-duced, at the end of the day, less satis-factory domestic services than the high income alternative. Spending more time in unpaid work, such households had less time available for domestic con-sumption and enjoyed much lower stan-dards of food and shelter. A minority were well provided with domestic ser-vices; the majority were substantially underprovided.

How would it be possible to increase the extent of satisfaction of the society's needs for domestic services? It certainly would be possible, in the 1930s, to increase the capital equipment used in the high-income mode, making servants somewhat more efficient at their work. This might have the effect of marginally improving the welfare of the high-income households, or of slightly reducing the amount of paid domestic labor necessary to provide the same level of welfare. Marginal additions of capital equipment to be used by servants could hardly make a very substantial impact on the major problem, which was that the majority could never expect to employ servants. If some want servants, others must be servants; it might be possible to increase the output from the high-income mode of provision marginally, but not in such a way as to make a substantial impact on the overall welfare of the society.

What actually happened was a radical innovation. More capital equipment was introduced—but in conjunction with the unpaid labor. Economic development during the 1950s and 1960s was dominated by a particular sort of consumer expenditure, which we might helpfully think of as capital investment in the informal economy—investment in vacuum cleaners, washing machines, electric or gas stoves, refrigerators—that served to increase the efficiency of unpaid domestic production. In effect, a new mode of provision of domestic services emerged, involving different sorts of paid work—manufacturing rather than service employment—and new sorts of housework requiring less physical drudgery.

Figure 1 shows the results of an attempt to reconstruct the evolution of domestic work time for women—nonemployed or very part-time employed—in the United Kingdom.[10] It may be interpreted as showing (1) the very substantial disparity between middle-class and working-class housewives in the 1930s, reflecting the differential effects of the high-income and low-income modes of domestic service provision on unpaid work time; (2) the increase in middle-class women's domestic work time through the 1950s as the high-income

mode became progressively more inaccessible to all except a minority of the rich; and (3) the convergence, and continuing decline through the 1960s and 1970s, of the domestic work of both classes. The same evolution of women's domestic work through the 1960s and 1970s is found in the United States, Canada, Holland, Denmark, and Norway (Figures 2A and 2B).[11]

We have here an example of radical innovation in a chain of provision for a particular need. There are different ways that a given purpose can be satisfied—alternative modes of provision—which have different mixes of costs and advantages. Different groups in the society will have differential access to the alternative modes, at any point in time, and accordingly receive different levels of benefit. In the example of domestic services in the 1930s, the rich minority had access to a mode of provision that gave them very substantial benefits, whereas the majority enjoyed much less satisfactory domestic conditions and at a considerable cost of unpaid work time. Over time, the relative costs and advantages of competing modes of provision changed, altering the distribution of advantages across the society. Through the 1950s and 1960s the monetary costs of the high-income mode of provision rose, so that it very nearly disappeared

10. The data for this figure are drawn from surveys carried out by Mass Observation during the 1930s and 1950s, the British Broadcasting Corporation (BBC) during the 1960s and 1970s, and the U.K. Economic and Social Research Council. See BBC, *The People's Activities and the Use of Time* (London: BBC Publications, 1978); Jay I. Gershuny et al., "Time Budgets: Preliminary Analyses of a National Survey," *Quarterly Journal of Social Affairs,* 2(1):13-39 (1986).

11. The multinational comparative data set used is not properly documented in a published form, but a brief description will be found in Jonathan I. Gershuny, "Time Use, Technology and the Future of Work," *Journal of the Market Research Society,* 28(4) (Oct. 1986). The estimates in Figures 2A, 2B, 4A, and 4B have been reweighted so as to remove the effects of increases in the proportions of employed women and unemployed men in the national samples. Note the increase in men's domestic work in figure 2B reflecting, we might guess, cultural rather than technological change.

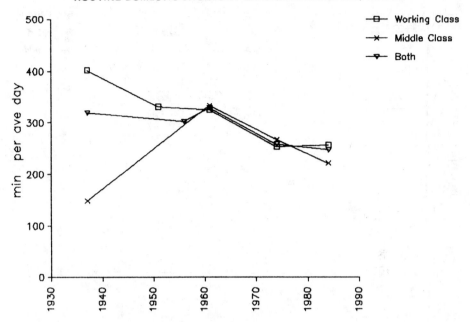

FIGURE 1
ROUTINE DOMESTIC CHORES OF BRITISH HOUSEWIVES, 1937-84

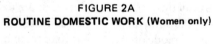

FIGURE 2A
ROUTINE DOMESTIC WORK (Women only)

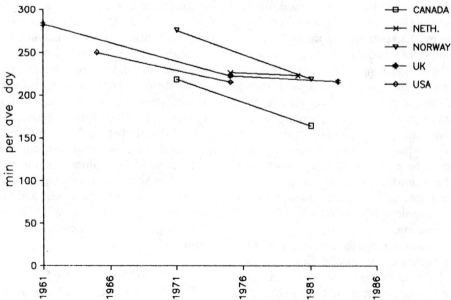

FIGURE 2B
**ROUTINE DOMESTIC WORK (Men only)**

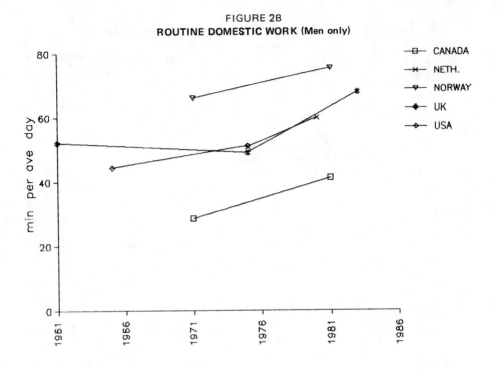

from this chain of production. At the same time the costs of the innovative, domestic-capital-intensive mode of provision fell, and its performance improved, so as to replace the high-income mode of provision. Hence, over time, the acquisition of domestic services, which used to demand paid service labor, came instead to require very much more manufacturing employment. And though the better-off minority of the population, who in the 1930s had very little unpaid domestic work, now have more, the consequence for the majority has been a substantial reduction in unpaid work input to this chain of provision.

To summarize the conceptual scheme: a society's time may be divided up into chains of provision for particular purposes or needs; these chains consist of the amounts of time, spent in paid or unpaid work or in leisure and consump-

tion, that are devoted to the satisfaction of each class of human purpose; all of the time spent by members of the society can be attributed to one or another category of production or consumption, in one or another of the chains. Over a historical period, the allocation of time among these categories changes, in three distinct ways: (1) there is change in the organization of the formal economy, such that different kinds, or different quantities, of paid labor time are required for the production of different commodities; (2) the society redistributes its time among various of the purposes; and (3) there is a change in the mix of activities involved in the satisfaction of particular purposes.

A SYSTEM OF ACCOUNTS

The notion of chains of provision provides a straightforward basis for a system of socioeconomic accounts that includes both the formal and informal economy. We can relate time use outside paid employment to final expenditure on—or state provision of—goods and services and hence to employment. Since both paid employment and extra-economic activities may be measured in terms of time, we arrive at a time-based account of changes in life-style and economic structure.

The first step relies on the observation that each sort of activity is associated with the use of particular final goods and services. Time spent at the cinema requires an entry fee, travel time requires a passenger ticket, time at school requires either state expenditure on a final service or, more occasionally, some household expenditure on private education. Washing clothes may require laundry services, or household expenditure on soap, water, and electricity, a washing machine, and its servicing. Each time-use category is associated with a distinct bundle of goods and services, although, of course, each category of good or service may be associated with more than one category of activity. For example, the same kitchen table may be used for food preparation and for eating and for school homework.

In principle, these associations between categories of activity and the commodities used while engaged in them could be determined empirically. We could, for example, ask within the time budget diary not only "What were you doing? Where? With whom?" but also "Using what?" For the moment, I have allocated commodities to their appropriate activities purely on the basis of a priori reasoning; Table 1 summarizes this set of assumptions.

These associations between activities and commodities are crucial in forming the link between the time-budget-based

life-style indicators and conventional economic statistics. The time expenditure categories in Table 1 include the full range of activities other than paid work; the money expenditure categories cover all the sorts of final goods and services consumed in the economy. The table thus enables us to translate time use into final demand, and using the conventional economic statistical sources—input-output and industry-occupation matrices—we can in turn translate final demand into industrial output, industrial employment, and thence into occupational employment patterns.[12]

Employment is itself a time-use category; furthermore, it is the one category missing from Table 1. So in the time-use column of Table 1 we have all the activities other than paid work; and the money-expenditure columns may be translated into time spent at work in different occupations. We can, in short, replace Table 1 with an alternative formulation, which represents all the society's activities, inside and outside the economy, in terms of a single indicator, time.

Table 2 provides a very simplified version of such a system of accounts, which divides paid work summarily into just two categories, manual and nonmanual. The table covers the population 14 years of age and older in the United Kingdom. For each of two years, the time-use columns sum to the total 1440 minutes of the average day of this population. In 1961, for example, this average day was made up of 236 minutes of paid work, 989 minutes of leisure or consumption time—if we were to look at more

12. This process of translation is a nontrivial task, requiring an intricate sequence of calculations that I shall not attempt to outline here; the general principle is nevertheless quite straightforward, and the set of associations in Table 1 is really the only unconventional aspect of it.

## TABLE 1
### ACTIVITIES, TIME USE, AND RELATED EXPENDITURES

| Purpose | Time-Use Activities* | Goods (Family expenditure survey) | Marketed Services (Family expenditure survey) | Non-Market Services (National accounts) |
|---|---|---|---|---|
| Shelter and clothing | Housework | Housing (rent, rates, other charges), power and fuel, clothing, furniture (including cutlery, china, and oddments), cleaning materials, matches, etc. | Repairs, maintenance, decoration, household and other insurance, laundry and cleaning, domestic help, other repairs not allocated elsewhere | Sewerage, refuse disposal, fire, local welfare, and other welfare services |
| Food: Cooking | Cooking, washing up | | | Agriculture, fishing, and food |
| Meals | Eating meals, snacks | All food and nonalcoholic drinks | | |
| Child care | Child care | | | Child care |
| Shopping | Shopping | | | |
| Travel and communications | Domestic travel / Leisure travel and excursions | Postage, telephones, telegrams; purchase of car, bicycle, etc. | Maintenance and running costs of motor vehicles; bus and train fares, etc. | Roads, lighting, transport, and communications |
| Personal care | Dressing, toilet, sleep | Toilet requisites, cosmetics | Hairdressing | |
| Restaurants | Restaurants | | Meals bought away from home | |
| Pubs | Pubs and social clubs | Alcoholic drinks | | |
| Cinema, theater | Cinema, theater, dances, parties, etc.; at church; civic duties; watching sports | | Cinema, theater, and other events | Libraries, museums, etc. |
| Playing sports | Playing sports | | | |
| Walking | Walks | | | |

| | | | | |
|---|---|---|---|---|
| Visiting and entertaining | Entertaining or visiting friends | | | |
| Television, radio | Television, radio, music | Radio and television, and musical instruments, including repairs | Radio and television licenses and rental payments | |
| Reading, study | Reading books or papers, or studying | Books, magazines, and periodicals | | |
| Talking, relaxing | Conversation, relaxing | Cigarettes, tobacco, pipes, etc. | | |
| Odd jobs, gardening | Odd jobs, gardening | Seeds, plants, flowers, and pets | | |
| Games, hobbies | Hobbies and pastimes, knitting, sewing | | | |
| Holidays | | | Hotel and holiday expenses, and miscellaneous other services | |
| Medical services | Personal services | Medicines and surgical goods | Medical, dental, and nursing fees | National Health Service |
| Education | | | Educational and training expenses | Education |
| Administration and defense | | | Pocket money and other expenditure not assigned elsewhere; life assurance, pension contributions; sickness and accident insurance, savings of all kinds, including contributions to Christmas and holiday clubs | Defense, external relations, Employment services, research and other industry, police, prisons, parliament, financial records, and other services |

*Measured in mean number of minutes per average day.

detailed activity data, we would find that it includes 560 minutes of sleep and 98 minutes eating—and 215 minutes of instrumental activity, such as cooking, cleaning, shopping, and so forth, which I summarily classify as unpaid work. The table is organized around six groups of activities, or purposes, of which two—"shelter, household maintenance" and "shopping, travel"—involve just instrumental activities, two involve only consumption activities—"out-of-home leisure" and "medicine and education"—and two—"home leisure, child care" and "food, sleep"—include a mixture of unpaid work and nonwork activities. Most of the paid employment in the economy can be explained in terms of the final demand for commodities associated with these six classes of activities.

Most, but not all. We have to take into account, in addition, employment associated with foreign demand for U.K. products, which generates in all 38 minutes of the total of 236 minutes of paid work in the average U.K. day but is not related to any unpaid work or consumption time in the United Kingdom. Of course, these exports are related to consumption time in foreign countries—and similarly, some U.K. consumption time is related to expenditure on imports, which serves to explain some foreign employment. The column headed "foreign work" related to U.K. activities—which I have estimated crudely by assuming that the productivity levels in countries exporting to the United Kingdom are on average the same as those in the United Kingdom—approximately balances the 38 minutes of U.K. work associated with foreign consumption activities.

Another category of U.K. production that cannot be matched with particular consumption or domestic work activities

is the provision of background, or environmental, services—law and order, defense, public administration—which have effects that are diffused through all of our experiences. An alternative way of handling these might be to treat them as an intermediate product the costs of which are distributed evenly across all branches of production. For the purposes of Table 2, these services have been grouped into a single category together with employment associated with the provision of analogous private background services such as life insurance, pensions, and personal savings.

Consider the change, over the period from 1961 to 1984, in the shelter maintenance chain. Unpaid work in this category, for the adult population as a whole, fell, by about 15 minutes per average day. This is the phenomenon we discussed in the previous section, social innovation in the production of domestic services. Now we can see the connection of the change in domestic work to change in paid employment. The reduction in unpaid work was enabled by increases in households' purchases of capital equipment and materials in the formal economy. Though less time was spent in the unpaid instrumental non-market tasks—indeed, precisely because less time was spent in them—unpaid work time became more intensive in its demand for purchased commodities. The reduced housework time is in effect purchased by an increase in domestic equipment.

So in spite of very high rates of productivity growth—an approximately threefold increase—in the manufacturing sector over the period, paid work time related to this category of purpose did not fall very fast—compared, for example, with paid work related to food, where an increase in agricultural and manufacturing productivity was not balanced by increasing consumption intensity. Indeed, when we consider that the normal hours of work per employee actually fell by about 10 percent over the period, we find that the number of jobs only declined by about 0.5 million from the 1961 total of 6.1 million, and white-collar and other service work associated with the provision of shelter rose over the period we are considering. Thus, associated with this purpose and as a result of the process of social innovation I have described, there is less time spent in unpaid production, but this time provided overall very nearly as many paid jobs in 1984 as in 1961.

Of course, the time freed from unpaid domestic work, and from the reduction in employed people's paid work time, must be spent somehow. One use to which this extra time is put is in the consumption of out-of-home recreational, educational, and medical services. This sort of change does not involve increasing consumption intensity—that is, increased expenditure and hence paid employment per moment of consumption time—but rather the increase of the total amount of time devoted to activities in which consumption intensity remains constant. A sit-down meal at a restaurant, for example, involves just about as much labor time now as it did thirty years ago; but more people eat out in the 1980s than in 1961. This increase means more consumption time and hence more paid labor time—though the argument is complicated by the emergence of the fast-food industry over this period. In the chain of provision of shelter, a reduction of the total of unpaid work time was balanced by an increase in the consumption intensity of that time, so that levels of paid employ-

ment hardly fell in spite of very substantial increases in labor productivity. In the out-of-home leisure category—pubs, restaurants, sports—an increase in time devoted to time-extensive service consumption leads to an increase in jobs. And a similar process may serve to explain the growth in employment in the chain of provision connected with medical and educational services.

Consider, finally, the category of shopping and related travel. Time spent by consumers in this activity increased from about 45 minutes per average adult in 1961 to about 70 minutes in 1984. As we see from Figure 3, this increase is part of a longer-term trend in the United Kingdom and corresponds to a similar increase, shown in Figures 4A and 4B in a number of other European countries. The North American data in Figures 4A and 4B are at a higher overall level but do not show the same upward trend. The explanation of the increase seems to be innovation in the retail industry, leading to larger, self-service shops. The shopper spends more time selecting and paying for goods in shops that are geographically removed from the city center, which means more travel time. The lower prices of goods bought from one-stop markets are in effect paid for by the increased nonmoney transaction costs—the increased time spent in shopping. We might, from a European perspective, interpret the multinational comparative evidence in Figures 4A and 4B as the Americanization of retail distribution.

The very substantial amounts of time devoted to shopping and related activities suggest a likely future effect of technical innovation on time use. The new technologies of the 1930s—valves, small electric motors, plastics—were em-

## TABLE 2
## A TIME-BASED SYSTEM OF ACCOUNTS

| | Time outside Employment* | | Time in Employment* | | All Paid Work in U.K.* | Foreign Work from Imports* | All Employment (000s of employees) | Distribution of Employment |
|---|---|---|---|---|---|---|---|---|
| | Nonwork | Work | White-collar work | Manual work | | | | |
| **1961** | | | | | | | | |
| Shelter, household | 0 | 93 | 25 | 36 | 61 | 14 | 6,278 | .26 |
| Food, sleep, etc. | 659 | 68 | 16 | 24 | 40 | 10 | 4,123 | .17 |
| Home leisure, child care | 268 | 12 | 7 | 10 | 16 | 4 | 1,672 | .07 |
| Shopping, travel | 0 | 41 | 6 | 7 | 13 | 1 | 1,344 | .06 |
| Out-of-home leisure | 45 | 0 | 8 | 3 | 11 | 2 | 1,169 | .05 |
| Medicine, education | 16 | 0 | 20 | 7 | 27 | 2 | 2,814 | .12 |
| Background service | 0 | 0 | 15 | 14 | 29 | 1 | 3,018 | .12 |
| Exports | 0 | 0 | 13 | 25 | 38 | 6 | 3,919 | .16 |
| All time use | 989 | 215 | 110 | 126 | 236 | 40 | 24,337 | 1.00 |
| **1983** | | | | | | | | |
| Shelter, household | 0 | 73 | 25 | 21 | 46 | 16 | 5,591 | .24 |
| Food, sleep, etc. | 647 | 63 | 8 | 8 | 16 | 6 | 1,934 | .08 |

60

| | | | | | | | | |
|---|---|---|---|---|---|---|---|---|
| Home leisure, child care | 284 | 17 | 7 | 5 | 12 | 3 | 1,411 | .06 |
| Shopping, travel | 0 | 70 | 5 | 4 | 9 | 2 | 1,119 | .05 |
| Out-of-home leisure | 70 | 0 | 9 | 2 | 11 | 2 | 1,386 | .06 |
| Medicine, education | 22 | 0 | 30 | 5 | 36 | 3 | 4,347 | .18 |
| Background service | 0 | 0 | 17 | 7 | 24 | 1 | 2,951 | .13 |
| Exports | 0 | 0 | 19 | 21 | 39 | 10 | 4,824 | .20 |
| All time use | 1,023 | 224 | 120 | 73 | 193 | 43 | 23,564 | 1.00 |
| Change 1961-83/4 | | | | | | | | |
| Shelter, household | 0 | −21 | 0 | −15 | −15 | 2 | −687 | −.02 |
| Food, sleep, etc. | −12 | −5 | −7 | −17 | −24 | −4 | −2,189 | −.09 |
| Home leisure, child care | 15 | 5 | 0 | −5 | −5 | 0 | −261 | −.01 |
| Shopping, travel | 0 | 29 | −1 | −3 | −4 | 0 | −225 | −.01 |
| Out-of-home leisure | 24 | 0 | 1 | −1 | 0 | 0 | 217 | .01 |
| Medicine, education | 6 | 0 | 10 | −2 | 8 | 1 | 1,533 | .07 |
| Background service | 0 | 0 | 2 | −7 | −5 | 0 | −66 | .00 |
| Exports | 0 | 0 | 6 | −5 | 1 | 4 | 905 | .04 |
| All time use | 34 | 9 | 10 | −53 | −43 | 3 | −773 | .00 |

*Measured in minutes per average day.

61

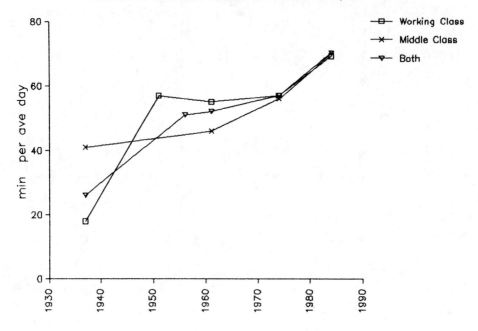

FIGURE 3
TIME SPENT SHOPPING BY BRITISH HOUSEWIVES, 1937-84

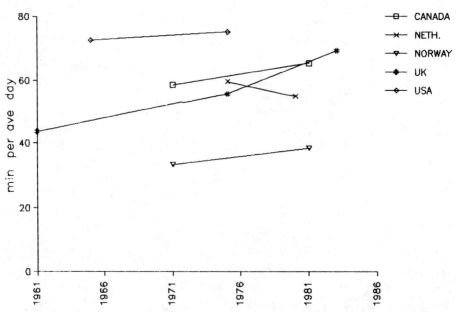

FIGURE 4A
SHOPPING AND ASSOCIATED TRAVEL (Women only)

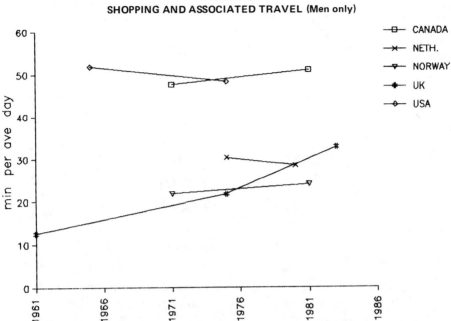

FIGURE 4B
SHOPPING AND ASSOCIATED TRAVEL (Men only)

bodied in consumer durable goods—washing machines, vacuum cleaners, and the like—used in innovative informal modes of provision of domestic services, which led to new jobs and a reduction of unpaid work time from the 1940s to the 1970s. Might not the new technologies of the 1980s—microchips, fiber optics—be embodied in new ways of organizing the provision of retail services? Tele-shopping, ordering goods from computer terminals in homes, making use of a range of associated services—consumer advice, funds transfers, home delivery, for example—could substantially reduce the amount of time currently devoted to marketing and could increase the paid employment associated with the distribution chain. And just as, in the past, time freed from domestic work went in part to enable the consumption of time-extensive leisure services, so in the future might time freed from the burden of shopping.

This brief presentation hardly scrapes the surface of the potential applications of an analysis of the interrelationships between technical innovation, production in the money economy, informal production, and consumption. The model outlined in this article shows how life-style—in the quite concrete sense of the allocation of time among alternative activities—relates to demand for products from the formal economy and how technical innovations affect the relationship between activity patterns and final demand. If our needs are met by a combination of formal and informal production, and if technical change alters the relationship between these, can we be satisfied with an economics that concentrates just on the formal economy?

ANNALS, *AAPSS*, **493,** September 1987

# Female Participation in the
# Informal Economy:
# A Neglected Issue

### *By* MICHELE HOYMAN

ABSTRACT: The author examines three questions: how much females participate in the informal economy; why they participate; and what the policy implications of their participation are. In the process of examining these issues, the author develops a behavioral theory of female participation, involving exit, voice, loyalty, and dual loyalty, following Hirschman's work. Using three measures—the number of individuals; the amount of time; and dollars—she finds that women participate in the informal economy as much as, and probably more than, men do. In the course of trying to explain why females participate in the informal economy, she discusses a variety of different explanations and then rejects them because they are too value laden and/or they make too many assumptions. Finally, she discusses the policy implications of more and more women having dual loyalty, such as the need for government-regulated, safe day care, and the need for revising the definition of labor force participation to reflect some of the informal activity of women.

*Michele Hoyman is associate professor of political science and a fellow in the Center for Metropolitan Studies, University of Missouri, Saint Louis. She received her Ph.D. in political science from the University of Michigan in 1978. Her primary areas of research are Title VII compliance, sexual harassment, labor unions, and litigiousness of workers, particularly women. She has recently published an article on the participation of blacks in local unions. Currently she is involved in an analysis of joint labor-management training programs in several industries and work on the informal economy.*

NOTE: The author is deeply indebted to William Miller, whose yeomanlike research assistance in drafting this article was enormous.

DESPITE all of the changes brought about by recent developments in the economic system, by women's liberation, and by the feminist movement, women still experience a significantly different economic reality in the formal economy from that experienced by men. This is true not only in the level of earned income, but in employment expectations and the whole variety of work opportunities. In light of this different economic reality, it is necessary to look at the informal economy as a whole, and to examine the character of women's participation in it particularly.[1] In this article, "informal economy" will refer to work activities or economic transactions, paid or unpaid, that occur outside of the conventional market economy and are not regulated, mentioned, audited, or counted by any official agency in the society.[2]

There are several critical questions that this article attempts to answer. First, do women participate less than, as much as, or more than men in the informal economy? Second, what is the explanation for women's participation in the informal economy? Are they motivated by the same factors as men? Third, is there a theory that can encompass the variety of different modes of participation, the differing reasons why

women may leave the formal for the informal economy, stay in the informal, stay in the formal, or leave the informal for the formal? Fourth, what are the policy implications of women's participation in the informal economy? These public policy considerations are focused on American women, as these women are the subject of this article. Before proceeding, however, we need to define the informal economy.

## DEFINITION OF THE INFORMAL ECONOMY

For the purpose of addressing the relative participation of women and men and to explore the motivation for female participation in the informal economy, I will focus on the two areas of participation that writers have classified as irregular and as household. I will refer throughout to these areas as the informal economy except when talking about either one in particular. Irregular or off-the-books employment is work activity, from the simple to the complex, that involves workers who do not report the work, pay social security taxes, or pay income taxes on earnings from customers or employers. Household-based work activities involve housekeeping, child care, home repair, maintenance, and do-it-yourself building activities.

The domains of the informal economy that I have excluded from my definition, such as the social or communal sector[3] and the illegal sector, are no less important. Female participation in the social area, for example, is extensive.

1. There is little work of a systematic nature on women in the informal economy. The notable exceptions are Louis Ferman, "Participation in the Informal Economy," mimeographed (Ann Arbor: University of Michigan, 1983); Ray E. Pahl, *Divisions of Labour* (New York: Basil Blackwell, 1984).

2. This definition follows most closely the definition of Mattera, for whom the unofficial nature of the informal economy is of paramount importance in demarcating the formal from the informal. Phillip Mattera, *Off the Books: The Rise of the Underground Economy* (New York: St. Martin's Press, 1985), p. 1.

3. Paola Vinay, "Family Life Cycle and the Informal Economy in Central Italy," *International Journal of Urban and Regional Research,* 9:82-98 (1985); for reference to Pahl and Gershuny, see esp. ibid., p. 84.

The contribution of women in the form of volunteer labor for churches, political parties, and charities is enormous. In the criminal area, which historically and stereotypically has been labeled as a male domain, there is increasing evidence that females are becoming more active, even though their crimes are less serious than those of men. In addition, the criminal activities of females more nearly approach those of males when we move from official crime statistics to data based on self-reporting.[4]

### EXTENT OF PARTICIPATION OF WOMEN IN THE INFORMAL ECONOMY

To answer the question of how much females participate in the informal economy is to answer the question of whether they participate as much as, more than, or less than males. But this is not an easy question to answer.

The difficulty is due partly to the immense conceptual and practical ambiguity about the distinctions between some of the activities in the informal economy and those in the formal, as well as between some of the different sectors of the informal. Defining what activities are taken to be informal is very problematic.

There is also the obvious problem of procuring the data. The reliability of survey responses is questionable since

the activity being measured often involves tax evasion or other illicit practices that people are unwilling to reveal to researchers. Thus solid and objective data are not widely available. Any attempt to obtain data on the participation of a subset—females in this case—only makes the task that much more difficult.[5]

There are three possible ways of measuring the amount of participation in the informal economy: (1) counting the number of individuals of each sex who participate; (2) measuring the relative time spent by each sex in terms of average hours a week or minutes a day per person; and (3) measuring the relative dollar value of the wages or amount of gross national product (GNP) generated by male and female participants. Let us consider each in more detail.

### Proportion of female to male participants

To determine whether more men or more women participate in informal economic activity, one must compare the fraction of the number of women participating over the absolute number of women in the population with the equivalent fraction for men. Although this is the optimal way to compare the numbers of male and female participants, the data to construct the numerator are generally not available.

One of the best quantitative studies was done by Vinay in Italy, where the sex differential in participation in the

4. Stuart Henry, *The Hidden Economy: The Context and Control of Borderline Crime* (Oxford: Martin Robertson, 1978); Michael J. Lynch, "The Social and Economic Marginality of Female Offenders: Implications for a Structural Level Theory of Women in Crime" (Paper delivered at the meeting of the American Society of Criminology, San Diego, CA, 1985); Bruce Frederick and Steven Greenstein, "Recent Trends in Arrest, Conviction, and Sentencing of Female Offenders in New York State" (Paper delivered at the meeting of the American Society of Criminology, San Diego, CA, 1985).

5. There are some relevant data. See Vinay, "Family Life Cycle," p. 89; Ferman, "Participation in the Informal Economy"; J. Smith, T. Moyer, and E. Trzcinski, "The Measurement of Selected Income Flows in Informal Markets" (Report, Survey Research Center, Institute of Social Research, University of Michigan, 1982); Harold C. Barnett, "Tax Evasion by Proxy: The Grey Market in Welfare Capitalism," *Contemporary Crisis*, 8:107-23 (1984).

informal economy was found to be quite dramatic. According to the official census data from 1971 for the area in central Italy—Marche—that Vinay studied, the official rate of participation for males in the formal economy was 59.2 percent; for females it was 23.8 percent. However, the 1975 study that Vinay cited revealed participation rates of 66.0 percent and 51.0 percent for males and females, respectively. This shows a jump in the male rate of only six points when informal activities were included, but the female rate nearly doubled.[6] Thus the formal participation rate underestimated the number of females working by a much greater amount than it underestimated the number of males.

For the United States, there are no comparable data as there is no national or regional survey asking whether or not people work in the informal economy. Thus we must use measures other than participation rates. One useful measure is the General Accounting Office's data on nonreporting, which provide the percentage of those engaged in certain occupations who are self-employed but not reporting. The General Accounting Office did an exact-match analysis of social security data to estimate unreported self-employment earnings.[7] It should be noted that these data only encompass self-employment. Since much of the off-the-books employment involves an employer, not self-employment, these figures understate the gross amount of activity, although this fact should not necessarily affect the proportionate amount of male to female activity.

6. Vinay, "Family Life Cycle," p. 83.
7. U.S., General Accounting Office, *Growth of the Underground Economy, 1950-81: Some Evidence from the Current Population Survey* (Washington, DC: Government Printing Office, 1983).

Many of the occupational categories in the General Accounting Office's data are so sex-segregated that we can assume that nearly all the workers in a specified occupation are female or that all are male, depending on the occupation.[8] Given this occupational segregation, one can identify certain occupations as female or male dominated and then relate the amount of activity associated with that particular occupation. Table 1 shows the occupations and the percentage of workers in them not paying their social security tax.

As can be seen from this table, all of the occupations are female segregated and all of them show a fairly high percentage of nonpayment of social security. The lowest percentage, for dressmakers and seamstresses, is still an impressive 20 percent for those who do not go on the books for purposes of paying their social security. The percentage not reporting in the child care occupational category—where child care occurs outside of private homes—is 84 percent, and it is 48 percent for child care in private households. A good half of the registered nurses reported nonpayment of social security. Given that nonpayment is illegal both for the employee and for the employer, actual figures would be higher than these reported figures.

8. Although the definition of occupational segregation varies, it is generally accepted that if 60 percent or more of the workers in an occupation—some say 80 percent or more—are of one sex, the occupation is segregated. See Suzanne M. Bianchi and Daphne Spain, *American Women in Transition* (New York: Russell Sage Foundation, 1986). For an excellent volume on the work patterns of contemporary women, see Francine D. Blau and Marianne A. Ferber, *The Economics of Women, Men, and Work* (Englewood Cliffs, NJ: Prentice-Hall, 1986).

TABLE 1
WORKERS NOT PAYING SOCIAL SECURITY TAX BY OCCUPATION

| Occupation | Percentage not Paying Social Security |
|---|---|
| Child care workers not in private households | 84.2 |
| Hairdressers and cosmetologists | 24.6 |
| Dressmakers and seamstresses | 19.7 |
| Registered nurses | 49.5 |
| Child care workers in private households | 48.2 |

SOURCE: U.S., General Accounting Office, *Growth of the Underground Economy, 1950-81: Some Evidence from the Current Population Survey* (Washington, DC: Government Printing Office, 1983), p. 13.

The same picture emerges when the breakdown is done by broad industry categories in which a largely female work force is employed. Examples of such industries are beauty shops, where 16 percent of employees do not report social security; dressmaking shops, with 47 percent not reporting social security; personal services, with 29 percent not reporting social security. Of course, industry categories are by definition broad enough to encompass several different occupations so that some of the variation by occupation vanishes. Nevertheless, the percentage not reporting social security varies from 16 to 47 percent,[9] which are rather substantial fractions of whole industries that are off the books for purposes of social security.[10] The three industries cited are female dominated. They provide us with some measure of the amount of female activity, although they provide no corresponding baseline data for males.

Another measure of female participation is the amount of activity reported either by the participants themselves or by households who use informal vendors. The former is the optimal source of data, but such data are the most difficult to obtain. The most valid way to secure the information may be to use what has been called the Ferman methodology.[11] Ferman's classic study used 10 ethnographers, who tracked participants for months and whose reports were cross-validated with anonymous surveys. Such an approach is enormously expensive and large in scope, however. The next best alternative is the use of household surveys concerning the amount of irregular vendor activity.

The most recent and thorough use of vendor activity data was a study of households done by James Smith for the Internal Revenue Service.[12] It helps us examine female participation in the informal economy by drawing again on the fact that occupational segregation is so

9. General Accounting Office, *Growth of the Underground Economy*, p. 14.

10. Aside from nonpayment of social security, there are other measures of informal activity, such as nonreporting of income tax, but this is the most difficult data to acquire since respondents who have not paid their income taxes are reluctant to admit this.

11. Louis A. Ferman, Louise E. Berndt, and Elaine Selo, "Analysis of the Irregular Economy: Cash Flow in the Informal Sector," mimeographed (Ann Arbor: University of Michigan; Detroit, MI: Wayne State University, 1978).

12. Smith, Moyer, and Trzcinski, "Measurement of Selected Income Flows."

severe that many occupations are identifiably male or female. Table 2 shows the number of households in Smith's study that report the use of informal vendors and what percentage they form of all households. Notice that the figures are based on households, so the figures for individuals would be even higher. Three identifiably female-dominated occupations are included in the table: personal care, child care in the home, and child care outside the home. The fourth category, adult care, is probably not occupationally segregated. Between 9 and 16 percent of all households use informal vendors in the female-dominated occupations. Off-the-books child care vendors are used by 10 percent of all households. It is my suspicion that these figures understate the amount of activity since respondents may hesitate to report that they use off-the-books vendors.

While these data provide some assessment of female participation, they only indirectly address the issue of the proportionate amount of male and female activity. Pahl collected some data in a U.K. survey that directly addresses this issue.[13] Pahl found that the percentages of females and males, respectively, in occupational categories were unequal. Looking at different occupations within the informal economy, he found that females constituted 92 percent of those in routine domestic work, 82 percent of the workers in personal support services, and 65 percent of the workers in formal community activity. In contrast, men formed the majority in only one category, the home-improvement sector of the informal economy. Yet even here

there was still a female participation rate of 13 percent. Other categories, especially domestic ones, were overwhelmingly female. In conclusion, Pahl's data support the notion that most occupations within the informal economy are female dominated, and they show that certain occupations are as segregated in the informal economy as they are in the formal.

Yet another way of trying to measure the relative amount of female and male participation in the informal activity is based on the number of mentions given to certain occupations reported in household surveys. In his survey of U.S. households, Smith measured the number of times the household mentioned buying certain services by occupation. Based on the Smith data, baby-sitting and house-cleaning were the second most often sought-after services.[14] Sewing and laundry were fifth and beauty care was sixth. Thus many of the female-segregated occupations were among the top in terms of selling services.

To summarize, when we measure the proportionate amount of female and male activity by the number of individuals participating, there are no direct survey data on participants. We have to rely instead on household respondents reporting how much they purchase from

13. Raymond E. Pahl, "Does Jobless Mean Workless? Unemployment and Informal Work," this issue of *The Annals* of the American Academy of Political and Social Science.

14. The number of mentions for each category of selling goods was as follows: door-to-door sales, 5.3; arts, crafts, furniture, and household, 2.2; fresh fruits, vegetables, and other food items grown, 1.5; cordwood, 0.4. The number of mentions for each category of selling services was: carpentry, painting, 2.7; baby-sitting and house-cleaning, 2.1; lawn and gardening care and one-time cleanups, 1.8; repairs of vehicles, furniture, and appliances, 1.7; sewing and laundry, 1.3; beauty care, catering, typing, and income tax preparation, 1.1; lessons, 0.6; other services, 4.5. The totals for both goods and services were 17.8. Smith, Moyer, and Trzcinski, "Measurement of Selected Income Flows."

TABLE 2
**HOUSEHOLDS PURCHASING PERSONAL SERVICES FROM VENDORS**

| Occupation of Vendor | Number of Households | Percentage of All Households |
|---|---|---|
| Personal care | | |
| Licensed and Unlicensed | 13,041 | 15.8 |
| Unlicensed | 10,510 | 12.7 |
| Child care in home, licensed and unlicensed | 7,507 | 9.1 |
| Adult care, licensed and unlicensed | 644 | 0.8 |
| Child care outside home, licensed and unlicensed | 7,250 | 8.8 |

SOURCE: J. Smith, T. Moyer, and E. Trzcinski, "The Measurement of Selected Income Flows in Informal Markets" (Report, Survey Research Center, Institute of Social Research, University of Michigan, 1982), p. 49.

informal vendors—an indirect measure at best. Thus our results are inconclusive, but they strongly suggest that females are as active as or more active than males.

*Proportion of time spent by females in informal work*

It is when one examines the time spent in an activity within the informal economy that the evidence is most convincing that female participation exceeds that of male participation. This excess of female involvement is a result of the relative amount of effort exerted by each partner in the household arena. It is safe to say that housework is an unpaid job.[15] Given the traditional division of labor in families, the number of hours of usually unpaid household work is more often than not an outcome of gender-role specialization. Taking a job in the formal economy does not significantly reduce the number of hours of household work; it concentrates such work in hours after formal economy

15. Bettina Berch, *The Endless Day: The Political Economy of Women* (New York: Harcourt Brace Jovanovich, 1982), p. 19.

work or on weekends. Pahl, in his historical examination of the division of labor in the household, makes the point that the exclusion of men from household chores and the exclusion of women from paid labor is a tradition of only the past seventy or eighty years or so.[16] He documents countless earlier examples of a very integrated division of labor where men and women were sharing the work of plowing and child rearing.

Pahl goes on to say that most of the world's work is done by women.[17] Women are put in the position of having multiple ties—to work, to husband or partner, and to family—and they adjust in pragmatic ways to changes in their marital status and status as mothers. The label of "chief earner" may be more appropriate for males, although the increasing number of single-parent households in the United States headed by

16. Pahl, *Divisions of Labour*, chap. 2 and p. 61. For the opposite view, see Ivan Illich, "Vernacular Gender," *CoEvolution Quarterly*, pp. 4-23 (Spring 1982). Illich's concept is that throughout time there has been a strict division of labor, with women using different tools and having different functions.

17. Pahl, *Divisions of Labour*, p. 81.

working women may even put a dent in that label. However, the label of "chief worker" is the more appropriate label for females.[18] In other words, Pahl draws a valuable distinction between work—often unpaid—and employment—paid—that is critical in terms of estimating the time and effort put forth by women in the informal economy. Much of the household and irregular activity falls under the rubric of work rather than employment. It is Pahl's suggestion, echoing Burns's,[19] that this lopsided emphasis on employment leads to the implication that formal or paid work is the only significant form of work. Such emphasis erroneously focuses on the individual male income earner, not the household, as the basic economic unit.[20] The issue is important since, were women's work counted, its value would greatly affect income figures, such as the GNP, as will be discussed later in the section on the value of women's participation.

The difficult question is, How much housework in terms of hours per week do women do? One estimate, in a study by Chase Manhattan Bank, is that women do 99.6 hours of housework per week.[21] Burns, in his study of 1200 Seattle family households, found that the number of hours of housework varied directly with the number of children. The women in the average house-

hold performed 49 hours of housework per week. In households without children, women's housework averaged 35 hours per week; with between one and three children, 56 hours per week; with four or more children, 62 hours per week. Burns also cites a Cornell study that attempted to measure the value of household work, taking into account the amount of time spent and the effect of taking a job outside the home. The researchers there came to the conclusion that women who both held a paying job and did household work worked a significantly higher number of hours per week on housework than their spouses.[22] They also found that, although the effect of working outside the home raises the value of the husband's work in the home, it lowers the value of the woman's work in the home.[23] Finally, and ironically, the study estimated the value of women's work contribution to the household and compared it to the value of the average employed woman's work. The difficulty of "costing out" the contributions of a housewife's work to a household has arisen in divorce cases recently.

An important issue in the use of time is whether the relative average amount of time a woman spends per day or per week doing housework has increased or decreased. Gershuny has done the most thorough examination of this and has found that the efforts of U.S. women in routine domestic work decreased from 250 minutes per day in 1966 to about 220 minutes in 1975 and 190 in 1986. The time men expended in housework increased from about 46 minutes per day in 1966 to about 50 minutes in 1975 to about 56 minutes in 1981.[24] According

18. Ibid.

19. Scott Burns, *The Household Economy: Its Shape, Origins, and Future* (Boston: Beacon Press, 1975), p. 11; Pahl, *Divisions of Labour*, p. 84.

20. Pahl, *Divisions of Labour*, p. 84.

21. Burns, *Household Economy*, p. 17. Another more recent estimate is that women spend 11 hours per week compared with an average of 3 hours for men for nonroutine cleaning tasks. "State of the American Home Survey," 1987, as reported in the *St. Louis Post Dispatch*, 25 Mar. 1987, p. 2A.

22. Burns, *Household Economy*, p. 18.

23. Ibid., pp. 17-18.

24. Jonathan Gershuny, "Technology, Social Innovation, and the Informal Economy," this

to Gershuny, shopping and associated travel for women rose from about 73 minutes per day in about 1965 to about 75 in 1975 and to about 78 in about 1985. For U.S. men, there was a decline from about 53 minutes in 1965 to about 47 minutes in 1975.[25]

There are two notable factors that emerge: (1) in general, men's and women's relative contributions in time are becoming equal; and (2) there is a very large gap between the two figures: 50 minutes a day for the average U.S. male in 1975 as compared to about 220 minutes a day for the average U.S. female for the same year. That is approximately a four to one ratio of women's to men's efforts in households. Other estimates are equivalent or even more unequal.[26] The results in terms of the time measure are simple and dramatic: women spend much more time than men in the informal economy or at least in the household sector of it.

### The monetary value of female informal work

One of the most compelling ways of measuring female participation in the economy is by assigning a dollar value to such activity. It would seem that if women's participation in the informal economy is a real contribution to the total economy, then it would be reasonable to measure that participation in dollars, since this is the commonly accepted unit of measure.

There are, however, several problems with such a standard. It assumes that the market value of women's work is accu-

rate—and not uniformly depressed as a result of its being so-called women's work. One of the effects of women's work not being considered a job is that all the work that women do is stereotypically perceived as having no value—or at least it becomes undervalued.[27] This devaluation pollutes female-segregated jobs in the formal economy. Those jobs, which are the equivalents in the formal economy to jobs that are done for free by the housewife—cleaning, sewing, baby-sitting—have two characteristics: the concentration of women in these jobs, and a depressed wage level. Both the label "women's work" and a great concentration of women in an area of work tend to depress wage levels. The latter has been empirically demonstrated by tipping, the phenomenon of the relative wage level going down when there is a certain concentration of females in an occupation.

If the fact that women's work is largely invisible is substantially depressing its value, then the dollar value is not an unbiased measure. The blunt fact is that women do housework for free. This depresses the market value of cleaning, baby-sitting, and similar housework, even when these activities are marketed in the formal economy. I suggest, as do Illich, Pahl, and others, that to use a dollar measure would underestimate the value of women's work. In addition, if work in the informal economy is a statement of the rejection of market values, as some would argue, then a dollar measure is particularly inappropriate since it embodies the same set of values upon which mainstream, formal economics depends. Yet since the dollar is such a

issue of *The Annals* of the American Academy of Political and Social Science, figs. 2A and 2B.

25. See ibid., figs. 4A and 4B.

26. John P. Robinson, *How Americans Use Time: A Social-Psychological Analysis of Everyday Behavior* (New York: Praeger, 1977).

27. Pahl, *Divisions of Labour*, chap. 2; Illich, "Vernacular Gender."

common unit of measure for mainstream economics and for such concepts as the GNP, we would be remiss not to attempt to measure female participation in dollars.

The estimates of the dollar value of household work are nothing less than dramatic. The household economy is estimated to be one-third the size of the market economy. In terms of the global economy, the value of women's work in the household, given in dollar values, would add an estimated one-third to the world's GNP.[28] The precise dollar value assigned to household activities obviously depends on the wage level selected. Most estimates are based on minimum wage figures, many of which are now obsolete. For instance, Burns estimated that the contribution to national income of housework was $350 billion dollars of activity. This was based on a minimum wage figure of $2.00 per hour. At today's minimum wage of $3.35 per hour and assuming the 175 billion hours of total work that Burns used, a current conservative estimate would be almost twice Burns's—or upward of $590 billion. The enormity of this figure is particularly striking since the assumption of minimum wage would not always be met once the job is translated into comparable formal economic activity. For example, a seamstress's or tax preparer's work, which would be assigned minimum wage in the preceding computations, commands a much higher price than minimum wage when purchased in the formal market.

Until this point in our discussion, the estimates of dollar values have focused on the household only. There is another portion of the informal economy to be considered here, irregular, off-the-books

activity. On this subject, Smith acknowledged openly the problems of obtaining candid responses from vendors themselves. He opted instead for a research strategy that used measures of the value of purchases that households make from informal vendors.[29] Although Smith did not break down the amount of activity by sex, he did disaggregate by occupation. Again, based on information about occupational segregation, Smith's occupational groupings can be divided into three categories: male dominated, female dominated, and mixed or unknown. All of the male-dominated occupations can be added together and all of the female-dominated categories can be added together to determine the relative dollar value for which males and females are responsible in the economy.[30]

In Table 3, the dollar value of the male-dominated occupations exceeds that of the female-dominated occupations by a fairly large margin. In part this may be a result of wage differentials between males and females that parallel those in the formal economy.[31] It should be noted that with even one of the unknown or mixed occupations—with

28. World Priorities, *Women . . . a World Survey* (Washington, DC: World Priorities, 1985), p. 11; Burns, *Household Economy*, p. 24.

29. Smith, Moyer, and Trzcinski, "Measurement of Selected Income Flows," pp. 2-3. In a later application, Mattera came up with the same set of figures. See Mattera, *Off the Books,* chap. 4, for a useful discussion of methodological problems also.

30. In Table 3, the figures for each occupation category are Smith's, but the designations of female or male dominated are mine.

31. Female wages in 1986 were only 64 percent of male wages. If we take 64 percent of the total dollar value of the male-dominated occupations indicated in Table 3—$16,500—we get $10,560. In other words, if we adjust for the relatively depressed female wages we get near equity of figures. The source of the figure of 64 percent was the U.S. Census Bureau, *Women in the American Economy* (1987), as reported in the *St. Louis Post Dispatch,* 4 Mar. 1987.

the exception of catering—moving over to the female-dominated category, the outcome would change rather dramatically. The three unknown or mixed occupations that are potentially female-dominated are flea market exchange that includes yard sales, catering, and food. If these were moved over to the female-dominated column, the female-dominated column would exceed the male-dominated column.

When we combine the figure for female irregular activity purchased through vendors—just over $9 billion—with the estimates on the dollar value of household work done by females—$700 billion—the figure for female dollar contribution to the informal economy would exceed that of the dollar contributed identifiably linked to male sectors of the economy. This calculation assumes that much of the activity commonly referred to as housewife's duties are performed by women. With the advent of changing gender roles and the emergence of the househusband, this may change. Also, this estimate is based on household and informal sectors only; it excludes the illegal sector and the social sector.

To summarize, the amount of activity found varies according to the the measure used. When we use a measure of time, the results most dramatically support the view that females participate more than males in the informal economy, largely as a result of the imbalanced effort according to sex in terms of household work. When we use a measure of the number of individuals, our results are inconclusive but suggest that females are as active as or more active than males in the informal economy. Finally, using dollars as a measure, we find that results vary depending on whether the irregular and household sectors are combined or not. If we look only at irregular

activity, we see that females participate less than males as measured by dollars. However, if we combine irregular activity and household activity and estimate the dollar values of both, we find that females participate more than males. It is my speculation that female participation would still exceed male participation even were we to include the remaining two sectors, the deviant, or illegal, and the social, or communal.

### EXPLAINING FEMALE PARTICIPATION IN THE INFORMAL ECONOMY

There are as many differing viewpoints as to why women participate in the informal economy as there are potential perspectives or values behind researchers and disciplines. However, the question of whether women self-select into the informal economy, are pushed into the informal economy by problems in the formal economy, or end up in the informal economy because of both barriers in the formal economy and certain attitudinal characteristics will be explored in the rest of this article.

### Do women choose to participate in the informal economy?

There are an estimated 1 million women in the United States who operate businesses out of their home, and the rate of increase of small businesses headed by women exceeds that headed by men.[32] Some authors have gone so far as to say that "working at home has always been the preferred option of women"[33] because it affords flexible work schedules. This argument has been

32. This figure comes from Internal Revenue Service data as reported in the *St. Louis Post Dispatch,* 9 Mar. 1987, p. 13A.

33. Elinor Lenz and Barabara Myerhoff, *The Feminization of America* (Los Angeles: Jeremy P. Tarcher, 1985), p. 92.

TABLE 3
**DOLLAR VALUE OF OCCUPATIONAL GROUPINGS BY GENDER (In millions)**

| Female-dominated | | Male-dominated | | Unknown or Mixed | |
|---|---|---|---|---|---|
| Occupation | Value | Occupation | Value | Occupation | Value |
| Child care | 4,955 | Home repair | 12,245 | Food | 9,003 |
| Domestic service | 3,882 | Auto repair | 2,810 | Sidewalk vendor | 1,782 |
| Adult care | 442 | Lawn and garden | 442 | Flea market goods | 1,698 |
| Cosmetic service | 411 | | | Lessons | 933 |
| Sewing | 392 | | | Fuel | 749 |
| | | | | Catering | 300 |
| | | | | Appliance repair | 744 |
| Total | 9,082 | Total | 16,502 | Total | 5,209 |

SOURCE: Smith, Moyer, and Trzcinski, "Measurement of Selected Income Flows," p. 25.

extended to informal work generally because of a unique match between the characteristics of female gender roles and what are often said to be the characteristic qualities of work arrangements within the informal economy.[34] This argument is intuitively appealing. The informal sector does provide more flexibility, greater probability of being household-based, and greater potential for part-time or occasional work, and it requires less stringent credentials to gain entry. Moreover, many of the household duties that are defined stereotypically as women's work and that women perform at no charge in their own home can be marketed in the informal economy.

Ironically, perhaps, one of the strongest statements claiming that women choose the informal economy comes from feminist writers. Recognizing that the values that represent success in corporate America may lead to apathy, even alienation, from self, from family, and from community,[35] some feminists

see the informal economy representing an alternative value system and a rejection of macho, corporate, rationalist, and materialist values. The argument is that the values women experience in the informal economy can humanize the employment experience and thereby reduce the conflict or disjuncture between work and household life.[36]

The most systematic treatment of women's self-selection into the informal economy was part of a study of female entrepreneurs conducted by Robert Goffee and Richard Scase. They indicated that there were four types of women: conventional, innovative, domestic, and radical. The conventional woman is high on attachment to conventional gender roles and high on attachment to conventional entrepreneurial ideals. The domestic woman is high on attachment to conventional gender roles but low on attachment to entrepreneurial ideals. The innovative woman is low on attachment to conventional gender roles and high on attachment to entrepreneurial ideals. The radical woman is low

34. Vinay, "Family Life Cycle," p. 89; Ferman, "Participation in the Informal Economy."

35. Diane Rothbard Margolis, *The Managers* (New York: William Morrow, 1979), p. 25.

36. Lenz and Myerhoff, *Feminization of America*, p. 82.

on attachment to conventional gender roles and low on conventional entrepreneurial ideals.[37]

The two types that were identified as likely to be involved in starting small businesses or getting involved in irregular activity were the innovative type, who were low on conventional gender roles and high on entrepreneurial values, and the radical type, who were low on conventional gender roles and low on entrepreneurial values. For the radicals, the business was not for profit so much as it was an alternative life-style statement.

However, we should not assume the functionalist fallacy that the presence of women in the informal economy indicates a preference for it. There are at least two other theories that explain women's participation in informal work. First, the informal economy may be thrust upon women as an economy of last resort rather than of choice. Barriers to participation in the formal economy such as discrimination, rigid schedules, and low wages all push women to work informally. Another possibility is that the limited access to only the lower-status, service-oriented jobs in the formal economy in combination with the low self-esteem and acceptance of conventional gender roles by many women causes them to revert back often to a traditional maternal role. It is this combination of factors that drives them back to the informal economy.[38] In what follows, I shall look at these arguments in more detail.

## Are women forced into the informal economy?

The most extreme version of this argument is held by Marxists and Marxist feminists. Dorothy Smith, for example, has argued that women are marginalized by the capitalist economic system such that

women's work must take up the slack created by the depreciation of the value of wages and irregularity and uncertainty of income from wages when rates of unemployment are high. At the same time as married women must try to get work because the family needs her wage, the difficulties of doing so are increased. When money is short, women's work in the home substitutes for labor embodied in goods bought at the store. There is a very straightforward relation here. You put more time in. You do more darning. You do more mending. You make more of your own clothes. You do more processing of food if you can't afford to buy labor embodied in commodities.[39]

Obviously, the Marxist perspective is distinguishable from the Marxist-feminist one just illustrated, but the cause—capitalism as an economic and political system—is common to both schools.[40] Socialism is the common solution advocated by both schools for the oppressed classes.[41] It is possible that Marxists and Marxist socialists see the irregular economy not only as a symbol of decay of the capitalist economy, but also as an arena for the practice of socialism without the constraints of the capitalist system. But Henry has argued that some of the irregular economy penetrates the capitalist structure and brings about evolutionary changes, just as women moving into

37. Robert Goffee and Richard Scase, *Women in Charge* (London: George Allen & Unwin, 1985).

38. Judith B. Agassi, *Comparing the Work Attitudes of Women and Men* (Lexington, MA: Lexington Books, 1982), p. 252-53.

39. Dorothy D. Smith, *Feminism and Marxism, a Place to Begin, a Way to Go* (Vancouver: New Star Books, 1977), p. 22.

40. Ibid.

41. Ibid.

jobs in the formal economy change the nature of work marginally if not radically.[42] Finally, it must be remembered that some of the alternative values of those participating in the irregular economy are not uniquely female linked.

There are variations on the general theme of women being forced into informal work, such as the life-cycle theory that Vinay presents for Italian women.[43] This theory suggests a pattern of family household participation based on the presence and number of preschool children. When preschool children come on the scene, the woman moves from the formal to the informal economy. In the United States, however, the data show an increasing trend toward participation of females as a whole in the formal economy and a most notable increase in the presence of young mothers in the economy. From 1970 to 1984, the participation of mothers in the informal economy with children under the age of one almost doubled. Participation within this group rose from 24 percent to 47 percent.[44] The participation rate increased generally in line with the age of the youngest child.[45] It seems that the paradigm of a fatalistic reversion back to maternal roles may no longer hold in the United States. At least the trend in the United States is very clearly in the opposite direction.

Many authors, including myself, feel that the roles that women play in the informal economy—and certainly the occupations they fill in the informal economy—closely mirror their status in the formal economy. The more objective analysis shows that women are certainly no better off in the informal than in the formal economy. In the words of Ivan Illich:

In shadow work much more intensely than in wage labor women are discriminated against. Less measurably, but even more massively than in wage labor, there is a sex differential in the bondage to this work. They are tied to more of it, they must spend more time on it, they have less opportunity to avoid it, its volume does not diminish when they take outside employment, and they are penalized more cruelly when they refuse to do it. What women are cheated out of in wage labor through discrimination is only a small fraction of the shadow price due them for their unpaid shadow work.[46]

The point is that participation in the informal economy may not be a halcyon experience—an escape from the shackles of the wage economy[47] or an escape from what Marx would call the world of necessity. It may as well be the case that the informal economy reinforces the strong division of roles and the inferior status of women. As Vinay states, there is a difference between "work imposed by necessity by the sexist division of the workforce on the one side—and activities performed for self-achievement and self-satisfaction on the other."[48]

42. Stuart Henry, "Can the Hidden Economy Be Revolutionary? Towards a Dialectical Analysis of the Relations between Formal and Informal Economics," mimeographed (Norfolk, VA: Old Dominion University, 1986).
43. Vinay, "Family Life Cycle," pp. 92-93.
44. Howard Hayge, "Working Mothers Reach Record Number in 1984," *Monthly Labor Review*, p. 31 (Dec. 1984).
45. Ibid. There is one exception. The figure dips or flattens slightly for mothers with children between four and five years old.
46. Illich, "Vernacular Gender," p. 9.
47. Ray Pahl, "Employment, Work and the Domestic Division of Labour," *International Journal of Urban and Regional Research,* 4:14-17 (1980).
48. Vinay, "Family Life Cycle," p. 95.

*Does women's coping through
   informal work enhance the
   formal economy?*

There is a perspective that looks at the informal economy as a buffer to or an enhancement of the formal economy. The empirical work that Ferman has done strongly suggests that the opportunities of the informal economy make the flaws in the formal economy bearable. Further, he argues that participation in the informal economy really becomes a deliberate and critical coping strategy when formal employment fails to meet the individual's economic and psychological needs.[49]

Thus irregular work—and off-the-books payment for it—may be used by women who receive one or more forms of transfer payment, such as disability payments under Social Security, Aid to Families with Dependent Children (AFDC), and Veterans Disability Payment. If the income were reported, it would result in the woman's being removed from public assistance. If the person did not earn extra income, she would not be able either to make ends meet or to achieve certain of her needs. An example from the Ferman study follows:

Mrs. Scruth is 53 years old, divorced, unemployed, and ill. She is receiving AFDC and public assistance. She is physically unable to care for her home and a housekeeper is provided once a week through a social service agency. She has housed at least two roomers over the last five years. They are charged monthly rent for room and board and the income is not reported for tax purposes. Mrs. Scruth requires her tenants to pay their rent promptly as this income is vital to her.[50]

49. Ferman, "Participation in the Informal Economy," p. 24.
50. Ibid.

Another role that the informal economy may play for women is the opportunity to try out some job skills. Opportunities are not nearly so bound by formal credentials in the informal economy and so are more accessible to women. The notion that blocked opportunities in the formal economy spawn informal activity has also been argued by both Pahl and Gershuny,[51] who have observed that economic recessions lead to many experiments with small entrepreneurs. For example, some argue that small businesses in the informal economy are used as a springboard to start more legitimate businesses.[52]

There is no reason to assume that this relationship between the informal and formal economy is simple. As Henry has written in his work on the political economy of the informal economy, the existence of the informal both signals the deterioration of the formal and at the same time supports the formal economy.[53]

Looking at the motivation on the individual woman's level, there are probably a multiple set of factors driving an individual from the formal economy to the informal. There may be as many different individual reasons for women participating in the informal economy as there are for men doing so. In other words, the possibility exists that women's reasons are idiosyncratic and individual, not systematic or gender linked. As Agassi states, the combination of factors may include greater unemployment, wage differentials, and occupational seg-

51. Gershuny, "Technology, Social Innovation"; Pahl, "Employment, Work and the Democratic Division of Labour."
52. Graeme Shankland, "Towards Dual Economy," *Guardian,* 23 Dec. 1977, p. 18.
53. Henry, "Can the Hidden Economy be Revolutionary?"

regation, as well as attitudinal characteristics of women, such as the greater importance given to instrumental values and a greater tendency to revert back to a conventional maternal role.[54]

Does the fact that the informal economy performs this function in relation to the formal economy mean that we can view it as an equalizer? Does it tend to make the distribution of income from the formal economy more uniform and less gender biased? Some recent empirical evidence suggests that the informal economy is not necessarily a salve for unemployment. Pahl, for example, suggests that those already in the formal economy have a much better chance of engaging in the informal. Therefore, some people may have one and a half jobs—one in the formal and another one part-time and off the books—and others may have none. This, in addition to the fact that wage rates in the formal parallel those in the informal, means that those who are "more equal" in the formal may be "more equal" in the informal. Thus the role of the informal economy as being an equalizer is not supported.[55] Similarly, Alden shows that double job-takers and moonlighters are not so much the poor but those already most active in the formal economy who spend holidays doing extra work and overtime.[56]

The most significant encumbrance to the potential egalitarianism provided by

simultaneously participating in the formal economy part-time and devoting the rest of the time to communal activities as suggested is "both the actual social division of labour and the sexist division of work tasks."[57] To Vinay and to me, it seems clear that no society, least of all our society, has overcome this.

The theories so far considered as explanations of women's participation in informal activity have several flaws. First, some theorists impute their own values to the observed behavior of women in the informal or formal economy without independent evidence that women have those values as their motivation; it is best not to espouse a theory that works a priori from an assumption as to why. Thus a theory is needed that is both agnostic and value free regarding the motivation of females. The theory I shall put forth is a behavioral interpretation of an individual's response to the formal or informal economy. Assumptions of atomized individuals in the marketplace choosing the formal or informal based on rational criteria may be mistaken. Similarly mistaken is the notion that the entry of females into the informal economy represents a feminist statement or even a statement rejecting market values. Since the woman may be participating in the informal economy for as many reasons as the male, a theory that neutrally describes this behavior is desirable.

54. Agassi, *Comparing the Work Attitudes,* pp. 65, 265; see also Larry DeBoer and Michael Seeborg, "The Female-Male Unemployment Differential: Effects of Changes in Industry Employment," *Monthly Labor Review,* pp. 8-13 (Nov. 1984).

55. This does not negate the fact that the irregular economy does help low-income individuals cope. See Pahl, *Divisions of Labour.*

56. Jeremy D. Alden, "Holding Two Jobs: An Examination of 'Moonlighting,' " in *Informal Institutions,* ed. Stuart Henry (New York: St. Martin's Press, 1981), pp. 43-59.

57. Vinay, "Family Life Cycle," p. 95. See also J. I. Gershuny, "Post-Industrial Society: The Myth of the Service Economy," *Futures,* 9:103-14 (1977); idem, *After Industrial Society?* (New York: Macmillan, 1978). idem, *Social Innovation and the Division of Labour* (New York: Oxford University Press, 1983); Rolf G. Heinze and Thomas Olk, "Development of the Informal Economy: A Strategy for Resolving the Crisis of the Welfare State," *Futures,* pp. 189-204 (June 1982).

A further flaw in the theories we have considered is that they are lacking in any organizational context. Decisions to take a job, leave a job, or combine two jobs usually occur within a context of a specific organization. The theory of motivation that I shall develop tries to accommodate these two qualities: the first is that it is neutral or value free, and the second is that it has an organizational perspective.

### A theory of participation and motivations: exit, voice, loyalty, and dual loyalty

The explanatory categories that Hirschman developed to explain an individual's exit from or bonding to an organization provide a theoretical framework with which to examine a person's decision regarding participation in the informal economy, the formal economy, or both.[58] Exit is the person's decision to move from the formal to the informal economy. Voice is a decision to stay within the formal but to do something about the objective conditions there, such as to unionize or to file a lawsuit. Loyalty is the person's decision to stay in the formal, not to exit, and not to exercise voice. Finally, dual loyalty is a decision to participate in the formal economy as well as to absorb a job, paid, or unpaid, illegal or legal, in the informal economy. It seems plausible, based on recent survey data of Pahl's and estimates by Feige and Gutmann[59] of the

enormous scope of activities subsumed under the rubric of irregular, that this status of dual loyalty is the norm rather than the exception.

The framework is a general one, broad enough to explain both male and female behavior. However, I would posit the following conclusions based on the evidence adduced in the previous empirical and theoretical discussion. The dual-loyalty status is one more frequently occupied by women than by men. It is a particularly good match for women who are mothers. Since there is an increasing trend for these mothers to adopt the dual-loyalty status rather than the exit strategy, does this mean that there will be a net decrease in the amount of informal activity performed by women? Probably not. Although gender roles are changing, it is generally the case that male spouses are not changing their relative contribution as quickly as their wives are changing from exit to dual loyalty.[60] Who then is going to do the extra work generated by the advent of another—or even the first—child in the household, chores like child care, laundry, and cleaning, if the mother is dually loyal? The answer is that the work will be done in the informal economy and no doubt by a woman. The only alternative, and there is some evidence that this happens also, is for the woman to compress extra work into the evenings and the weekends.

It is my strong assertion that the presence of women, or their predominance, in the informal economy cannot be said to reflect a preference for informal work, nor is it a feminist rejection of the formal economy's macho values. It is at least as likely that women are forced

58. Albert O. Hirschman, *Exit, Voice and Loyalty: Responses to Decline in Firms, Organizations and States* (Cambridge, MA: Harvard University Press, 1970).

59. Edgar Feige, *The Irregular Economy: Its Size and Macro-Economic Implications* (Madison: University of Wisconsin, 1979); Peter Gutmann, "The Subterranean Economy," *Tax and Spending*, pp. 4-11 (Apr. 1979).

60. The reader will recall the figures on the relative amount of household effort men and women contributed to the household.

by a combination of economics and sex bias to be there. Many are there out of necessity rather than choice.

The trend from exit to dual loyalty is not the only trend in the work force. Influenced by, though not determined by, feminist values and changing gender roles, there are more and more women participating in the formal economy who remain single or who marry and remain childless. In other words, loyalty is increasing among women. I submit, though, that the social reinforcement for loyalty—formal participation—among men still grossly exceeds that among women. Thus the househusband is a deviant role; the housewife is not. The career woman is a more deviant role for a woman than the career man is for a man. Note that "career man" sounds awkward or redundant merely because the societal assumption is so strong that not only will men have jobs, but they will have careers. Thus the outcome is a differential tendency for women to exit, or never to have entered the formal market.

### CONCLUSION: POLICY IMPLICATIONS

By way of conclusion, I would like to sketch the policy implications that follow from the changing role of women in the economy and their heavy participation in the informal economy. One of the key policies that is needed is day care. Federal support for—or regulation of—low-cost and safe day care is rather critical both to the working mother's ability to choose either the formal or informal economy and to her ability to hold any form of employment. Given the very low wages of many women workers, the provision of inexpensive day care often means the difference

between being on welfare and being employed, at least for a particular—and rather large—group of women, that of single parents who are heads of households. Even with middle-class and upper-class working mothers, this is an important issue since women with young children no longer drop out of the labor force. In fact, their participation rate is now identical to that of working women in general.

A second policy implication is that jobs in the informal economy are without the protections enjoyed by jobs in the formal economy, such as the benefits of protective legislation and a union contract. Since the latter only protects approximately 20-25 percent of the work force currently, it is the government regulation that would be the most useful to most workers, even though the scope of issues it controls is much narrower than the average union contract.

The discussion of the informal economy is often fragmentary and reductionist, failing to consider the context of the broader political system. To omit the government as an actor from analyses of the informal economy is an obvious and unfortunate omission, since governments can with a stroke of a pen change the status of an activity from legal to illegal and vice versa. Both the stance of the government and the laws themselves can serve to limit, tolerate, or reenforce the informal economy. The government can decide to round up those who do not pay their income taxes, can bring actions against employers who do not extend employee protections to their small business endeavors, and can bring actions against employers and individuals for nonpayment of social security taxes. Alternatively, the government can choose to ignore the problem. The main government activity in the United States has been initiated by the Internal Revenue Service and has been aimed at finding noncompliers.

The Department of Labor has moved in a different direction recently. It has endorsed the informal economy to the extent that it has lifted the ban on homework, much to the chagrin of unions, feminist groups, and female unionists, such as the Coalition of Labor Union Women. In the words of Joyce Miller, the Coalition of Labor Union Women president, "Homework will bring back the industrial dark ages of long hours at low wages with health and safety abuses."[61]

The main policy choice for a government is whether to acknowledge the existence of the informal economy. If it does, it must provide subsequent regulation extending the available protections for formal workers to workers in the informal economy. Obviously, the other policy choice is whether and how to collect income taxes and social security from those in the informal economy.

Another policy implication is that labor force participation of women may be grossly underestimated, given the extent of their activity in the informal economy. The government statistics should be revised in order to give an alternative and more accurate reading of the level of female participation in the labor force.

Finally, there are some policy issues raised by both the unprecedented entry of more and more women workers into the formal economy and the increasing numbers of women who have dual loyalty. This development should create more demand for day care, flextime,

61. *C.L.U.W. News,* no. 60, p. 1 (Nov.-Dec. 1986).

and, ironically, according to my analysis, more—not less—informal economy work at the same time.

There are two converging factors that will change the fundamental character of female participation in the work force. The first is the increasing number of women who are in the formal economy; the second is the important—in fact, predominant—role that females play in the informal economy. These two developments pose a challenge both to researchers and to policymakers. What we are seeing, if not a new development, is the official recording of a historical development.

Summing up, I argue that women's contribution to the informal economy is so dramatic—although invisible—that if ever recorded, it would usher in a new chapter in the book of women in the work force. Although women's role in the informal economy may well be exploited, rather than being the romantic alternative experience of escaping from the bondage of the formal wage labor economy, the entry into the formal labor market has not been as self-actualizing and liberating as the women's liberationists and feminists had hoped. This fact has led some feminists such as Betty Friedan to challenge the value of superwoman as a realistic goal. Referring to the rigors of dual-loyalty status, the popular writer Erica Jong is quoted as saying, "We have liberated ourselves into a state of exhaustion."

What is certain is that any analysis of women's contribution to work that does not take account of the informal economy will be seriously flawed. Similarly, any examination of the informal economy that ignores the contribution of women's hidden labor does not deserve to be taken seriously.

ANNALS, *AAPSS*, **493**, September 1987

# Measuring the Informal Economy

*By* JAMES D. SMITH

ABSTRACT: This article presents results from a study of the informal economy carried out by interviewing a national probability sample of approximately 2100 families. Each family was asked about purchases it had made from vendors who were selling goods and services on the side. A number of questions were asked about each vendor to help verify that vendors were indeed functioning as informal suppliers. Although not all characteristics had to be present for any single supplier, informal suppliers were characterized as individuals who had casual record-keeping systems, lacked a fixed place of business, and relied upon word of mouth and other casual means of advertising. Typical of such vendors are automobile mechanics operating in a home garage, produce sellers operating from a roadside stand, and craftsmen who operate from a pickup truck or in a home workshop. It was found that about $42 billion in informal economic activity took place in 1981 and that four out of every five American families purchased something from an informal vendor. Home repairs, accounting for over $12 billion, constituted the largest form of informal economic activity. The second most important was food sales.

*James D. Smith is a research scientist and program director at the Survey Research Center of the University of Michigan. He has written widely on the distributions of income and wealth and on the application of microanalytic simulation models for informing public policy. His work on the informal economy is a natural extension of his work on income distribution.*

THE informal economy is defined as a subeconomy of what one might call the nonformal economy: all those economic activities, legal and illegal, that elude the national income accounts because vendors' operating styles are such that the final counting mechanisms of the national income accountants do not detect them. There has been a paucity of research on the informal economy in the United States, and what there is focuses on macroeconomic issues: the magnitude and size of the informal economy expressed in financial terms, the evasion of tax payments, and corrections in national income accounts when we add the monetary value of informal exchanges. Two studies have used a microeconomic approach, surveying users of informal exchanges to identify the characteristics of participants in the informal economy as well as their motivations, values, attitudes, and norms of exchange. The purpose of this article is to report the results of one of these surveys, focusing on the following questions:

1. What is the size of the informal economy in the United States?
2. Who are the vendors that operate in this economy?
3. Who are the purchasers of goods and services in this economy?
4. What are the motivations that predispose consumers to use the informal rather than the formal economy?

An understanding of how the informal economy operates and how it contributes to our national economy must focus on the decisions and behavior of individuals who participate in informal exchanges. Any consequent public policy on informal economics must take into account the social reality of economic exchange that flows from these decisions and behavior.

The informal economy includes all types of market economic activity conceptually in the national accounts that is undermeasured due to the informal business styles of vendors. Put another way, it includes all activity that is conceptually within the national income accounts definitions but not captured for lack of any adequate auditing trail. Major sources of national accounts data are business and personal income tax returns. If returns are not filed by entrepreneurs, the sources are deficient. If entrepreneurs report only part of their activities, the tax records again are deficient. The informal economy is not defined, however, by the failure to pay taxes. Some informal vendors file returns and pay taxes, others file returns but do not owe taxes, and still others neither file returns nor pay taxes.

SCOPE AND PROCEDURES FOR
MEASURING THE
INFORMAL ECONOMY

Although entrepreneurs operating in the informal economy are not likely to be as sensitive to researchers' questions as those who ply their wares in the illegal economy, it is nevertheless difficult, if not impossible, to make national measurements of informal economic activity by interviewing vendors. Although the source of their income may be legitimate, they frequently operate at the margin of conformity with requirements for licensing, permit filing, and performance codes. Even if they do not owe taxes, some will be in technical violation of filing requirements of state, local, and federal governments. Hence informal economy vendors are sensitive about discussing their entrepreneurial activities. Even if they were willing to provide information to researchers, one despairs of designing a probability sample from which national estimates can be derived.

The approach taken in the study reported here was to measure the size of the informal economy by measuring the value of purchases households made from informal vendors. By definition, a dollar spent by one person is a dollar of income to another. This approach has both advantages and disadvantages. The advantages are that (1) purchasers are willing to talk about their transactions with informal vendors; and (2) it is relatively easy to design a national probability sample of households. The disadvantages are that (1) purchasers are often hard-pressed to differentiate between vendors in the formal economy and those in the informal; and (2) we are in a position to collect only a limited amount of information about vendor characteristics. Therefore, purchasers must be asked about proxies denoting an informal entrepreneurship.

The point should be made, however, that people have a well-developed sense that there are vendors who "work off the books" or "on the side." Indeed, the latter terminology was found in focused discussion groups and national pretests to be a part of the national vocabulary. It also became clear from the informal discussion groups that there is a general belief that on-the-side vendors are evading tax obligations. Furthermore, the generally expressed view was that such tax evasion was only a little wrong, like driving 60 miles an hour. If one gets caught, one pays the fine, but it is a minor and technical violation of an unjust law. Indeed, the view was frequently expressed that taxes were unjustly distributed because loopholes allowed persons with large incomes to avoid paying their fair share. Informal economy transactions were seen by some as do-it-yourself tax reform.

A national sample of approximately 2100 households was interviewed by phone. The interviews were taken in August, September, October, and November of 1981. Questions about purchases in the informal economy were included within a set of questions broadly economic in nature that are asked in the monthly Surveys of Consumer Attitudes by the University of Michigan's Survey Research Center. When the responses to these questions are weighted, national estimates of the amount spent and the types of goods and services purchased are produced.

The questionnaire used for the informal economy study was developed after focused discussion group sessions with persons who were living in both urban and suburban areas and who had incomes representative of a cross section of Americans. The questionnaire proceeded through three pretests before a final instrument emerged.

Three waves of interviews, each consisting of a sample of about 700 households, were conducted beginning in August and ending in November of 1981. Respondents were asked to report amounts spent on a variety of goods and services during the "last 12 months." The three waves were pooled and treated as though they were a single set of interviews taken at a point in time. The information thus collected is best thought of as representing the purchases of consumers in the 12 months from November 1980 through October 1981. For ease of expression, the estimates are referred to at times in the text as for the year 1981. For a few goods and services, respondents were asked about the amounts they spent in the three months preceding the interview, and in a few other cases, in the six months preceding the interview. This was done to facilitate recall where individual purchases tended to be both irregular and small. The amounts reported were adjusted to annual values.

As noted, the questions regarding informal economic transactions were conducted as part of the monthly Surveys of Consumer Attitudes. The surveys have a large economic component. Thus the questions on informal transactions were asked in the context of many questions about related economic activity. Before asking respondents the questions related to the informal economy, we straightforwardly stated, "We would like to ask you some questions about the opportunities people have to buy goods and services from persons who sell them on the side."

For each of the areas of consumption the focus on informal activity was reinforced by giving examples or by restating the request for information about purchases made from vendors doing business "on the side."

A number of questions about the vendor's occupation, the place where services were performed or goods received, how respondents learned about the vendor, and whether payment was requested in cash were asked to help filter out of the estimates formal economy activities that might otherwise creep into respondents' answers.

The use of checks for payment certainly does not denote a formal economy transaction, nor does the request for cash provide a positive indicator of an informal economy transaction. Even with illegal activities, such as political payoffs, prohibited contributions to political parties, bribes, and the like, a check may provide the wrongdoer's undoing only if an intense investigation takes place. It is not likely that informal economy transactions are traced through checks, even when the vendor is underreporting income to official taxing bodies. On the other hand, a vendor might ask

for cash simply because the customer is not known or the merchant has experienced excessive numbers of returned checks. Particularly when dealing with customers who are transient, such as might be the case with roadside stands, checks that bounce may, for practical purposes, be uncollectable. In any case, a request for cash is taken to be only mildly corroborative evidence of an informal economy transaction.

When it was not obvious where a transaction or a service took place, respondents were asked this information to aid in excluding from their reports amounts spent in the formal economy. As with a request for a payment in cash, the location of a transaction provides only weak evidence of the proper classification of an expenditure in the formal or informal economy. Nevertheless, it is one of a set of weak indicators that, when taken as a group, can often provide reliable guidance.

Respondents were asked how they learned about the provider. Here the concern was to identify modes of advertising or other indicators that the vendor was in fact a formal economy vendor. In the case of personal care, respondents were asked if the provider was licensed. Other things being equal, licensed vendors are more likely to be found in the formal as opposed to the informal economy.

THE SIZE OF THE
INFORMAL ECONOMY

The upper limit of the informal economy, as defined here, is estimated to be about $42 billion dollars in 1981. Internal Revenue Service analysts believe that about $10 billion of this was reported on income tax returns. This compares to a gross national product of $2.9 trillion and personal consumption expenditures of $1.9 trillion during the same period.[1] The $42 billion is the gross value of sales and should not be construed as the net income of informal vendors. Whether a business operates in the formal, informal, or illegal economy, it faces operating expenses that reduce net income; profits are but a fraction, and sometimes a negative fraction, of gross receipts. The Internal Revenue Service reports that its records indicate that the net income on tax returns with business income is about 59 percent of gross receipts. If the Internal Revenue Service proportion is correct, about $25 billion of unreported income existed in the informal economy in 1981. Some of this would not have been taxable, however.

The range of goods and services sold in the informal economy is quite extensive. Table 1 shows the value of informal transactions in 15 broad classes of goods and services measured in this study. The two largest components of the informal economy are home repairs and food; they accounted for about $12 billion and $9 billion, respectively, in 1981. They are quite different components from the standpoint of their underlying production processes. Food, which is sold in informal markets by producers, has a relatively capital-intensive production process. Home repairs, on the other hand, are labor intensive. What the two areas have in common with all informal market activities is that they can be carried on by a sole proprietor working alone or with the assistance of only one or two employees.

The need for record keeping is minimal. It is entirely possible for a farmer to produce an ancillary crop—say, ber-

1. Gross national product and personal consumption expenditures are annualized preliminary second-quarter figures.

ries—for which he keeps no production, sales, or cost records. Indeed, such record keeping may not be cost effective. If he has no employees or only employs family members, he may also avoid keeping records for unemployment compensation, tax, and occupational safety or health agencies. Since he purchases very little from suppliers in the production of berries, his record keeping is minimal on this score as well. Furthermore, his merchandising style can be very casual. A simple sign proclaiming "Fresh Berries," temporarily set up each season and staffed by his children, can be adequate to bring customers to his door or a roadside stand and provide a significant volume of sales.

Expenditures for child care in unlicensed establishments and/or in the homes of the families buying such care came to $5 billion. When child care was provided in the purchaser's home, vendors were classified as informal suppliers. Some child care provided in the vendor's home is, of course, in the formal economy, but it is believed to be a relatively small amount.

Domestic services were classified as informal or formal by whether or not providers were directly engaged or employed through a commercial cleaning firm. An amount of $3.9 billion was measured for the former whereas very little of the latter was found.

The repair of automobiles has an upper limit of about $2.8 billion in the informal economy. The classification of automobile repair services reported in the survey presents greater problems than do domestic services or child care, where the purchaser is likely to have a significant knowledge of the vendors' characteristics.

All purchases from sidewalk vendors and at flea markets were classified as

TABLE 1
VALUE OF PURCHASES FROM INFORMAL VENDORS BY TYPES
OF GOODS AND SERVICES, 1981 (Millions of dollars)

| Goods and Services | Amount |
| --- | --- |
| Home repair and additions | 12,245 |
| Food | 9,003 |
| Child care | 4,955 |
| Domestic service | 3,882 |
| Auto repair | 2,810 |
| Sidewalk vendor goods | 1,782 |
| Flea market goods | 1,698 |
| Lawn and garden services | 1,447 |
| Lessons | 933 |
| Fuel | 749 |
| Appliance repair | 744 |
| Adult care | 442 |
| Cosmetic service | 411 |
| Sewing and related services | 392 |
| Catering | 300 |
| Total | 41,793 |

SOURCE: J. Smith, T. Moyer, and E. Trzcinski, "The Measurement of Selected Income Flows in Informal Markets" (Report, Survey Research Center, Institute of Social Research, University of Michigan, 1982).

taking place in the informal economy. Flea markets are a less peripatetic form of sidewalk vending. The degree to which flea markets are organized varies. Depending upon the political jurisdiction, flea market vendors may be required to acquire permits or licenses in addition to paying a booth fee, but otherwise flea market vendors have the earmarks of informal economy entrepreneurs.

Respondents were asked about the purchase of lawn and garden services. These are typically supplied by youths of high school and college age, in spite of a growing lawn and garden care industry in affluent suburbs. Respondents were queried about whether such services were provided by a firm or business providing lawn care services, or by a person operating more casually. The estimates are believed very clean, with little of the formal economy having

crept into the $1.4 billion of reported transactions.

Lessons, ranging from academic tutoring to flamenco dancing, accounted for $0.9 billion of informal market activity. Many lessons involve a single instructor and a single student. Payments are often made on a lesson-by-lesson basis, and the instructor frequently operates in his or her own home or the home of the purchaser. All these conditions lend themselves to an informal economy activity.

Soaring fuel costs in 1981 rekindled interest in coal and wood as sources of heat. We asked about the purchases of coal and wood from vendors operating on the side as opposed to established businesses. For practical purposes we did not find any informal market in coal, but we did uncover a substantial informal cordwood market, yielding

about $0.7 billion. For a small invest-
ment in a chain saw and a used but
serviceable pickup truck with aging
springs that may be stiffened by an extra
leaf installed on a Saturday afternoon,
many a young man appears to have gone
into the cordwood business. These entrepreneurs may be found on weekends in
an A&P parking lot or slowly plying
their wares door-to-door, asking customers if they have friends who might
also want a cord of wood delivered and
racked.

Appliance repairing, except for major
items, has largely disappeared in mass-
consumption societies because it is labor
intensive and hence costly relative to
replacement. Households spent about
$0.75 billion in the informal economy
for such repairs, however.

Although the care of adults represents
a much smaller part of the informal
economy than does child care, nearly
$0.4 billion was spent with unlicensed
suppliers of such services. About the
same amount was spent for cosmetic
services.

### VENDORS IN THE INFORMAL ECONOMY

Who were the recipients of the $42
billion spent by consumers in the informal economy? Because the estimates
were derived from consumers' reports of
their purchases in the informal economy,
the study relies on information provided
by purchasers about vendors. Where an
arm's-length transaction occurs, neither
party to it necessarily knows much about
the other. For some transactions, however, a significant knowledge of vendors
may be held by buyers. For instance, a
vendor of child care is usually known
relatively well by a buyer.

All respondents were asked about
vendors' usual occupations—whether
they were full-time on-the-side entrepreneurs, had regular jobs, were retired,
and so on. In Table 2 this information is
shown without regard to what was purchased. About a quarter of the value of
informal economy transactions involved
vendors who were regularly employed.
For these vendors the income from their
informal economy activity supplements
wages from a regular job. The remaining
three-quarters of the value of transactions in the informal economy involved
vendors whom one would not expect to
have large amounts of other income, on
average. A possible exception is retirees,
who accounted for approximately $1.5
billion of informal economy transactions.

Transactions worth $1 billion were
conducted in the informal economy with
vendors who were full-time on-the-side
vendors. About $4 billion in informal
transactions were with friends or relatives. It is not evident from the data
what the economic status of the vendors
or purchasers is in this kinship networking of transactions. It seems likely
that such transactions take place in all
economic strata and are not limited to
reciprocity among friends and kin of
low- and middle-income individuals. Indeed, the nature of the services suggests
that the activities took place across a
broad economic spectrum. Most of them
were for the care of family members and
for lawn maintenance. Included in the
"other" category are combinations of
occupational status and statements such
as "he does odd jobs" or "he is a
handyman." The $2.2 billion in "don't
know or undetermined" arose partly
because of an inappropriate response of
"yes" to the question "Does this person
also have a regular job and do repairs on
the side, is he retired or what?" It was
impossible to tell whether the respon-

TABLE 2
GROSS SALES IN THE INFORMAL ECONOMY BY OCCUPATIONAL
STATUS OF VENDORS, 1981 (Millions of dollars)

| Occupation | Gross Sales |
|---|---|
| Regular job | 11,732 |
| Unemployed or laid off | 675 |
| On strike | 99 |
| Retired | 1,496 |
| On-the-side operator | 1,126 |
| Housewife | 112 |
| Student | 329 |
| Part-time worker | 69 |
| Student with regular job | 29 |
| Friend or relative | 4,071 |
| Nurse | 77 |
| Babysitter | 477 |
| Day care center | 6 |
| Nursing home | 302 |
| Friend or relative day care operator | 9 |
| Other | 648 |
| Don't know or undetermined | 2,159 |
| Inappropriate to ask | 18,378 |

SOURCE: Smith, Moyer, and Trzcinski, "Measurement of Selected Income Flows."

dent was answering "yes" to the first thing he heard, "regular job," or the last, "retired." A "yes" response was therefore coded as undetermined. This was clearly an interviewing error that slipped by supervisors.

There were several sections where it was inappropriate to ask consumers about vendor occupational status. In some cases, the question would have seemed absurd—such as with purchases from a farmer, at a roadside stand, or at a farmer's market, which amounted to $9 billion—or the respondent would find it impossible to know, such as with sidewalk vendors and flea market vendors, transactions with whom totaled $1.8 billion and $1.7 billion, respectively. The large value in this category is due largely to food purchases.

## PURCHASERS OF INFORMAL ECONOMY GOODS AND SERVICES

Over 80 percent of U.S. households purchased some goods or services in the informal economy in 1981. In this section, we will present information about education, income, race, marital status, and number of children as it relates to participation in the informal economy.

### Education

Purchasing households and respondents were slightly above average in numbers of years of education completed compared to the population as a whole. There is a very discernible relationship between education and consumer activity in the informal economy. Of all households, 83 percent purchased something in the informal economy. On the other hand, 90 percent of families represented by respondents with more than 12 years of education made purchases in the informal economy in 1981. A chi-square statistic computed for the data is significant at the .0001 level, supporting the observed relationship between education and activity in the informal economy.

Not only does the probability of being a consumer in the informal economy increase with number of years of education, but the amount spent systematically increases with increasing levels of education. Families represented by a respondent with 8 or fewer years of education spent about $159, but the amount increased to $293 for those with 9 to 11 years of education and to $424 for those with a high school degree, and still further, to $672, for families represented by a respondent with more than 12 years of education. In Table 3 nonpurchasers have been excluded from the calculation, thus showing for purchasing families the average amount spent according to the number of years of education completed by the respondent representing the family.

This same pattern of increasing consumption with education is, of course, true of formal economy purchases. What is being observed is not simply a relationship between education and consumption in the formal and informal economies, but to a significant extent, a mixture of income and education acting upon families' propensities to consume because of the positive correlation between income and education.

*Income*

The higher a family's income the more likely that family is to participate in the informal economy. In Table 3, families are also distributed by their annual income and expenditures in the informal economy. There is a relatively strong tendency for the average amount spent in the informal economy to increase as family income increases. This also holds true for average expenditures in the formal economy. The mean amount spent in individual categories of consumption, although not evident in the table, is far less correlated with income than total expenditures in the informal economy.

*Race*

Given the size of the sample, it is not possible to provide information by detailed racial characteristics. The estimates are limited to those families in which the respondent was white and those in which the respondent was nonwhite. Nearly 85 percent of white families purchased something in the informal economy whereas only about 75 percent of nonwhite families made such purchases. Furthermore, as can be seen in the distribution in Table 3, white families tend to spend more in the informal economy than do nonwhite families. This is expected due to the higher income level of white families.

*Age*

Looking at informal economy expenditures by age of respondent, it was found that the percentage of nonpurchasers decreases with age. Referring back to Table 3, it can be seen that the amount spent increases until about age 35 and then systematically declines until it reaches approximately the same level that it had been at less than 19 years of age.

TABLE 3
MEAN VALUE OF ANNUAL PURCHASES IN FORMAL AND
INFORMAL ECONOMIES FOR HOUSEHOLDS MAKING
PURCHASES IN THE INFORMAL ECONOMY, 1981

| | Purchases in | |
| | Formal | Informal |
| --- | --- | --- |
| Income | | |
| $1-$4,000 | $2,990.91 | $366.95 |
| $5,000-$9,999 | 2,707.85 | 237.03 |
| $10,000-$14,999 | 3,142.58 | 417.07 |
| $15,000-$19,999 | 4,226.39 | 455.24 |
| $20,000-$24,999 | 4,089.61 | 532.74 |
| $25,000-$29,999 | 4,662.07 | 572.15 |
| $30,000-$34,999 | 4,855.86 | 668.50 |
| $35,000-$39,999 | 4,830.25 | 1,384.33 |
| $40,000 or more | 8,458.40 | 1,103.39 |
| Education | | |
| 0-8 years | $2,965.32 | $263.63 |
| 9-11 years | 3,796.32 | 408.08 |
| 12 years | 4,249.79 | 512.65 |
| More than 12 years | 5,015.18 | 747.36 |
| Age | | |
| 1-18 years | $5,100.44 | $320.56 |
| 19-25 years | 3,815.41 | 493.40 |
| 26-35 years | 4,618.63 | 788.62 |
| 36-45 years | 5,812.64 | 685.20 |
| 46-55 years | 4,982.32 | 575.05 |
| 56-65 years | 4,000.44 | 463.20 |
| 65 years or older | 2,710.67 | 304.39 |
| Number of children | | |
| 0 | $3,705.37 | $545.99 |
| 1 | 5,148.47 | 515.73 |
| 2 | 5,318.94 | 765.12 |
| 3 | 5,718.00 | 780.44 |
| 4 | 6,977.01 | 747.78 |
| 5 or more | 4,922.44 | 454.17 |
| Race | | |
| White | $4,405.30 | $615.75 |
| Nonwhite | 4,366.52 | 527.79 |

## Marital status

Marital status does not make a great deal of difference with respect to whether one is a purchaser or nonpurchaser in the informal economy. Nonpurchasers in all marital categories but "widowed"

were 14 to 21 percent of all families. A slightly higher percentage—30 percent—was found for the widowed, but this is partly attributable to age. As was noted, purchasing dropped off at ages over 65, and we would expect to find a greater number of widowed in the older age groups. Looking only at families who purchased, the amounts spent tend to be larger for families headed by married and never married persons than for other family types.

## Number of children

Finally, looking at household expenditures in the informal economy by the number of children, it was found that the number of children had little effect on whether a family was a purchaser or nonpurchaser in the informal economy. Looking at Table 3, it is seen that expenditures increase with family size, up to three children, and then decline. This probably reflects an interplay of needs and level of income as family size increases.

### ECONOMIC PERCEPTIONS AND MOTIVATIONS RELATED TO THE INFORMAL ECONOMY

In addition to the information needed to estimate the size of the informal economy, households were asked whether they had ways of making extra money, such as extra jobs or sideline businesses to help keep their income from falling behind prices. They were also queried about trading activities in which they may have been involved. Further, they were asked what they perceived to be the major advantages and disadvantages of buying from people selling on the side and how the current expenditures with informal sources compared to the past and expected future expenditures. Findings based on these questions are now presented.

## Means of making extra money

Over one-fifth—22 percent—of the population reported they had ways of earning extra money. In fact, many families were involved in several extra-income activities. The activities reported are presented in Table 4. Respondents were anxious to report on these activities. Some, in fact, offered their views as to whether they thought the activity should be considered an on-the-side activity.

The largest number of mentions, 5 million (weighted), involved the selling of manufactured goods such as Avon, Amway, and Tupperware products. This activity is on the borderline between the formal and informal economies. The information is of interest because some vendors of such products in fact operate in the styles of the informal economy.

The largest response, for what were considered strictly on-the-side methods of earning extra money, was for selling services such as carpentry, painting, plumbing, masonry, and related services—approximately 3 million (weighted) mentions. Other activities mentioned were training and grooming dogs, buying and selling cars, photographic services, moving services, transportation services for the handicapped or elderly, playing in bands, and selling goods at flea markets.

## Trading activities

Respondents were asked if they were involved in any trading activities, either through organized clubs or on their own. It was found that 10 percent of U.S. households engaged in trading goods and services on their own, but less than 1 percent belonged to formal clubs.

In response to the question "Please tell me what you traded and the things you got in exchange in the last 12 months," trading services for services was the most frequently reported, amount-

TABLE 4
**REPORTS OF ON-THE-SIDE ACTIVITIES OF HOUSEHOLDS, 1981 (Millions)**

| Ways of Making Extra Money | Number of Mentions |
|---|---|
| Selling goods | |
| Door-to-door sales of manufactured products—Avon, Amway, Tupperware, and similar products | 5.3 |
| Arts, crafts, furniture, and household items produced by households | 2.2 |
| Fresh fruits, vegetables, and other food items grown or produced by households | 1.5 |
| Cord wood | 0.4 |
| Selling services | |
| Carpentry, painting, plumbing, masonry, and related crafts | 2.7 |
| Baby-sitting and house cleaning | 2.1 |
| Lawn and gardening care and one-time cleanups | 1.8 |
| Repairs of vehicles, furniture, appliances, and lawn equipment | 1.7 |
| Sewing or laundry | 1.3 |
| Beauty care, catering, typing, and income tax preparation | 1.1 |
| Lessons—music, dance, cooking, art, or other lessons | 0.6 |
| Other services | 4.5 |
| Total | 17.8 |

SOURCE: Smith, Moyer, and Trzcinski, "Measurement of Selected Income Flows."
*Number of mentions does not sum to total due to multiple mentions.

ing to 44.5 percent of trading activities. (See Table 5.) The types of exchanges included mechanics' services for carpentry, fixing a car for installing a carpet, baby-sitting for baby-sitting, lawn care for helping put in dry wall, sewing for hair cuts, and medical services for legal services.

### Perceived advantages and disadvantages of buying from on-the-side vendors

Respondents were asked what they considered to be the major advantages and disadvantages of buying from informal vendors. The most frequently reported advantage—in 57 percent of the

reports—was lower costs. Better quality was the next most frequently mentioned, in 12 percent. The most frequently stated disadvantage, accounting for 45 percent of the reports, was the absence of guarantees and exchange and return privileges. Lack of a guarantee caused households to fear the loss of money if goods were defective or service unsatisfactory. Of the reported disadvantages, 31 percent concerned questionable or uncertain quality.

### Level of activity relative to the past and future

Households were asked whether they bought "more," "less," or the "same"

TABLE 5
**TYPE OF TRADING BY HOUSEHOLDS REPORTING TRADING ACTIVITIES, 1981**

| What Was Traded | Percentage of Reports |
| --- | --- |
| Services for services | 44.5 |
| Services for goods | 13.1 |
| Goods for goods | 22.9 |
| Goods for services | 8.9 |
| Services for money | 5.1 |
| Goods for money | 5.5 |

SOURCE: Smith, Moyer, and Trzcinski, "Measurement of Selected Income Flows."

amount in the current year from informal vendors relative to the preceding year. They were also asked if they intended to buy "more," "less," or the "same" in the year ahead compared to the current year. Of the households, 9 percent reported they bought more than in the previous year, while 20 percent reported they bought less. Intending to buy more in the year ahead were 17 percent, and 14 percent said they intend to purchase less. In Tables 6 and 7 intentions to buy and current purchases relative to the past are shown by whether the household is currently a purchaser or nonpurchaser.

Households intending to buy more on-the-side goods and services next year most frequently—in 30 percent of reports—cited lower prices as the reason. Greater accessibility to on-the-side operators and prior good experience with informal economy sources were reported about 15 percent of the time (Table 8).

The most frequently stated reasons families gave for spending less in the informal economy was that their needs for goods or services would decline in the year ahead—given 34 percent of the time—or that their personal economic condition would decline—18 percent. (See Table 9.)

It is of interest that the reasons for increased activity in the informal econ-

omy are related to favorable experience in dealing with informal suppliers—lower prices and good quality—while the reasons for decreasing activity have to do with changes in a family's own situation—reduced consumption needs or reduced income. This argues against the informal economy as a second-class market to which one goes in hard times, and it supports the hypothesis that the informal vendor is becoming a more important part of the economic system.

Turning to why households bought more in the current year than in the previous year, households reported lower prices most frequently—25.1 percent of the reports. To overcome the erosion of consumption by inflation, households may find it increasingly important to purchase goods and services inexpensively. The second most stated reason, accounting for 18.7 percent of the reports, was prior good experience with informal economy sources. (See Table 10.)

Finally, the reasons households bought less in the current year than in the previous year were, in 33.7 percent of reports, that their needs for goods and services had decreased and, in 20.4 percent, that a decline in their personal economic condition forced them to buy less. (See Table 11.)

## TABLE 6
### INTENTIONS TO BUY INFORMAL GOODS AND SERVICES
### BY PURCHASING AND NONPURCHASING HOUSEHOLDS, 1981

| Intend to Buy Next Year | Purchaser | Nonpurchaser |
|---|---|---|
| More | 19.6% | 11.3% |
| Less | 16.8% | 8.6% |
| Same | 63.5% | 80.1% |
| Total | 100.0% | 100.0% |
| Number of households (in millions) | 66.8 | 12.9 |

SOURCE: Smith, Moyer, and Trzcinski, "Measurement of Selected Income Flows."

## TABLE 7
### CURRENT PURCHASES OF INFORMAL GOODS AND SERVICES
### RELATIVE TO IMMEDIATELY PRECEDING YEAR BY PURCHASING
### AND NONPURCHASING HOUSEHOLDS, 1991

| Current Purchases Were | Purchaser | Nonpurchaser |
|---|---|---|
| More | 11.6% | * |
| Less | 23.3% | 11.8% |
| Same | 65.2% | 86.3% |
| Total | 100.0% | 100.0% |
| Number of households (in millions) | 68.3 | 13.1 |

SOURCE: Smith, Moyer, and Trzcinski, "Measurement of Selected Income Flows."
*Fewer than 400,000 households reporting.

## THE SIGNIFICANCE OF THE STUDY

The most significant aspect of the study is that it provides a systematic estimate of the size of the informal economy. That underground and informal economic activities exist in this society has long been acknowledged. The problem has been one of estimating the magnitude of such activities. A number of attempts have been made to estimate the size of the underground economy using macro indicators. Such approaches rely on plausible but documented relationships between informal economic activity and such things as currency in circulation, large bills in circulation, and unemployment rates. They also often include informed guesses by law enforcement officials about the level of undetected criminal activities such as arson, drug trafficking, and prostitution.

In this study we have singled out that portion of the underground economy that involves inherently legal economic transactions, and we have measured it directly by asking a national probability sample of families the amounts spent for the acquisition of goods and services from vendors who are dealing on the side. Clearly, there are limitations to our

TABLE 8
**REASONS HOUSEHOLDS INTEND TO BUY MORE FROM
ON-THE-SIDE VENDORS IN THE YEAR AHEAD, 1981**

| Reason | Percentage of Reports |
|---|---|
| Improvement in personal economic condition: earning or working more, more people in family working, got married | 2.5 |
| Desire to save money; decline in personal economic conditions: unemployed, lower income, divorced or widowed | 11.6 |
| Economy in general poor or static; inflation or unemployment | 4.4 |
| Prices of on-the-side goods or services lower | 30.1 |
| Need for more goods or services: home addition, special purchase, unexpected or emergency situation | 12.8 |
| Change in availability of informal sources: more access to on-the-side operators | 15.3 |
| Prior good experience with informal economy sources | 15.1 |
| Other or no particular reason given | 8.2 |

SOURCE: Smith, Moyer, and Trzcinski, "Measurement of Selected Income Flows."
NOTE: 17 percent of households reporting.

TABLE 9
**REASONS HOUSEHOLDS INTEND TO BUY LESS FROM
ON-THE-SIDE VENDORS IN THE YEAR AHEAD, 1981**

| Reason | Percentage of Reports |
|---|---|
| Improvement in personal economic condition: earning or working more, more people in family working, got married | * |
| Decline in personal economic conditions: unemployed, lower income, less work, divorced or widowed | 18.0 |
| Economy in general poor or static; inflation or unemployment | * |
| Prices of on-the-side goods or services too high | * |
| Fewer goods or services needed | 34.3 |
| Change in availability of informal sources: less access to on-the-side operators | 15.2 |
| Prior poor experience with informal sources; poor quality; no guarantee | 14.5 |
| Other or no particular reason given | 13.1 |

SOURCE: Smith, Moyer, and Trzcinski, "Measurement of Selected Income Flows."
NOTE: 14 percent of households reporting.
*Fewer than 400,000 households reporting.

TABLE 10
## REASONS HOUSEHOLDS BOUGHT MORE FROM ON-THE-SIDE
## VENDORS THAN IN THE PREVIOUS YEAR, 1981

| Reason | Percentage of Reports |
|---|---|
| Improvement in personal economic conditions: earning or working more, more people in family working, got married | * |
| Desire to save money; decline in personal economic conditions: unemployed, lower income, divorced or widowed | 11.5 |
| Economy in general poor or static; inflation or unemployment | * |
| Prices of on-the-side goods or services lower | 25.1 |
| Need for more goods or services: home addition, special purchase, unexpected or emergency situation | 12.3 |
| Change in availability of informal sources: more access to on-the-side operators | 14.5 |
| Prior good experience with informal economy sources | 18.7 |
| Other or no particular reason given | 12.8 |

SOURCE: Smith, Moyer, and Trzcinski, "Measurement of Selected Income Flows."
NOTE: 9 percent of households reporting.
*Fewer than 400,000 households reporting.

TABLE 11
## REASONS HOUSEHOLDS BOUGHT LESS FROM ON-THE-SIDE
## VENDORS THAN IN THE PREVIOUS YEARS, 1981

| Reason | Percentage of Reports |
|---|---|
| Improvement in personal economic condition: earning or working more, more people in family working, got married | * |
| Decline in personal economic conditions: unemployed, lower income, less work, divorced or widowed | 20.4 |
| Economy in general poor or static; inflation or unemployment | * |
| Prices of on-the-side goods or services too high | * |
| Fewer goods or services needed | 33.7 |
| Change in availability of informal sources: less access to on-the-side operators | 19.4 |
| Prior poor experience with informal sources; poor quality; no guarantee | 8.8 |
| Other or no particular reason given | 12.0 |

SOURCE: Smith, Moyer, and Trzcinski, "Measurement of Selected Income Flows."
NOTE: 20 percent of households reporting.
*Fewer than 400,000 households reporting.

approach. We rely upon buyers to provide us sufficient information about vendors for us to classify the latter as informal suppliers. We also face all of the problems of survey research, such as memory bias and voluntary participation. By no means proof of the quality of our estimates, but certainly corroborative, is the fact that each respondent was asked about purchases in both the formal and the informal economies for each of the goods and services that was measured in the study. When the reports of formal economy purchases were compared to national income and product accounts, they compared very favorably.

Although the magnitude of the informal economy as we have measured it accounts for less than 3 percent of the gross national product, the findings have significance for the way we think about employment status for certain parts of the labor force. It suggests, for instance, that craftsmen and tradespeople move easily between states of being employees and being self-employed. The findings suggest that the perceived swings in economic status of such workers as measured by traditional employment statistics may be overstated. It also suggests that if such workers exercise claims to unemployment insurance while in fact they are self-employed in the informal economy, tighter administration of the unemployment system could result in lower unemployment insurance premiums or greater benefits to other workers who are unemployed and do not so easily shift to self-employment status.

ANNALS, *AAPSS*, **493**, September 1987

# Developing Economies and the Informal Sector in Historical Perspective

*By* CHRIS GERRY

ABSTRACT: In the 1970s, social scientists used the term "informal economy" to describe the economic survival strategies of many of the working poor in Third World cities. Now, both terminology and analysis are applied in the advanced, industrialized countries to the often proliferating variations in nonwage employment that have emerged during the world recession of the late 1970s and 1980s. In this article, social science's understanding of the relationship between the informal economy and socioeconomic development is traced back to the early nineteenth century. It is argued that this interest has tended to wax and wane according to the cycle of boom and slump in national and international economy alike. It is in this broader historical context that the policies and reality of small-scale informal economic activity in the Third World can best be elucidated.

---

*Chris Gerry holds a bachelor's and a doctoral degree in economics from Leeds University, England. He has been a staff member of the Centre for Development Studies at the University College of Swansea for ten years and has worked in Senegal, Colombia, Mozambique, Tanzania, Ghana, and Portugal. The author of several essays and articles on small-scale producers in the Third World, he coedited with Ray Bromley* Casual Work and Poverty in Third World Cities.

EVER since feudalism began to be overthrown in Europe, scholars have been concerned with the contribution that could be made to economic growth and equity by the smaller-scale manufacturing and service activities that were organized along noncapitalist, precapitalist, protocapitalist, or even ostensibly anticapitalist lines. In classical political economy the nature and role of what is now referred to as the informal economy or informal sector was closely connected to both the theory and the practice of economic development. Such studies have as long a historical pedigree and as wide a geographical coverage as the more general theoretical analysis of the rise of capitalism. They certainly have a deeper heritage than the 1970s' literature on urban poverty and employment problems in the Third World would imply. However, in the last hundred years, the force with which these specific ideas have shaped development theory and policymaking has tended to vary according to the relative success of large-scale, increasingly transnational capitalist enterprises. Put simply, interest in the informal economy varies according to whether the international economy has been experiencing conditions of boom or slump.

Thus any discussion of the informal economy will benefit from examining this relationship. An appropriate starting point is the debate over the small producer in the emerging industrial capitalist societies of Europe. Before this is undertaken, some introductory clarification must be made with regard to the theories that have underpinned the analysis of growth and development in general and, in particular, the place of the small producer in this process.

## GROWTH, DEVELOPMENT, AND SMALL ENTERPRISES: HOW MANY PARADIGMS?

Four theories of how prices are determined, markets work, and incomes are generated and distributed have competed over the last 150 years to influence political decision making in general and, in particular, that relating to economic growth and social development. Though the four theories have coexisted over that period, each has exerted different degrees of influence at different times.

### Free marketeers

Free market, liberal, or laissez-faire theorists hold that markets, if left to operate without interference from the government or artificial monopolies, will automatically satisfy both individuals' and society's preferences. The roots of this assertion lie in Adam Smith's late-eighteenth-century philosophical conclusion that "publik and national, as well as private opulence" is based upon "the uniform, constant and uninterrupted effort of every man to better his condition."[1] The small independent producer, pursuing his or her own self-interest, continued to be idealized by the proponents of laissez-faire long after the power of master craftsman and workshop had been superseded by the capitalist employer and the factory. In the interwar years of the twentieth century, free marketeers argued that the liberation of home and international markets from government interference was the only defense against national stagnation and global recession. Today, such views are often referred to as neoliberal and have been most closely

1. Adam Smith, quoted in I. I. Rubin, *A History of Economic Thought* (London: Ink Links, 1979), p. 169.

associated with the monetarism of Milton Friedman and the current privatization and deregulation policies of many governments throughout the world.

In the long run, it was argued, market forces would also permit the gradual modernization of all less developed countries in the image of the capitalist economies that had often been their colonial masters. In the meantime, small enterprises and what is described today as the informal economy would provide the indigenous entrepreneurs such countries lacked. Foreign capital and entrepreneurs would withdraw as and when their local counterparts were able to compete successfully with respect to prices and quality in home and overseas markets.

*Reformists*

Second, there is the structuralist theory found in the work of the early-nineteenth-century English economist David Ricardo. He favored free markets and is perhaps best known for his theory of comparative advantage whereby countries specializing and trading in what they can most efficiently produce gain mutual benefit. However, he was skeptical that markets would automatically reflect everyone's preferences. His analysis of the English economy and society of his day convinced him of the inevitability of conflicts between classes over the distribution of the growth that took place. Rather than accepting the laissez-faire proposition of a minimal state, Ricardians proposed a more active role for government. Government institutions would become professional and impartial arbiters of antagonistic class interests, and, through institutional reforms to promote greater equality of incomes and opportunities, social conflict would be minimized and the capital-

ist system preserved.

Late in the last century, such ideas manifested themselves in trade protectionism. In this century, their influence has been most notable in post-World War II Keynesian economic theory and policy, itself a product of the Great Depression. At that time, it was argued, the market had shown itself incapable of ensuring full employment. Keynesianism advocated a greater degree of government regulation of the economy, often culminating in substantial direct intervention in production and the market. In the 1970s, however, influenced by more radical interpretations of Keynes, by interwar South American protectionist industrialization policies, and by the growing Non-Aligned Movement of poor and middle-income countries in the 1960s, the so-called dependency school of developmental theory emerged. In most respects this was a pro-planning, anti-laissez-faire perspective that explained underdevelopment predominantly in terms of the chronic inequality in trade between rich and poor countries.

Dependency theory viewed the problems of small enterprises in the informal sector as being those of the Third World economy in microcosm. Just as the poor country's underdevelopment was perpetuated by its subordinate exchange relations with the industrialized economies, so the informal sector could never develop its own dynamic of capital accumulation and growth so long as it coexisted unequally with mainly foreign-owned large-scale capitalist enterprises.[2] The suggested answer was to create a more radical state to support small indigenous entrepreneurs against large foreign capi-

2. Chris Gerry, *Petty Production and the Urban Economy: A Case Study of Dakar,* Working Paper no. 8 (Geneva: International Labor Office, World Employment Program, 1974).

talists, as part of a relatively autarkic development strategy. Despite its often Marxist terminology, and the fact that it was often referred to as neo-Marxist development theory, dependency theory's preoccupations were demonstrably nation-to-nation rather than interclass, and its proposals reformist rather than revolutionary.

## Marxists

Third, there is the Marxist school. It maintains that the capitalist market system, which the free marketeers seek to conserve and Ricardian reformists would wish to modify, has a built-in tendency to generate periodic slumps. Government policy is used to force the major social and financial burden of these crises onto the working class. Nevertheless, the development of capitalism gives rise to its own grave digger in the form of a large wage-earning class that, once fully conscious of its own independent power, can organize to overthrow the system. The type of state ownership of productive assets found in the centrally planned economies of the USSR, Eastern Europe, China, and other countries is conventionally but inaccurately believed to reflect Marx's ideas. Those styling themselves as Marxists often disagree over (1) how directly workers' power should be exercised after capitalism has been overthrown; (2) the political form that workers' control should take under socialism; and (3) how sustainable socialist revolution is if limited to one country.

The authentic Marxist development theory would, I feel, argue that the isolated attempt by a backward, embattled, and boycotted Russia to construct socialism after 1917 produced bureaucratic deformities, structural transformation from above, and an eventual

negation of much that was humane and progressive in Marx's thinking. Little that has happened in China, Cuba, or elsewhere would modify that conclusion. Trotsky argued that the existence of a weak capitalist class in a backward country with a massive peasantry did not necessarily exclude the possibility of socialist revolution. Indeed, an accelerated transition from near-feudal autocracy to socialism could be effected by a small working class, if it were able to convince the peasantry to accept its revolutionary leadership. But national economic backwardness would prevent the most basic problems of socialism from being solved, unless unity could be forged with similar movements in more advanced countries and the revolution could be internationalized.[3]

Consequently, a revolutionary Marxist solution to Third World poverty would require that both the USSR and China desist from extending their support to or withdrawing it from dissident movements in developing countries merely as a function of their own national economic and foreign policy interests. Additionally, mature, well-supported, and independent revolutionary movements would have to exist or, indeed, have taken power in a number of today's key capitalist states. This conclusion seems to imply that Marxists and free marketeers alike consider the Third World to be rather marginal to world events. Does the Third World appear to be as much of a sack of potatoes to contemporary Marxists as the French peasantry did to Marx? Not really. Third World countries will continue to figure prominently as weak links in capitalism's international system. As new

3. Leon Trotsky, *Permanent Revolution, Results and Prospects* (New York: Pathfinder Press, 1969), pp. 276-79.

areas unevenly develop greater industrial and market potential, new generations of grave diggers are born, whose struggles act as an example and a stimulus to workers in the more advanced countries. Thus there is a tendency of capitalism to reproduce periodic crises that give rise to the potential for challenging and overthrowing the system both nationally and internationally.

With this perspective in mind, Marxists could be expected to see small entrepreneurs and those active in the informal sector in very much the same light as Trotsky viewed the peasantry. Despite the value they attach to private property and their susceptibility to the ideology and values of capitalism, most small producers fare badly in both boom and slump, since it is large capital that profits in prosperity and transfers the cost burden in times of recession. In this respect, and to the extent that the informal sector is brought into close contact with large capitalist and state enterprises—for example, in its search for both inputs and markets for its output— small entrepreneurs and particularly their employees should not be ignored by those seeking to develop a revolutionary consciousness among the poor, exploited, and oppressed in the Third World. Rather than commenting on what the state or large corporations should do to help the informal sector, Marxists would struggle to establish greater and closer contact between workers in both formal and informal sectors as a means of achieving a revolutionary transformation of society.

## Populists

There has long existed a school of social, political, and economic thought that, to a greater or lesser extent, denied the uniqueness, desirability, or practicability of progress based on large-scale industrialization. This factor distinguishes populism from the laissez-faire, reformist, and Marxist models so far discussed. Its roots are quite varied: the nostalgic agrarian romanticism of Sismondi (1773-1842) and the late-nineteenth-century Russian narodniks, which reflected the views of an increasingly ruined agrarian petite bourgeoisie; the anarchist writers Godwin (1756-1836), Proudhon (1809-65), and Kropotkin (1842-1921), who hoped to replace the capitalist system with a commonwealth of artisans and small cultivators; the early-nineteenth-century utopian followers of Ricardo, who articulated the fears and aspirations of a fledgling working class.

Populists tended to juxtapose an idealized natural justice or natural liberty with the injustice and wage slavery they identified with capitalism. Like Sismondi and Proudhon, utopian socialists saw capitalist categories such as profit and wages as being unnatural. Populist writers and activists were more than skeptical with regard to the ability of a market economy, dominated by an industrial ethic, to provide adequately and distribute equitably the benefits of growth to the majority of citizens. Most populists regarded the capitalist market with a suspicion bordering on hostility, because there appeared to be no guarantee that products would exchange at prices reflecting their labor content. Their solutions to the ills of capitalism ranged from the abolition of false money and its replacement by a more just measure of value, such as the labor certificate, to the establishment of interest-free cooperative banks. Lenin summarized Marx's criticisms of early agrarian populism as follows:

Sismondi regarded small-scale production as a natural system and was up in arms against big capital, which he regarded as an extraneous element . . . [he] failed to understand the inseparable and natural connection between big capital and small independent production, [and] . . . that these are two forms of commodity economy . . . [he] is up in arms against . . . commodity economy in one form while, utopian-like, he praises the small producer . . . i.e. commodity economy in . . . its rudimentary form.[4]

Marx's assessment of Proudhon's arguments was much the same.[5] Rubin criticizes the utopian socialists, saying, "Their ethical rejection of capitalism was too readily transformed into a theoretical disregard for its inherent laws. Being overly preoccupied with constructing plans for what ought to be, the utopian socialists gave insufficient study to what is."[6]

Seen in the more recent context of the Third World, populism has tended to espouse development strategies that are institutionally based, for example, upon the ostensive equality and collectivism of the precolonial era, such as the various African socialisms of East and central Africa. It has also preached much greater autonomy, as in Tanzania's strategy of *ujamaa*, or self-reliance, or in the advocating of appropriate technology. In this respect, its own nationalism has sometimes become indistinguishable from that of the reformists. Clearly, small enterprises and the informal sector would play almost as central a role in the development rhetoric as would the peasantry. Whether that rhetoric would be matched by concrete attempts to base economic development predominantly on small-scale cooperative undertakings is more doubtful.

## DEVELOPMENT AND EARLY POPULIST ANTI-INDUSTRIALISM

Early reflections on the small urban and peasant enterprise sector were rooted in either moral or pragmatic opposition to the impact of rapid industrialization. First among such critiques of industrialism was the work of Simonde de Sismondi.[7] On reading of the social impact of the English crises of 1815 and 1818, Sismondi pointed to the contradiction between the growing productive capacities of agriculture and industry and the stagnating purchasing power of the population. The former was the result of mechanization while the latter was caused by rural-urban migration and the growing urban poverty engendered by the spread of wage-labor unemployment and by the international capitalist competition for markets.

Sismondi's solution was for less developed European countries to reject what he felt was the "erroneous path" of industrialization and rely instead on what was seen as the preexisting balanced and harmonious institutions of small property owners. The idea was that the benefits would be shared more equitably between property owners and laborers. Later, the anarchist Pierre-Joseph Proudhon drew similar conclusions while speculating on how new forms of productive, distributive, and credit arrangements, might be adopted.[8] Marx,

4. Vladimir I. Lenin, *A Characterization of Economic Romanticism: Sismondi & Our Native Sismondists* (Moscow: Progress, 1967), pp. 71-72.

5. Karl Marx to P. V. Annenkov and to J. B. Schweizer, in *The Poverty of Philosophy* (Moscow: Progress, 1975), pp. 165-87.

6. Rubin, *History of Economic Thought*, p. 349.

7. Simonde de Sismondi, *Nouveaux principes d'économie politique ou de la richesse dans ses rapports avec la population* (Paris, 1819).

8. Pierre-Joseph Proudhon, *Le système des*

who referred to the sphere of the small producer as "the pygmy property of the many,"[9] also contributed to the early debates, denouncing both Sismondi and Proudhon as ideologues of the petite bourgeoisie, because of their idealist philosophical notions and their atavistic anti-industrialism.

It is easy to forget the conditions prevailing in the second half of the nineteenth century. Much labor in the advanced industrial economies had still to be organized under the factory system. The self-employed small master typified the enterprise of the day much more than the captain of industry and his giant textile mill or ironworks and was characterized by very cramped and crowded workshops. Though each was unique, these workshops were similarly unmechanized and had a rudimentary division of labor compared to the factories they supplied or with which they competed. Their internal hierarchy was based not only on property—such as who owned the building, whether craftsmen owned their own tools, and who provided the raw materials—but also on differences in skill, age, and time served. Relations between the different grades of workers and their masters were characterized by a seemingly feudal set of relations of personal dependence and paternalism.

However, the apparent independence of such petty producers belied the fact that most were squeezed by cutthroat competition and subordinated to much larger enterprises through the market. Viewed from the outside, these small enterprises often appeared to be little more than satellites of the factory system and, along with their workers, mere adjuncts to the industrial wage-labor force.[10]

The logic of capitalist industrialization was to substitute exploitation of wage labor for old-style paternalism. This compelled small masters either to develop along increasingly capitalist lines in order to compete and survive or to be condemned, along with their journeymen and apprentices, to become a part of the growing factory proletariat or the industrial reserve army of labor. Under boom conditions, some of this reservoir of labor would cease its economic survival activities. In place of casual labor, informal employment, domestic service, crime, or the workhouse, workers would be drawn back into full-time wage employment. In the downswing of the business cycle, wage labor would be expelled from the factory system and returned to the pool. The more fortunate might find themselves laboring as a small proprietor or working for one, perhaps in some dingy backstreet satellite of the very factory in which they had formally been employed.

Evidently, those owning and/or working in small enterprises at the turn of the century were no less subject to social differentiation than any other class or stratum. Lenin, for example, argued that, though a minority of small proprietors might become successful capitalists, and some of their laborers might

contradictions économiques, ou philosophie de la misère (Paris, 1845).

9. Karl Marx, Capital (Harmondsworth: Penguin, New Left Books, 1976), 1:762. For his major works dealing with small property and his critique of Proudhon's views, see idem, The Poverty of Philosophy: Answer to the 'Philosophy of Poverty' by M. Proudhon, rev. ed. (Moscow: Progress, 1975); idem, Grundrisse (Harmondsworth: Penguin, New Left Books, 1972), pp. 471-514; idem, Capital, vol. 1, app., pp. 1014-38.

10. Frederick Engels, The Condition of the Working Class in England: From Personal and Authentic Sources (London: Panther Books, 1969), pp. 225-26.

themselves become small proprietors, it was in the nature of capitalist development that the majority would be absorbed into the factory labor force.[11] Small-scale activities and refuge occupations would not disappear, but neither would they remain the same, as capitalism developed.

By the late nineteenth century, industrial capitalists had to confront the growing militancy of labor unions, as well as what Engels termed the "puny, dwarfish and circumscribed" capital of small self-employed producers.[12] Nevertheless, the political views and values of these petty producers remained more bourgeois and conservative than proletarian and revolutionary, so long as they were able to retain some of the formal trappings of business independence.

As industrialization spread across Europe, competition for markets and colonies caused greater booms and deeper slumps. A new wave of populist anti-industrialism was engendered, again condemning the exploitation, misery, and poverty that had accompanied economic growth.

The Russian anarchist Prince Peter Kropotkin believed global industrialization to be inevitable. All populists agreed that the most desirable form it could take would be a combination of small agricultural and manufacturing units, organizationally decentralized, spatially dispersed, and oriented toward local consumption needs.[13] While anarchists wanted to see society based upon libertarian principles, other populists—such as the Russian narodniks—saw a modification of the existing village institutions as the appropriate means of its organization.[14] Lenin argued that capitalism had developed too far in Russia for its critics usefully to propose tactics to avoid its detrimental social side effects; the system had to be overthrown.[15]

## EMPLOYMENT, POVERTY, AND DEVELOPMENT IN THE POSTWAR BOOM

In the Great Depression and the war that followed it, academic interest in the less developed territories of the world was at a low ebb. It was the wave of post-World War II decolonizations that brought development issues to the notice of a wider audience. In the more advanced South American economies that had achieved independence much earlier, the interwar period had been one of relative economic growth, often achieved by nationalist governments with somewhat protectionist policies of industry and trade. The 1930s' depression in Western economies had supported the contention that the persistence of a small, apparently independent sphere of the economy provided two essential components for future growth. First, it provided an immediate refuge for the structurally and/or technologically unemployed. Second, in the boom that followed, it provided a launchpad for would-be entrepreneurs, whose enterprise would help to absorb the remaining unem-

11. Vladimir I. Lenin, *Collected Works*, vol. 3, *The Development of Capitalism in Russia* (London: Lawrence & Wishart, 1972), p. 536.

12. Engels, *Condition of the Working Class*, pp. 216-38.

13. Peter Kropotkin, *Fields, Factories & Workshops Tomorrow*, ed. C. Ward (London: George Allen & Unwin, 1974).

14. Lenin, *A Characterization of Economic Romanticism;* idem, *Development of Capitalism in Russia.*

15. Lenin, *Characterization*, pp. 81-92 (sentimentality), pp. 92-97 (petit bourgeois nature of Sismondism and Narodism), pp. 111-24 (its ultimately reactionary character).

ployed. How true this was to be for the developing countries in the postwar boom remained to be seen.

Political independence and a degree of postwar economic growth for most developing countries stimulated a wave of rural-urban migration that the proponents of laissez-faire welcomed. Once labor had been transferred from its low-productivity or zero-productivity agricultural activities in the countryside to the high-productivity opportunities of the city, the same industrialization that had been experienced by the Western capitalist economies could proceed. Migrants constituted the surplus labor that, according to the dualist growth model of W. Arthur Lewis, would constitute the raw material for this process of industrializing emulation.[16]

## The reformist position

In Latin America and the ex-colonies of Africa and Asia, falling adult and infant mortality meant an increased population growth rate and a massive expansion of the working-age population. The pace of rural-urban migration and the general failure of comprehensive industrialization spelled more unemployment. Many politicians feared that political instability could be provoked by disenchanted, unemployed urban so-called marginals. There was also a wider acceptance that emulative industrialization guaranteed neither economic growth nor broader social development, even in a postwar boom. Without better prices for agricultural, mineral, and industrial exports, growth would be further inhibited in the Third World, it was argued;

the state should adopt policies to stimulate income and employment growth in both rural and urban areas.

There were two major policy developments in both the urban and rural areas that gave greater priority to job creation. First were government policies emphasizing rural income and employment initiatives, which were aimed at raising labor productivity in cash cropping, stemming out-migration, and increasing food production. Second, to complement these policies, there was to be a stimulation of urban small-scale production and services. This latter sector was thought to be cheaper in terms of start-up capital; more labor intensive and therefore capable of absorbing more of the urban unemployed and underemployed; and subject to fewer leakages via profit repatriation abroad than large, Western-style industry.[17] Particular stress was laid on the latent income and employment-generating potential of the urban informal sector.

If this reformist policy worked, the sector composed of the ubiquitous Third World handicrafts workers, petty traders, and peasants would act as a buffer to the worst traumas of underdevelopment. This would be the case at least until takeoff was achieved. While support for cottage industries and small businesses might add marginally to a poor country's gross national product, it by no means guaranteed that the resultant benefits would be directly enjoyed by those active in the sector.

This reformist approach, as exemplified by the policy guidelines of *Redistribution with Growth* and the policies enacted

---

16. W. Arthur Lewis, "Economic Development with Unlimited Supplies of Labour," *The Manchester School* (University of Manchester) (1954).

17. Ray Bromley, ed., *Planning for Small Enterprises in Third World Cities* (Oxford: Pergamon Press, 1985), pp. 3-35; Meier Malcolm Harper, *Small Business in the Third World* (Chichester: John Wiley, 1984), pp. 10-24.

in many countries by the World Employ-ment Programme of the International Labor Office (ILO),[18] was aimed at achieving income transfers to benefit the poor, without prejudicing too much the preexisting capitalist basis for economic growth. Government deregulation—where price policies, credit criteria, licensing norms, and so forth had discriminated against small enterprises—was to be combined with government intervention in the fields of training, subcontracting, and marketing. But an essential ingre-dient of the approach was to invest in the poor by putting productive assets into their hands, after which they would presumably be able to compete more effectively for upward economic and social mobility.

The conclusion drawn by many of the studies and policy experiments was that with certain reforms and innovations the small-enterprise sector could be trans-formed from a stagnating and inward-looking complex of coping mechanisms of the urban poor into an authentic engine of economic growth. Thus there was some degree of optimism that the informal economy could fuel, if not instigate, economic development in these countries.

### Reformists and the informal economy: last hope for the least developed?

The reformists involved in policy formulation and research in government

departments, aid agencies, and academic institutions in the 1970s quickly adopted the term "informal sector." This was used to describe economic activities that were characterized by low levels of labor and/or capital; simple or primitive tech-nology; limited conformity to state regula-tion; and/or the provision of goods and services for a predominantly poor clien-tele.

The concept of informality has its origin in American sociology. It referred to the parallel system of labor organiza-tion and wage bargaining that had grown up alongside the formal labor-employer structures in industrialized economies. The concept of informality, as applied to developing countries, implied a par-allel system that tried to mimic or emu-late, while simultaneously flouting, the dominant economic and organizational norms that the developed, industrialized countries were now encouraging in the developing economies. Perhaps the best résumé of the characteristics that ana-lysts have attributed to this sector is to be found in the work of the Brazilian geographer Milton Santos, who uses the notion of upper and lower circuits' for-mal and informal sectors, as shown in Table 1.

The ILO attempted to develop further the concept of informality that Keith Hart had originally applied to urban, small-scale, and often illegitimate self-employment in the shantytowns of Accra, Ghana.[19] The term "informality" was first operationalized in its 1972 employ-ment report on Kenya. S. V. Sethura-man, who did more than anyone within the ILO to popularize the term, felt it was appropriate to widen the term's currency beyond Hart's anthropological

18. Hollis Chenery et al., *Redistribution with Growth* (New York: Oxford University Press, 1974); International Labor Office, *Towards Full Employment: A Programme for Colombia* (Geneva: International Labor Office, 1970); idem, *Employment, Incomes and Inequality: A Strategy for Increasing Productive Employment in Kenya* (Geneva: International Labor Office, 1972).

19. Keith Hart, "Informal Income Opportuni-ties and Urban Employment in Ghana," *Journal of Modern African Studies*, vol. 11 (1973).

TABLE 1
CHARACTERISTICS OF THE TWO SECTOR ECONOMY

| Characteristic | Formal Sector | Informal Sector |
|---|---|---|
| Technology | Capital intensive | Labor intensive |
| Organization | Bureaucratic | Family based |
| Capital | Abundant | Scarce |
| Work hours | Regular | Irregular |
| Wages | Normal; regular | Rare; irregular |
| Inventories | Large; quality | Small; low-grade |
| Prices | Often fixed | Often negotiable |
| Credit | From banks and similar institutions | Personal; non-bank |
| Profits | Large on high turnover | Low on small turnover |
| Client relations | Impersonal | Personal |
| Fixed costs | Large | Negligible |
| Publicity | Necessary | Little or none |
| Re-use of goods | None; wasteful | Frequent recycling |
| Overhead capital | Indispensible | Dispensible |
| State aid | Large | Almost none |
| Foreign dependence | Great; often export-oriented | Small or none |

SOURCE: Milton Santos, *The Shared Space: The Two Circuits of the Urban Economy in Underdeveloped Countries* (London: Methuen, 1979), p. 38.

concern with the underworld of illegal brewers, unlicensed traders, prostitutes, and others to embrace the entire urban working poor. The grounds for expansion were that

it takes a very long time for the benefits of general development policies to trickle down to the poorest sections of the population. Effective development needs to be focused directly on a specific "target" population, and the [Kenyan] employment mission considered that perhaps the most important such target group in urban areas was what it described as the informal sector.[20]

Colin Leys repeated the conclusion that the conventional industrialization strategy could not solve the growing problems of rural-urban migration, underemployment, and inequality. He char-

acterized the income-generating activities of the urban poor in Kenya as follows:

The informal sector means economic activities which largely escape recognition, enumeration, regulation and protection by the government. . . . Labour-intensive, competitive, using locally produced inputs, developing its own skills and technology, locally owned and controlled, the informal sector is, in the ILO Kenya Report mission's view, the model of the kind of economy Kenya needs; but instead of being encouraged to the maximum, it is restricted and harrassed so that it, too, fails to furnish adequate incomes to those who are engaged in it.[21]

With the benefit of hindsight, it can now be seen that there could be two

20. S. V. Sethuraman, "The Urban Informal Sector: Concept, Measurement and Policy," *International Labour Review*, 114:69 (1976).

21. Colin Leys, "Interpreting African Development: Reflections on the ILO Report on Employment, Incomes & Inequality in Kenya," *African Affairs*, 72:420 (1973).

principal strategic responses to this familiar contradiction between growth and development. First is a policy of reformist economic nationalism—based explicitly or implicitly on dependency theory—by which an enlightened and more independent state would liberate, protect, and nurture these indigenous entrepreneurs, who previously had been restricted to the poorest end of a limited market by a history of state and foreign capital collusion and monopoly. The second major response could be a policy of greater liberalization—based on laissez-faire economic theorizing—by which an enlightened and outward-looking government would free aspirant entrepreneurs from state monopolies and regulations, thereby expanding income-earning opportunities among the poor, without threatening the established interests of either indigenous or foreign private enterprise. But, as Leys concluded, if the promotion and stimulation of the informal sector was a task to be undertaken by governments and their agencies on behalf of the urban poor, it was idealistic to expect them to legislate against their own economic and class interests. Leys believed that whichever strategy was adopted, the class interests of the government would ensure that its verbal support for the poor self-employed would not be matched by policies to improve their living standards.

### Neo-Marxism:
### a radical reformist critique?

Alongside the income-redistributing and employment-creating reformism of the 1970s, there emerged a minority view of the current role and future potential of the small enterprise sector. This alternative approach argued from a neo-Marxist or dependency theory per-

spective that the poverty found in the informal sector was due to its relations with capitalist production and distribution and with a state that furnished conditions propitious for capital accumulation. The supposed incapacity of small enterprises to contribute as fully as they might to national economic growth was intimately connected to the very nature of the growth process itself.[22] Further-

22. See Anibal Quijano, "The Marginal Pole of the Economy and the Marginalised Labour Force," *Economy and Society*, vol. 3 (1974); Gerry, *Petty Production and the Urban Economy*; idem, "Petty Production & Capitalist Production in Dakar: The Crisis of the Self-Employed," in R. Bromley, ed., *The Urban Informal Sector: Critical Perspectives*, special issue of *World Development*, vol. 6 (1978); Manfred Bienefeld, "The Informal Sector and Peripheral Capitalism," *Bulletin of the Institute of Development Studies* (Brighton, Sussex), 6(3) (1974); Milton Santos, *The Shared Space: The Two Circuits of the Urban Economy in Underdeveloped Countries* (London: Methuen, 1979); Terry McGee, "Peasants in Cities: A Paradox, a Paradox, a Most Ingenious Paradox," *Human Organisation*, vol. 32 (1975); Alejandro Portes, "The Informal Sector and the World Economy: Notes on the Structure of Subsidised Labour," *Bulletin of the Institute of Development Studies* (Brighton, Sussex), vol. 9 (1978). See the collections of essays such as R. J. Bromley and Chris Gerry, eds., *Casual Work and Poverty in Third World Cities* (New York: John Wiley, 1979). See also critiques and literature reviews of the informal sector concept: Jai Breman, "A Dualist Labour System? A Critique of the Informal Sector Concept," *Bombay Economic and Political Weekly*, vol. 2 (1976); Philippe Hugon, A. N. Le, and Alain Morice, *La petite production marchande et l'emploi dans le secteur 'informal'* (Paris: Université de Paris, Institut d'étude du developpement économique et social, 1977); Caroline Moser, "Informal Sector or Petty Commodity Production: Dualism or Dependence in Urban Development?" in *Urban Informal Sector*, ed. Bromley; Alison MacEwan Scott, "Who Are the Self-Employed?" in *Casual Work and Poverty*, ed. Bromley and Gerry; Priscilla Connolly, "The Politics of the Informal Sector: A Critique," in *Beyond Employment: Household, Gender and Subsistence*, ed. Nanneke Redclift and Enzo Mingione (New York: Basil Blackwell, 1985).

more, the very concept of the informal sector was rejected because of its dualism. The dissidents argued that the economic characteristics on which the concept was based were more the result of the domination of small enterprises by large ones than the cause of small enterprises' low incomes and productivity. Though their analyses had different emphases, they saw the economic activities of the nonwaged urban poor as constituting a subordinate petty commodity form of production coexisting with a dominant capitalist mode of production. Alison Scott defines these producers as follows:

(a) the production of commodities for the market . . . (b) small scale production [in terms of] volume of output, size of work force, size of capital and level of technology . . . (c) ownership of the means of production by the direct producer.[23]

Capital benefited in two ways from the provision of cheap essential goods such as transport, housing, recycled materials, clothing and shoes, entertainment, and petty commerce.[24] It benefited

from the downward pressure directly exerted on urban wage levels and also from the indirect effect on the value of urban labor power resulting from these producers' preeminence in the industrial reserve army. Nevertheless, many petty commodity producers were little more than disguised wage workers indirectly exploited in particular through the subcontracting system.[25]

For these reasons, the neo-Marxists dismissed government policies that made marginal administrative reforms in the hope of unleashing the pent-up productive energies and enterprise of small producers as being either naive in their approach or cynical in their intent. The promotion of the informal sector, and the proliferation of its relations with capital—for example, through subcontracting to private and state enterprises—would merely facilitate the expanded transfer of value from the working poor to national and foreign capitalists. For a minority of these small-scale producers, discriminatory access would be facilitated to the few profitable niches foreign and state capital had left unoccupied. For the majority of petty producers, however, there would be no real help. All but formal autonomy would be lost as the exploitative relations

23. Alison MacEwan Scott, "Notes on the Theoretical Status of Petty Commodity Production," mimeographed (Colchester: University of Essex, Department of Sociology, 1977), pp. 1-2.

24. On these subsectors, see, respectively, Dean Forbes, "On Urban-Rural Interdependence: The Trishaw Riders of Ujung Padang," in *Food, Shelter & Transport in South East Asia and the Pacific,* ed. P. Rimmer, D. Drakakis Smith, and T. McGee (Canberra: Australian National University, Department of Human Geography, 1978); Rod Burgess, "Petty Commodity Housing or Dweller Control? A Critique of John Turner's Views on Housing Policy," in *Urban Informal Sector,* ed. Bromley; Chris Birkbeck, "Garbage, Industry and the Vultures of Cali, Colombia," in *Casual Work and Poverty,* ed. Bromley and Gerry; Chris Gerry, "Small Scale Manufacturing & Repairs in Dakar: A Survey of Market Relations within the Urban Economy," in ibid.; Nikki

Nelson, "How Men and Women Get By: The Sexual Division of Labour in the Informal Sector of a Nairobi Squatter Settlement," in ibid.; Terry McGee, *Hawkers in Hong Kong: A Study of Policy and Planning in the Third World City* (Hong Kong: University of Hong Kong, Centre of Asian Studies, 1974).

25. See, for example, Chris Gerry and Chris Birkbeck, "The Petty Commodity Producer in Third World Cities: Petit Bourgeois or Disguised Proletarian?" in *The Petite Bourgeoisie: Comparative Studies of the Uneasy Stratum,* ed. F. Bechhofer and B. Elliott (New York: Macmillan, 1981); Bromley and Gerry, eds., *Casual Work and Poverty,* pp. 5-7.

that already existed between capital and the urban working poor expanded and intensified. Additional repercussions of the proliferation of such relations would be the incorporation of more and more women into industrial out-working and the potential challenge to patriarchy that this implied.[26]

In summary, the neo-Marxist critics of government policies to promote small enterprises believed that both the small proprietor and his or her coworkers would be transformed into disguised wage workers serving the interests of capitalist growth and the perpetuation of poverty. At the same time, the myth of the independence of the small enterprise sector and its potential for growth, crucial to the reproduction of bourgeois values, would be nurtured. In this way, the persistence of apparently precapitalist relations of production within the household and workshop was not only compatible with but also functionally beneficial to capital accumulation in the economy as a whole.

## The continuity of populist dissent

Populist anti-industrialism was at a low ebb during the 1930s and the wartime period; only Gandhi's lone voice could be heard occasionally from the colonial sidelines. The period of reconstruction among major industrial nations and the period of attempted industrial emulation in their colonies nevertheless caused a few dissenting ideas to be formulated. Much later, these began to be articulated publicly. The continuity of populist dissent during the later postwar period is

best exemplified by writers such as Schumacher[27] and Illich.[28] These commentators suggest that small-scale production might moderate the excessive centralization of power and concentration of wealth in both core and peripheral economies—hence small is beautiful. They were much less concerned with the more quantitative issue of how the sector might be used to support a more independent style of Third World industrialization.

However, for as long as the postwar boom lasted any such criticism of so-called modern industrial society was likely to be dismissed by both reformist and laissez-faire policymakers as the utopian dreams of the dissidents, hippies, armchair revolutionaries, and neo-Luddite labor unions. Conventional wisdom argued that such anti-industrial ideas were evidence of a failure to understand the practical managerial problems of the real world. Nevertheless, the ideas struck a responsive chord among a minority of liberal and libertarian thinkers, and so Schumacher, Illich, and others kept alive this populist idealism. Once the boom in the world economy finally gave way to an unprecedented period of stagnation and contraction during the late 1970s and 1980s, the stage was set for these ideas to thrive once more.

### INFORMALITY AND THE CURRENT RECESSION: NEOLIBERALISM ON THE OFFENSIVE

The current world recession has created the conditions for yet another re-

26. Marta Roldán, "Industrial Outworking, Struggles for the Reproduction of Working Class Families, and Gender Subordination," in *Beyond Employment*, ed. Redclift and Mingione.

27. E. F. Schumacher, *Small Is Beautiful: A Study of Economies As If People Mattered* (London: Sphere Books, 1974).
28. Ivan Illich, *Deschooling Society* (London: Calder and Boyars, 1972); idem, *Celebration of Awareness* (London: Calder and Boyars, 1972).

habilitation in the industrialized world of the idea that small-scale, alternative, or apparently noncapitalist institutions might contribute more effectively to economic recovery and growth. With the onset of the most severe global capitalist crisis since the 1930s, and the recognition that the recession was likely to be both protracted and profound, postwar Keynesian development theory steadily lost its preeminent role.[29] Since the late 1970s, there has been a rolling-back of state intervention. In its place has come a reassertion that the market is the motor of capital accumulation. This has been voluntarily adopted by the governments of many industrialized countries as a means of rekindling economic growth and profitability. It has been forced on other governments, particularly those of the Third World, as a condition of the rescheduling of existing debts and/or the extension of new credit lines.

In the industrialized countries, the international recession of the late 1970s and 1980s demanded far-reaching social, economic, and political changes. With conservative governments in office in many of the countries of the Organization for Economic Cooperation and Development, this meant that labor costs had to be held in check. This was accomplished in part by using the law to dissuade labor unions from militant action. In addition, public expenditure was firmly controlled and the market encouraged to operate with less restraint than there had been in decades. Later, stock ex-

changes were revitalized by a wave of corporate mergers, and the slogan of popular capitalism was launched on the back of the privatization of public industries.

High unemployment has ensured that policies seeking to promote small business and self-employment have been attractive to the governments of industrialized countries. Neoliberal policymakers in the advanced countries understandably emphasize a revitalization of capitalist values such as that of enterprise at the grass-roots level. This has been done at the expense of what they argue is an overblown, outdated, and inefficient state-dominated mixed economy. The shift in emphasis constitutes a key element in shaping the values, structures, and practices upon which such governments feel a new boom can be constructed.

At the same time, the supposedly informal means of securing a livelihood adopted by a growing stratum of the unemployed and impoverished has attracted a more punitive attention from state institutions. The rapidly expanding shadow, or irregular, economy, in which undeclared incomes are generated often alongside the receipt of state benefits, was denounced by many as both an obstacle to the success of laissez-faire economic restructuring and a double burden on a faltering, if not negative, growth rate.

INFORMALITY AND THE
CURRENT RECESSION:
A RADICAL
REFORMIST DEFENSE

Radical reformist contributions have been heavily influenced by the works of writers Gorz and Bahro.[30] Indeed, in

29. See John Toye's recent defense of development economics against the neoliberal attacks of Deepak Lal, Bela Balassa, and others in *Dilemmas of Development* (New York: Basil Blackwell, 1987); Deepak Lal, *The Poverty of Development Economics*, Hobart Paperback no. 16 (London: Institute of Economic Affairs, 1983).

30. Rudolf Bahro, *Socialism & Survival:*

many respects, the radical reformists of the current recession have become difficult to distinguish from the populists, who would argue that the slump offers an opportunity to move away from both capitalist and Soviet-style industrialism, an opportunity that must be seized if the environment and even the human species is to be preserved. Both Gorz and Bahro have argued that the principal struggles determining the welfare of the mass of the population are no longer those of class. Rather, they are struggles of East versus West over the proliferation of nuclear armaments and North versus South over the distribution of income in an era of global economic restructuring. In this vein some radicals commenting on the economic downturn have bid "farewell to the working class" and its outmoded forms of economic and political struggle.[31] Others have argued that the recession and the unemployment and self-employment it promotes may offer ex-wage-slaves the opportunity for liberation and self-emancipation. Some progressive city governments have even argued that greater local autonomy from central government will be achieved and ethnic and gender discrimination challenged by actively promoting self-employment and cooperatives[32] rather than by defending jobs in the limited sense of

minimizing the losses of public-sector wage employment.

Thus promoting the informal sector and small businesses has been given greater legitimacy both by neoliberal governments, if offensively for purposes of economic, political, and social restructuring, and by those who wish to deploy it defensively, to protect those who have fallen victim to the worst effects of the slump. What are termed informal, black, irregular, community-based, or cooperative economic activities have tended to lose their lumpen or hippie image. They have instead become legitimate objects of government and academic interest viewed as employment-creating, enterprise-generating, wealth-creating, or even liberating and self-emancipating options, located outside of large corporate, unionized manufacturing industry. Though the mechanism by which small and/or informal enterprises may induce economic growth and social progress in a period of slump may be viewed differently by neoliberals and radical reformists, the policies they propose may be more complementary than contradictory. This is especially so when seen in terms of the need for the state to sell a crisis-resolving strategy to its own political constituency and to the wider electorate. But do the ideas and policies being discussed today in the advanced countries bear any resemblance to those previously devised for developing countries?

*Articles, Essays & Talks, 1979-82* (London: Herche Books, 1982); Andre Gorz, *Farewell to the Working Class: An Essay in Post-Industrial Socialism* (London: Pluto Press, 1982).

31. See Gorz, *Farewell to the Working Class*; James Robertson, *Future Work: Jobs, Self-Employment and Leisure after the Industrial Age* (London: Gower/Maurice Temple Smith, 1985).

32. W. M. Kazuka, *Why So Few Blacks?* (London Borough of Hackney: Hackney Business Promotion Project, 1980); Greater London Council, *The London Industrial Strategy* (London: Greater London Council, 1985).

## THE CURRENT RECESSION AND THE THIRD WORLD

In the 1970s, international agencies such as the ILO and the World Bank advised Third World governments that the informal sector should be actively promoted by marginally and highly selectively redistributing incomes, assets, and opportunities. Though growth and employment were to be stimulated within reformist-dominant economies, it was employment creation to which policy advisers gave priority. If entrepreneurship were deemed to be in short supply, then both state and foreign aid institutions would fill the gap either directly or through management-training inputs. However, the scale of the employment problem, and the predictable reluctance of those in government in developing countries to give up the economic power they hold, exposed the pious idealism in much of what the reformists had to say.

In the developing countries today, the crisis manifests itself in terms of downward-spiraling export revenues, deepening indebtedness, and declining food production. The potential for new production locations, investment opportunities, and markets for both ailing and aspirant transnational corporations is being created by the imposition by international financial agencies of greater economic, organizational, and political discipline on governments, which in turn transfer the burden to the people in the form of increased austerity. The vital steps in the renaissance of free-market capitalism involve both a liberalization of national and regional markets for most commodities, including investment funds and labor, and a substantial privatization of the state and state-related enterprises. International financial and banking institutions have offered developing countries the limited choice of adopting laissez-faire capitalism or surviving without Western support.

Though this formulation may contain an element of bluff, the majority of developing countries, with little money and even less credit, may not be in a position to call it. Military dictatorships, such as those in Chile and Pakistan, fear

the restoration of parliamentary democracy and may consequently accede to external demands for economic liberalization. Democracies, especially of the fledgling variety, may agree to such measures because failure to do so could lead to either a right-wing military coup or a Left-inspired popular insurrection, as in Brazil, Argentina, or the Philippines. Self-styled Third World socialisms, as in Nicaragua, Mozambique, and Zimbabwe, may see the acceptance of International Monetary Fund conditions as a lesser evil than the continuation of externally backed economic and political destabilization and the perhaps terminal decline in internal popularity this may imply.

Thus the form, speed, and scope of restructuring is extremely uneven between and among rich, middle-income, and poor countries. Competition between transnational corporations, between states, and between economic and political power blocs, each with its own shifting array of Northern and Southern allies and client-states, has intensified in the 1980s almost to the point of open trade war. From the rich countries' viewpoint, as long as the debt crisis and political instability constitute major obstacles to a revival of foreign investment, any likelihood of defeating the recession on a global scale seems remote. The impact of this particular impasse on the informal economy and small enterprises in developing countries remains unclear. It will vary considerably from case to case. Undoubtedly, in the coming years, the theoretical categories and formulations reviewed here will again be put to the test.

### AN ORTHODOX
### MARXIST REAPPRAISAL?

In recent years, Marxists interested in peasant agriculture have reappraised the theoretical and empirical work on the persistence and problems of petty commodity production within capitalism that was undertaken by radicals opposed to the theory and practice of informal sector promotion.[33] For example, Gibbon and Neocosmos have critically examined a number of propositions that have dominated radical approaches to both urban and rural small-scale production in the last decade. Their aim has been to make Marxist analytical categories more effective for empirical investigation. This relatively recent Marxist reappraisal calls into question the notion that petty commodity producers are disguised wage laborers exploited by capital. It also questions the functionalist proposition that small-scale production subsidizes peripheral capital accumulation by providing cheap essential consumer goods for the mass market and by holding down wage levels through the role it plays as a major part of the industrial reserve army.[34] Gibbon and Neocosmos begin by arguing that

to suggest that a social formation is capitalist by virtue of being founded on the contradiction between labor and capital, is not to assert that *all* or even the majority of enterprises in [it] . . . will conform to a "type" in which capitalists and wage-labourers are present, and which constitutes the measure in relation to which all other forms deviate.

What makes enterprises . . . capitalist or not, is not their supposed essential features, but the relations which structurally and historically explain their existence.[35]

Consequently, petty commodity production is seen as being just as much the product of the contradiction between capital and labor as is a stereotypical, fully fledged, and unequivocally capitalist enterprise.

Far from being inherent in a universal or ahistorical sense, the persistence of this form of production is the result of the operation of the law of value and corresponding changes in the social division of labor. The allegedly natural advantages possessed by petty commodity producers included their tendency toward self-exploitation—that is, the ability to intensify their own or their household's labor under severe market pressure[36]—their low capital and skill requirements, the ease of newcomer entry into petty commodity production, and the use of multiple sources of income. But, according to Gibbon and Neocosmos, they derive from the concrete and specific operation of the law of value under capitalism. Bernstein observes that

petty commodity production will exist as long as capitalism exists. An understanding of the general reasons for this, helps rescue the analysis of petty commodity production from tendencies to treat it as residual, whether as a manifestation of incomplete or "blocked" transitions to capitalism, or as the site of inevitably "backward" or reactionary politics. On the basis of an analysis of the general conditions of existence, and production, of petty commodity production within capitalism . . . it should prove possible to

33. For example, P. Gibbon and M. Neocosmos, "Some Problems in the Political Economy of 'African Socialism,'" in *Contradictions of Accumulation in Africa: Studies in Economy & State*, ed. H. Bernstein and B. Campbell (Newbury Park, CA: Sage, 1985); Henry Bernstein, *Capitalism and Petty Commodity Production*, Development Policy & Practice Working Paper no. 3 (Milton Keynes: Open University, 1986); Harriet Friedmann, "Postscript: Small Commodity Production," in *Rethinking Petty Commodity Production*, ed. Jonathan Barker and Gavin Smith, special ed. of *Labour, Capital and Society*, vol. 19 (1986).
34. Bernstein, "Capitalism and Petty Commodity Production," pp. 2-3.
35. Gibbon and Neocosmos, "Some Problems," p. 169 (emphasis in original).
36. Henry Bernstein, "Notes on Capital & Peasantry," *Review of African Political Economy*, vol. 10 (1977).

118                                    THE ANNALS OF THE AMERICAN ACADEMY

advance the concrete investigation of specific types of petty commodity production—their fluctuations, diversity, and differentiation.[37]

By also focusing attention on the political implications of their analysis, Gibbon and Neocosmos help to clarify the connection that is often made in a mechanistic way between occupations, enterprises, and the political practice that is assumed to follow automatically. By emphasizing that petty commodity producers are not themselves exploited, either by another class or by another type or scale of capital, Gibbon and Neocosmos also alert us to the fact that petty commodity producers are not necessarily petit bourgeois in their political behavior and orientation. Bernstein correctly points out that this realization is as important in the context of developing countries as the realization, particularly in advanced industrial societies, that "those occupying proletarian class spaces, necessarily form a working class or pursue revolutionary ideology and politics."[38]

Gibbon and Neocosmos draw their conclusions predominantly from an analysis of peasant agriculture in Africa and explicitly define petty commodity producers as those who "are capable of reproducing themselves as private producers of commodities without employing wage-labour and without selling (part of) their labour-power."[39] Consequently, the mass of small, often unregistered craftsmen and traders in Third World cities, for whom small numbers of family members, unwaged apprentices, and waged or semi-waged employees simultaneously work, cannot easily

be differentiated from much larger, undeniably capitalist enterprises exclusively employing wage labor. Nor are we able to form any clearer picture of the economic and political position of the very heterogeneous and essentially propertyless labor working for these small producers.[40] Such insights are necessary if we are to elucidate theoretically the specific place of such enterprises, their proprietors, and workers in capitalist development and to predict how they might fit, if at all, into governments' future liberalization policies.

CONCLUSION

In the developing countries in the latter years of the postwar boom, state intervention and a degree of economic nationalism was the most familiar approach to solving the problems of faltering industrialization, arrested growth, growing inequality, and poor income and employment prospects. The transformation of the economic survival strategies characterizing the urban and rural poor into a veritable engine of economic growth and employment generation proved to be either a reformist or a populist pipe dream. Many of the theoretical confusions and policy errors that marked that period are today being repeated in the heartlands of the advanced industrial countries, from the capitalist West to the centrally planned economies of the Soviet bloc.

The conclusion I draw from the previous analysis would rule out any serious contribution by populist theory and policy to resolving the problems of poverty and underemployment in developing countries. In underestimating the powerful ideological and real-world links between small enterprises and the

37. Bernstein, "Capitalism and Petty Commodity Production," pp. 38-39.
38. Ibid, p. 31.
39. Gibbon and Neocosmos, "Some Problems," p. 169.
40. Friedmann, "Postscript."

dominant state, industrial, and commercial structures, the informal economic activities, which are both product and sustainer of large-scale capitalism, are elevated to the status of a practical alternative and a panacea for modern ills.

Reformist approaches are under sustained attack by the laissez-faire theorists and policymakers and are in internal turmoil themselves. Facing conditions of economic crisis throughout much of the Third World, reformists confront a sort of paradigmatic no-win situation. If they accept a reduced role for state intervention, their credibility becomes very difficult to maintain. If they opt for greater state regulation, they start to resemble Soviet-bloc and Chinese regimes. These regimes are gradually and with difficulty introducing their own economic reforms, including a less hostile attitude to their own informal, or second, economies. If reformists hold their ground, they will appear to be atavistically holding on to postwar boom policies that have lost their relevance.

This leaves only the neoliberal or laissez-faire policies and those of authentic Marxism. The former is clearly on the offensive in these years of economic downturn and restructuring. The slogan of "popular capitalism" appeals not only to those who have lost wage employment, but also to those of a populist orientation who are convinced that the era of the small man has returned. But it remains little more than a slogan, either in the industrialized or the developing countries. Neoliberalism seeks to change attitudes toward self-employment and enterprise while restructuring national

and international markets more in favor of large corporate enterprises, which have a degree of monopoly power under less threat than the power of labor unions and the public sector.

In the Third World, the turn toward more market-oriented policies will continue. It may well bring more and more people into often indirect contact with large and medium-sized enterprises, as subcontractors, casual laborers, and outworkers. This may give rise to the types of situation outlined in recent Marxist contributions to the debate, whereby labor's closer relations with capital in the less developed countries may spark new challenges to the system. For such challenges to be successful, they must embrace those working in relative isolation both in the informal sector and in peasant agriculture.

Today's neoliberal advice that self-employment, enterprise, and the free play of market forces should play a greater role in economic growth is being widely, if sometimes grudgingly, accepted. It is extremely doubtful that the poor of the Third World can look forward to a new international economic order that, paradoxically, will be ushered in by economic neoliberalism rather than state-fostered economic nationalism. It is far more probable that new ground is being prepared for a faltering recovery in the condition of the world economy. If this is the case, it will be the realigned dominant classes in rich, middle-income, and poor countries that will benefit. It is my opinion that few lasting benefits will be enjoyed by those for whom life is always informal by comparison with that of their rulers.

ANNALS, *AAPSS*, **493**, September 1987

# The Second Economy of the
# Soviet Union and Eastern Europe

By STEVEN L. SAMPSON

ABSTRACT: The second economies of the Soviet Union and other East European countries derive from structural inadequacies in the socialist planning system and from the cultural and historical evolution of each East European society. This article combines the structural and cultural approaches to the second economy and focuses on four of its most prevalent forms: peasant household production, the shadow economy within socialist enterprises, the underground factories of Soviet Georgia, and the hidden economy within the retail and service sectors. In all cases, social linkages and cultural values provide frameworks for economic activities. The second economy helps to alleviate consumer shortages and bureaucratic bottlenecks in all these societies. It also acts as a social mollifier, channeling dangerous political frustrations into consumerism, swindling, or petty corruption. Yet the overall effect of the second economy is a corrosive one: as a surrogate reform, a second economy tolerated by the authorities only reproduces the fundamental flaws of the formal economy. Moreover, it exacerbates the gap between society and the state, between "us" and "them."

*Steven L. Sampson, a cultural anthropologist, received his Ph.D. in 1980 from the University of Massachusetts, Amherst. He has carried out ethnographic fieldwork on town planning and local politics in Romania and is the author of* National Integration through Socialist Planning: An Anthropological Study of a Romanian New Town *and articles on various aspects of informal systems in Eastern Europe. He has recently coauthored a book on the anthropology of Denmark's second economy, entitled* Uden Regning *[Without receipt] and is preparing an extended anthropological study of the informal sector in Eastern Europe.*

WERE an international commission of experts asked to design a society where the second economy would thrive best, they would probably design the Soviet Union.[1] Press reports and scholarly analyses have shown that the second economy is an integral part of everyday life in all the socialist societies. Ironically, the second economy in these countries is often the equivalent of the market or primary economy in capitalist countries.

Some of these activities are simply what we would term capitalist entrepreneurship: the peasant who cultivates her private plot and sells the produce on the free market, speculative trading, middleman fees, renting property, money lending, and operating a private firm.

Other forms of the second economy found in Eastern Europe are common to all advanced economies, socialist or capitalist. These include producing or selling illegal goods such as narcotics or providing illegal services such as prostitution; pilfering from the workplace; skimming cash receipts; conducting unregistered or untaxed trade; and paying off police or inspectors to ignore such activities.

Finally, there are second economy activities that are neither typically capitalist nor universally illegal: the informal or illegal activities that enterprises use to fulfill their plan; underground factories; paying bribes or tips in order to buy something in a store or to induce planners and controllers to revise plans; buying and reselling goods obtained from shops for foreigners; and selling scarce or rationed goods taken from the state.

Popular accounts have tended to term the second economy of Eastern Europe—hereafter "Eastern Europe" is meant to encompass the USSR and other countries of the Eastern bloc—"islands of capitalism" in which the spirit of free initiative thrives in spite of stifling bureaucracy.[2] The official East European press looks on the second economy as a "corrosive" factor, robbing the formal economy of essential goods, services, and labor time. Illegal or informal economic activity is an example of a "backward mentality" destined to disappear as the socialist system is "perfected."[3]

This only begs the question of why—after 70 years of socialism in the Soviet Union, 40 in the other East European countries—these backward mentalities

1. This sentence is paraphrased, by permission, from Gregory Grossman and Vladimir G. Treml, "Measuring Hidden Personal Incomes in the USSR," in *The Unofficial Economy,* ed. Sergio Alessandrini and Bruno Dallago (Aldershot: Gower Press, 1987).

2. For example, Yuri Brokhin, *Hustling on Gorky Street* (London: W. H. Allen, 1976); Hedrick Smith, *The Russians* (New York: Quadrangle, 1983); Robert Kaiser, *Russia: The People and the Power* (New York: Pocket Books, 1976); Konstantin Simis, *USSR: The Corrupt Society—The Secret World of Soviet Capitalism* (New York: Simon & Schuster, 1982); David Shipler, *Russia: Broken Idols, Solemn Dreams* (New York: Times Books, 1983); David Willis, *Klass: How Russians Really Live* (New York: St. Martin's Press, 1985); Lev Timofeev, *Soviet Peasants—or the Peasants' Art of Starving* (New York: Telos Books, 1985).

3. Speaking of corruption in the Soviet Republic of Georgia, Eduard Shevardnadze, who was then first secretary of the Georgian Communist Party—and is now the USSR's foreign minister—made the very un-Marxist statement that "there are people in whom the spirit of private ownership seems to be inborn." *Zarya Vostoka,* 3 Nov. 1973, quoted in David Law, "Corruption in Georgia," *Critique* (Glasgow), no. 3, p. 103, (Autumn 1974). The current Soviet campaign against persons with "unearned incomes" stresses the particular need for "improving ideological and political work and . . . molding in each person an attitude of irreconcilability toward the private-ownership mentality." "Alien to Our Morality," TASS report, 10 Aug. 1986.

not only exist, but seem to be thriving as never before. This has led some analysts, including some East Europeans, to see the second economy in terms of its "lubricating" function.[4] Some go so far as to assert that "were it not for the second economy, the entire system would collapse."[5]

In fact, the second economies of Eastern Europe are at once liberating, corrosive, and lubricating. The starting point for an analysis of Eastern Europe's second economy is to see it in the context of the total economic system. The second economy is an integral part of the official, planned economy, sometimes complementing it, sometimes hindering it directly, sometimes competing with it.

This article examines Eastern Europe's second economies as both a structural aspect of socialism and as cultural and historical products of specific East European societies. Because the second economy has been studied largely by economists, much of its noneconomic character has been overlooked. Recent studies by anthropologists show the

second economy to be an expression of deeply rooted social and cultural features of each society. These features are best revealed not by aggregate data but by micro-level everyday interactions that form the core of most anthropological field studies. Hence the combination of the political-economic and sociocultural factors can help explain both the tenacity of the second economy in Eastern Europe and the variations from one socialist society to another.

SECOND ECONOMY RESEARCH
ON EASTERN EUROPE

Within Soviet studies, the analysis of the second economy commenced a decade ago with the seminal articles by Simes, Katsenelinboigen, and especially Grossman.[6] A recent bibliography on the Soviet/East European second economy now lists over 150 items.[7] A major collection has been edited by Grossman, and the Hungarian economists have been especially productive.[8] Anthro-

4. Cf. Charles Schwartz, "Corruption and Political Development in the U.S.S.R.," *Comparative Politics*, 11:425-43 (July 1979); Gregory Grossman, "The Second Economy of the USSR," *Problems of Communism*, 26(5):40 (Sept.-Oct. 1977). Among East Europeans, the Hungarians have particularly emphasized a lubrication approach. Cf. Istvan Gabor, "The Second (Secondary) Economy," *Acta Oeconomica*, 22:291-311 (1979).

5. Smith calls it "an essential lubricant for the rigidities of the planned economy." Smith, *Russians*, p. 86. Meanwhile, a U.S. Select Committee on Soviet Internal Developments concluded that it "lubricates the joints of a creaking system." Quoted from Stuart Henry, "The Informal Economy: How Revolutionary Is It?" *Crime and Social Justice*, 2:8 (1987). See also Istvan Kemeny, "The Unregistered Economy in Hungary," *Soviet Studies*, 34:364 (July 1982).

6. Dimitri K. Simes, "The Soviet Parallel Market," *Survey*, 21(3):42-52 (Summer 1975); Aron Katsenelinboigen, "Coloured Markets in the Soviet Union," *Soviet Studies*, 29:62-85 (Jan. 1977); Grossman, "Second Economy of the USSR"; idem, "Notes on the Illegal Private Economy and Corruption," in *The Soviet Economy in a Time of Change*, by U.S., Congress, Joint Economic Committee (Washington, DC: Government Printing Office, 1979), pp. 834-55.

7. Gregory Grossman, "The Second Economy in the USSR and Eastern Europe: A Bibliography" (Berkeley-Duke Occasional Papers on the Second Economy in the USSR, no. 1, University of California, Berkeley, and Duke University, updated, March, 1987).

8. Gregory Grossman, ed., *Studies in the Second Economy of Communist Countries* (Berkeley: University of California Press, 1988); Janos Kenedi, *Do It Yourself: Hungary's Hidden Economy* (London: Pluto Press, 1982); Istvan Gabor, "The Second Economy in Socialism: General Lessons of the Hungarian Experience," *Papers on*

pological studies have appeared on Poland, Soviet Georgia, and Central Asia, and Grossman and Treml's survey of 1900 Soviet émigrés promises to give valuable information on the second economy in the USSR.[9]

Nevertheless, our knowledge remains limited by the geographic areas studied and by political restrictions placed on the research, both of which skew or bias the research. Many studies of the Soviet second economy focus on the non-Russian republics, while our information on the East European states aside from Hungary and Poland is confined to descriptive studies or press reports of corruption.[10] Research is also hampered

by a lack of empirical data, due to deliberate concealment by the authorities, simple ignorance, or conceptual confusion.[11] Consequently, as in other areas of Soviet studies, second economy

---

*Labor Economics* (Budapest: Karl Marx University of Economics, 1984); Peter Galasi, "Peculiarities and Limits of the Second Economy in Socialism (the Hungarian Case)," in *Economics of the Shadow Economy,* ed. Wulf Gaertner and Alois Wenig (New York: Springer-Verlag, 1985), pp. 353-61; Peter Galasi and Gyorgy Sziraczki, eds., *Labour Market and Second Economy in Hungary* (New York: Campus, 1985).

9. Janine Wedel, *The Private Poland: An Anthropologist's Look at Everyday Life* (New York: Facts on File, 1986); Gerald Mars and Yochanan Altman, *Private Enterprise in the USSR: The Case of Soviet Georgia* (Aldershot: Gower Press, 1987); idem, "The Cultural Bases of Soviet Georgia's Second Economy," *Soviet Studies,* 35(4):546-60 (Oct. 1983); idem, "The Cultural Bases of Soviet Central Asia's Second Economy (Uzbekistan and Tajikistan)," *Central Asian Survey* (in press); Grossman and Treml, "Measuring Hidden Personal Incomes in the USSR"; introduction to Grossman, "Second Economy: A Bibliography."

10. Examples from Simis's *USSR: The Corrupt Society* and Smith's *Russians* overwhelmingly concern Georgians, Armenians, and Azerbaijanis. Law's "Corruption in Georgia" also infers that the same is true for the Russian republics. Other studies of East European—that is, non-USSR—second economies used in this survey include the following: Horst Brezinski, "The Second Economies in Eastern Europe," in *East European Economic Trends and East-West Trade: U.S., West*

*and East European Perspectives,* ed. P. Marer and P. Van Veen (forthcoming); Steven Sampson, "The Informal Sector in Eastern Europe," *Telos,* no. 66, pp. 44-66 (Winter 1985-86); Horst Brezinski and Christoph Roos, "The Development of the Second Economy in Hungary," *Korean Journal for East-West European Studies,* 1:95-127 (Fall 1985); Andrzej Korbonski, "The 'Second Economy' in Poland," *Journal of International Affairs,* 35(1):1-15 (Spring-Summer 1981); Anders Åslund, *Private Enterprise in Eastern Europe: The Non-Agricultural Private Sector in Poland and the GDR* (New York: St. Martin's Press, 1985); idem, "Private Enterprise in Poland, the GDR and Hungary," in *Bidrag til Öststatsforskning,* 11(1):26-34 (Jan. 1983); Horst Brezinski, "The Second Economy in the GDR—Pragmatism Is Gaining Ground," *Arbeitspapiere des Fachbereichs Wirtschaftswissenschaft,* Neue Folge Nr. 7, Universität-Gesamthochschule Paderborn, BRD (Feb. 1987); Ilse Grosser, "Personliche Wirtschaften in Bulgarien—Jungere Entwicklungen," *Südosteuropa,* 33(9):491-507 (1984); Per Ronnås, "The Role of the 'Second Economy' as a Source of Supplementary Income to Rural Communities in Romania: A Case Study," *Bidrag til Öststatsforskning,* 11(1):34-43 (Jan. 1983), Steven Sampson, "Rich Families and Poor Collectives: An Anthropological Approach to Romania's Second Economy," ibid., pp. 44-77; Horst Brezinski and Paul Petrescu, "The Second Economy in Romania—A Dynamic Sector," *Arbeitspapiere des Fachbereichs Wirtschaftswissenschaft,* Neue Folge Nr. 6, Universität—Gesamthochschule Paderborn, BRD (Dec. 1986). Finally, the best sources of press reports from the Soviet Union are the *Current Digest of the Soviet Press* and *Radio Liberty Research* (Munich) and for the other East European countries *Radio Free Europe Research* (Munich).

11. These issues are elucidated in Peter Wiles, "What We Still Don't Know about the Soviet Economy," in *The CMEA Five Year Plans (1981-1985) in a New Perspective: Planned and Non-Planned Economies* (Brussels: North Atlantic Treaty Organization, Economics and Information Directorates, 1982).

analyses often rely on anecdote, media reports, and speculative estimation.[12]

In the East European context, the study of second economy activities would include those that are unplanned, unregulated, unreported, privatized, and/or illegal. This would cover a wide range of activities, and scholars differ over precisely what should be included.[13] Considering the second economy as extraplan behavior, which may or may not have beneficial consequences for the official economy, Marresse's syncretic definition is useful: "The second economy includes all of the nonregulated (legal and illegal) aspects of economic activities in state and cooperative organizations, *plus* all unreported activities, *plus* all forms of private (legal, semilegal, and illegal) economic activity."[14]

Measuring the extent of the second economy has proven difficult due to lack of data and conceptual confusion. It appears less widespread in heavy industry, banking, finance, and the military and more pervasive in sectors such as construction, food, repairs, light industry, transport, wholesale and retail trade, and personal services from doctors' services to waiters' services.[15] Because second economy activity may vary widely from one sector to another, and because definitions of the second economy may differ for different researchers, statements that estimate the second economy as being from 10 to 50 percent of a country's gross national product have little comparative value.[16]

Private agriculture, for example, is a key component of the second economy

12. Prospects for empirical research, personal fieldwork, or scientific collaboration with East European researchers remain dim, if not nonexistent. Hungary, where second economy research is officially sanctioned, remains the exception.

13. Cf. Grossman, "Second Economy of the USSR"; Dennis O'Hearn, "The Consumer Second Economy: Size and Effects," *Soviet Studies,* 32(2):218-34 (Apr. 1980); Peter Wiles, "The Second Economy, Its Definitional Problems," in *Unofficial Economy,* ed. Alessandrini and Dallago; Peter Galasi, "Peculiarities and Limits."

14. Michael Marrese, "The Evolution of Wage Regulation in Hungary," in *Hungary—A Decade of Reform,* ed. P. Hare, H. K. Radice, and N. Swain (London: Allen & Unwin, 1981), p. 51. This definition is discussed in particular by Brezinski in his "Second Economies in Eastern Europe."

15. Peter Wiles, using "commonsense and literary evidence," states that larger objects are harder to steal, divert, or sell; hence trains and planes are not part of the black economy. Similarly, "where audit is easy (banks) or important (weapons) there will be less corruption." At the other end of the scale, building and car repairs are such that "there seem to be few uncorrupt transactions." See Peter Wiles, "What We Still Don't Know," *CMEA Five Year Plans,* by North Atlantic Treaty Organization.

16. The figure of 10-50 percent is a summary of statements by knowledgeable Soviet émigrés. The variation most likely reflects differing perceptions of the second economy as being strictly black or illegal transactions, or including black plus legal private production, kolkhoz marketing, and trading. See Zev Katz, "Insights from Emigres and Sociological Studies on the Soviet Union," in *Soviet Economic Prospects for the Seventies* (Washington, DC: Government Printing Office, 1973), p. 90. Hungarian estimates of up to 50 percent of gross national product derive from a second economy that includes criminal theft, black theft of raw materials and labor time, all "black value added," "benign plan violation" within socialist factories in order to achieve the plan—the shadow economy—legal private and cooperative production, plus bribes and tips. Wiles makes a good case for excluding benign plan violation from the second economy, thereby bringing it down to 7-25 percent worldwide. See Peter Wiles, "Second Economy, Its Definitional Problems," p. 10. A final note of caution regarding estimates of the second economy comes from Istvan Gabor, who states that "the widely quoted estimate of 16-19 percent of the entire GNP being created in the second economy draws its credence solely from the prestige of the person who made the estimate." Gabor, "Second Economy in Socialism," p. 29.

in all the socialist countries. The output of collective farmers' personal plots provides from 30 to 42 percent of total agricultural output in the USSR, Hungary, Bulgaria, and Romania.[17] In Poland, where 77 percent of all agricultural land is in private hands, the legal private sector occupied almost 32 percent of the labor force in 1983.[18]

In commerce, the second economy is pervasive. O'Hearn's analysis of Soviet press reports indicates that 80-85 percent of all gasoline ends up on the black market, 25 percent of the internal fish catch is poached from state lands, and 25 percent of all distilled alcohol is produced and sold outside the state sector.[19] Soviet emigre interviews suggest that 18 percent of all consumption expenditures were given to private individuals and that 30 percent of all home food was purchased outside the public sector or via connections.[20] The Soviet Union has permitted the lowest level of

legal private commercial activity in Eastern Europe. The largest amount is in Hungary, where between 1970 and 1983 the number of private shops and restaurants doubled, to 19,293, to constitute 26 percent of all shops.[21]

The second economy service sector is similarly extensive, inasmuch as personal relations between seller and client—established via bribes, tips, or friendship—determine whether the service will be of acceptable quality. Despite the fact that second economy labor can be from two to five times more expensive than that procured by the official economy, a Moscow survey showed that 70 percent of house repairs were carried out privately, most of this by illegal or unregistered repairmen.[22] In Georgia from 97 to 99 percent of repairs to home and household items were done privately.[23] Soviet investigations routinely show that on days when state service enterprises are audited, receipts are one and one-half to two times higher than on "normal" days.[24]

Private construction brigades, agricultural harvest and forest-clearing brigades are common throughout the USSR and Eastern Europe. They often receive two to five times the official wage, even though they are hired by state enterprises.[25] In Poland, private firms con-

17. Brezinski and Petrescu, "Second Economy in Romania," p. 3; Horst Brezinski, "The Second Economy in the Soviet Union and Its Implications for Economic Policy," in *Economics of the Shadow Economy,* ed. Gaertner and Wenig, p. 363; Allen Kroncher, "CMEA Productive and Service Sector in the 1980's: Plan and Non-Plan," in *The CMEA Five Year Plans,* by North Atlantic Treaty Organization, p. 204.

18. Andrzej Bloch, "The Private Sector in Poland," *Telos,* no. 66, pp. 129, 131 (Winter 1985-86).

19. O'Hearn, "Consumer Second Economy," pp. 232, 227; Vladimir Treml, "Alcohol in the USSR: A Fiscal Dilemma," *Soviet Studies,* 27(2):161-77 (1972); idem, "Alcohol in the Soviet Underground Economy" (Berkeley-Duke Occasional Papers on the Second Economy in the USSR, University of California, Berkeley, and Duke University, 1986; reprinted in *Studies in the Second Economy of Communist Countries,* ed. Grossman).

20. Gur Ofer and Aaron Vinokur, *Private Sources of Income of the Soviet Urban Household* (Santa Monica, CA: Rand, 1980), pp. 70, 58.

21. Brezinski and Roos, "Second Economy in Hungary," pp. 104-5.

22. O'Hearn, "Consumer Second Economy," p. 225.

23. Ibid.

24. S. P. Artemov, "Sluzhba byta v desiatoi piatiletke," *Den'gi i Kredit* [Money and credit], no. 12, p. 23 (1976), cited in Dennis O'Hearn, "The Second Economy in Consumer Goods and Services," *Critique* (Glasgow), no. 15, p. 103 (1982).

25. Kroncher cites a ratio of nearly 11:1 in his "CMEA Productive and Service Sector," p. 200. Other descriptions of these brigades are described in Simis, *USSR: The Corrupt Society,* pp. 258-61,

structed 52 percent of urban housing and 66 percent of housing in rural areas.[26]

Income and employment figures for the second economy give additional indication of its extent. Poland's 470,000 private enterprises accounted for 24 percent of total employment and generated 20 percent of money income in 1980, the latter rising to 32 percent in 1983.[27] In Hungary about three-quarters of the population receives additional income from the second economy.[28] Incomes from the second economy often greatly exceed official wages in Georgia.[29] A Soviet emigre survey indicated that 11 percent of all households' total income derived from private sources.[30] However, among the 10 percent of Soviet families who reported income from tips, bribes, and speculation, extra income

averaged 79 rubles per month, or about 2 weeks of the average wage.[31]

The extent of second economy activity seems to be greater in the southern Soviet republics, especially in Georgia and Central Asia. Second economy activities are also more extensive in outlying regions, ethnic enclaves, and the more ruralized republics. There are several reasons for this: inadequate supplies of consumer goods and services combined with persistently high demand that force people to use private or illegal channels; more autonomous rural households able to carry out private production; higher birth rates making for larger and stronger networks of kin, friends, and connections; family-centered moral codes that view the state and its officials as enemies; poor chances of upward mobility into the Soviet establishment for non-Russian minorities; and the Soviet state's inability to enforce laws or carry out control in outlying zones or among traditionally hostile ethnic groups.[32] Czechoslovakia and the German Democratic Republic, both industrialized and urbanized, probably have more reduced second economies than other areas of Eastern Europe.[33]

An integral part of second economy activity is corruption. Although difficult

and in Grossman, "Second Economy of the USSR," p. 36. Sizable incomes for such traveling brigades of agricultural and forest workers are reported in Romania by Ronnås and Sampson, in Hungary by Kenedi, and in the German Democratic Republic by Brezinski, where such "after-work brigades can easily charge 3 to 4 times the official wages plus 'fringe benefits.' " See, respectively, Ronnås, "Role of the 'Second Economy,' " p. 38; Steven Sampson, National Integration through Socialist Planning: An Anthropological Study of a Romanian New Town (Boulder, CO: East European Monographs, 1984), pp. 153-56; Kenedi, Do It Yourself, passim; Brezinski, "Second Economy in the GDR," p. 9; Die Welt, 20 June 1980.

26. Wedel, Private Poland, p. 40.
27. Korbonski, " 'Second Economy' in Poland," p. 2; Bloch, "Private Sector in Poland," p. 157.
28. Gabor, "Second Economy in Socialism," p. 32; Kroncher, "CMEA Productive and Service Sector," p. 205, citing Wall Street Journal, 22 Mar. 1982.
29. Law, "Corruption in Georgia"; Wiles, "What We Still Don't Know"; Mars and Altman, Private Enterprise in the USSR.
30. Ofer and Vinokur, Private Sources of Income, p. 51.

31. Ibid., p. 33. This would also include income derived from pilferage or sale of pilfered items, but not private wages, such as from moonlighting. Grossman's "Notes on the Illegal Private Economy" provides an excellent summary of such income sources.
32. See Mars and Altman, Private Enterprise in the USSR. Non-Russian ethnic groups also rank high on Peter Wiles's "continuum of dishonesty." Wiles, "What We Still Don't Know," app. II.
33. Brezinski, "Second Economies in Eastern Europe," p. 9; idem, "Second Economy in the GDR." Czech data are sparse, though see Leonard Silk, "The Mystery of Czech Affluence," New York Times, 20 June 1986.

to quantify, the extent of corruption—bribes to planners, hush money to police, nepotism and influence peddling—is indicated by the continuing stream of reports in the official press. The importance of this is also revealed in periodic campaigns against illegal, nonlabor, or speculation incomes in Poland, the USSR, and Romania and in the spectacular corruption scandals recently revealed in Moldavia, Uzbekistan, and Kazakhstan, where millions of illicit rubles were made over several years.[34] Bribes and payoffs are a normal part of daily life in the USSR, beginning with the payoff for a good room in the obstetric ward, ending with the payoff for a quality burial plot.[35]

THE SECOND ECONOMY<br>IN OPERATION

A closer look at the operation of the most widespread aspects of a typical second economy will enable us to see how the second economy is integrally

related to the wider structure of socialist society.

## Peasant household production

Domestic production of food has always been a source of household consumption and personal income for East Europeans. One form of this private farming, in which farmers own their own lands and livestock and grow food for personal consumption, on contract to the state, or sale on the market. Another form of household production is the combining, by collective farm families, of domestic resources with the small plots of land allocated to them by the collective.

Private farming is the principal form of peasant production in Poland, while such farms occupy less than 5 percent of peasant households in the rest of Eastern Europe. Often these peasants resort to the illegal second economy to procure fertilizer, tractors, and transport to market. Moreover, since the free markets may have regulated price ceilings, peasants may also engage in various subterfuges to obtain desired prices for their produce.

The typical collective farmer uses the collective as a resource to be exploited, working not for the collective but on the collective for the household enterprise. Collective farm wages are low, but fodder payments and the production of the personal plot are channeled into household production. Other resources of the collective may be borrowed, purchased, or stolen.[36]

34. See fn. 10; Philip Hanson, " 'Nonlabor Incomes' in the USSR," *Radio Liberty Research,* 172/86, 24 Apr. 1986. As several observers have noted, campaigns against economic crime seem to concentrate disproportionately on the non-Russian republics and on non-Russian nationalities, thus appealing to Russian nationalist sentiments as well. During the early 1960s, for example, most of the black marketeers who were executed had Jewish surnames.

35. Detailed especially in Simis, *"USSR: The Corrupt Society,"* pp. 205-47. See also Wojciech Markiewicz, "A Small Hand-Book for the Bribe-Giver: Tokens of Gratitude," in *Survey,* 29(3):195-98 (Autumn 1986), translated from *Polityka* (Warsaw), 30 Aug. 1986. Romania, Bulgaria, and Poland, where the bribes are often in dollars or dollar coupons, are similar in this respect, as they suffer from extreme shortages in virtually all spheres of social, economic, and cultural life, from procuring social services and consumer goods to obtaining cultural products such as books.

36. Sampson, "Rich Families and Poor Collectives." See Joel Halpern and David Kideckel, "Anthropology of Eastern Europe," *Annual Review of Anthropology,* 12:277-310 (1983), for further references on the relation between the collective farmer and the household. On the peasant-worker

A third form of family food production is the complex household enterprise produced when peasant-worker households add wage income from nonagricultural employment plus the resources of their workplace to agricultural wages, fodder inputs, and household labor. This combination of homegrown food, wages, payments in kind and income from sale of household produce can give these suburban households a standard of living that is often higher than those in nearby towns. Extra income from this household economy is often used in extravagant status displays, such as in the building of giant three-story houses.

Urban dwellers throughout Eastern Europe frequently complain about price-gouging peasants who demand speculative prices for their goods or who in Poland refuse to accept anything but Western currency. Yet the peasants must cover additional costs such as illegal transport, living in the city, security for bad harvests, and so forth. The collective farm's personal plot system can be viewed as a form of exploitation in which the collective frees itself from the obligation of paying the peasants a decent wage.[37] The point is that private plot production is an integral part of the collective farm wages and not something carried out beyond normal work. That is, private plot production is necessary for peasant subsistence. The peasants are forced to use the second economy to earn this wage. The peasants and peasant-workers cultivate this plot on their second shift.

There is ample evidence to show that first economy production suffers as a result—both on the collective and in the factory.

## The shadow economy of the socialist factory

Managers of Soviet factories are constrained by central planning decisions, central allocations of supplies, and limitations on wages and labor discipline. Plan fulfillment is every manager's prime concern, if only because this is the only way his or her career can advance. Hence, various extra-plan strategies are used to cut through bureaucratic bottlenecks or to procure supplies, transport, repair, extra labor, and spare parts. This shadow economy involves misreporting to the authorities and bribing or making connections with other managers in what are known as family circles.[38] Most factories retain a fixer (in Russian, *tolkach*), who functions as middleman, broker, and network entrepreneur. In order to procure these scarce resources, managers resort to what Grossman calls "the Four B's: barter, black market, bribe and *blat*" (Russian for "connections" or "influence").[39] The most important application of the Four $B$'s is with planners. Influencing them to decrease the plan norms or increase allocations of supplies is crucial for any manager who contemplates plan fulfillment.

The Four $B$'s are not a new develop-

strategy, see in particular John Cole, "Family, Farm and Factory: Rural Workers in Contemporary Romania," in *Romania in the 1980's,* ed. Daniel N. Nelson (Boulder, CO: Westview Press, 1981), pp. 71-116.

37. See, in particular, Timofeev, *Soviet Peasants,* and the review symposium on this book in *Telos,* no. 68, pp. 109-27 (Summer 1986).

38. "Family circles" is a term used by Joseph Berliner in *Factory and Manager in the USSR* (Cambridge, MA: Harvard University Press, 1957), pp. 259-63. My use of "shadow economy" comes from Gregory Grossman, "The 'Shadow Economy' in the Socialist Sectors of the USSR," in *CMEA Five Year Plans,* by North Atlantic Treaty Organization, pp. 99-115.

39. Grossman, " 'Shadow Economy' in the Socialist Sectors," p. 108.

ment. Berliner's informants from the 1930s and 1940s describe similar strategies.[40] However, there is evidence that as the East European economies grow more complex, production bottlenecks are increasing.[41] This means that shadow economy behavior must be tolerated even more, even though "benign plan fulfillment" can easily be transformed into embezzlement and illicit production.[42]

## The underground factories

Underground factories in the Soviet Union tend to specialize in small, simply manufactured, easily transportable and marketable consumer items such as "ladies underwear, meat *pirozhiki,* brooches made of a couple of plastic cherries or fashionably tailored artificial leather jackets."[43] Numbering in the "tens of thousands,"[44] they comprise mostly workshops producing high-demand consumer goods in moderate quantities. Underground factories normally coexist inside a state factory, using it as a cover to conceal the illicit use of supplies, funds, labor, transport, and distribution networks. While the state enterprise operates normally and achieves its plan, the surplus capacity is unofficially used to manufacture additional goods. These may be identical or may differ slightly from the goods described in the official profile of the factory.

Profits from the underground factory can only be partially invested. These second economy entrepreneurs may spend their profits as conspicuous consumption on big houses, vacations, cars, and feasts and to help offspring or godchildren pay their bribes to get good job placements or enter medical school.

Many underground entrepreneurs are Jews, who have been denied avenues of social mobility in the universities, army, policy, or party apparatus.[45] Many factories are located in the USSR's ethnic republics, where ethnicity serves as a mobilizing network and as a shield against controls. Considerable factory production costs go for bribing planners, inspectors, police, and even party officials.[46] Bribe expenses usually average 15-20 percent of illicit earnings.[47]

Take, for instance, Mars and Altman's study of an illicit biscuit factory in Soviet Georgia. The factory was inherited by two Jewish owners from their fathers; a third owner, a Gentile, was added later. The Gentile's social network was important for keeping the factory safe. A hidden production of four times the quantity of biscuits allowed in their plan was being produced.[48] Excess capacity was created by bribing planners and functionaries in those ministries that allocated the ingredients for biscuits. Additional ingredients were purchased from outside suppliers who themselves

40. Berliner, *Factory and Manager in the USSR;* idem, "The Informal Organization of the Soviet Firm," *Quarterly Journal of Economics,* 66(3):342-63 (Aug. 1952).
41. Grossman, " 'Shadow Economy' in the Socialist Sectors," p. 115.
42. Peter Wiles discusses the difference between "benign" and "malign plan fulfillment." The terms are his. Wiles, "What We Still Don't Know."
43. Simis, *USSR: The Corrupt Society,* p. 157.
44. Ibid., p. 147.

45. Ibid., p. 153.
46. Simis writes that the "black" millionaire Laziashvili had an annual income of R10-12 million and paid out R1 million yearly to Georgian party officials, including the minister of internal affairs. Ibid., p. 166. See also "The 'Black' Millions," *Radio Liberty Research,* 179/177, 27 July 1977.
47. Simis, *USSR: The Corrupt Society,* p. 166.
48. Mars and Altman, *Private Enterprise in the USSR,* chap. 6.

may have been pilfering from their own factories. Packaging and labeling were carried out via links with a paper and printing plant. Workers were paid extra, but the full details were concealed from them. Distribution was always a key problem, since police watch all the main roads and can stop trucks to examine their bills of lading. Successful distribution thus entailed bribes to virtually the entire police department of the region. The extra production was sold to retailers at a 15 percent discount off the normal wholesale price. Retail outlets sold the biscuits at official state prices and pocketed the income.

At every stage, personal support networks were necessary to ensure production and distribution and to cope with periodic crises. Anyone in a higher position in the second economy must have large networks of kin, friends, clients, or patrons. In the biscuit factory, the three owners had complementary networks: one had kin within the factory, one had friends and kin in other factories, and the third had a social network that included particularly important police officials. Combining these network linkages and their entrepreneurial talents, the factory owners achieved a comfortable profit.

### Private and illegal trade and services

The second economy operates extensively both in socialist retail outlets and among legal private traders and service people. Quality goods are frequently held back by managers and warehouse attendants and allocated to friends or black marketeers. Only the remainder reach the shop, where the salesclerk may hide more desirable goods under the counter. Via bribes or tips—or by virtue of friendship—the salesclerk sells the privilege to buy the item, which may cost more than the item itself.

Legal private traders are often discriminated against by the state in the allocation of merchandise, as well as subject to high taxes and controls. Hence they are often forced to resort to illegal strategies such as selling contraband, defrauding customers, or skimming receipts. Hungarian shopkeepers defraud their customers out of 8 billion forints each year. In Szczecin, Poland, 20 percent of all private entrepreneurs were convicted and fined for tax evasion in one year.[49] Bribes to obtain supplies and protection money to controllers are part of normal business operations. A Polish study showed artisans admitting to have paid 12 percent of their turnover in bribes and having received 18 percent of their supplies from illegal sources.[50]

For East European consumers, the key to procuring anything in the second economy is to establish some kind of private relationship with the seller. Kenedi describes three possible bases for such a relationship: the cash payment, bribe, or tip given when buyer and seller do not know each other and do not expect to have a long-term relationship; the mutual favors exchanged between friends and acquaintances in which services are exchanged reciprocally; and the wide-ranging social obligations founded on kinship and friendship in

49. Åslund, "Private Enterprise in Poland, the GDR and Hungary," p. 28.

50. J. Urban, "Prywatna Inicjatywa" [Private initiative], Zycie Gospodarcze, 22 Dec. 1968, cited in Åslund, "Private Enterprise in Poland, the GDR and Hungary." The difference between the Polish and East German private traders' problems is summarized by Åslund when he says that the Polish trader must pay a bribe to the supplier, whereas his East German counterpart need only give a tip—Iapowki versus Trinkgeld. Ibid., p. 29.

which the exchange is permanently unbalanced.[51]

It is common for cash payments to develop into favors or favors to evolve into a more stable friendship. Friendship relations are more dependable and less risky, since no cash is passed around. In the East European situation, where so many goods and services are in short supply, there is a crucial need to establish wide-ranging social exchange networks. Hence, the second economy brings together widely disparate social categories: professors become friends with shoe salespeople, engineers court butchers, and so forth.[52] East European traditions of commensality and drinking help forge and solidify these relations, especially where certain foods and beverages are themselves difficult to obtain. In Romania, for example, offering a guest a cup of coffee is not just a sign of hospitality but an indication that one has the networks to procure coffee and may also be willing to share them.[53]

In the East European second economy, who one knows is more important than the money one has. Those who stand in line for coffee, theater tickets, or bureaucratic permits may have the requisite cash but are without the necessary social connections. Those with strategically placed kin, friends, colleagues, clients, and patrons can bypass the lines.

Such private arrangements attest to the inventiveness of many East Europeans, but these also demand time, energy, and exasperation and create obligations that cannot always be fulfilled. There are winners and losers. The losers are those who lack the money, the connections, and/or the ability to turn their official job into an unofficial source of income.

Finally, space does not permit a discussion of the hard currency shops to which most East Europeans—Poles excepted—are denied access. In some countries, payment in Western currency or goods from these shops competes with payment in local currency. In Romania, Western cigarettes, particularly Kent, function as a currency of the country's second economy. Available only in the hard currency shops, they are procured via special relations with foreign tourists or students, with diplomats, or via family visiting from abroad. Like money, Kents are anonymous, divisible, and relatively long lasting. They can even be counterfeited by stuffing empty packs with Romanian cigarettes!

51. On the establishment and maintenance of such personal relations, see especially Kenedi, *Do It Yourself;* Wedel, *Private Poland;* Mars and Altman, *Private Enterprise in the USSR;* idem, "Cultural Bases of Soviet Georgia's"; Sampson, "Rich Families and Poor Collectives"; idem, "Informal Sector in Eastern Europe."

52. On the role of friendship in Eastern Europe, see Sampson, "Informal Sector in Eastern Europe"; Vladimir Shlapentokh, *Love, Marriage and Friendship in the Soviet Union* (New York: Praeger, 1985).

53. On food and drink symbolism in Eastern Europe, see Charlotte Chase, "Symbolism of Food Shortage in Current Polish Politics," *Anthropological Quarterly,* 56(2):76-82 (Apr. 1983); *East European Quarterly,* 18(4), *Special Issue on Alcohol in Eastern Europe* (1985).

## STRUCTURAL AND CULTURAL VARIATIONS

East European second economies vary from country to country. These variations are based on specific interactions between structural, cultural, and historical factors.

Taking structural factors first, it appears that second economies will tend to be more extensive in those countries where (1) there is a large private sector, as in Poland and Hungary; (2) where the rural populations are relatively large, as in Poland, the Balkans, and the USSR; (3) where the official economy is less effective due to the predominance of "reds" over experts, resulting in irrational planning policies, as in Albania, Romania, the USSR, and Bulgaria; (4) where the regime has not resolved basic problems of distributing food and consumer goods, as in Romania, Poland, and the USSR; (5) where foreign influences, tourism, and Western currency are more extensive, as in Poland, Hungary, the Baltic states, and the German Democratic Republic; and (6) where the control organs are less effective due either to laxity at the center, as in Poland and Hungary, or to resistance of a hostile periphery or ethnic minority. This resistance occurs in the non-Russian republics, the less urbanized Balkans, and minority areas throughout Eastern Europe, such as Kosovo and Transylvania, and among Gypsies, Jews, Armenians, Volga Germans, and so forth.[54]

These structural factors give each socialist state a different type of second economy, even though their relative sizes—as a proportion of gross national product—might be similar.

The structural variables cited operate in the cultural-historical context of each society. Cultural factors are manifest as specific cultural behaviors, value orientations, or institutions especially conducive to second economy production, exchange, or consumption or compatible with the kinds of informal social networks on which the second economy is based.

Some cultural behaviors conducive to the second economy are those that stress conspicuous display as indicators of personal prestige: skills in the ability to fast-talk bureaucrats or police; in squeezing favors or obligations out of people who are in high positions; in establishing patron-client or friendship networks with wide-ranging groups of people; and in publicly expressing one's linkages to others via gift giving, social togetherness, commensality, or alcohol use.

Cultural values compatible with an extensive second economy at least in the Soviet Union and the Eastern bloc countries are those that prioritize primary kin affiliations over allegiance to formal institutions like workplace, party, trade union, or state. Where nepotism is a moral duty and "faith in the state" is low, there will be little moral disapproval in appropriating state resources for private ends. As Kenedi says, "We must not allow the state to wither away. It's the only one we have. And if there were no such thing as the state, it would have to be invented."[55] In addition, societies that place a high value on personal honor and risk-taking behavior to prove one's honor will also be compatible with second economy behavior. Georgia and Soviet Central Asia are very much kin based, "honor and shame" societies.[56] Poland and Romania are notable for their lack of any "faith in the state."[57]

Finally, there are cultural institutions

54. A preliminary attempt to deal with the ethnic nature of the second economy in Yugoslavia has been carried out by Vjeran Katunaric, "The Socioethnic Nature of the Hidden Economy" (Manuscript, Department of Sociology, University of Zagreb, 1984).

55. Kenedi, *Do It Yourself,* p. 57.
56. Mars and Altman, *Private Enterprise in the USSR;* idem, "Cultural Bases of Soviet Georgia's"; idem, "Cultural Bases of Soviet Central Asia's."
57. Sampson, "Rich Families and Poor Collectives"; idem, "Informal Sector in Eastern Europe"; Korbonski, " 'Second Economy' in Poland"; Wedel, *Private Poland.*

such as having large families, clan systems, godparenthood, ritual friendship, and feasting that help to form social networks of deep obligations based on long-term trust. Large networks, obligations, and trust are keys to success in any second economy. They can help to procure money, whereas money cannot always procure obligations and trust. Large family traditions are obvious facilitators. An Uzbek or Kazakh—from Soviet Central Asia—with six siblings has available to him the networks of a dozen cousins and six other in-laws and their networks.

Since cultural and structural factors interact over time, historical factors also determine the nature of the second economy in each East European society. Poland's second economy seems to have achieved a head start as a result of the Nazi occupation.[58] Many anti-Nazi patterns regarding the importance of informal connections and suspicion of higher authority were continued under the Soviet occupation. In Romania, the nepotism and bribery that developed during the Ottoman occupation have continued today as patterns of deference to authority, misrepresentation, bribes, gifts to local elites, and the overt nepotism of General Secretary Ceausescu, whose wife, children, brothers, and in-laws occupy high party and state posts.

The existence of historical precedents

does not mean that East Germany, Hungary, or Czechoslovakia could not develop Georgian or Balkan cultural patterns. Political oppression and economic mismanagement could easily stimulate them. Hence a Soviet émigré sociologist has bemoaned the gradual Georgianization of Soviet society.[59]

We should not be surprised to see cultural factors achieving their own momentum such that they aggravate preexisting structural inadequacies. This has clearly been the case in the USSR, Poland, and the Balkans.

## ORIGINS, CAUSES, AND EFFECTS

While some second economy activities are intrinsic to socialist economies and can be found in the earliest accounts of Stalinist industrialization, most analysts maintain that they have blossomed in the last 10-15 years.[60] There are several reasons for this: the proletarianization of farmers and housewives and their integration into large-scale collective farms or factories; the spread of large workplaces to outlying republics and rural areas; urbanization, foreign influences, and rising consumer aspirations that have not been met by the state

58. Korbonski writes, "The fifteen-year period spanning the wartime German occupation, the postwar Communist takeover, and the Stalinist era was accompanied by the presence of a dynamic parallel market." This has meant that "Poland, most likely ahead of the other East European countries, became a good example of the coexistence of two socioeconomic systems: the *pays legal* and the *pays reel*." Korbonski, " 'Second Economy' in Poland," pp. 8-9. This same continuity argument is stressed as well in Wedel, *Private Poland*.

59. Shlapentokh, *Love, Marriage and Friendship*, p. 213.

60. Cf. Grossman, "Second Economy of the USSR," pp. 31, 36-37; idem, "Notes on the Illegal Private Economy," p. 46; idem, " 'Shadow Economy' in the Socialist Sectors," p. 113; Brezinski, "Second Economies in Eastern Europe," p. 8; idem, "Second Economy in the Soviet Union," p. 367; Kroncher, "CMEA Productive and Service Sector," p. 195; George Schöpflin, "Corruption, Informalism and Irregularity in Eastern Europe: A Political Analysis," *Südosteuropa*, 34(4):210 (1985); Dieter Cassel and E. Ulrich Cichy, "Explaining the Growing Shadow Economy in East and West: A Comparative Systems Approach," *Comparative Economic Studies*, 28(1):34 (Spring 1968).

sector; the decline of terror as a control mechanism; the population's increasing disrespect for state institutions as the institutions show themselves permanently unable to meet basic needs for housing, goods, and services; and the increasing degree of sophistication in second economy strategies, replacing simple bribes with intricate networks of friendship and exchange.[61]

Why do East Europeans use so much of their time and energy and put themselves at such great risk to pursue second economy activity? Clearly, the manifest reason is that people want to make more money and managers want to fulfill the plan. Yet these human motives have political, economic, and sociocultural foundations.

East European economies are politicized economies. A wide range of economic decisions are made by political organs. The political priorities that lie in the plan, the priority of heavy over light industry, production over consumption, industry over services, all generate political responses. Strikes, protests, and riots are one type of response. The second economy is another.

The immediate economic cause of the second economy is the shortage of desired goods and services. The underlying cause of *these* shortages is the shortage of labor. Workers hold back their labor in the first economy in order to use it for consumption—standing in line; leisure—or for moonlighting.[62]

These structural causes feed into the East Europeans' feelings of estrangement from their workplaces, institutions, and the bureaucracy. Workplaces remain institutions to be exploited—"them"—rather than collective property to be safeguarded. The pervasive attitude that "everybody is doing it" and that the elites are getting their own special fringe benefits—what might be called the third economy—creates a moral atmosphere that makes it natural to resort to second economy strategies.

The second economy clearly has a lubricating effect insofar as it helps supply goods and services that the formal economy does not. In its shadow form, it provides the "baling wire and chewing gum" that keep the socialist enterprises from breaking down completely.[63]

In adding extra incomes and raising living standards, the second economy also functions as a social mollifier.[64] Resentment at the privileges of the elite is ameliorated by the masses' petty swindling, bribes, and moonlighting. Outlying republics or ethnic groups attain living standards in the second economy that surpass those of Moscow or

61. Janos Kenedi summarizes this trend: "It's not enough to know how to read between the lines—one has to squeeze through them." Kenedi, *Do It Yourself,* p. 97.
62. This statement is supported not only by virtually all Western journalistic accounts but by East European émigrés in the West who are amazed at the intensity of labor in most Western factories. Istvan Gabor has stressed "labor withholding" as the key to understanding the second

economy. Moreover, he cites several Hungarian studies where between 75 and 98 percent of the workers stated that they could be working harder. Moreover, low work intensity also leads to "negligent and indolent work, 'notorious' absenteeism, being late, frequent changing of workplaces, arbitrary shortening of worktime," and so forth. With labor withholding as the norm, workers earn extra money either by working overtime or in the second economy. See Gabor, "Second (Secondary) Economy," p. 296.
63. O'Hearn, "Consumer Second Economy," p. 231. As Grossman, Brezinski, Gabor, and Cassel and Cichy have all stated, the second economy is itself a kind of surrogate reform, insofar as what was once illegal is now tolerated.
64. The term "social mollifier" is used by Cassel and Cichy, "Explaining the Growing of the Shadow Economy," p. 34.

Leningrad. Instead of protesting, people find individual solutions. This may explain why some of the officially low-paid groups in these societies, such as peasants and service workers, are so politically passive: their second economy incomes make up for it.[65]

Yet the lubricating and mollifying functions are offset by its corrosive function. By stealing labor time, materials, or funds from the first economy, the second economy makes the formal system even more inefficient than it is already. Labor is wasted, goods are shoddy, and no one really seems to care. Inside the enterprises, extra-plan improvisation covers up for the fundamental deficiencies of central planning.

Moreover, the constant swindling of the state perpetuates a moral gap between individuals and institutions. The "us"-"them" dichotomy or "underground society"[66] rhetoric may sound romantic, but the reality of the second economy is inequality, exploitation, and a lack of solidarity among those not part of the social networks. People are expected to defraud each other, lie to each other, falsify statistics, and misrepresent them-

selves in public encounters. People are kept off balance by the paradox of pervasive shortage and by the fact that nothing is every totally unavailable. There are always success stories of people who got hold of the seemingly unobtainable item—from an American record album to an exit visa. Hence people blame themselves if they cannot get hold of a desired commodity: they simply are not smart enough.

Due to the political, economic, and moral effects of the second economy, society degenerates into competing bands.

CONCLUSION: CAN THE
SECOND ECONOMY
BE REFORMED?

Each new second economy scandal brings renewed calls for "strengthening ideological training" and "perfecting the organs of control." To this Mikhail Gorbachev has added a policy of "openness" (*glasnost*) in revealing instances of corruption and second economy activities. Yet a genuine solution to the corrosive aspects of the second economy must attack it at its political, economic, and sociocultural roots. Ideological exhortations, propaganda, threats of more control, and revelations of scandals in this or that enterprise or republic are not directed toward these roots. This is why they invariably do not work.

One step toward reducing the second economy's corrosive effects with respect to societal integration would be to legalize certain forms of second economy entrepreneurship now illegal and to give the private sector priority equal to that of the socialist sector in allocations, support, and expertise. To date, the East European regimes have largely tolerated the private sector, typically leaving it to

65. By contrast, workers in heavy industry, often in large homogeneous towns, are heavily dependent on state supplies via shops or direct deliveries to the factory. When these supplies fail—as occurred in Poland—the second economy channels are only of limited usefulness. Hence the only alternative is political action. See John Montias, "Economic Conditions and Political Instability in Communist Countries: Observations on Strikes, Riots and Other Disturbances," *Studies in Comparative Communism*, 13(3):283-301 (Fall 1980); Ole Norgaard and Steven Sampson, "Poland's Crisis and East European Socialism," *Theory and Society,* 13(4):773-99 (1984).

66. Cf. Kemeny, "Unregistered Economy in Hungary," p. 363; Kemeny speaks of "an underground country." See also Elemer Hankiss, "The Second Society" (Manuscript, Institute of Sociology, Hungarian Academy of Sciences, 1986).

fend for itself, often illegally.

A second solution must attack the problematic nature of the first economy. Since one cause of first economy inefficiency is lack of information due to the population's general lack of interest, some ways of stimulating workers' allegiance to these institutions might be sought. The easiest way would be to institute a form of genuine workers' control, a key demand in the Polish labor movement. Workers' control over both plan formulation and the profits that accrue from it might stimulate attitudes in which pilferage would be discouraged.

Of course, both these solutions touch on the sacrosanct leading role of the party in economic decision making. Just as the second economy is a political reaction, these solutions are also political ones.

As it stands today, East Europeans continue to cultivate their metaphorical private plots, squeezing every last bit of value from them whether it be legally or illegally. Peasants who sell their sacks of vegetables at the market, workers who pilfer parts from the factory, truck drivers who sell state gasoline, bureaucrats who arrange residence permits to Moscow, the Romanian kiosk woman who rents out her sole copy of *Newsweek* by the hour to the locals, all are cultivating their private plots. Anticorruption campaigns and control measures cannot eliminate "personal plot socialism."[67] They are not intended to. Rather, their scope is to reset the boundaries of how much private activity is tolerated, how much in the way of materials can be pilfered, how much state labor time can be used for personal needs.

Real efforts to eliminate the personal plot would only produce more problems for the first economy and a politically volatile populace. Here the Hungarian solution seems to offer a probable course of action for other East European regimes. Encouraged by the state to take second jobs and set up private businesses, each Hungarian citizen now has the right to work 16 hours per day. If someone cannot attain the good things in life, they now have only themselves to blame. Socialism, once a reaction to the capitalists' lengthening of the working day, has now found in it a solution to its own problems.

Legitimating the second economy in this way only covers up its political, economic, and moral roots. Such reforms bode ill for the first economy. The history of socialist Eastern Europe shows that economic difficulties produce political aftershocks. The institutionalization of personal-plot socialism will be no exception.

67. See my review of Timofeev's *Soviet Peasants* in *Telos*, no. 68, pp. 114-17 (Summer 1986), for a fuller exposition of "personal plot socialism."

ANNALS, *AAPSS*, **493**, September 1987

# The Political Economy of
# Informal Economies

*By* STUART HENRY

ABSTRACT: This article considers the mutual interrelationship between informal economies and the wider political economy of capitalism. Four dimensions are discussed: (1) the generation of informal economies as a paradoxical outcome of distinguishing them from capitalism; (2) the support given by capitalism and reciprocated by informal economies that enables each to gain strength from their similarities; (3) the opposition to informal economies that is reflected back on the wider economy; and (4) the destruction capitalism inflicts as it attempts to colonize and co-opt informal economies and the simultaneous transformation of capitalism that occurs with their absorption into the wider structure. The article argues that as a result of these complex interrelations, the development of, and intervention in, informal economies is neither simple nor linear. Failure to take these relations into account can lead to policy and its implementation that produce many unforeseen outcomes.

*Stuart Henry received his doctorate in sociology from the University of Kent in Canterbury in 1976. He is currently visiting associate professor of sociology at Eastern Michigan University, where he teaches criminological theory and white-collar crime. He has taught at polytechnics and universities in England and the United States and has written numerous articles for journals and magazines. His books include* Self-Help and Health, *which he coauthored with D. Robinson;* The Hidden Economy; Informal Institutions, *which he edited; and* Private Justice.

A NY consideration of informal economic activity, however much that is concealed from the management of the state, will be incomplete if account is not taken of the wider structural context in which the activity is set. Just as it was a mistake for the study of political economy to become divorced from the study of households,[1] so the relatively recent study of the underground, irregular, and hidden economies would be seriously flawed if it ignored their interconnectedness to the wider society. The political economy of informal economies conceives of the face-to-face informal economic activities that go on in households and in informal social networks in relation to the broad macro-features of the political and economic system of capitalism.

It is important to recognize, however, that this interconnectedness between informal economies and the wider capitalist structure is not one-way. In this article I shall attempt to demonstrate that not only do informal economies emerge from the contradictions of capitalism, but they are simultaneously supportive and undermining of capitalism, as that system is of them. Put simply, informal economies both are shaped by and shape the wider political economy in which they are set. Moreover, this is also true for global capitalism's relationship with Third World informal sector employment[2] and for socialist second

economies in their relationship with the state planned economy.[3]

## CAPITALISM AND ITS COMPONENT INFORMAL ECONOMIES

I take the view that the political economy of Western capitalism, rather than being a unified whole dominated by a capitalist free market economy and a facilitative state, is much more fragmentary and contradictory. As I have argued elsewhere,[4] Western industrial societies are multiplex economies containing a range of qualitatively different, conflicting, and coalescing subeconomies under the overarching domination of capitalism. These constituent economies of capitalism are not discrete or separate entities but are overlapping and interrelated, each with its own discernible identity, each also sharing features in common with the wider structure of which it is a part. For these reasons it is very difficult to be precise about where the boundaries of one subeconomy end and those of another begin.

I take the term "informal economies" to be the generic term for the range of

1. Siegwart Lindenberg, "An Assessment of the New Political Economy: Its Potential for the Social Sciences and for Sociology in Particular," *Sociological Theory*, 3:99-114 (1985).

2. Chris Gerry, "Developing Economies and the Informal Sector in Historical Perspective," this issue of *The Annals* of the American Academy of Political and Social Science. See also Ray Bromley and Chris Gerry, eds., *Casual Work and Poverty in Third World Cities* (New York: John Wiley, 1979); Priscilla Connolly, "The Politics of

the Informal Sector: A Critique," in *Beyond Employment*, ed. Nanneke Redclift and Enzo Mingione (New York: Basil Blackwell, 1985).

3. Steven L. Sampson, "The Second Economy of the Soviet Union and Eastern Europe," this issue of *The Annals* of the American Academy of Political and Social Science.

4. Stuart Henry, ed., *Informal Institutions* (New York: St. Martin's Press, 1981); idem, "The Working Unemployed: Perspectives on the Informal Economy and Unemployment," *Sociological Review*, 30:460-77 (1982); idem, "Can the Hidden Economy Be Revolutionary? Towards a Dialectical Analysis of the Relations between Formal and Informal Economics," mimeographed (Norfolk, VA: Old Dominion University, Department of Sociology and Criminal Justice, 1986); John Davis, "Gifts and the UK Economy," *Man*, 7:408-29 (1972).

overlapping subeconomies that are not taken into account by formal measures of economic activity. Although this term is a relatively arbitrary choice, it seems to be the least emotive or value laden of those available. It should not, however, be taken to mean that the regular economy of capitalism is wholly formal, but that informality is the predominant characteristic of the economies that we are considering here.[5]

Defining and classifying what counts as informal economies is further complicated because those who define and construct taxonomies are themselves selecting criteria based on their own structural position and interests. Indeed, this problem is reflected in the profusion of names that informal economies have attracted. As Carol Carson has observed, in addition to the catchy titles of "underground," "unobserved," and "hidden," these activities have been described as

cash, black, unofficial, informal, irregular, unrecorded, moonlight, twilight, gray, shadow, subterranean, marginal, dual, second, parallel and illegal. The choice of names sometimes reflects an author's point of view: for employment, moonlight; for tax administration, unreported; for law enforcement, illegal. Some authors have drawn distinctions among the names according to the activities they intend to cover. Others, although they have used different names, do not appear to have different coverage. In summary, a generally accepted taxonomy has not yet emerged.[6]

Accepting this position could be grounds for dodging the issue of definition and classification. However, to do so would be unhelpful, if only because the default position is likely to be one of assuming market economic assumptions and motives that, as Gaughan and Ferman point out,[7] and as I have demonstrated elsewhere,[8] are often a highly inappropriate description of much of the activity with which we are dealing.

Any all-encompassing description of the activity is bound to fail to convince. In part, this is because it will clash with ethnographic and participant accounts steeped in their own unique experience. In part it is because it will challenge observers' carefully constructed abstract categories, and in part it is because the very diversity of these subeconomies defies generalization. In commenting on the conceptual confusion resulting from lumping together a diverse range of informal activity including domestic do-it-yourself work, consumption and leisure-time activities, black labor, tax evasion, smuggling, alternative communal projects, self-help, and mutual aid, it is little wonder that Joseph Huber is moved to exclaim that "the result is conceptual 'tuttifruitti' which leads to political hodgepodge, if it leads anywhere at all."[9]

What these diverse activities have in common is certainly difficult to describe

5. Also it is important to recognize that although it is often referred to in the singular, we are clearly talking about a number of interrelated subeconomies; hence I prefer the term in the plural.

6. Carol S. Carson, "The Underground Economy: An Introduction," *Survey of Current Business*, p. 21 (May 1984).

7. Joseph P. Gaughan and Louis A. Ferman, "Toward an Understanding of the Informal Economy," this issue of *The Annals* of the American Academy of Political and Social Science. See also Louis A. Ferman and Louise E. Berndt, "The Irregular Economy," in *Informal Institutions*, ed. Henry.

8. See Stuart Henry, *The Hidden Economy* (Oxford: Martin Robertson, 1978).

9. Joseph Huber, "Conceptions of the Dual Economy," *Technological Forecasting and Social Change,* 27:65 (1985).

without first specifying the total societal context. Under socialist states, for example, informal economies often have more in common with capitalist free market activities than with the communal forms that these activities sometimes take under capitalism.[10] For advanced Western capitalist societies in times of relatively full employment, informal economies seem to share the following characteristics. They are (1) concealed from the state accounting system and are largely unregistered by its economic and criminal measurement techniques; (2) small scale; (3) labor intensive, requiring little capital; and (4) locally based, with trading taking place through face-to-face relationships between friends, relatives, or acquaintances in a limited geographical area. Beyond this, characteristics such as whether altruistic or avaricious, autonomous or parasitic, legal or illegal, using cash or using kind as a medium of exchange are generally less applicable. These are, in fact, criteria used by commentators to distinguish different constituent subeconomies.

Of the variety of classification schemes available in the literature[11] I shall adapt that used by Gaughan and Ferman in this volume and based on Sahlins's seminal work in economic anthropology.[12] Sahlins's analytical framework distinguishes exchange in any society on

the basis of the extent to which reciprocity is a central organizing principle. This produces three basic kinds of exchange: (1) intimate, which is governed by the principles of generalized altruistic reciprocity and takes place among close friends, relatives, and socially recognized kin; (2) associational, which is governed by the principle of balanced reciprocity and takes place among friends and neighbors who are members of a loose-knit social network; and (3) entrepreneurial, which is governed by the principle of negative reciprocity, self-interest, or avarice and takes place largely among strangers.[13]

Each of these kinds of exchange can be considered on a vertical plane as differing depths or levels overlapping with each other as one moves from altruistic reciprocity among intimates to negative reciprocity among strangers. At the same time each basic kind of exchange is more or less present in the variety of informal economies that we can consider on a horizontal plane.[14] For example, the social or communal economy is mainly characterized by the intimate type of exchange.[15] The do-

10. Sampson, "Second Economy of the Soviet Union"; Istvan R. Gabor, "The Major Domains of the Second Economy in Hungary" (Paper delivered at "The Informal Economy: Social Conflicts and the Future of Industrial Societies," First World Conference on the Informal Economy, Rome, Nov. 1982).

11. For a discussion of these, see Henry, "Working Unemployed"; Huber, "Conceptions of the Dual Economy."

12. Marshall Sahlins, *Stone Age Economics* (Chicago: Aldine-Atherton, 1972).

13. These terms are derived from the work of Sahlins and Thompson; for discussion, see Gaughan and Ferman, "Toward an Understanding"; see also Robin Cantor, Stuart Henry, and Steve Rayner, *Markets, Distribution and Exchange after Societal Cataclysm* (Oak Ridge, TN: Oak Ridge National Laboratory, 1987).

14. A similar analytical framework was developed by Georges Gurvitch for analyzing the varieties of law, each of which could exist at different levels of formality or informality. See Georges Gurvitch, *The Sociology of Law* (Boston: Routledge & Kegan Paul, 1947).

15. Carol B. Stack, *All Our Kin: Strategies for Survival in a Black Community* (New York: Harper & Row, 1974); Martin Lowenthal, "The Social Economy in Urban Working Class Communities," in *The Social Economy of Cities*, ed. G. Gappert and H. Ross (Newbury Park, CA: Sage, 1975).

mestic or household economy, while characterized by intimate exchange, also has elements both associational and, as many critics of patriarchy have argued, entrepreneurial.[16] The irregular economy is more typically found to be associational and entrepreneurial in character, although it too has aspects of intimate exchange.[17] The hidden economy is also largely associational with elements both intimate and entrepreneurial,[18] but it can operate with a high level of entrepreneurial exchange[19] such that it approximates the extreme end of avariciousness found to be typical of criminal economies of trade in stolen goods, prostitution, drugs, and gambling.[20]

While it is possible to break these informal economies down into their own constituent subeconomies, to do so becomes cumbersome and needlessly complex. Moreover, it forces us to choose between observer-based and participant-based criteria with insufficient data on which to base a decision. For the

purpose of the following discussion, therefore, I shall simply describe the activity and indicate the term that has typically been applied to it as this becomes relevant to the discussion of the interrelationship between constituent subeconomies and the wider social structure.

The first two dimensions of the interrelationship between these informal economies and the wider societal structure I shall consider are those of mutual support. I shall show that support occurs either (1) because of the strain toward separation that emerges as the regular economy of capitalism is growing and being established as the primary economy; or (2) because the wider capitalist economy coalesces with informal economies, exploiting, co-opting, and colonizing them as it transforms them into its own likeness. I will then go on to consider the mutual relations of opposition between informal economies and the wider structure.

16. This is why the feminist writers often opt for the phrase "domestic labor" or "hidden labor." See, for example, Jane Taylor, "Hidden Labour and the National Health Service," in *Prospects for the National Health*, ed. Paul Atkinson et al. (London: Croom Helm, 1979).

17. Ferman and Berndt, "Irregular Economy"; Leslie M. Dow, "High Weeds in Detroit," *Urban Anthropology*, 6:111-28 (1977).

18. Henry, *Hidden Economy*; Gerald Mars, *Cheats at Work: An Anthropology of Workplace Crime* (London: George Allen & Unwin, 1982).

19. Jason Ditton, *Part-time Crime: An Ethnography of Fiddling and Pilferage* (New York: Macmillan, 1977).

20. It is worth mentioning here that even regular economy market exchange can be interspersed with intimate exchange—see, for example, Harvey A. Faberman and Eugene A. Weinstein, "Personalization in Lower Class Consumer Interaction," *Social Problems*, 17:499-57 (1970)—and under imperfect competition, or monopoly, is characterized as much by avaricious exchange as are criminal economies.

## THE PARADOX OF SUPPORT THROUGH OPPOSITION

Support through opposition means that in distinguishing the overarching structure of capitalism from that which it is not, proponents inadvertently create counter structures. These take the form of subeconomies that are based on exchange structures that have been excluded from the capitalist system. Simultaneously, proponents of the subeconomies, in elaborating their own activities' differences from the wider system, help support its clarification.

As early capitalism emerged from feudalism, definitions and boundaries were created to establish bourgeois legality. The newly emerging capitalist society changed what had previously been acceptable practices, such as payments in kind, into illegal activity, parasitic on the development of capitalism. Jason Ditton, for example, has argued that the extended package of common rights enjoyed by feudal tenants had made a major contribution to household budgets but that these were stripped away by the eighteenth-century Acts of Enclosure.[21] Wood gathering, game rights, and grazing rights became the crimes of wood theft, poaching, and trespassing.[22] This was not a sudden event but one that took place at different rates and to differing degrees in different parts of the country. John Styles has shown that workers in the newly founded manufacturing industries of late-seventeenth- and eighteenth-century England constantly borrowed, bartered, and sold small quantities of materials among themselves and that "the boundaries between legitimate dealing of this kind, receiving embezzled goods and even receiving goods stolen by outsiders from workshops and warehouses were not always well defined and were disregarded by many."[23] Criminalization of the consumption of a part of one's daily labor was redefined in conjunction with capitalist development of the factory to become employee theft and embezzlement; the trading of embezzled goods came to constitute a hidden economy.

Again, it must be pointed out that although the right to enjoy the direct products of labor was denied and the activities of those who continued this practice were seen as parasitic on the wider host economy, this was not a total transformation but one of emphasis and definition. Styles reasons that workers were prepared to argue for their right to previously recognized perquisites against campaigns by employers to redefine them as frauds through the creation of laws. But, he says,

it would be wrong to imagine that such attacks [by employers] always brought about a once-and-for-all transformation of this component of a worker's income, or were intended to do so. . . . Indeed, most *employers* appear to have been decidedly unwilling to eradicate perquisites permanently, despite the insistence by some modern historians that this was one of the "main tasks" of capitalist development.[24]

As will be seen when I examine the supportive relations between capitalism and informal economies, there are good reasons why employers wish to retain an element of the hidden economy.

It is important to recognize, then, that informal economies can be transformed by redefinition from activity that was previously no more than innocent trading into a criminal enterprise. Although some of the original substance of the activity may remain—in the case of the hidden economy the original substance is that of an intimate and associational network of exchange—this interpretation is publicly suppressed, and the illegality and corresponding avaricious motives are drawn out as the significant dimension. As Ditton defines it, the hidden economy is seen as "the sub-commercial movement

21. Jason Ditton, "Perks, Pilferage and the Fiddle: The Historical Structure of Invisible Wages," *Theory and Society*, 4:39-71 (1977).

22. Douglas Hay et al., *Albion's Fatal Tree: Crime and Society in Eighteenth Century England* (Harmondsworth: Allen Lane, 1975); E. P. Thompson, *Whigs and Hunters* (Harmondsworth: Allen Lane, 1975).

23. John Styles, "Embezzlement, Industry and the Law in England, 500-1800," in *Manufacture in Town and Country before the Factory*, ed. Maxine Berg et al. (New York: Cambridge University Press, 1983), p. 179.

24. Ibid., pp. 204-5.

of materials and finance, together with the systematic concealment of that process for illegal gain . . . a microscopic wry reflection on the visible economic structure upon which it parasitically feeds."[25]

However, in its very drawing of boundaries, capitalism is signifying areas that may be more attractive to those dissatisfied with the existing system and it is also providing the grounds justifying participation in the hidden economy. As David Matza has observed, "The criminal law, more so than any comparable system of norms, acknowledges and states the principled grounds under which an actor may claim exemption. The law contains the seeds of its own neutralization."[26]

In addition, the banning of behaviors provides the conditions of what first Wilkins and then Young describe as "deviancy amplification."[27] Amplification occurs when those who publicly condemn and react to behavior that is deemed unacceptable exaggerate its negative aspects. Distorted presentation, such as negatively labeling informal economies as black, underground, hidden, secret, nether, and so on, creates a new situation for participants, who are then forced to respond by concealing other related information and practices. This secrecy brings new deviant solutions, increased contact with other excluded groups, and further reaction by control agents as the whole cycle is repeated in a seemingly endless spiral of negative signification.

Another sense in which the separation or distinction between informal economies and the wider system of capitalism enables both realms to grow in opposition to one another is through ongoing pronouncements that are part of the politics of oppositional discourse. These, paradoxically, generate mutual support for that which is opposed.[28] For example, when advocates of the regular capitalist economy publicly discredit irregular economy work as dangerous for employees because of the absence of protective legislation, insurance, and benefits, they simultaneously imply that regular work is safe and responsible. When they denounce the products of irregular work as unreliable and without guarantee, they are, by implication, simultaneously promoting the formal economy as accountable, predictable, and efficient. But such pronouncements also, paradoxically, invite comparisons on price, personal relations, spontaneity, flexibility, and uniqueness that may inform many regular economy participants that there are alternatives of which they might otherwise have been unaware; the pronouncements may encourage them to participate in informal economies, which they might not otherwise have done.

A further way in which the politics of defining the boundaries of capitalism can simultaneously generate informal activity is in the role played by the state. The growth of the state as a facilitator of the growth of capitalist enterprise requires that it accrue revenue from those

25. Jason Ditton, "The Fiddler: A Sociological Analysis of Blue Collar Theft among Bread Salesmen" (Ph.D. diss., University of Durham, 1976), p. 275.

26. David Matza, *Delinquency and Drift* (New York: John Wiley, 1964), p. 60.

27. Leslie Wilkins, *Social Deviance: Social Policy, Action and Research* (London: Tavistock, 1964); Jock Young, "The Role of the Police as Amplifiers of Deviancy," in *Images of Deviance*, ed. Stanley Cohen (New York: Penguin, 1971).

28. See Michel Foucault, *The History of Sexuality: An Introduction* (New York: Penguin, 1978); Elizabeth R. Morrissey, "Power and Control through Discourse: The Case of Drinking and Drinking Problems among Women," *Contemporary Crisis,* 10:157-79 (1986).

on whose behalf it acts. Taxation laws, however, not only define who and what is taxable; they also specify who and what is nontaxable. As Gutmann, an advocate of a more laissez-faire capitalism, says, "The subterranean economy ... is a creature of income tax, of other taxes, of limitations on the legal employment of certain groups and of prohibitions on certain activities."[29] He argues that the redistributive economy and the welfare state, growing employment protection legislation and sex and racial equality legislation are actually creating the grounds for capitalist employers to go outside the system, employ workers off-the-books, and so facilitate participation in the irregular economy. The problem of high levels of government involvement is particularly acute in times of high inflation. "Inflation redistributes income from income earners to government as taxpayers are pushed into higher tax brackets; squeezed taxpayers in turn try to push part of the cost of inflation onto the government by getting off-the-books income."[30]

But we need not imagine that informal economies would weaken with the withering of the welfare state. The very structure of capitalism is such that it generates its own historically specific types of informal economies, as Ferman and Ferman were first to demonstrate.[31] In their seminal article they claim that the very origins of irregular economies "lie in structural conditions and processes in the larger society, and cannot be divorced from them."[32] They argue that modern capitalist industrial society encourages such economies by creating structural inequalities based on class, ethnic, and cultural segregation. In addition, economic specialization, protectionist trade unions, and professional associations coalesce so that some goods and services are not widely available or are too expensive for those with low or nonexistent incomes. The direct result is that a market is created outside of the formal regular economy for cheap goods and services, and, say Ferman and Ferman, "once regular patterns are established they provide training and opportunity for those members of the community who choose to earn their livelihood this way and [the patterns] are supported by a population that has few viable alternatives for the purchase of goods and services."[33]

We can see, therefore, that in its political attempt to develop, define, and protect itself from that which it is not, capitalist economic structure simultaneously creates and generates the contradictory possibilities of internal subeconomies. As these counter and parallel economies themselves gain strength from the wider structure, they also give it strength by allowing its boundaries to be defined and by providing a safety net for those who are unable to survive its competition of interests. Nowhere is this mutuality of support more apparent than when we consider the second major dimension of the interrelationship between informal economies and the wider capitalist structure, that of convergence or coalescence.

29. Peter M. Gutmann, "The Subterranean Economy," *Financial Analysts Journal*, 34:26 (1977).

30. Peter Gutmann, "Latest Notes from the Subterranean Economy," *Business and Society Review*, p. 29 (Summer 1980).

31. Patricia R. Ferman and Louis A. Ferman, "The Structural Underpinning of the Irregular Economy," *Poverty and Human Resources Abstracts*, 8:3-17 (1973).

32. Ibid., p. 5.
33. Ibid., p. 17.

## COLONIZATION THROUGH COALESCENCE

We saw in the previous section how developing capitalism did not completely remove informal economies, though it did transform their definition. The reason why employers retain that to which they are ostensibly opposed becomes clearer when the functions of informal economies are examined. Scraton and South have captured the nub of this dialectical relationship:

Essentially workers' involvement in the hidden economy represents a dynamic form of opposition to the interests of capital by the daily enactment of processes which inhibit the exploitative relations of capital over labor. . . . It constitutes an attack on the hegemony of class discipline from what "autonomous space" is available, both mental and material, to workers. It is precisely for this reason that attempts are made to incorporate pilfering and fiddling into the wage relation. Thus these activities cannot be considered outside the historical dynamic of class relations.[34]

The existence of a system of payments in kind that are not part of a formal wage or salary structure, and that can be redefined as theft or perquisites depending upon the state of the business cycle, gives employers a hidden arm of control. It allows them to reward employees for service "beyond the call of duty,"[35] but it also allows them to establish individual reward systems for the control of their overall wage bill. Gerald Mars and his colleagues have shown, for example, how in the restaurant industry certain core workers are granted the right to pilfered food and access to the best tips in return for loyalty in policing peripheral workers who may wish to form unions and push for higher wages.[36]

Jason Ditton has similarly shown that service workers are often placed in low-wage situations by their employers who "connive at corruption" by turning a "blind eye" to employees who cheat customers. This serves as a means of deflecting employees from making losses for the company. However, once such pilfering and fiddling has been learned by novice employees as a method to cover their potential losses from mistakes, these activities are extended, often against the company and in connivance with the customer, to make a little extra side money.[37] Here we see supportive relations begin to turn into negative relations of coalescence, as I shall discuss later.

It has been argued that allowing a degree of employee theft is healthy for worker morale and helps relieve the boredom of monotonous work routines and so facilitates the wider production process.[38] More cynically, Ditton, like Scraton and South, has observed that embezzlement and other related hidden economy activities, where they are seen

34. Phil Scraton and Nigel South, "The Ideological Construction of the Hidden Economy: Private Justice and Work Related Crime," *Contemporary Crisis*, 8:11 (1984).

35. Melville Dalton, *Men Who Manage* (New York: John Wiley, 1964).

36. Gerald Mars and Peter Mitchell, "Catering for the Low Paid: Invisible Earnings," *Bulletin*, no. 15 (London: Low Pay Unit, 1977); Gerald Mars, Don Bryant, and Peter Mitchell, *Manpower Problems in the Hotel and Catering Industry* (Farnborough: Saxon House, 1979); Gerald Mars and Michael Nicod, "Hidden Rewards at Work: The Implications from a Study of British Hotels," in *Informal Institutions*, ed. Henry; idem, *The World of Waiters* (London: George Allen & Unwin, 1983).

37. Ditton, *Part-time Crime*.

38. Lawrence R. Zeitlin, "Stimulus/Response: A Little Larceny Can Do a Lot for Employee Morale," *Psychology Today*, 5:22, 23, 26, 64 (1971).

as "beating the boss" or "defeating the system," are cheap symbolic concessions for a device that actually entrenches the dependency of employees since the concession can be granted or withdrawn at will, to suit market conditions.[39]

If further evidence were needed of the functionally supportive relations between capitalism and the range of informal economies, one would only have to look at what, in the literature on the Third World, has been described as "informal income opportunities."[40] Although some argue that the informal sector is a residual form of petty commodity production operating independently of capitalism,[41] others recognize that it is relied upon in times of crisis as a means of labor absorption for the wider capitalist society, serving to disguise unemployment and stimulate new employment. Informal sector workers are disguised wage laborers since their production is subject to control by industrial capital, which sets the volume, type, and quality of the goods produced and fixes the prices below their true value.[42] Bromley

and Gerry, for example, argue that where the employees are subcontracted out-workers, or where they are self-employed, they are harnessed to the needs of large capitalist enterprises; they are dependent upon the enterprises' credit, rental of space or equipment, and supply of raw materials; or the larger enterprise is the sole buyer of the employees' product.[43]

But there is a sense, too, in which informal economies in capitalism are more than an appendage and its participants more than a marginal surplus population. Informal economies are valued as contributing to economic growth by providing low-cost consumer goods, being a test bed for innovations in business, and for oiling the wheels of industry, enabling bureaucratic restrictions to be overcome.[44]

Indeed, it is in this vein that some futurists have celebrated the usefulness of informal economies to advanced industrial capitalism. Shankland, for example, notes that "in a healthy society" formal and informal economies "sustain each other and their relationship should be a symbiotic one of mutual support." He says,

The formal sector effectively controls the commanding heights of the economy and the political system, but the informal sector is essential, not parasitic or residual . . . it operates rather at the interstices of the formal institutions of modern urban society; it cannot offer an alternative society but a complementary economic activity to the

39. Jason Ditton and Richard Brown, "Why Don't They Revolt? Invisible Income as a Neglected Dimension of Runciman's Relative Deprivation Thesis," *British Journal of Sociology*, 32:521-30 (1981).

40. Keith Hart, "Informal Income Opportunities and Urban Employment in Ghana," *Journal of Modern African Studies*, 11:61-89 (1973).

41. J. Bremen, "A Dualistic Labour System: A Critique of the Informal Sector Concept," *Economic and Political Weekly*, 11:1870-76 (1976); R. Davies, "Informal Sector or Subordinate Mode of Production? A Model," in *Casual Work and Poverty*, ed. Bromley and Gerry.

42. D. Mazumdar, "The Urban Informal Sector," *World Development*, 4:655-79 (1976); John Bryant, "An Introductory Bibliography to Work on the Informal Economy in Third World Literature," in *Bibliographies on Local Labour Markets and the Informal Economy*, ed. Ray Pahl and Julian Laite (London: Social Science Research Council, 1982).

43. Bromley and Gerry, ed., *Casual Work and Poverty*.

44. Michael Carter, "Issues in the Hidden Economy—A Survey," *Economic Record*, 60:209-21 (1984). This functional role for informal economies is particularly well documented for second economies under socialism. See Sampson, "Second Economy of the Soviet Union."

formal with a different, informal and more personal life style.[45]

Shankland argues that the benefits of encouraging the informal economy are enormous and are particularly useful as a way of getting new business started on a trial basis.[46] Indeed, some early capitalists founded their enterprises on materials acquired from the hidden economy. The use of materials thus acquired, as Styles says, "was widely believed to be a very common route of entry into manufacturing for men with little capital."[47]

Gershuny, in his early writings on postindustrial society, has been most credited with the benign futurist position toward the informal economy.[48] He predicts a growth of labor productivity resulting from a declining manufacturing sector and spurred on by the microtechnological revolution. This growth will continue to reduce employment opportunities in the formal sector. Fiscal and legitimacy crises will halt the traditional Keynesian public-spending solution to unemployment and will encourage the ideological shift from public provision to privatization. Rather than continuing the expansion of the service sector, argues Gershuny, we are more likely to see an expansion of the "self-service" economy. Unable to afford formal economy services because of higher unemployment and lower income in the formal economy, people will turn to the household, the community, and the irregular economy.

Leading government officials in Western capitalist societies have claimed that the irregular economy of work off-the-books is actually indicative of the spirit of capitalism. In Britain, both Prince Charles and Prime Minister Thatcher have claimed that the irregular economy "proves that the British are not work shy." Similarly, Ronald Reagan has said that the cut-price, irregular work done by wetbacks employed off-the-books may contribute more to the U.S. economy than they take out in benefits. Their unregistered status does not allow them to draw state benefits for fear of being caught. More recently he has suggested that the necessary cut in welfare services demanded by the budget deficit creates the opportunity for local self-help and mutual-aid initiatives, from psychological support groups to neighborhood housing construction and project management, and from parent-run day care to self-help for the elderly.

There are numerous examples of the ways in which benign symbiotic relationships exist between regular capitalist enterprise and informal economies. Every time do-it-yourself tools are sold to consumers by hardware stores or when department stores sell food mixers and other household appliances, they are clearly contributing to capitalist production. They are simultaneously contributing to the household, communal, and irregular economies since these goods enable self-servicing and self-provisioning in ways that the sale of finished consumer goods do not. The phenomenal growth in industries pro-

45. Graeme Shankland, "Towards Dual Economy," *Guardian*, 23 Dec. 1977, p. 18.

46. Graeme Shankland, *Our Secret Economy* (London: Anglo-German Foundation, 1980).

47. Styles, "Embezzlement, Industry and the Law," p. 179.

48. J. I. Gershuny, "Post-Industrial Society: The Myth of the Service Economy," *Futures*, 9:103-14 (1977); idem, *After Industrial Society?* (New York: Macmillan, 1978), idem, "The Informal Economy: Its Role in Post-Industrial Society," *Futures*, 11:3-15 (1979); Jonathan Gershuny, *Social Innovation and the Division of Labour* (New York: Oxford University Press, 1983); Jonathan Gershuny and Ian D. Miles, *The New Service Economy: The Transformation of Employment in Industrial Societies* (London: Francis Pinter, 1983).

ducing home-improvement materials and tools, such as paint, paper, laminates, wood, power tools, step ladders, workbenches, screws, and nails, is not only indicative of the adaptability of capitalism to profit from new demand but also reflects the emerging contradictions that informal economies represent. People are no longer content with finished products but are increasingly demanding those that require participatory production and control, if not in the factory, then in the home, the community, and on the street: dinner sets to Tupperware parties, dining room suites to do-it-yourself. Each of these rely on domestic production or social networking or both to complete consumption.

Heinze and Olk have argued against such stabilizing strategies for capitalism based on the colonization of people's desire for participatory control. However, their preference for a "complementary network" strategy involving a deliberate policy of state encouragement and support for the informal sector seems politically naive.[49] Suggestions that laws could be amended to provide flexibility of working hours, financial support for decentralized community decision making, and legal status for alternative concerns seem to ignore the experience of other decentralized alternative projects, such as neighborhood courts and community justice.[50]

Ironically, decentralization and privatization are, as we shall see in the next section, not always benign for capitalism. The growth of informal economies can undermine some aspects of the capitalist system that spawned them, although these economies are themselves very vulnerable to being undermined.

## MUTUAL DESTRUCTION THROUGH OPPOSITION

It has been well documented that capitalist employers considerably influence the legislative content of capitalist industrial democracies.[51] In this way capitalist interests can control, undermine, or destroy informal economies, especially where these are found to be obstructive or threatening. People engaged in irregular work can be prosecuted and sanctioned under federal tax laws as can those who employ them. Similarly, those who trade in pilfered goods are subject to theft laws. Even communal economy exchanges of services can be policed through licensing laws. Clearly, direct control is cruder than co-optation, but, as Pashukanis reminded us long ago, "the judicial element in the regulation of human conduct enters where the isolation and opposition of interests begins" and where legitimation breaks down.[52]

49. See Rolf G. Heinze and Thomas Olk, "Development of the Informal Economy: A Strategy for Resolving the Crisis of the Welfare State," *Futures*, pp. 189-204 (June 1982).

50. Richard L. Abel, "Conservative Conflict and the Reproduction of Capitalism: The Role of Informal Justice," *International Journal of the Sociology of Law*, 9:245-67 (1981); James P. Brady, "Sorting out the Exile's Confusion: Or a Dialogue on Popular Justice," *Contemporary Crisis*, 5:31-38 (1981); Christine B. Harrington,

*Shadow Justice: The Ideology and Institutionalization of Alternatives to Court* (Westport, CT: Greenwood Press, 1985).

51. Richard Quinney, *Class, State and Crime* (New York: Longman, 1980); David F. Greenberg, *Crime and Capitalism* (Palo Alto, CA: Mayfield, 1981); William J. Chambliss and Robert Seidman, *Law, Order and Power* (Reading, MA: Addison-Wesley, 1982).

52. E. B. Pashukanis, *Law and Marxism: A General Theory*, ed. Christopher J. Arthur (London: Ink Links, 1978).

A less direct way of undermining informal economies is through the politics of labeling. Many of the labels such as "black," "hidden," "underground," and "subterranean" carry negative connotations. Much of the popular media accounts of these activities portray participants in the informal economy as twilight operators who are out to make a fast buck and cannot be trusted.[53] However, as with support through opposition, discussed earlier, the influence is mutual rather than one-way. When agents of capitalism attempt to control informal economies through the politics of public condemnation, the effect can be counterproductive; it can bring contempt for the established institutions of capitalism.

One very good illustration of the generation of contempt for capitalist institutions is in the growth of self-help groups to fill the gaps in care that professional care services were forced to leave owing to fiscal crises and technical limitations to growth. The success of self-help support networks in the health and social services has made self-help activities respectable in spite of much hostile criticism of their benefits from professional interest groups, such as doctors, psychiatrists, and some social workers. In so far as criticism continues, it only serves to undermine the credibility of those uttering it, not least because of their economic interests. The result is that people are now more prepared to try alternatives to professional services.[54]

An excellent illustration of the way public condemnation of informal economies undermines capitalism can be seen from the way the news media responded to the hidden economy of pilfering and fiddling at work in Britain in the mid-1970s. Until this time hidden economies had remained undiscovered and ignored by journalists. When it was found that, rather than being the practice of a few bad apples, hidden economy activity was widespread, engaged in by all sections of society and all occupations,[55] it became both newsworthy and grounds for moral outrage. On its front page the most widely circulated British newspaper, the *Sun*, reprimanded the nation with the banner headline: "STOP THIEF!" Its editorial blazed, "The truth is we are all at it. Which doesn't make it any more acceptable morally. And it doesn't make much sense either. For in the end someone has to pay. And who is that? Us!"[56] However, such categorical condemnation disregards the reality of people's experiences in informal economies. It also forces journalists to discuss difficult issues for a capitalist society such as why even its moral standard-bearers in the professions are found cheating. When doctors are found to be siphoning off clients from their practices into private care or defrauding Medicare with fictitious claims for nonexistent patients, then, as one journalist observed, the hidden economy starts to "eat away at the moral fabric of society. Very soon the line between fiddling and outright theft becomes blurred. . . . A nation on the fiddle is usually a nation in financial and moral trouble. After all when everyone else is fiddling you tend to go along."[57]

---

53. Stuart Henry, "Fiddling as a Media Issue," *Media Reporter,* 6:41-43 (1982).

54. Alfred H. Katz and Eugene I. Bender, *The Strength in Us: Self-Help Groups in the Modern World* (New York: Franklin Watts, 1976); David Robinson and Stuart Henry, *Self-Help and Health: Mutual Aid for Modern Problems* (Oxford: Martin Robertson, 1977).

55. Gerald Mars, *Cheats at Work.*

56. *Sun,* 9 Aug. 1976.

57. Jane Walmsley, "London on the Fiddle: Part 2," *Evening Standard,* 18 Mar. 1980, pp. 20-21.

The undermining of the wider capitalist system by informal economies is a fear that has been recognized and expressed by governments. As Walmsley has shown, in Britain, the Public Accounts Committee of the House of Commons has said, "There is a real danger of tax evasion spreading beyond the limits of the present black economy." Its chairperson said, "If people see others breaking the law without any chance of being caught it could affect tax payers who might say, 'If it's good for them, lets see if we can break the law in some other way.' " As a former chairperson of the revenue service said, "It is eroding what you might call the integrity of tax paying generally."[58]

Paradoxically, the very public condemnation of informal economic activity alerts others to its existence and serves to attract new participants who might have either remained outside or remained ignorant of its existence. These people may feel cheated by a society that claims to control such activity and especially when they find that some of its very figureheads are secretly engaged in activity from which they have been refraining.

## MUTUAL DESTRUCTION THROUGH COALESCENCE

In the course of what appear to be supportive gestures, informal economies are transformed by their relations with capitalism. The principle of co-optation operates such that underground, unofficial, and informal activities are absorbed by the larger and more profuse capitalist organizations, which take what they need and leave the rest. The most extreme version of this position has been well captured by what has become known as Geiger's Law: "When the counter culture

58. Ibid.

develops something of value the establishment rips it off and sells it back."[59] Geiger was talking about the professionalization of the intimate communal economy of self-help groups and mutual aid. What often start out as informal support groups for those who have found formal professional services unable to serve their needs may become professionalized, taken over, managed, advised, and funded by private corporate or government agencies. It is for this reason that the more successful and longest-established self-help networks have found it necessary to decline all outside support; however, many more have ambivalent relations with professionals.[60]

While, as we have seen, the domestic economy facilitates capitalism, the household's domestic system of production has also traditionally been a prime candidate for undermining from the wider matrix of capitalism. That it is a primary focus for intimacy and informal networks should not blind us to the fact that much of what we take to be the household's economy has been based on the unpaid domestic labor of women in such activities as gardening, food preparation, cleaning, child care, social support, nursing of the elderly and dependents, and medical care of sick family members.[61] Indeed, in this context, some

59. Cited as Geiger's Law by S. F. Jencks, "Problems in Participatory Health Care," in *Self-Help and Health: A Report* (New York: New Human Services Institute, 1976).

60. O. H. Mowrer, "The 'Self-Help' or Mutual-Aid Movement: Do Professionals Help or Hinder?" in *Self-Help and Health*; T. Dewar, "Professionalized Clients as Self-Helpers," in ibid.

61. Michele Hoyman, "Female Participation in the Informal Economy: A Neglected Issue," this issue of *The Annals* of the American Academy of Political and Social Science. See also Scott Burns, *The Household Economy* (Boston: Beacon Press, 1977); Ivan Illich, "Vernacular Gender," *CoEvolu-*

have argued, women's labor is marginalized and now serves as a reserve army of labor.[62] In some industrial societies motherhood and women's shadow domestic labor are being emphasized by a conservative social policy that "tends toward the marginalization and pauperization of those sections of the population who have lost the battle for the remaining jobs" rather than a policy that extends employment opportunities for women.[63]

Perhaps the most dramatic illustration of the way the wider structure of capitalism undermines intimate informal economies by coalescing with them is the use of social networks as a marketing device to sell capitalist consumer goods for profit. This has obviously been done in the commercialization of gift exchange, but it is at its most blatant in Tupperware parties or in the Amway perfume pyramid selling or in home-agent mail-order catalogs.[64]

We can gain considerable insight into how capitalism undermines informal economies from what members of intimate networks and communal economies say about their experiences in attempting to retain a separate identity. For example, one member of a community theater cooperative whom I interviewed during a study on co-ops[65] told me,

No more do I believe we operate perfectly as a collective could operate. Obviously it's contradicted by lots of things in the outside world. We are on one level a cooperative experimenting with new ways of doing things and on another we are a small company developing plays. One thing beyond anything else that makes that possible is economic survival. If you want to eat and do community theatre it's necessary to earn money and that means endless concessions.

Concessions to capitalism mean that capitalist principles and solutions to problems are drawn on to solve informal economy problems. For example, when a self-help housing cooperative abandons its informal social-control policy for collecting rent arrears and starts issuing court-ordered eviction notices, it is not an autonomous alternative economy. One member of a short-life self-help housing co-op echoed the inevitability of such dependence:

If you send them a notice to quit, they say, "Oh that's a bit heavy, isn't it . . . getting the law involved?" But if the law wasn't involved, people wouldn't be secure in their short-life housing. . . . So the law is already involved. I think it's a drag giving credibility to the law because the law doesn't particularly like co-ops or the people who are in them. . . . We are allowing the police to harass our members, which is very heavy but . . . if there isn't another way, then you've got to do it.[66]

By resorting to landlord-tenant law, the cooperative helps validate both capitalist society's view of credit and debt and the value of impersonal, rational, and predictable procedures. At the same time, use of capitalist remedies enables the cooperative to survive in a capitalist environment, but in a form different from and less intimate than what its members intended. It is in just such a way, then, that informal economies are undermined.

*tion,* pp. 4-23 (Spring 1982); idem, *Shadow Work* (London: Marion Boyars, 1981); Ray Pahl, *Divisions of Labour* (New York: Basil Blackwell, 1984).

62. Enzo Mingione, "Social Reproduction of the Surplus Labour Force: The Case of 'Southern Italy,' " in *Beyond Employment,* ed. Redclift and Mingione.

63. Heinze and Olk, "Development of the Informal Economy," p. 197.

64. John Davis, "Forms and Norms: The Economy of Social Relations," *Man,* 8:159-76 (1973).

65. Stuart Henry, *Private Justice: Towards Integrated Theorizing in the Sociology of Law* (Boston: Routledge & Kegan Paul, 1983), p. 218.

66. Ibid., p. 206.

It is clear that, as islands of intimacy in a sea of capitalism, informal economies are more likely to erode than are the numerous institutions of the wider social structure. However, to say this is not to deny that the reverse process occurs. Ironically, informal economies and institutions are likely to do more to modify the shape of capitalist structure than the ostensibly oppositional structures such as cooperatives and communes, since these latter are generally marginal and rarely encountered in capitalist society. Capitalism may be very successful in undercutting such opposing orders, but it cannot destroy its own institutions and therefore must continually contend with the opposing internal tendencies that informal economies sometimes represent.[67]

As I have already said, it would be an inaccurate representation to suggest that informal economies are wholly opposed to the capitalist system in which they occur, even if they often emerge from its contradictions. Indeed, as Ditton points out, the hidden economy of pilfering and fiddling, for example,

shares many structural and substantive features with business. . . . Fiddling is not in opposition to these values; salesmen [who fiddle] do not believe that fiddling will eventually overthrow the capitalist economy . . . they fully believe themselves to be part of the same commercial army. . . . Fiddling, like selling, epitomizes the capitalist "spirit." The subculture of fiddling reflects a sort of dutiful anti-hedonism . . . which provides the normative bedrock of capitalism.[68]

But here Ditton is picking up only the avaricious dimensions of the hidden economy. The hidden economy, like all informal economies, also contains communal, social, and intimate strains.[69] It is founded in part on a network of altruistic and balanced reciprocity where status may be achieved and prestige gained based more on how much is given away than on how much is made; where members of trading networks are prepared to give as much as they can and where goods and services can be traded because they are needed by others; where commodities become valued because of their special history and origins, because of who obtained them and how; and where little money is made from friends and trading partners because the rewards are more social than monetary. Insofar as the hidden economy is founded as much on altruism as on avarice, on love as on money, then this meaning is available to penetrate the wider structure of capitalism. The more that people engage in the communal dimensions of informal economies, the more they carry that experience into their relations in capitalism and the more that capitalism is changed. Such change is not major. Rather, it is a rounding of the corners of impersonal market exchange.

## CONCLUSION

The foregoing analysis demonstrates that simple statements about informal economies being caused by this or that factor or this or that system, by tax laws, capitalist inequalities, opportunism, altruism, and the like capture only some aspects of what is a dynamic and complex set of relations. At best these statements are partial accounts that leave much unsaid. At worst they are part of the politics of informal economies that seeks to impose a particular view of the world,

67. Stuart Henry, "Community Justice, Capitalist Society and Human Agency: The Dialectics of Collective Law in the Cooperative," *Law and Society Review*, 19:303-27 (1985).

68. Ditton, *Part-time Crime*, pp. 173-74.

69. Henry, *Hidden Economy*.

to control, manipulate, or influence it in order to serve a particular interest.

Informal economies in capitalism exist in contradictory relations with the wider structure. We have seen how they emerge from and are constantly being transformed by the wider capitalist industrial matrix; they are sometimes in opposition to and sometimes in support of capitalist institutions. We have also seen how capitalism is sometimes in opposition to them and sometimes in support of them. This interrelationship is both positive and negative, mutually supportive and mutually destructive. And, importantly, these contradictory aspects can and often do operate simultaneously. Part of the explanation for this comes from the very duality of the existence of informal economies within capitalist society. Informal economies have a degree of autonomy but are also considerably dependent. They might best be described as semi-autonomous parts of the capitalist whole.[70]

These circumstances suggest that any policy that attempts to intervene to shape informal economies is going to have many more effects than the direct effects that are intended. Simple interventionist policies will have numerous unintended consequences some of which may be constructive, others of which will be less so. Any policymaking that seeks to address informal economies, such as those directed at curbing off-the-books employment or those designed to provide welfare services or to crack down on employee theft, will need to be aware of the full range of possible interrelated effects of its action. This will necessitate an appreciation of the complexity of the dialectical interconnectedness of informal economies and the wider structure in which they are set, the multifarious dimensions of which have only been sketched in this article.

---

70. For a treatment of law as a semi-autonomous field, see Sally Falk Moore, *Law as Process* (Boston: Routledge & Kegan Paul, 1978). For an elaboration of this dialectical approach, which Peter Fitzpatrick calls "integral plurality," see Peter Fitzpatrick, "Law and Societies," *Osgood Hall Law Journal*, 22:115-38 (1984).

ANNALS, *AAPSS*, **493**, September 1987

# Issues and Prospects for the Study of Informal Economies: Concepts, Research Strategies, and Policy

*By* LOUIS A. FERMAN,
STUART HENRY, and
MICHELE HOYMAN

ABSTRACT: This article considers the current state of knowledge about informal economies. Criticism of the value of the informal economy concept is addressed by considering the multiple disciplinary interests in the topic, the confusion over an appropriate definition, and the problems of classification and explanation. A multidisciplinary, macro-micro approach is suggested. The joint ethnography-survey method has been found to be the most productive research tool for empirical study, and the principles of such methodology are outlined. In the context of a discussion on the politics of research funding, major areas for future research are identified. These include historical surveys; local-area studies; changing household work patterns in relation to the wider formal economy; informal work and illegal markets; class, ethnic, and sexual composition of the participants; informal institutions, particularly information and skill exchanges; media and their representation of the informal economy; and the role of informal economies in coping with national disasters. Finally, the implications of the informal economies for government policy on taxation, labor, welfare, and crime and criminal justice are drawn out.

---

*Louis A. Ferman is professor of social work and research director of the Institute of Labor and Industrial Relations, University of Michigan.*

*Stuart Henry is visiting associate professor of sociology at Eastern Michigan University.*

*Michele Hoyman is associate professor of political science and a fellow in the Center for Metropolitan Studies, University of Missouri, Saint Louis.*

IN this article we draw attention to some of the many unresolved issues in the study of informal economies and draw out the implications of informal economies for attempts to manage social life. The article considers four broad areas: conceptual issues, methodological perspectives, research gaps, and policy implications.

## CONCEPTUAL ISSUES

It has been argued that the concept of the informal economy is confused and of questionable usefulness. The editors of a recent collection of papers on the social dimensions of economic life reflect a common ambivalence about its role:

Our early discussions revealed disagreement about the utility of the concept and over the extent to which it referred to an identifiable sector of economic activity. Indeed, there is not a single paper in the present volume that uses the term for analysis. . . . The earlier concept of the informal economy as a separable and, as it were, autonomous economic sector has turned out to be unproductive . . . as have ideas of a set of different subeconomies . . . between which people could move at will. The basic realities, however, that stimulated the interest in the informal economy . . . still remain a challenge to social scientists: the existence of whole series of economic activities which do not fall easily within the definitions and analysis of traditional economics or get measured by government.[1]

Rather than attempt a resolution of this confusion, our aim here is to outline some of the numerous conceptual issues in order to invite future clarification. Four broad issues will be addressed: (1) disciplinary; (2) definitional; (3) typological; and (4) explanatory.

### Disciplinary issues

It is perhaps trite to reassert that disciplines have their own values and assumptions. However, one of the major features of writings on informal economies is that they very much reflect the social scientists' disciplinary affiliation. Economists, for example, are interested in alternative modes of allocation and distribution, particularly how far these constitute extra-market activities and whether they constitute imperfections.[2] They have sought to measure the size and extent of informal economies and have not been concerned with the issues of socially constructed meaning and motivation, beyond the economic rationalist reduction that people participate for the money. In contrast, anthropologists and ethnographically oriented sociologists have framed their concern in terms of relations of kinship, friendship, neighborliness, partiality, sympathy, and altruism, and the extent to which these constitute a social glue that binds and ties.[3] Here the focus has been on norms

1. Bryan Roberts, Ruth Finnegan, and Duncan Gallie, eds., *New Approaches to Economic Life* (Manchester: Manchester University Press, 1985), pp. 8-12. For a similar view, see Priscilla Connolly, "The Politics of the Informal Sector: A Critique," in *Beyond Employment: Household Gender and Subsistence*, ed. Nanneke Redclift and Enzo Mingione (New York: Basil Blackwell, 1985). Others, while recognizing the problems, wish to refine rather than abandon this and related concepts; see, for example, Joseph Huber, "Conceptions of the Dual Economy," *Technological Forecasting and Social Change*, 27:63-73 (1985).

2. Not all economists take this view. Dual labor market theorists, for example, show that social and economic heterogeneity can coexist where labor segmentation occurs between primary jobs that are skilled and highly rewarded and semiskilled and unskilled jobs. See David M. Gordon, Richard E. Edwards, and Michael Reich, *Segmented Work, Divided Workers* (New York: Cambridge University Press, 1982).

3. John Davis, "Rules Not Laws: Outline of an Ethnographic Approach to Economics," in *New Approaches to Economic Life*, ed. Roberts, Finnegan, and Gallie, p. 503.

of exchange and the role of reciprocity. It could be argued that this approach neglects the wider political economy that has been the preserve of structural sociologists and developmental theorists. Other sociologists have taken a middle-range approach, viewing informal economies in terms of exchange relationships and how these are related to the stability or instability of social organizations. Feminist writers have for many years focused on the issue of the value of women's work or domestic labor, as have anthropologists in studying the households of subsistence economies. Recent feminism has challenged this ghettoization, arguing that studies of economic life must consider gender constraints on men as well as women in both the household and the wider society. For political scientists, the issue is couched in terms of its historical and contemporary policy implications, where it is seen as evidence of, grounds for, or reasons against government intervention. A surprising omission has been an analysis of the class and power dimensions of informal economies.[4] Quite clearly, the assumptions of one discipline can become the research problems of the next.

Put simply, the phenomenon of informal economies has developed a multidisciplinary rather than interdisciplinary interest, with little interchange between the various disciplinary approaches.[5] It would seem that rather than allowing disciplinary dominance, the field would benefit from approaches that addressed the concerns raised by each of the disciplines. As Roberts, Finnegan, and Gallie say, one of the chief features of these new approaches to economic life is their interdisciplinary nature: "Not only are some of the older, taken-for-granted boundaries between disciplines being challenged, but much recent research is now drawing on insights from a number of disciplines, not just from one."[6] However, any move to an all-embracing theory seems premature, and much more may be gained from the jostling of different paradigmatic approaches, which may also help overcome the disciplinary boundaries.

## Definitional issues

Such is the diversity of disciplinary interest and the diffuse nature of the topic that from the outset a central difficulty has been to specify precisely what counts as the phenomenon under study. Are these informal activities an economy, a sphere of exchange, a market, or merely the practice of trading? Are we dealing with a single economy, a subeconomy, many subeconomies, or sectors of the economy? There are also grounds for describing the phenomenon as self-servicing,[7] self-provisioning,[8] or more broadly as self-help.[9] Alterna-

4. But see R. E. Pahl, *Divisions of Labour* (New York: Basil Blackwell, 1984); Redclift and Mingione, ed., *Beyond Employment*; John A. Denton, "The Underground Economy and Social Stratification," *Sociological Spectrum*, 5:31-42 (1985).

5. But for a joint work from an economist, a sociologist, and an anthropologist, see Robin Cantor, Stuart Henry, and Steve Rayner, *Markets, Distribution and Exchange after Societal Cataclysm* (Oak Ridge, TN: Oak Ridge National Laboratory, 1987).

6. Roberts, Finnegan, and Gallie, ed., *New Approaches to Economic Life*, p. 14. Roberts, Finnegan, and Gallie ironically rely on a multidisciplinary approach bringing together sociologists, anthropologists, social psychologists, and economists.

7. J. I. Gershuny, "The Self-Service Economy," *New Universities Quarterly*, pp. 50-66 (Winter 1977).

8. Pahl, *Divisions of Labour*.

9. Barry Knight and Ruth Hayes, *The Self Help Economy: Social and Economic Develop-*

tively, why not just opt for the terms "labor" or "work"?

Informal economic activities are difficult to be precise about because they are typically defined as an inversion, alternative, or negation of the conventionally accepted administrative categories, institutions, and structure of the wider societal system. Therefore, what counts as informal economic activity will depend very much upon the feature of the wider system to which it is being related. This, along with the different disciplinary interests, accounts for why there are upward of thirty different terms for the activity, each with a different scope and connotations. Whether the activity forms one economy or many, the adjectives used to describe it emphasize that it is: (1) qualitatively different from the wider economic arrangements as implied by such terms as "informal," "irregular," "nonmarket"; (2) based on social units rather than atomized individuals, as in the designations "domestic," "household," "neighborhood," "community," "green"; (3) separate, when it is described as "parallel," "second," "dual"; (4) oppositional, as indicated by "alternative," "counter"; (5) peripheral, as in "marginal," "gray," "colored"; (6) concealed from official records and accounting systems, as implied by "hidden," "underground," "subterranean," "black," "submerged," "shadow," "nonregistered," "unrecorded," "invisible," "moonlight," "twilight," "unofficial," "cash"; and (7) inferior, as implied by the terms "illegal" and "nether."

A crucial issue here is not only which of these numerous terms best captures the essence of the phenomenon or whether each refers to something slightly different, but also whether distinguishing between the activity and something else is useful. What is gained in clarification may be lost by artificially separating those that are inextricably intertwined. Moreover, such distinctions may falsely attribute autonomy to the activities, separating them from other informal economies and from the wider system of which each is a part. And that calls for more imaginative definitions rather than none at all.

## Typological issues

The last point really begs the question of how to classify the numerous informal activities, and it also has implications for deciding on an appropriate methodology.[10] Given that no generally accepted typology is available,[11] should students of informal economies adopt the naturalistic, inductive stance and formulate their categories based on the participants' meaning of their trading networks? Alternatively, should classifiers select the central criteria on which to base a normatively imposed order? A third possibility would be the construction of a Weberian ideal type where logical categories are synthesized from the available empirical and historical data so that particular instances can be compared to the general type. Whichever

10. A number of the issues raised in this section have emerged from exchanges with Alison Lever, to whom the authors are grateful.

11. Carol S. Carson, "The Underground Economy: An Introduction," *Survey of Current Business* (May 1984); but for some attempts at classification, see Stuart Henry, "Introduction" in *Informal Institutions*, ed. Stuart Henry (New York: St. Martin's Press, 1981); idem, "The Working Unemployed: Perspectives on the Informal Economy and Unemployment," *Sociological Review*, 30:460-77 (1982); Huber, "Conceptions of the Dual Economy."

*ment in the Inner City* (London: London Voluntary Service Council, 1982).

approach is adopted, and a synthesis of all three seems likely to be most useful, particular attention must be given to the starting point.

If informal economies cannot be considered in isolation from the wider social and political matrix, what do we take to be the social whole? From the normative perspective, to take one characterization of the starting point is to color the parts that we abstract. For example, beginning with global capitalism would give us different parts from those that would be derived if we began with U.S. industrial society, and different again if we began with the Western market economy. Can socialist informal economies even be compared with capitalist ones? It is an impossible task unless we begin with industrial society as the whole—and then how do we compare the informal sector of the Third World?

Take, for example, the notion of irregular work defined as paid work outside formal employment, done on a part-time basis. This is a highly ethnocentric stance since it implies that formal employment is the norm, which on a global scale it is not. In most countries a small proportion of the population have registered stable employment; the larger proportion depend on unregistered, precarious employment that may be full-time casual work, or full-time stable work without legal guarantee because of its unregistered nature. Indeed, the distinction between work, employment, and self-employment is particularly colored by the whole from which these abstractions are derived. An illegal immigrant in U.S. industrial society can be in full-time work for an employer but not in employment from the bureaucratic perspective of this society because she or he is not registered. This is why some prefer the term "shadow employment" or even "shadow wage labor" for off-the-books work where the employee does not own the means of production.[12]

Parts of a whole can be subdivided into their own constituent parts. An obvious example is the U.S. capitalist economy, which may be considered both a part of the world economic system and a whole containing numerous subeconomies that at once both reflect and constitute its character. For example, the capitalist economy may be said to comprise a formal economy, defined as economic production, exchange, and consumption that are registered, legal, and use money as a medium, and an informal economy, where activities are either illegal or unregistered. The informal economy then becomes the whole containing a variety of subeconomies, such as the cash-based unregistered irregular economy, the criminal economy, and the social economy, defined as being exchange that is not formally registered and that does not involve cash. We might then conceptually distinguish constituent economies of each of these subeconomies. The social economy under this scheme would contain the household or domestic economy, the communal or neighborhood economy, and the self-help or mutual-aid economy. Each of these could then itself be further subdivided and so on.

"The point," as Swingewood has said, "is that the totality is always part of something larger and the part is simultaneously a totality."[13] From the perspective of dialectical analysis, "the part"—in this case, informal economies—"cannot be abstracted from the whole and sociologically examined apart from it and then mechanically inserted again after analysis." Rather, the parts, like empiri-

12. Pahl, *Divisions of Labour*.
13. Alan Swingewood, *Marx and Modern Social Theory* (London: Macmillan Press, 1975), p. 57.

cal facts, "must be integrated into a whole or they remain abstract, and theoretically misleading."[14]

Acknowledging the wider context in considering component parts avoids a number of errors. For example, analyzing parts of a whole in isolation could easily lead a researcher intent on highlighting the reciprocal nature of exchange among members of social networks to the view that workers in the informal economy are unaffected by market forces. Considering the wider capitalist context, it would be absurd to suggest that just because a worker is unregistered she or he is somehow freed from market forces, and there may be some grounds for arguing that such a worker would be more subject to them. However, does this alone warrant calling his or her work market economic activity? Other criteria might be important in distinguishing informal work from the work done by formal employees.

From the naturalistic perspective, normative typologies that draw clear distinctions between types of informal economy are problematic. In the real world people are not divided neatly among types of informal economy, though they may spend more of their time doing some kinds of activity than others. It is for this reason that a useful typology may be one that addresses the interrelated nature of the types identified within it; these are overlapping and blurred rather than clearly distinct. To fail to acknowledge this might be particularly unhelpful given that the subject is in part characterized by its belying of boundaries.

*Explanatory issues*

The typological discussion implies that analysis that reifies the parts and

14. Ibid., pp. 44-45.

the whole from the human agents who produce them might be best avoided, since informal economies are nothing if they are not recurring outcomes of human action whose very production serves as the medium for further production. Put simply, informal economies exist only in the acts of doing; there are no institutional props to serve as reminders or cues.[15] This leads us to consider the macro-micro dimensions that influence the phenomenon.

At the macro level, we need to know the forces that have shaped the emergence of informal economies and the way these economies relate to the emergence of the wider structure. The process seems not to be one-way but mutually interactive, as some of us have tried to illustrate in our contributions to this volume. Nor is the informal economy consistently positive or negative in its effects. What are the abilities of informal economies to resist or reproduce the class, sex, and gender divisions within the wider structure? Under a capitalist economic system, do those with a communal or alternative base generate a different internal order from those founded on less intimate relationships? And if they do, is this necessary for the existence and further development of capitalism? Does this inversion and opposition of the formal explain why private entrepreneurial markets emerge under socialism?

It might also be possible to explain the existence of informal economies from a functional perspective as fulfilling some need, as with second economies in socialist societies; or overcoming restric-

15. For a theoretical perspective that takes account of the agency-structure relationship and that sees all human activities as recursive, meaning that they are continually recreated by social actors via the very means whereby they express themselves as actors, see Anthony Giddens, *The Constitution of Society* (Oxford: Polity Press, 1984).

tions such as market regulation, high taxes, or shortages; or providing testing grounds for innovation and enterprise. They may simply be residues from the past, in the process of being replaced or emerging to herald a postindustrial, postmaterialistic, people-oriented era. Without some sense of their historical context we would be unable to make sense of these trends.

At the micro level, we need to consider what motivates people to participate in informal economic activities. Do they have a choice? Some people, such as the single parent who takes up home-working, may have severely restricted choices. Others, such as the single academic who dabbles in farming, may be relatively free.

What are the satisfactions that are derived from the activity? Some of the evidence suggests that more than money is involved. To what extent are these activities motivated by the desire for status, prestige, social relations, reciprocity, competitive play, control over one's life, or simply the fun and excitement of beating the system? Or are we dealing here with what Goffman originally described as "secondary adjustments," the angles, ropes, gimmicks, dodges, deals, ins, and so forth that enable a person to survive as a social identity in a structured setting?[16]

Up to this point the discussion has focused on the conceptual issues raised by informal economies, but there are also substantial methodological issues, to which we now turn.

METHODOLOGICAL PERSPECTIVES

Developing empirical research on informal economies offers a number of

major difficulties and challenges. We are dealing with a phenomenon that has only recently emerged from the realm of speculation and conventional wisdom, where anecdotal description has predominated over systematic and rigorous research. These earlier approaches emerged largely due to the often concealed nature of the activities. The lack of conceptual clarity and the presence of disciplinary factionalism have created considerable difficulties in formulating an appropriate methodological perspective from which to study the phenomenon.

An approach that respects both individual human agency and the structural forces that shape and enable action is preferable to one biased in either direction. Of course, it is never easy to use methods that are simultaneously interpretive and positivistic, designed to elicit members' categories, shared meaning, and understanding and designed to obtain general empirical data on large numbers of people. The combined ethnography and follow-up survey method seems the most enlightened in this regard.

The logic of such a method for the study of informal economies was first formulated by Louis Ferman's team for his 1977 Detroit study and has become known as the Ferman Methodology.[17] Its objective was to develop and integrate two data bases, one ethnographic and the other survey. The aims of the ethnographic component of the study were to (1) obtain in-depth micro-level information on the processes and structures of exchange; (2) establish the meaning, attitudes, values, and norms concerning the activities of the parties to the transac-

16. Erving Goffman, "Characteristics of Total Institutions," in *Symposium on Preventative and Social Psychiatry* (Washington, DC: Government Printing Office, 1957).

17. See Louis A. Ferman, Louise E. Berndt, and Elaine Selo, *An Analysis of the Irregular Economy: Cash Flow in the Informal Sector* (Ann Arbor: University of Michigan; Detroit: Wayne State University, 1978).

tions; and (3) generate hypotheses.

Within a specific neighborhood the ethnographic observers were to focus on exchange as a specific unit of analysis, looking at what was being exchanged, the norms governing the exchange, the characteristics of the buyers and sellers, the place exchanges occurred, whether money was present, and how unique the exchange proved to be. These observations were to be made at different intervals so that some sense of whether exchanges were one-shot or patterned, repetitive occurrences could be established. Another consideration was the ecological context or spatial framework in which the exchange occurred. This involved cartographic sketching of the different spacial units, from the community and neighborhood to the particular dwellings, taking account of the commercial-residential mix and the economic history of the area. Important, too, were compiling portraits of how people became vendors and consumers; how informal exchanges were knitted together with formal work; how, over time, this formed a total work career; how economic and noneconomic resources and support systems underpinned these exchanges over a lifetime; and how, and under what conditions, informal exchanges evolved into increasingly more organized work efforts to become formal businesses. Finally, the ethnographic component was concerned to document the patterns of communication of information about bids to buy and offers to sell that were believed to be significant factors in shaping local informal economic activity.

The aim of the survey was to obtain a macro-level statistical portrait of (1) the frequency of informal exchanges; (2) the variety of types of exchange; (3) the monetary value of exchange; (4) the extensiveness of exchange; (5) the charac-

teristics of sellers and buyers; (6) the attitudes of consumers about such exchanges; and (7) the testing of hypotheses formulated from the ethnography. The survey was a study of household members' decision making in provisioning. It aimed to answer questions concerning how the goods and services were procured, who in a household was to be serviced, who bought and who supplied goods, and the attitudes and perceptions of these participants concerning the meaning of the exchanges, whether they were for economic necessity or intrinsically satisfying, and why some people may have resisted participation.

The two data bases were seen as complementary, the ethnographic permitting a microscopic examination and the survey data providing the broad, generalizable results. These were then interrelated to establish the reliability of observations. This was particularly important in a study where participants might conceal or mask their behavior or mislead the researchers because of the fear, anxiety, and danger of potential discovery.

Based on this methodology the University of Michigan-Wayne State University study of ten Detroit neighborhoods was begun. The study identified ten administrative school districts as neighborhood units, which were selected to represent income and racial composition as well as occupational variations. Ten trained ethnographers took up residence in these neighborhoods for a four-month period. Using the technique of participant observation, each ethnographer kept a daily log of observed informal exchanges, mapped the ecology of the neighborhood, recorded critical incidents of exchanges, developed portraits of typical informal economy participants, and charted the social and communication networks that were associated with the

informal exchanges. Based on the ethnographic information, a questionnaire
was constructed and administered by an
independent research team, using personal interviews with 284 households in
the ten neighborhoods. The results of
the study have been reported elsewhere.[18]

Subsequently, two further large-scale
empirical studies on informal economies
have explicitly been influenced by the
Ferman Methodology. In England in
1979 Ray Pahl and his team from the
University of Kent began a combined
ethnographic and household survey of
730 households on the Isle of Sheppey,[19]
and in 1981 James Smith and his colleagues at the University of Michigan's
Institute of Social Research undertook
a national survey of 2753 households
using an adapted version of the same
approach.[20] These three studies represent
exemplars of a pioneering methodological approach; its founding principles
have proven to be essential for the
generation of comprehensive accounts
of informal exchanges.[21]

18. Ibid.; Louis A. Ferman and Louise E.
Berndt, "The Irregular Economy," in *Informal
Institutions,* ed. Henry.
19. See Pahl, *Divisions of Labour.*
20. Kevin McCrohan and James Smith, "Informal Suppliers in the Underground Economy,"
*Statistics of Income Bulletin,* 3:27-34 (1982); idem,
"A Consumer Expenditure Approach to Estimating the Size of the Underground Economy,"
*Journal of Marketing,* 50:48-60 (1986).
21. In considering innovative methodologies
for studying informal economies, mention must be
made of the work of Gerald Mars and Yochanan
Altman. While not using survey techniques, Mars
and Altman studied the second economy in Soviet
Georgia by employing ethnography, structured
interviews, and life histories of a community of
5000 recently arrived immigrants from Soviet
Georgia to Israel. The "retrospective reconstruction" enabled them to obtain a rich data base on an
otherwise nonresearchable area. See Gerald Mars
and Yochanan Altman, "The Cultural Bases of
Soviet Georgia's Second Economy," *Soviet Studies,*
35:546-60 (1983).

## RESEARCH GAPS

Substantive research on informal economies has been no less a controversial
issue than the concept itself. As Duncan
Gallie points out:

By far the most controversial area of research
. . . concerns the informal economy. There
are those who think that the SSRC was
mistaken . . . to make this a central area for
financial support; there are those who consider that . . . it was worth initiating research,
but that the results of this research have
effectively destroyed the theories that stimulated it. And finally there are those who argue
that this remains one of the single most
important areas in which there should be
further funding.[22]

Limited by disciplinary interests and
by the politics of research funding,
studies in informal economies have been
narrowly channeled. Despite their critical stance, says Davis, researchers have
bought into "the established categories
of the system of analysis they seek to
revise." As he sardonically laments, "If
they have found a princedom by kissing
the toad of falseness, they should now
embrace imperfection. But in fact they
have at best been tentatively rebel-
lious."[23]

Part of the problem is that researchers
go where the money is greatest and the
resistance least. Just as criminologists
have traditionally taken crime to be
street crime and largely ignored crimes
of powerful corporations and government, so informal economy researchers
concentrate on irregular trade among
those on survival incomes. Government
agencies such as the Internal Revenue
Service interested in tax revenue loss are
able to offer funding to researchers who

22. Duncan Gallie, "Directions for the Future,"
in *New Approaches to Economic Life,* ed. Roberts,
Finnegan, and Gallie, p. 522.
23. Davis, "Rules Not Laws," p. 503.

seek to identify who the "scroungers" and "tax dodgers" are among the poor and welfare recipients,[24] leaving more critical research to be independently financed. Less attractive to such agencies have been local-area studies, and as a result there have been few of these conducted. Instead of concentrating on areas of urban poverty it might be instructive for such studies to explore whether "the informal economy flourishes best in areas of relative prosperity where it can feed upon a growing industrial base and where households have the disposable income to buy the services it can provide."[25]

Also missing are historical studies of informal economic activities. Particularly useful would be studies of the shift from the medieval principle of a "berth" for everyone, irrespective of their employment status, to the notion, peculiar to industrial societies, of the right to employment and with it the idea of work outside employment.[26] This raises the whole issue of the work of livelihood as opposed to work for income. It signals the importance of status and social position in relation to making a living and denotes the centrality of fulfilling ourselves socially, which cannot be wholly replaced by formal employment.[27]

Considerable research has been done

on household work and women's hidden labor, but studies showing the interrelationship between these and changing patterns of formal employment would be useful, as would those that focused upon household work strategies and how these have changed over time.[28]

While studies of illegal trading in stolen goods and services are available,[29] little has been done on the relationship between irregular work and illegal activity.[30] There have been one or two recent studies of the relationship between young people, irregular work, and drug use[31] and reports on the informal economy and female sexual slavery,[32] but much more needs to be done. The broad issue of how different informal economies sustain each other is one that has been particularly neglected outside of Marxist contributions.

Studies that focus on the social class, ethnic, age, and sex composition of participants in informal economies have

24. See esp. Carl P. Simon and Ann D. Witte, *Beating the System: The Underground Economy* (Boston: Auburn House, 1982).

25. Gallie, "Directions for the Future," p. 522.

26. Krishan Kumar, "The Social Culture of Work: Work, Employment and Unemployment as Ways of Life," *New Universities Quarterly*, vol. 34 (1979); idem, "Unemployment as a Problem in the Development of Industrial Societies" (Paper delivered at the meeting of EEC-FAST programme, Marseilles, France, 23-26 Nov. 1981). See also J. I. Gershuny and R. E. Pahl, "Work Outside Employment: Some Preliminary Speculations," in *Informal Institutions*, ed. Henry.

27. For an approach that is critical of this perspective, see Roy Carr-Hill, "Whither (Research on) Unemployment?" in *New Approaches to Eco-*

*nomic Life*, ed. Roberts, Finnegan, and Gallie.

28. See esp. Jonathan I. Gershuny, *Social Innovation and the Division of Labour* (New York: Oxford University Press, 1983); Roberts, Finnegan, and Gallie, eds., *New Approaches to Economic Life*, sec. 6, which discusses household roles in a changing economy.

29. See esp. Marilyn Walsh and Duncan Chappell, "Operational Parameters in the Stolen Property System," *Journal of Criminal Justice*, 2:113-29 (1974); Carl Klockars, *The Professional Fence* (New York: Free Press, 1974); Marilyn Walsh, *The Fence* (Westport, CT: Greenwood Press, 1977).

30. See, however, Stuart Henry, *The Hidden Economy: The Context and Control of Borderline Crime* (Oxford: Martin Robertson, 1978); Simon and Witte, *Beating the System*; Philip Mattera, *Off the Books: The Rise of the Underground Economy* (New York: St. Martin's Press, 1985).

31. John Auld, Nicholas Dorn, and Nigel South, "Irregular Work, Irregular Pleasures: Heroin in the 1980's," in *Confronting Crime*, ed. Roger Matthews and Jock Young (London: Sage, 1986).

32. Kathleen Barry, "The Underground Economic System of Pimping," *Journal of International Affairs*, 35:117-27 (1981).

not been conducted, although some of the work on ethnic business is relevant here.[33] How far informal activities are the province of children, youth, the disabled, and the retired is an empirical question that at present we cannot answer.[34] Indeed, there is a case for relating demographic information about who participates in local labor markets, who participates in self-help and mutual-aid groups, who holds double jobs, and so on to produce a composite picture of who participates most actively in informal economies.

Less obvious is to examine whether there exist informal information networks and informal knowledge exchanges in which people "list their skills, the condition under which they are willing to serve as models for others who want to learn these skills and the addresses at which they can be reached."[35] This information may be part of a network of gossip, and the way it is communicated could tell us much about the way an informal system of education may underpin informal economies.[36]

Informal institutions within existing formal institutions may also be usefully researched from the perspective of informal economies. How far are formal decisions dependent upon an informal exchange of information? Clearly, this has been the hallmark of insider trading and covert foreign policy operations by the U.S. government. Instead of imagining that openness in business and government characterizes Western industrial democracy, perhaps we should make the assumption that beneath every formal institutional arrangement there is an informal set of customs and practices that are not themselves wholly explicable as rules or norms. Studies of such informal networks of information trading would be invaluable to our understanding of the way social life functions. Instructive, too, would be an examination of the way the media constructs and manages information about what counts as the informal economy, how it presents the motives of those who are involved, and whether the media's management of information is politically manipulated.[37]

Finally, an important but less obvious direction for research on informal economies is to examine their contribution to disaster management. It is clear, for example, that in the initial stages of natural disasters, such as earthquakes or floods, informal neighborhood networks are often first on the scene. We need to know how far informal support and coping networks are available, whether they are instantly formed in such situations, how their effectiveness is impeded, and how they may better function. Some research is currently under way, for example, to look into the role informal economies might play in reconstructing economic exchange following a cataclysmic event such as an asteroid impact, or a nuclear war, which would destroy the U.S. industrial infrastructure.[38]

33. See Sandra Wallman, "Structures of Informality: Variation in Local Style and Scope for Unofficial Economic Organisation in London," in *New Approaches to Economic Life*, ed. Roberts, Finnegan, and Gallie; Roger Waldinger, "Immigrant Enterprise and the Structure of the Labour Market," in ibid.

34. See Ferman and Berndt, "Irregular Economy."

35. Ivan Illich, *Deschooling Society* (London: Calder Boyars, 1971), p. 79.

36. See Leslie M. Dow, "High Weeds in Detroit," *Urban Anthropology*, 6:111-28 (1977); Colin Ward, "Community Education," in *Informal Institutions*, ed. Henry.

37. Stuart Henry, "Fiddling as a Media Issue," *Media Reporter*, 6:41-43 (1982); Peter Golding and Sue Middleton, "Why Is the Press So Obsessed with Welfare Scroungers?" *New Society*, 46:195-97 (1978).

38. Cantor, Henry, and Rayner, *Markets, Distribution, and Exchange*.

## POLICY IMPLICATIONS

Many academic discussions of informal economies, with the exception of some writings by tax economists, are noticeably lacking in their treatment of the government as an actor and, more specifically, in their treatment of public policies. Yet governments vary radically in their reactions to informal economies and specifically to irregular work and those engaged in it. Government policy on tax, welfare, and crime shapes—if not creates—informal economies by defining what is formal and legitimate and thereby what is not.

### Taxation policy

Tax policy issues include such questions as whether or not tax policy creates incentives to participate in informal work or whether it simply changes the sectors in which such work would occur, and how or whether to control noncompliance.

We can observe both different amounts and different government tolerances of informal activity across different countries. Table 1 shows the range of estimates of a composite of informal economies described as the underground economy for different countries. Thus in Italy, which tops the league for amounts of informal activity, there is a high tolerance of it on the part of government and the public. In contrast, in West Germany, where there is much less of it, there is also much less tolerance. The pattern of government attempts to control it also vary almost directly with changes in unemployment; the higher the unemployment, the greater the enforcement. In the United States there is a paradox that remains to be explained: there is a very high level of informal work activity with an implied public acceptance and tolerance of it coexisting with a vigorously expressed, if not enforced, government policy to apprehend noncompliant citizens, spearheaded by the Internal Revenue Service.

In one of the most sophisticated attempts to measure the relative sizes of informal economies for different countries, Frey and Weck-Hanneman argue that the burden of taxation and of regulation as well as tax morality significantly influences the size and development of the informal sector.[39] Because of their simultaneous consideration of multiple unobserved variables, their approach produces rankings that question the accepted truth among many economists that high-tax countries have larger than average informal economies.

As can be seen from Table 2, high-tax countries such as Sweden, Denmark, and Holland do have a relatively high level of informal economic activity. Similarly, Spain, Japan, and Switzerland, being low-tax countries, have a relatively low level of informal economic activity. However, Italy is a low-tax country and has, on most estimates, one of the highest levels of informal economic activity. This circumstance suggests that tax levels are not a sole determinant. This is explainable by incorporating other measures such as tax morality. On the measures available, Frey and Weck-Hanneman show that Switzerland has the highest tax morality while Italy has the lowest, but other influential factors are the country's rate of unemployment and its level of economic development.

In a review of these issues Carter distinguishes between the incentive and the opportunity for informal economic activity. He says, "High tax rates and

39. Bruno S. Frey and Hannelore Weck-Hanneman, "The Hidden Economy as an 'Unobserved' Variable," *European Economic Review*, 26:33-53 (1984).

TABLE 1

ESTIMATES OF THE SIZE OF THE UNDERGROUND ECONOMY
IN SELECTED COUNTRIES

| Country | Range of Estimates as Percentage of Gross National Product |
|---|---|
| Italy | 10-33 |
| United States | 4-33 |
| Soviet Union | 20-25 |
| Canada | 5- 22 |
| Sweden | 1-17 |
| Norway | 2- 16 |
| Japan | 4-15 |
| United Kingdom | 1-15 |
| Australia | 3-13 |
| West Germany | 2-12 |
| France | 8-10 |
| Netherlands | 5-10 |
| Austria | 4- 8 |
| Spain | 1- 6 |
| Switzerland | 3- 4 |

SOURCE: Adapted from Carol S. Carson, "The Underground Economy: An Introduction," *Survey of Current Business*, p. 33 (May 1984); Michael Carter, "Issues in the Hidden Economy— A Survey," *Economic Record*, 60:209-21 (1984).

TABLE 2

SIZE ESTIMATES OF THE HIDDEN ECONOMY AS PERCENTAGE OF
GROSS NATIONAL PRODUCT IN 17 COUNTRIES OF THE ORGANIZATION
FOR ECONOMIC COOPERATION AND DEVELOPMENT, 1978

| Country | Percentage of Gross National Product |
|---|---|
| Sweden | 13.2 |
| Belgium | 12.1 |
| Denmark | 11.8 |
| Italy | 11.4 |
| Netherlands | 9.6 |
| France | 9.4 |
| Norway | 9.2 |
| Austria | 8.9 |
| Canada | 8.7 |
| Federal Republic of Germany | 8.6 |
| United States | 8.3 |
| United Kingdom | 8.0 |
| Finland | 7.6 |
| Ireland | 7.2 |
| Spain | 6.5 |
| Switzerland | 4.3 |
| Japan | 4.1 |

SOURCE: Bruno S. Frey and Hannelore Weck-Hanneman, "The Hidden Economy as an 'Unobserved' Variable," *European Economic Review*, 26:46 (1984).

pervasive regulation supply the incentive for hidden activity." The opportunity for evading taxes and regulations depends upon development, social structure, and tax compliance. Some countries may have high incentives but low opportunities or vice versa. Those with low opportunities and low incentives, such as Switzerland, are thus found on the bottom of any hierarchy of size, while those with high incentives and high opportunities, such as the Scandinavian and Benelux countries, are found high in the rankings of informal economic activity.

Carter also points out that the relationship between tax and informal economic activity, in general, is not one-way. Thus countries like Italy have low tax rates in part because people rely on social networks to provide mutual support, thus requiring less in the way of formal services and therefore less taxation.

We suggest that more work of a comparative nature that looks systematically across countries should be done. Of particular interest would be a comparison of the different policies that governments have toward off-the-books employment, the different sanctions they use to enforce these, and the relative rates of prosecution to apprehension. Also, it would be interesting to relate the relative difference between the rates of informal economic activity for different countries to the relative difference in their crime rates. For the United States, for example, the crime rate and the level of informal economic activity are both relatively high, whereas for Switzerland they are both relatively low.[40]

In the United States, one of the most interesting policy questions is raised by the passage of the 1986 Tax Reform Act, most sections of which become effective in 1987. For those people at the bottom end of the socioeconomic scale who have relied upon informal income sources to get by and make out, this legislation has effectively decriminalized their work. Will this result in their ceasing to do informal work or will they now engage in extra work and follow the increased threshold to remain in the off-the-books category?

The same law produced tax-rate changes for all categories of income, not just the marginal working poor. There was also elimination of many of the itemized deductions available to, and heavily used by, the middle-income and upper-income earners to lower their effective marginal rate. It remains to be seen whether and to what extent the new lower rates will bring changes in these persons' use of off-the-books workers and irregular services. How will these changes affect the class distribution of irregular work, and will the changes further reinforce exploitation by the most powerful and active members of the society?

Another and related issue is the effects of the enforcement of tax laws on the public and the social costs of these. If informal economic activity is being used to supplement welfare for the poor, which some studies now seriously question,[41] is its control debilitating for that section of the population? Would it make more sense to put all the emphasis on major tax evaders and leave the bottom end of the social hierarchy rela-

40. Marshall B. Clinard, *Cities with Little Crime: The Case of Switzerland* (New York: Cambridge University Press, 1978); Martin Killias, "Switzerland," in *International Handbook of Contemporary Developments in Criminology: Europe,*

*Africa, the Middle East and Asia,* ed. Elmer H. Johnson (Westport, CT: Greenwood Press, 1983).
41. Pahl, *Divisions of Labour.*

tively unpoliced? In the absence of effective policies for the transition of the unemployed to the formal work force, informal work may provide a means of work training and a source of integrity that countertrend the dependency notion of welfare checks. Alternatively, is heavy policing likely to force to the surface contradictions that might otherwise be masked and through their exposure bring structural changes in the formal economy? From this perspective, policing evasion might indirectly be an agent of social change, while failure to police it might better sustain the status quo.

Put simply, when tax policy and its enforcement are altered, changes occur in the relationship between informal economies, the formal market economy, and the redistributive economy, and we need to know about these changes if we are to formulate and implement effective policy. The current situation provides the opportunity for a quasi-experimental design to measure the effects of tax reform on the amount of participation and which groups are affected by such reform. For example, if a panel survey could be done for each of the next three years, we could get a sense of irregular participation and how this changes, as the public's behavior changes, in relation to the new tax law. It would also be useful to follow up such work at five-year and ten-year intervals to examine the long-term effects.

*Labor policy*

In considering labor policy it is worth distinguishing informal work inside employment, such as the pilfering and fiddling of goods and services, and the unofficial use of company time, from work outside employment such as irregular, off-the-books work and household or domestic labor.

A particularly important area of labor policy concerns industrial relations. Without an understanding of the important role of informal work inside employment it is difficult to appreciate the way in which organizational and technological change can affect workplace relations, as Gerald Mars has convincingly argued.[42]

At a more macro level of labor policy we can see that an appreciation of informal work outside of employment is essential if a realistic assessment of a society's economic performance is to be gauged. The measure of labor force participation, as an indicator of a nation's economic activity, is severely understated it if excludes the estimated one-fifth to one-third of the population engaged in irregular work. Related to this is the question of what relationship exists between formal employment and informal work in terms of the relative participation rates. If the most active members of the formal economy are the most active in informal economies,[43] then what kind of unemployment policy would be most effective in stimulating those inactive in both these sectors?

As Hoyman points out in this volume, in no area of labor are the policy implications as great as in the work status of women. Not only would labor force participation rates be transformed were we to take account of women's participation in the irregular economy, but classic measures of economic activity such as the gross national product would increase by as much as one-third if the value of their contribution were counted.

42. Gerald Mars, *Cheats at Work: An Anthropology of Workplace Crime* (London: George Allen & Unwin, 1982), p. 184.

43. Jeremy Alden, "Holding Two Jobs: An Examination of 'Moonlighting,' " in *Informal Institutions,* ed. Henry.

This also has implications for the value of the work women do whether it is in the irregular economy or not, for the increasing visibility of their status, and for the effects that this may have on their self-image. One clear indication is that if women's hidden labor were included, the progress toward comparability would likely be shown to be inadequate since when all work that women do is included the overall wage of women relative to men is even lower.

Day care is a critical policy issue for women's emerging status in both formal and informal economies. It is noteworthy that the current debate about welfare reform has produced an overwhelming consensus for the workfare approach to welfare as a panacea for the problems of mothers receiving Aid to Families with Dependent Children. However, unless low-cost, safe day care is available, welfare and low-income mothers will be unable to pay for the day care costs let alone the other expenses. The provision of such day care could transform the options of those millions of women who currently are forced to accept employment at minimum wage.

*Welfare policy*

A related issue concerns welfare policy generally and government reliance on informal economies, particularly social economies of mutual aid and self-help, care networks that are often provided by women. The argument of some authors, that unemployment and the fiscal problems of the welfare state can be absorbed by encouraging a greater use of self-help solutions,[44] can be criticized because

such a solution would alleviate the pressure on government and professional care-givers to address the inefficiencies of their services.[45] Indeed, as Cornford says, "Self-help requires means, and it will be a bitter mockery if it becomes the excuse for a prosperous, secure and well paid majority to turn its back on the sick, the disabled and the poor and unemployed."[46] Similarly, some have questioned whether relying on informal economies as a lubricant for inefficiencies and inequities in the wider economy is wise, since "greater benefits might be achieved . . . by removing unwise regulations."[47]

Indeed, one of the dangers of informal economies is that they may actually prevent policy reform by providing grounds for governments to off-load their more difficult functions, to dodge their responsibilities, and to have a ready-made excuse to avoid social change. Moreover, informal economies may effectively palliate those with immediate needs and pacify the most vociferous of society's critics who are deluded into thinking that their problems are solvable through local action. Energy is then diverted from more fundamental criticism of the wider society because of the day-to-day demands of informal economic activity. Whether informal economies are socially beneficial or not, there is no question in our minds that adequate policy must address their presence if policymakers are going to gain a

44. J. I. Gershuny, "The Informal Economy: Its Role in Post-Industrial Society," *Futures*, pp. 3-15 (Feb. 1979); Rolf G. Heinze and Thomas Olk, "Development of the Informal Economy: A Strategy for Resolving the Crisis of the Welfare State," *Futures*, pp. 189-204 (June 1982).

45. Stuart Henry, "The Dangers of Self-Help Groups," *New Society*, 44:654-56 (1978).

46. Cornford, "The Revival of Self-Help," in *Informal Institutions*, ed. Henry, p. 197.

47. Michael Carter, "Issues in the Hidden Economy—A Survey," *Economic Record*, 60:219 (1984).

greater handle on the outcome of their interventions.

## Criminal justice policy

There are a number of ways that informal economies affect crime and criminal justice policy. It has long been recognized by criminologists that the official crime statistics only account for the tip of the iceberg as far as the actual level of crime is concerned. The vast bulk of criminal activity goes unreported and often undiscovered, even by the victims.[48] A portion of that undiscovered crime is the illegal supply and exchange of stolen goods and services.

One of the obvious policy implications for criminal justice is that if crime-control policies are based on the discovered official crimes and these are unrepresentative of all crime, then those that are undiscovered are likely to remain uncontrolled. A good example of this is the long-held assumption that stolen goods are the direct outcome of active predators such as thieves and burglars, who search for passive receivers of their stolen merchandise. Others, however, take the view that the fences of stolen goods are actually the driving force behind the thieves, controlling their operations. Some even suggest that the fences are unofficially permitted this role by politicians and police in exchange for favors, such as information on thieves in order to produce an overall satisfactory prosecution rate.[49] Once this is recog-

nized, the focus of crime-control policy will have to shift to the traders and the buyers rather than their predatory accomplices if it is to cut the parasitic behavior effectively.[50]

A similar revision of policy is necessary if we take into account the role of informal economies and drug addiction. The conventional view is that narcotics cause crime and that cutting addiction cuts crime. Auld, Dorn, and South argue that the low level of welfare payments is inadequate to satisfy basic needs for housing, clothing, heating, and food.[51] In order to meet these needs people engage in irregular work, and it is through their involvement in this partially illegal irregular economy that they sometimes encounter and come to buy and sell narcotics such as heroin. Thus crime, in the form of illegal trading in goods and services, can be seen to lead to heroin use. Auld, Dorn, and South pinpoint the policy implications of this exactly:

A shift in economic policies that reduced the extent to which the irregular economy permeates increasing numbers of inner-city and other areas would reduce petty crime, and with it much heroin use in its presently expanding forms. A direct assault by law enforcement agencies against episodic heroin users, by contrast, would do relatively little to dent the criminal aspects of the irregular economy in which they play only a part.[52]

Also important is the study of the motivations of those engaged in illegal

---

48. See Richard F. Sparks, *Research on Victims of Crime: Accomplishments, Issues and New Directions* (Washington, DC: Government Printing Office, 1982); Bureau of Justice Statistics, *Report to the Nation on Crime and Justice: The Data* (Washington, DC: Department of Justice, 1983).

49. Klockars, *Professional Fence*; Stuart Henry, "On the Fence," *British Journal of Law and Society*, 4:124-33 (1977).

50. On inhibiting traders, see Ted Roselius and Douglas Benton, "Marketing Theory and the Fencing of Stolen Goods," *Denver Law Journal*, 50:177-205 (1977); on inhibiting buyers, see Joseph F. Sheley and Kenneth D. Bailey, "New Directions for Anti-Theft Policy: Reductions in Stolen Goods Buyers," *Journal of Criminal Justice*, 13:399-415 (1985).

51. Auld, Dorn, and South, "Irregular Work, Irregular Pleasures."

52. Ibid., p. 173

trading activities. As numerous studies have shown,[53] the meaning of engaging in illegal activity can be social rather than monetary. People participate not only for material rewards but for the satisfactions of prestige, status, reciprocity, and even altruism. Acknowledging the existence of informal economies demands that we do not simply assume that the meaning of their informal illegal trading is the same as that of trading in the wider market economy of capitalism, that is, that their informal illegal trading is motivated by material profit. Where the underlying meaning of illegal trading is predominantly social, crime control policy based on increasing the material costs of trading is unlikely to be effective. More appropriate responses might involve increasing the legitimate opportunities for obtaining the social satisfactions, and placing greater reliance on informal networks of social control, since these operate through the very communities and networks that channel illegal trade.[54]

This does not, however, imply that we simply need to develop a more sophisticated undercover response in order to penetrate the underground. It means instead that we need to adopt a new perspective toward crime. As some commentators have recognized, traditional criminological and criminal justice research that accepts the fragmentation of crime from the communities and networks in which it is inextricably tied is unhelpful. Cyril Robinson, for example, says criminal justice should en-gage in "putting reality back together, of thinking whole" and calls for an approach to community justice research in which we

study the interpenetration of communal by societal structures and values, how each generates "different networks of social interaction," the competitive beckoning call of success and prestige from local and societal institutions, the pattern of local and national elites and their relative influence, the extent that community economic activities are embedded in the web of social relations, and how all these influence the problems, possibilities and interplay of formal and informal social control.[55]

## CONCLUSION

The challenge of informal economies to social science is that they offer a glimpse at the dark side of a moon. They at once enable us to see familiar structures and processes in their formation and to see how human agents manage their social creations. The task for anyone defining, classifying, and explaining informal economies is enormous, for its complexity defies any simplistic treatment and requires that we draw on all our disciplinary insights and knowledge simultaneously. Theoretically, informal economies offer an ideal context to explore some of the new directions in integrated theorizing that have emerged in the 1980s.[56] Empirically, the area is

53. Henry, *Hidden Economy*; Ferman and Berndt, "Irregular Economy"; Mars, *Cheats at Work*.

54. Stuart Henry and Gerald Mars, "Crime at Work: The Social Construction of Amateur Property Theft," *Sociology*, 12:245-63 (1978); Stuart Henry, "Controlling the Hidden Economy," *Employee Relations*, 1:17-22 (1979); idem, *Private Justice* (Boston: Routledge & Kegan Paul, 1983).

55. Cyril Robinson, "Criminal Justice Research: Two Competing Futures," *Crime and Social Justice,* no. 23, p. 122 (1985).

56. See especially Giddens, *Constitution of Society*; Karen Knorr-Cetina and Aaron Cicourel, eds., *Advances in Social Theory and Methodology: Towards an Integration of Micro- and Macro-Sociologies* (Boston: Routledge & Kegan Paul, 1981). For a seminal application of integrated theorizing to the relations between formal and informal institutions, see Peter Fitzpatrick, "Law and Societies," *Osgood Hall Law Journal,* 22:115-38 (1984).

perhaps one of the most important that social science has discovered since the recognition that industrialization was not going to unify all nations. What seems to be emerging from the last ten years of work is certain evidence that people can make a difference to the structures that shape their lives, that many more people are involved in them than their peripheral status would suggest, and that the rewards of participation are often as much social as material.

# Book Department

## INTERNATIONAL RELATIONS AND POLITICS

BLITZER, WOLF. *Between Washington and Jerusalem: A Reporter's Notebook.* Pp. xii, 259. New York: Oxford University Press, 1985. $15.95.

SHARKANSKY, IRA. *What Makes Israel Tick? How Domestic Policy Makers Cope with Constraints.* Pp. xii, 184. Chicago: Nelson-Hall, 1985. $22.95. Paperbound, $9.95.

For those who consider themselves close friends and determined supporters of Israel, *Between Washington and Jerusalem* offers much that they will find agreeable. In a descriptive and journalistic style Wolf Blitzer provides a ringing affirmation of U.S.-Israeli ties. Based on extensive interviews with major figures in the U.S., American Jewish, and Israeli political establishments, and on insights culled from many years of experience as the Washington correspondent of the *Jerusalem Post*, Blitzer focuses on the complex relationship between American Jews, the various branches of the U.S. government, and the government of Israel.

Yet for those who view U.S.-Israeli relations more open-mindedly, acknowledging both benefits and costs, or for those with greater experience of the issues raised by the U.S.-Israeli relationship, Blitzer's book is disappointing and disturbing. It is disappointing for several reasons. First, Blitzer's insider and reportorial perspective rarely sheds new light on the major issues that are at the heart of the events he has recorded. He is thorough in presenting the personalistic aspects of these events, but as a result the book is a forest of anecdotal details. It seems that the only criterion for including a fact, story, or quotation is that it reflect favorably on Israel. This leads to the second disappointing aspect of the book: it is so clearly one-sided. Blitzer has done an excellent job in his daily work as a reporter, but he has not applied his critical or investigative faculties as sharply in preparing this book. More accurately, he applies those faculties only to the Washington side of his story. Whenever he turns to the Jerusalem side, they are conspicuously absent.

Finally, the book is disappointing because in making his case Blitzer seems unable to escape the shopworn conventional wisdom that seeks to meld realpolitik and morality into a unified justification of U.S. support. Israel's status as a democracy and as a symbol of the Holocaust, its vulnerability to the Arab states, despite its power to deter Soviet ambitions in the region, its role as an intelligence asset for the West, all of these are called into play in an effort to persuade American readers that U.S. and Israeli interests in the Middle East are the same and that where they diverge, Israel's interests should prevail.

It is Blitzer's emphasis on the primacy of Israel's interests that is disturbing, especially in his portrayal of American Jews. Unless American Jews are actively supporting Israel, they are shown as failing in their "special responsibility." Whatever the Israeli government does, American Jews, especially those in positions of political power, are expected to fall into line. If not, as Blitzer points out, they will be "quickly brought into line." Support for Israel is seen as properly reflexive. He quotes a leading figure in the Jewish community: " 'Unless something is really pressing, really critical or fundamental, you parrot Israel's line.' " For another American Jewish leader the issue is very simple: " 'The [Amerian Jews] who are critical are the ones who are hostile to Israel.' " This is disturbing not only because it seeks to replace the emotional, intellectual, and political autonomy of American Jews with an unthinking commitment to Israel, and because it establishes a political litmus test upon which the identity of American Jews as Jews is shown to rest, but also because we cannot doubt that Blitzer is accurately depicting the mind-set of the leading figures in the American Jewish community. Only time will tell whether this abdication of a more critical role has helped to sustain Israel or has in fact contributed to developments that threaten Israel's future.

*What Makes Israel Tick?* is a descriptive survey of the management and organization of political interests in Israel from a public policy or public administration perspective. In this sense, the policies that Blitzer presents to us as given are shown by Sharkansky as the consequence of an involved and contentious process. Taking the historic 1977 elections, which brought the Likud Party to power for the first time, as an opportunity to explore the learning process of a new government, Sharkansky primarily covers the politics of economic policymaking. Though he includes a chapter on religion and politics, it is weaker than the sections on budgetary issues, where he brings the insights of firsthand experience in the policy process to his work. Overall, Sharkansky finds that despite significant distinctions between the Labor and Likud parties on the level of rhetoric, the constraints on policymakers lead to relatively high levels of consistency in actual policies. At the same time, the recognition and acceptance of these constraints constitute the great and painful lesson that the Likud Party must learn. In short, Sharkansky has produced a good introduction to public administration in Israel, which is strongest on budgetary and fiscal matters. Though it contains few new insights in other areas, the book nonetheless manages to cover a lot of ground quite succinctly.

STEVEN HEYDEMANN

University of Chicago
Illinois

BUEHRIG, EDWARD H. *The Perversity of Politics.* Pp. 116. Wolfeboro, NH: Croom Helm, 1986. $27.50.

This volume expresses Buehrig's "lack of certainty as to exactly what lesson the pursuit of political science for some fifty years has taught me" and does so in elegant, lapidary prose. But since Buehrig is not certain how to reduce politics to a science, it is hard for a reviewer to summarize his argument in less space than he takes to set it forth. Suffice it to say that he emphasizes the unforeseen and incalculable aspect of politics, a "quest for security" that involves both conflict and cooperation—inevitably and inescapably. But, to cap the complexity, "conflict can have a positive effect in and of itself," largely through the stimulus to cooperation within a particular group that conflict with an outside enemy may arouse.

Buehrig devotes an interesting chapter to the ambiguous and changing relationships between religion and secular government. As he points out, religious collision created the modern pattern of politics:

Always theoretically incompatible, universalisms, whether Islamic, Christian, or Chinese, became practically so when discovery—joined by philosophy—exposed their ethnocentrism.... Legitimisation of authority and its allocation could no longer pander to ideological fantasy. The upshot was transition to a pattern of authority below the pretension of universal rule. International law—newly conceived—lodged sovereignty in territorial units and prescribed legal equality between them. Thus personal jurisdiction natural to a community of believers—as in Islam and Christianity—gave way to territorial jurisdiction divided among independent entities. Further still, authority—no longer sanctified from above—came to rest on consent from below (p. 29).

But a world of sovereign, independent, and rival states has its difficulties, too. The book concludes:

The limited warfare of the eighteenth century bore a meaningful relationship to the attainment of political goals. As war has since become increasingly total and as its meaningfulness as an instrument of policy has steadily declined, it is ironical—testimony to the perversity of politics—that the sacrifices of conflict, rendered ever greater by science and technology, have yielded very little indeed to the inviting prospects of cooperation (p. 112).

The least satisfactory part of the book is the second chapter, entitled "The Power Overtone." The meaning of this unfamiliar phrase remains opaque to me. From the examples he uses, Buehrig makes clear that it refers to behavior aimed at asserting prestige and/or honor. But these intangibles seem interchangeable with "influence" in his vocabulary, and the chapter concludes by stating that it was none of these, but hope that provoked American entry into World War I, although he seems to be using that involvement as an example of the "power overtone" in action.

But such confusion—or seeming confusion—is uncharacteristic. Elsewhere the volume is clear, concise, well informed, and wise. His principal message, perhaps, is this:

The central importance of law—as a means of coping with the power overtone and of coordinating networks of personal relations—needs to be greatly emphasized. But alone, it is not enough. However impressive architecturally, its efficacy rests on a substratum of political culture affording a degree of trust among strangers (beyond family, clan and tribe) that tempers political competition and invests economic enterprise with confidence.

That trust, he goes on, "is a precarious achievement," historically conditioned, and depends on "responsiveness to rational and moral influence and practice of an accustomed civility."

Buehrig's book is eminently civil, and as such it counts as a real, if minor, contribution to the sort of politics he and other liberally minded persons seek to encourage.

WILLIAM H. McNEILL
University of Chicago
Illinois


CABLE, JAMES. *The Geneva Conference of 1954 on Indochina.* Pp. xii, 179. New York: St. Martin's Press, 1986, $32.50.

CHADDA, MAYA. *Paradox of Power: The United States in Southwest Asia, 1973-1984.* Pp. xi, 278. Santa Barbara, CA: ABC-CLIO, 1986. $35.00. Paperbound, $20.00.

At first glance these volumes have little in common. Despite its title, Cable's book is not an account of the Geneva Conference per se, but of the British diplomacy that led to and shaped the conference, while the Chadda study concerns U.S. foreign policy. Cable reviews events in 1954 that concerned Southeast Asia; Chadda begins two decades later with events in a quite different part of the world.

On further reflection, however, it is apparent that they overlap in various ways. Each concerns efforts by great powers to impose order and stability in sensitive areas of the Third World. Southeast and Southwest Asia were, and remain, arenas where the interests of major states intersect, raising the distinct possibility of direct confrontation. Next, each author emphasizes the impact of domestic political factors on foreign policy. Each points out how great powers displayed limited understanding of the powerful domestic forces at work in either geographical area. Third, despite the implications of the preceding point for theory in the field, neither book involves any serious application of theory or attempts to translate the findings into theoretical terms. For the most part, Cable and Chadda recount events and offer analysis only within the framework of the events that unfolded.

Finally, both give attention—modestly in one, centrally in the other—to the American tendency to overvalue and improperly employ military power and its related instruments—arms transfers, security assistance, and the like—at the expense of other tools of state-craft. With respect to Southeast Asia this led to Washington being odd man out at the Geneva Conference, and to a determined American effort—ultimately military in nature—to frustrate the intended results of the Conference. In Southeast Asia it has meant a heavy investment in arms transfers, military bases, and power projection forces with, Chadda concludes, no commensurate gains in U.S. influence or regional stability.

The Cable book is fine reading and will be of interest to students of either British foreign policy or the postwar history of Indochina. It offers an insider's perspective—Cable was on the British delegation to the Conference—and richly conveys the human dimension of diplomacy through brief but penetrating sketches of the leading personalities. It takes issue with certain myths about the Conference and sensibly concludes that the chief result of the Conference—and of Britain's role in it—was to get Europe well out of the disaster in Southeast Asia that American policy was eventually to produce.

Maya Chadda covers the international politics of the region from Egypt to Pakistan in a smooth and readable fashion, quite an accomplishment in view of the detailed information presented. The discussion of U.S. policy in the region consistently links it to American global problems and perspectives, and proceeds from one administration to the next in exploring the intellectual conceptions that have guided American actions. The ultimate thrust of her analysis is rejection of the Reagan administration's approach to overestimating Soviet influence and the Soviet threat in Southwest Asia, relying too

heavily on military instruments and failing to understand fully the regional and local dimensions of conflict and change in the societies in that area. Chadda does, however, find the administration being more flexible in Reagan's second term.

PATRICK M. MORGAN
Washington State University
Pullman

DOWER, JOHN W. *War without Mercy: Race and Power in the Pacific War.* Pp. xii, 399. New York: Pantheon Books, 1986. $22.50.

The war in the Pacific was, as a continuing stream of scholarship reminds us, a savage affair. Forty years of peace and friendship between the United States and Japan have done little to soften the images of the conflict: Pearl Harbor, the Death March on Bataan, the grim fighting afloat and on blood-soaked islands, the suicidal resistance of doomed Japanese troops, the fire-bombings of Japanese civilians, the atomic strikes on Hiroshima and Nagasaki. So harrowing was the conflict, and so voluminous the literature concerned with it, that one is almost startled to find a study that not only adds a virtually new dimension to the story, but offers a remarkably original interpretation of why the conflict proceeded along its particularly brutal path. The thesis of John Dower's *War without Mercy* is something of a shock: the struggle in the Pacific was a race war. That fact, Dower holds, is central to an understanding of why Americans and Japanese fought one another as long and as hard as they did.

According to Dower, many of the war's excesses—including the barbarous treatment of or unwillingness to take prisoners, and the massive assaults on civilians—stemmed from deeply ingrained racism on both sides. Centuries of tradition had taught the Japanese to exalt their Yamato race above all others, a view that easily bred contempt for their enemies; they were convinced that Americans were a decadent and unclean people with no stomach for a fight. This outlook extended even to other Asians—thus the ghastly slaughter of noncombatant Chinese—despite the fact that much of Asia applauded the humiliation of the white imperial powers. American racism was equally virulent. Generations of Americans had considered Japanese as inferior to whites, a belief that, before the war, allowed the United States habitually to underrate Japanese resolve and military potential. Yet after Japan's stunning early victories, this same racism portrayed the Japanese as mindless fanatics, apelike in manner, brutal beyond parallel, and willing to die as a nation for the emperor. Neither side could see the other in any but the grimmest of stereotypes.

This dark picture of the Pacific war derives from meticulous and impressive research. Dower drew on the official reports, military documents, and popular press and media—including cartoons and films—of both sides. In addition, he found that scholarly Japanese and American studies of the national character of the enemy generally reinforced popular racist perceptions. Thus, while fully acknowledging that racism was also a factor in the European struggle, *War without Mercy* holds that racial stereotypes more deeply characterized Pacific operations. If Americans hated the Nazis, they still saw Germans as white and Western; Allied propaganda found room for the good German while depicting the Japanese almost exclusively as unified and undifferentiated fanatics.

Using a clear organization and polished writing, Dower is a careful and persuasive historian; his path-breaking study oversteps the evidence only near the end of the book. He implies that racism, in great measure, kept the war going longer after both sides knew that Japan must lose—that is, after mid-1944—after which time the antagonists suffered more casualties than during the years when the issue still hung in the balance. Yet to assign such importance to racism is probably misleading. Warring nations seldom know when to quit: Germany also fought on long after most Germans knew they were finished; if Allied aircraft devastated Tokyo and other Japanese cities late in the war, they did the same to Dresden; peaking American war production and huge troop reinforcements from Europe would have inflicted crushing losses on Japan in any case. Unintentionally, Dower himself may have underrated the Japanese: backs to the wall, Japanese soldiers and sailors were skillful and brave; most civilians were stalwart amid fright and weariness. There is no reason to suspect that they would not have gone down fighting even in the absence of a race war—history is replete with examples of similar desperation.

Dower concludes on a note of caution. The war stereotypes did not die on V-J Day, but adapted to the circumstances of peace. Japan, for instance, drew on traditions holding that one could learn from outsiders without becoming like them. General MacArthur assumed a paternalistic attitude toward the conquered Japanese that was, if more benevolent, fully in keeping with prewar notions of Western superiority. Yet the stereotypes of race remained, even if on a more subtle level. Indeed, the vocabulary of conflict is still employed occasionally in the modern trade war between America and Japan—for example, "economic Pearl Harbor." This is a point worth considering, for given the events of forty years ago, the resurrection of war words is too serious a business to treat lightly. John Dower has explained why in one of the most important histories of the past decade.

MARK EDWARD LENDER
Kean College of New Jersey
Union

DWORKIN, RONALD. *Law's Empire.* Pp. xiii, 470. Cambridge, MA: Harvard University Press, Belknap Press, 1986. $20.00.

If "good wine needs no bush" and "a good play needs no epilogue"—and both assertions have the high authority of Shakespeare—then a good book is also its own assertion. Hence my hesitation to review this book of legal philosophy; it needs no review. The subject is of enthralling interest. The law concerns every human being, it is always with us, and it directs the path of our destiny from cradle to grave.

With erudition and provocative insight, Dworkin, utilizing the principles that ground the Anglo-American legal system, presents his theory of law by harmoniously combining philosophy with the abstract and law with the concrete.

Dworkin approaches the law, that expression of civilization that closely approaches perfection, by propounding the major philosophical question faced in all American complex cases: "In difficult cases how do and how should judges decide what the Law is?" Dworkin argues that judges must decide hard cases by interpretation rather than precedent. In his critique of what interpretation is, its structure, and how to best select one interpretation as better than others, he creates an imaginary judge of superhuman intellectual power and patience who accepts laws as integrity. Dworkin calls him Hercules.

At first, the title of this book seemed inappropriate to me, but upon reflection it is seen to be a term of reality. For in bearing on his or her shoulders the burdens of humanity, the American judge must cling to institutions that he or she knows and have been proven, while investing most of his or her energies in determining what the law is and applying it, with integrity, to the disputes at hand.

Through several chapters we follow Hercules' career by viewing the types of tensions and judgments he must face in delicately deciding hard cases. Intertwining sympathy, imagination, varied knowledge, and diction as clear as a mountain stream, Dworkin discusses how the judge's interpretation includes his delicate balance between political convictions of different sorts and contributes to decisions balancing individual rights versus the good of community.

Perhaps his best discourse stressing the primary theories on the general character of law is found in his six interpretations on the question of emotional damages in civil cases. He first explores the theory that the law of a community should be based on only what the established conventions of the community say it is. Then he moves to another major theory, which assumes that law is best understood as an instrument of society to achieve its goal. Dworkin argues forcefully and persuasively against both these views. He insists that the most fundamental point of law is not to report consensus or provide efficient means to social goals, but to answer the requirement that a political community act in a coherent and principled manner toward all its members.

It is rare to read a book on the philosophy of law written by a mind that so harmoniously combines the two. Books on the theories of American law will proliferate with the bicentennial of the Constitution in 1987, but few will be as strikingly original or readable as this one.

GERALD L. SBARBORO

Circuit Court of Cook County
Chicago
Illinois

LIVINGSTONE, NEIL C. and TERRELL E. ARNOLD, eds. *Fighting Back: Winning the War against Terrorism.* Pp. x, 268. Lexington, MA: D. C. Heath, Lexington Books, 1986. No price.

RA'ANAN, URI et al. *Hydra of Carnage: International Linkages of Terrorism, The Witnesses Speak.* Pp. xvii, 638. Lexington, MA: D. C. Heath, Lexington Books, 1986. No price.

Since the mid-1970s, the problem of terrorism, or—to use the neologism currently in vogue—low intensity violence, has increased dramatically. Not only has the sheer number of attacks multiplied, but the resultant number of casualties has continued to climb. Complicating this trend have been two extremely ominous developments. First, recent evidence indicates that there has been a tremendous increase in the amount of state sponsorship of terrorist organizations. Second, the technological sophistication of terrorist attacks has also continued to rise.

One of the few developments that has kept pace, or even perhaps surpassed, this increase in terrorism is the amount of airtime and ink being devoted to the problem of terrorism. Unfortunately, much of this has been excessively sensationalist and has ignored the many complexities of the problem. The two volumes reviewed here represent a long-awaited and welcome break from this trend. The volumes contain a plethora of articles written by specialists on terrorism drawn from academia, government, and the private sector. The articles address the varied causes of terrorism, its international linkages, and the ways in which terrorism and its effects might be alleviated. The proposals for inhibiting terrorism include various diplomatic, legal, economic, and military options. However, if there is a central theme that emerges from both of these volumes, it is that the United States must fight back to stem the tide of terrorism, and for most of the authors discussed here this means an explicit willingness to use force both for preemptive attacks and for reprisals.

Those articles that examine the causes of the recent increase in terrorism generally highlight three particularly salient factors: the ability of terrorists to gain media coverage, the inability or unwillingness of Western societies to defend themselves against terrorism, and the growing state sponsorship of terrorist activities. While a number of authors do sink to gleeful media bashing, an articulate defense of the news media is provided by Sander Vanocur. In short, Vanocur argues that the increased ability of terrorists to use the news media for their own ends is not so much a function of the liberal political philosophy of the media, but a direct result of recent technological and business trends, such as the development of cheaper, lighter-weight remote equipment and the proliferation of non-network news organizations. Since these trends are not likely to be reversed, Vanocur is pessimistic about any changes in the news media that might play a significant role in the fight against terrorism.

Many of the authors attribute much of the increase in terrorism to the support terrorist organizations now receive from the Soviet Union and many of its allies. In this area the editors of *Hydra of Carnage* are to be especially commended, as they have included more than 300 pages of testimony by those formerly involved with terrorist groups in order to back up this assertion. Together, the volumes contain articles that explicitly examine the historical and doctrinal antecedents of current Soviet support for terrorism.

While the two volumes more than satisfactorily establish the Soviet Union's ties to international terrorism, many of the authors seem to take the argument a step further by viewing terrorist organizations as Soviet surrogates or proxies. They imply, possibly intentionally, that the Soviet Union can and does control these organizations. While the Soviet Union and its allies are guilty of providing arms, training, money, and intelligence to these organizations, I have not seen the evidence that demonstrates Soviet control. While some may find this distinction trivial, in my opinion it is both academically and practically vital. When focusing on East-West dynamics, there is a clear tendency to give only cursory treatment to the terrorist organizations themselves. The problem is similar to the one that has been experienced by analysts and practitioners of Soviet policy toward the Third World, where a preoccupation with the East-West conflict has meant paying insufficient attention to the dynamics and problems of the Third World itself. Iran is merely the most glaring example of the disastrous results this tendency can have. Trying to force events in the Third World into the rubric of East-West conflict has often led to a dangerously distorted understanding of the dynamics and problems of the Third World. Thus it is regrettable that neither of these volumes contains a single chapter devoted solely to the terrorist organizations themselves.

Ironically, the organizations that do receive a considerable amount of attention in the *Hydra of Carnage* are revolutionary movements such as the South West Africa People's Organization in Namibia, the Vietcong, the Sandinistas, and the Popular Movement for the Liberation of Angola. While revolutionary organizations can, and often do, engage in terrorism, there is a logical distinction between organizations engaged in an active revolution—often for ethnic self-determination—on their own territory and organizations, such as the Baader-Meinhoff gang or the Red Brigades, that use random violence, often on foreign soil, against foreign nationalists simply to gain international attention. If all revolutionary movements that have used terrorism are to be labeled terrorist organizations proper, then I have considerable reservations with B. Hugh Tovar's notion that support for the Contras in Nicaragua and National Union for the Total Independence of Angola are positive steps in the fight against terrorism.

Along similar lines, I might agree with Malcom Wallop's assertion that one man's terrorist is not necessarily another man's freedom fight, although I would not call the notion "moral illiteracy." One can make some objective and moral distinctions between movements. Furthermore, as Wallop suggests, the difficulty of making such distinctions does not justify American inaction. But at the same time, I may still disagree with Wallop as to who the real freedom fighters are.

These particular criticisms aside, both of these volumes are a welcome addition to the ongoing debate on terrorism, its causes and remedies. For academics and policymakers alike, both volumes should prove an invaluable asset.

DANIEL R. KEMPTON
University of Illinois
Urbana-Champaign

SINGH, S. NIHAL. *The Yogi and the Bear: A Study of Indo-Soviet Relations.* Pp. viii, 324. Riverdale, MD: Riverdale, 1986. No price.

LU, CHIH H. *The Sino-Indian Border Dispute: A Legal Study.* Pp. x, 143. Westport, CT: Greenwood Press, 1986. $35.00.

These two works focus on specific issues in India's foreign relations. The Singh book, however, ranges much more widely, as it brings in regional matters and relations with the West, than does Lu's, which is targeted solely on the border issue.

Singh, a former journalist now engaged in research, has followed Indo-Soviet relations for many years and uses this experience well in his discussion. The major part of the book—the first ten chapters—is a chronology, interspersed with Singh's comments on events pertaining to the India-USSR relationship. There is a wealth of documentary support to which is added evidence from a number of conversations Singh has had with participants in the formulation and execution of Indian foreign policy. A more comprehensive index would have made this horde of information more readily available to one who wishes to use this book as a reference.

The key to the book, however, is Singh's appraisal of the relationship between India and the Soviet Union in chapter 11. In the introduction, Singh expresses his view that "this relationship has reached a dangerous stage and needs a close, hard look." He writes that the Soviets "are gradually seeking to give India no option but to attain its [India's] power ambitions through a secondary role to serve Soviet interests in Asia." In an action that Singh describes as "supine," he criticizes the statement of the Indian U.N. delegate on the Soviet invasion of Afghanistan. Although Singh calls his work "India-centered," it is an important book that should be read carefully by all interested in either Soviet or South Asian foreign policy.

The Lu book begins with the apocalyptic assertion that the dispute between China and India is one that could lead to World War III. This overstatement out of the way, Lu provides a careful historical analysis of the Tibet question and then proceeds to an evaluation of the specific border problem. He looks at the mediatory role led by Sri Lanka following the border conflict in 1962 and notes its failure. His solution seems to parallel that of the Chinese, namely, cession by India of the Aksai Chin area to China, which occupies the area now, and the acceptance by both countries of the McMahon line in the east and also of a line along the passes mentioned in the 1954 agreement in the center sector. The book would have been much more useful if it had maps to locate the many points Lu mentions. There are some errors; for example, Morarji Desai may have very much wished to be prime minister from 1969 to 1980, but his years in that office are 1977-80. The book is one of importance and is one of a very few to address a problem that for India remains high on the foreign policy agenda.

CRAIG BAXTER

Juniata College
Huntingdon
Pennsylvania

SMITH, R. B. *An International History of the Vietnam War: The Kennedy Strategy.* Pp. xii, 429. New York: St. Martin's Press, 1985. $25.00.

THAYER, THOMAS C. *War without Fronts: The American Experience in Vietnam.* Pp. xxvii, 276. Boulder, CO: Westview Press, 1985. Paperbound, $25.00.

At peak, 540,000 Americans fought in Vietnam, in 10,000 hamlets, 260 districts, and 44 provinces. The number of Americans who died was 58,000. These two books, both superbly crafted but strikingly different in style and approach, add impressively to the new literature growing out of the renewed interest in the Vietnam war. The authors are of different backgrounds. Smith is a historian who has published widely on Asia generally and on Vietnam in particular. Thayer was chief of operations analysis in Robert S. McNamara's Advanced Research Project Agency. His book is based on information classified during the period he collected it in his three years in Vietnam. Smith's book covers the war from Kennedy's initiation of his counterinsurgency policy in 1961 to Johnson's escalation of the conflict in 1965. Thayer's work focuses on American troop

involvement in South Vietnam from 1965 to 1972. Smith places his study within a global context. He argues that the Vietnam experience cannot be understood by examining merely the bilateral relations between the United States and Vietnam or by relying on documentary histories of American anticommunism. Rather, U.S. relations with China and the Soviet Union and the struggle for Southeast Asia must be included. Thayer's work, on the other hand, focuses on what actually happened in Vietnam while American troops were there. It does not deal with Hanoi, or Paris, or even Washington, D.C. It attempts to explain why we could not win the war given the strategies we adopted. Though dramatically different in these and many other ways, the two books cover the Vietnam involvement from 1961 to 1972 in a surprisingly complementary fashion.

Smith's principal thesis is that the Kennedy policy of counterinsurgency was not merely a prelude to a wider war—as conventionally conceived—but an attempt to resolve a paradox. Kennedy was aware of the global implications of the war in Vietnam by the end of 1961, both as part of the cold war and as an example of wars of national liberation. He did not want the war in Vietnam to become a focal point of major East-West confrontation lest it interfere with the main objectives of his foreign policy elsewhere. Thus, in 1961, Kennedy rejected both the suggestion of his advisers that a Southeast Asia Treaty Organization force be deployed along South Vietnam's borders with North Vietnam and Laos and the recommendation of the Joint Chiefs of Staff of unilateral military action by U.S. forces in South Vietnam. He opted instead for counterinsurgency: (1) expand trading programs in South Vietnam; (2) send more American advisers to work with Vietnamese officers in the field; and (3) supply logistic support teams of armored vehicles and helicopters staffed by American troops. All this was done to help South Vietnam defend itself. If Kennedy had lived, would things have worked out differently in Vietnam? While that question cannot be easily answered, Smith's conclusion seems to be that things might well have been different. Counterinsurgency itself failed not because of anything either Kennedy or Johnson did, but because Hanoi was able to defeat it.

The fighting itself was, of course, confusing to the public because it was impossible to follow by simple lines on a map. Thayer begins his book with a little story about a National Security Council meeting in 1963, shortly before Kennedy's death. A diplomat and a general, both just returned from Vietnam, report their findings. Kennedy asks, "You two did visit the same country, didn't you?" While Thayer's book does not claim to make a full, integrated account of the Vietnam conflict—it is a quantitative analysis of troop involvement, essentially— it does pick up where Smith's book leaves off. It goes well beyond the military trends in the conflict, providing fresh, often provocative, accounts of such critical dimensions as war damage, civilian casualties, and refugee flow. This book will not be without its critics, both as to methodology and as to the various inferences drawn. But it does have the definite advantage of being drawn from bimonthly reports written while the conflict was in progress. Historians may interpret Thayer's data differently in future years. But, if nothing else, Thayer's book explains why we lost the war without fronts.

WILLIAM C. LOUTHAN
Ohio Wesleyan University
Delaware

SOLOMON, RICHARD and MASATAKA KOSAKA, eds. *The Soviet Far East Military Buildup: Nuclear Dilemmas & Asian Society.* Pp. xv, 301. Dover, MA: Auburn House, 1986. $29.95. Paperbound, $16.95.

This book, edited by Richard H. Solomon and Masataka Kosaka, is an excellent, professional objective appraisal of the expansion in recent decades of the Soviet Union's ground, naval, and air forces into the Asia-Pacific region. It focuses on "the nuclearization of the Soviet military presence to a point that now threatens all of the countries of East Asia that are allied to or have friendly relations with the United States."

A central theme of this anthology concerns the nuclear dilemmas associated with the problems of coalition defense in the nuclear era. Such dilemmas have long plagued North Atlantic Treaty Organization (NATO) policy and strategy in Western Europe. They now confront the countries located on the eastern rim of the Soviet empire.

The introduction and part 1 of this book, comprising three chapters written by distinguished American scholars, attempt to evaluate the meaning of Moscow's military buildup in the global context of the Soviet military challenge.

In part 2, five authors from different perspectives describe how the Soviet military buildup affects the security of the People's Republic of China, Japan, the Republic of Korea, the states of the Association of Southeast Asian Nations, and Australia and New Zealand.

Part 3 deals with the potentially explosive confrontation in the Korean peninsula between the Republic of Korea and Kim Il Sung's regime in the north and also with the ongoing struggle for the complete control of former Indochina. The impact of the shifting nuclear balance of these Asian regional conflicts is addressed.

Part 4 discusses how the European NATO experience with the Soviet nuclear threat might help the nations of East Asia cope better with the already formidable Soviet nuclear deployments in that region of the globe.

This book represents a comprehensive survey by a multinational group of established defense and foreign policy experts associated with SECAP—the security conference on Asia and the Pacific—on how the United States and its Asia friends and allies should cope with a rapidly growing nuclear threat to the vast Asian Pacific region. The book's contributors argue that the United States should maintain a strong nuclear deterrent in the region while comporting itself in such a way so as not to give rise to political tensions among its allies. The military response that the editors advocate in order to achieve the desideratum is that

the United States should maintain an effective but low visibility nuclear retaliatory force in the region, composed of submarine-launched ballistic missiles and cruise missiles and nuclear capsule aircraft—buttressed by intercontinental nuclear forces based in the United States—to deter Soviet nuclear initiatives, and to assure allied governments that there is an effective "coupling" between American defense capabilities and their own security.

This book is not for the average reader, but serious students of strategy will find this book a useful volume.

WILLIAM R. KINTNER
University of Pennsylvania
Philadelphia

### AFRICA, ASIA, AND LATIN AMERICA

BENVENISTI, MERON. *Conflicts and Contradictions*. Pp. xii, 210. New York: Random House, Villard Books, 1986. $15.95.

BELING, WILLARD A., ed. *Middle East Peace Plans*. Pp. 240. New York: St. Martin's Press, 1986. $27.50.

Put simply, Meron Benvenisti's book is a personal memoir on the Arab-Israeli conflict in Jerusalem and the West Bank, while Willard A. Beling's edited volume is a survey of peace plans from the standpoint of major parties to this same conflict. Benvenisti has lived in the midst of this struggle, a sabra born in Palestine before Israel's independence, whereas the contributors to the Beling book have all been outsiders. In a sense the reader has before him or her the subjective and objective in these two books and so can judge the relative usefulness of each in understanding the past, present, and future of Arabs and Jews in Palestine.

When I first met Meron Benvenisti in Israel during 1969, he was the dynamic deputy mayor of Jerusalem engaged with Teddy Kollek in making this city, sacred to three major religions, a place of both political unity and ethnic peace. The West Bank itself was then held under strict occupation pending peace settlement that would trade land for peace, Arab rights for Israel's security. While this formula still stands, it has been emptied of meaning by the twenty years that have passed since June 1967. In essence, this vision of land for peace constituted a liberal Zionist dream that Arabs and Jews could live together in Palestine not as one, but as good neighbors. This dream proved an illusion because life together involves a dynamic of equal recognition of an otherness that is the most important and sacred characteristic of humanity. Constant warfare between Arabs and Israelis, waged in the name of extravagant political objectives, has incurred an ultimate cost: dehumanization of the other.

It is to Benvenisti's intellectual credit that he is not only acutely aware of this dehumanization within the fundamentals of Israel's existence as well as in the guiding principles of Palestinianism, but is also cognizant of his own personal engagement in this existence—errors, if not sins, of omission as well as commission. Yet his genius—and I use this in the most genuine sense of intelligence—has been his effort to transcend conflicting ideologies and political priesthoods to explore the human dimensions of the Arab-Israeli struggle and to search for ways to stop "eradicating each other's names" on two competing "maps" of Palestine.

At stake in the warfare between Israelis and Palestinians is less a formal politics of compromise that might emerge someday than everyday life questions of how children grow up and how adults behave toward their neighbors. Benvenisti's vision, once that of liberal Zionism to be later exposed in all its emptiness, is now that of existential actor: no area of human relations is free from conflict and none will be, so the problem is how to live at peace with this consciousness. How to exist with one's own contradictions and those of others? And will political leaders understand this in time to prevent even worse disasters in the Arab-Israeli conflict than we have seen so far? Benvenisti ends his brilliant memoir on a pessimistic note with words from a Catholic friend in Belfast: if Arabs and Israelis are changing names on maps as the English and Irish have done, "may God have mercy on you all!"

The various maps for settlement of the Arab-Israeli conflict—or, more correctly, settlement of the Palestinian-Israeli struggle for the land called Palestine—are provided in the Beling volume. In addition, a third part focuses on peace in Lebanon, covered by R. D. McLaurin, and the Iran-Iraq conflict, covered by Fariborz Rouzbehani. Of special interest in this review, however, are parts 1 and 2 on the Arab-Israeli peace process.

The first part has three essays on major actors in this process—Israel, the Palestinians, and Saudi Arabia—by Don Peretz, Helena Cobban, and David E. Long, respectively. On the one hand, the reader is hard pressed to treat any of the plans or proposals discussed as being seriously negotiable, while on the other hand, one has trouble explaining why Saudi Arabia is considered a major actor at all.

Part 2 deals with other principal actors in the peace process—the United States, the Soviet Union, and Western Europe—described by William B. Quandt, Vladimir N. Sakharov, and Adam M. Garfinkle. Only the United States has made any significant contribution to peace settlement prospects, aside from Begin and Sadat with American mediation, among the various parties covered in this volume, and yet Quandt's analysis of the U.S. role is perfunctory. Sakharov, described in the book as "a Soviet-trained diplomat who defected to the West" after KGB duty in the Middle East, provides perhaps one of two insightful essays in this volume, the other being by McLaurin on Lebanon. Garfinkle's treatment of West European involvement in the peace process is patronizing and polemical, treating powers

that bear great historical responsibility for the origins of the Arab-Israeli conflict as opportunistic interlopers.

In a word, the Beling volume provides an uneven, expert analysis of the various dimensions of peace in the Middle East, but it underscores what Benvenisti describes in another book as the tendency of the Middle East peace process to read better in Latin than in the colloquial Arabic and Hebrew that express the real dynamics of the Arab-Israeli struggle. Benvenisti's memoir, by contrast, takes us outside the realm of policy—where he once held high office himself and then was ostracized for his nonpartisan skepticism about the wisdom of those in high places—doubtful that a peace process manned by ambitious politicians and professional diplomats will heal a pathological condition between Israelis and Palestinians that converts everyday neighbors into historical enemies. Choices for peace must be made by ordinary citizens, Benvenisti suggests, on whether to side with those who lead the peace process nowhere or with those who refuse the pretensions of high politics for an existence of contradiction and accommodation in genuine human community with former enemies. Ultimately the line crossed from enmity to community is a divide between two political zones: in one realm are the high and mighty; in another those who are condemned to daily interaction with each other within a history where they have been forced to play victims and executioners. Benvenisti intimates that if the peace process is operated by the same politicians who also run the machines of war, then ordinary citizens must refuse this process and find their own *modus vivendi* with each other.

ROBERT J. PRANGER
American Enterprise Institute
Washington, D.C.

COOX, ALVIN D. *Nomonhan: Japan against Russia, 1939.* Two vols. Pp. xvii, 1253. Stanford, CA: Stanford University Press, 1985. $95.00.

This book is nothing less than a *tour de force* in institutional as well as military history. Its sweep is at once grandiose, covering the nearly four-decade development of the Kwantung Army, and painstakingly detailed, recounting the undeclared war with the Soviet Union in 1939 that Japan lost. Its massive length and prodigious research rightfully earn it the status of definitive history.

Readers approaching a work of such magnitude may well hesitate before attempting to digest it all. For those interested primarily in Japanese imperialism in Manchuria and the pivotal role of the Kwantung Army, the first and last quarters of the work will prove most beneficial. Here the principle of *gekokujō* ("domination from below") was in full swing as the Kwantung Army from its beginning operated without the approval of Tokyo. Early on, this took the form of intervention in warlord struggles, progressed to the assassination of the Old Marshall, precipitated the Mukden Incident, and led finally in 1939 to the unilateral decision to bomb airfields inside Mongolia, the ostensible cause of the Nomonhan Incident. Along the way, the army became convinced of its superiority over any foe—an attitude that would contribute to its downfall.

It is the second and third quarters of this work that concentrate mainly on the fighting on the Manchurian-Mongolian border. So detailed is the account here that practically every engagement, no matter how small, is described. One gets a sense of how the fighting looked from the perspectives of not only generals but also the lowest-ranking enlisted men. This approach allows Coox to note the weaknesses of the strategy and tactics of the Kwantung Army and conclude that Japan lost because it suffered from poor leadership and material deficiencies that could not be made up by "spiritual" factors.

Even on a much smaller scale, this work would be a welcome addition to the literature since little is known about the incident and its wider implications. The loss forced Japan to turn to the south in 1940, explaining in part why Pearl Harbor occurred, and had

the additional effect of allowing the Soviet Union to wage a one-front war against Germany. But this book represents scholarship on a grand scale, with research extending over decades, a complete mastery of both primary and secondary sources—mostly Japanese—and hundreds of interviews. The fact that this represents an undertaking of heroic proportions may well propel it into the status of a classic.

WAYNE PATTERSON
Saint Norbert College
De Pere
Wisconsin

HANLON, JOSEPH. *Beggar Your Neighbours: Apartheid Power in Southern Africa*. Pp. xi, 352. Bloomington: Indiana University Press, 1986. $35.00.

SOGGOT, DAVID. *Namibia, the Violent Heritage*. Pp. xvi, 333. New York: St. Martin's Press, 1986. No price.

These two books intersect at several points and both should be required reading for all those concerned with the developing tragedy of southern Africa, its effects upon Africa as a whole, and its role in international affairs, particularly the relationship between the West and the Third World. South Africa represents the most problematic legacy of imperialism, and the reason for this is that since the late nineteenth century, whites in South Africa have operated one of the most elaborate systems of subimperialism. The discovery of diamonds in Griqualand and later of gold on the Witwatersrand sent social and geopolitical shock waves throughout the region. That mineral revolution had both centrifugal and centripetal effects. It set in train fresh expansionist urges that were to result in the partitioning of the whole of southern Africa, and it began the process of creating a powerfully integrated regional economy cutting across territorial frontiers. Through labor migration, scarcely a village in the entire subcontinent escaped the pull of the mines and the urban agglomerations and services that developed around them.

Economic realities produced political imperatives. The British set about the rationalization of the political complexities of the region in the Boer War. Jan Smuts, the dominant political figure in South Africa for the first half of the twentieth century and the only white one with a truly international role, was converted to a British imperial ideal of world government. In pursuing his wholist big-is-beautiful philosophy, he set out to create a United States of southern Africa. World War I seemed to present him with his opportunity. He himself led campaigns against the Germans in South-West Africa (Namibia) and Tanganyika. At the end of the war he was instrumental in the founding of the League of Nations and was virtually the father of its mandate system. Yet he saw no paradox between those internationalist objectives and his overweening ambition for South Africa. He thought he could secure the High Commission territories—Botswana, Lesotho, Swaziland—from the British, the British South Africa Company lands—Zambia and Zimbabwe—from its dying commercial grasp, and the Portuguese territories—Angola and Mozambique—from a republic sick of imperial pretensions. At one stage he even saw the Congo (Zaire) and Tanganyika as within his grasp.

In fact he secured only Namibia through the mandate system, but his ambition to match economic dominance with political control has never left the considerations of South Africa's white rulers. Ironically, his Nationalist opponents were unimpressed with his visions, seeing them as endangering white supremacy and Boer influence, but they used Namibia to prop up their power. Moreover, as the processes of decolonization have swept over southern Africa they have transformed Smuts's imperial vision into a neocolonialist one.

Joseph Hanlon's excellent work examines their search for a "total strategy" through a "total onslaught" on their neighbors. He, together with a number of specialist collabora-

tors, examines South Africa's economic and political destabilization of Swaziland, Lesotho, Mozambique, Angola, Zimbabwe, Botswana, and Malawi. South African troops, South African intelligence, and South African-backed guerrillas are at work throughout the region. Hanlon suggests that the South Africans have generated a full-scale war through economic sanctions against their neighbors, invasions and bombings of both border areas and capitals, and attempted assassinations of political leaders, though we still await evidence that the death of President Samora Machel was a successful one. Hanlon argues that the West should recognize this and get off the fence. To support his arguments he offers excellent appendixes on the costs of South African destabilization and the effects of international sanctions on neighboring states, as well as useful statistical annexes.

War has long been part of the reality of Namibian existence. Since the German near-genocide of the Hereros and the World War I campaign, Namibia has been subjected to repeated aggressions. Now, in David Soggot's words, Namibia has achieved a tragic accession to international notoriety. Soggot, a defense lawyer who has been involved in many of the trials of Namibian activists, seeks to chart in his book both the large issues and, through individual stories, the human dimensions. He gives the Namibian tragedy human scale by revealing the "faith and sorrow of men and women who had dared to participate in history." Namibia has often been seen as South Africa's Achilles' heel, a piece of flagrant illegality, an affront to the international community, but also a symbol of the powerlessness of its institutions. In fact, Namibia has invariably acted as a bridgehead, and it is in that role that Soggot and Hanlon rightly cast the colony in South Africa's campaigns in its subcontinent. It is to be hoped that these two valuable books, both of them coolly analytical and impassioned by turns, well grounded in the political and economic facts of southern Africa, and both remarkably up-to-date in a fast-moving situation, will be read with real care and attention in the State Department.

JOHN M. MacKENZIE

University of Lancaster

United Kingdom

HONIG, EMILY. *Sisters and Strangers: Women in the Shanghai Cotton Mills, 1919-1949.* Pp. ix, 299. Stanford, CA: Stanford University Press, 1986. $37.50.

HERSHATTER, GAIL. *The Workers of Tianjin, 1900-1949.* Pp. viii, 313. Stanford, CA: Stanford University Press, 1986. $37.50.

Between 1895 and 1945 China's major cities greatly expanded in population, and the division of labor became more specialized. Factories and their industrial workers accounted for much of this new division of labor. This new mode of production was associated with far different worker-manager relations from those in any other economic organizations of that time. Higher real wages, cleaner work environment, and new skills served as incentives for young workers, especially females, to enter the factory and accept managerial discipline and authority. Between World War I and 1949 this new factory system flourished, but declined when violence and war occurred.

These two studies describe the new factory work discipline imposed upon workers and how they adjusted. From interviews with workers and former members of the Young Women's Christian Association, newspaper accounts, periodicals, government reports, and scholarly studies, Honig and Hershatter have pieced together historical narratives of workers' lives, their relationships, and factory conditions.

We learn that violence and hardship were constant companions for women in the Shanghai textile mills. These women workers formed sisterhoods for their protection. Whereas women textile workers rarely were active in the labor movement of the mid 1920s, they spearheaded violent protest against factory managers in early 1949 when 6000 women workers went on strike at a textile mill.

In Tianjin the working class always remained fragmented without any unified working-class activities except briefly in the mid 1920s and again between 1946 and 1948. Workers retained their rural ties, and they constantly moved from job to job. Vertical patronage between factory foremen and their workers greatly determined who worked and who did not and under what kind of conditions. In both Tianjin and Shanghai powerful urban gangs influenced who gained employment and who might be assaulted whether on or off the job.

As representing the new social history, how well do these two studies expand our understanding of what happened to workers under the new factory system?

While we learn that urban workers especially young females, experienced considerable violence, these studies make no attempt to determine if such violence was random, systematic, increasing, or decreasing over time. Did urban gangs control so much economic activity because these cities had no powerful, central municipal authority and police control? Did real wages rise for factory workers over the period, and how severe was the decline in real wages between 1937 and 1949, when China suffered foreign invasion and civil war? Were alternative employment and life-styles in medium-sized and small towns and villages more attractive than factory life in large cities? Did the existence of a large surplus labor force with considerable underemployment mean that factory workers were a privileged group?

Unfortunately, these studies do not provide answers to these questions to judge how the new factory system contributed to China's economic and social development during these crucial decades.

Perhaps the real contribution of these studies is to confirm that factory workers still retained their traditional ties with villages and developed personal networks to adjust to the new factory discipline. Factory workers retained their traditional values, and they also enjoyed greater independence and a better life-style although frequently at great personal risk. Although workers in factories devised their networks to resist management speed-ups to increase labor intensity, they lacked sufficient power to develop associations to change management rules until Communist Party cadres organized such efforts after 1945. But at that time China had become so chaotic that such protests could easily be orchestrated by revolutionists.

A serious omission in both studies is the failure to use Ming K. Chang's superb *Historiography of the Chinese Labor Movement, 1895-1949* (Stanford, CA: Hoover Institution, 1981) and the many sources cited in it.

Both Honig and Hershatter refer to 1949 as the year of liberation when actually the Chinese Communist Party only had unified China under its rule.

RAMON H. MYERS

Hoover Institution on
    War, Revolution and Peace
Stanford
California

KRAMER, MARTIN. *Islam Assembled: The Advent of the Muslim Congresses.* Pp. xi, 250. New York: Columbia University Press, 1986. $30.00.

SIVAN, EMMANUEL. *Radical Islam: Medieval Theology and Modern Politics.* Pp. xi, 218. New Haven, CT: Yale University Press, 1985. $18.50.

Islam, both in its institutional form and as a revolutionary movement, has proven to be a major social and political force in our times. The two books reviewed here should be read in the context of these two very different characteristics.

Martin Kramer's book presents an interesting study of the efforts made by Muslims between the last third of the nineteenth century and the end of World War II to bring about some sort of Islamic unity. Influenced by the winds of change in Europe, which had

by that time reached the Muslim world, Muslim leaders began to write and speak in favor of pan-Islamic unity. In this book we meet the well-known *ulama* (religious leaders)— Jamal al-Din al-Afghani, Muhammad Abduh, Rashid Ridha, al-Hajj Amin al-Husaini, and others—as they seek the establishment of an institutional foundation for Muslim unity that would cut across local and even continental boundaries. All of these Muslim figures, as the book shows, defended the organizational principle in Islam, not only in their writings but in a series of inter-Muslim conferences and congresses.

However, while Muslim thinkers could agree on unity in principle, there was much disagreement on its nature. While some merely desired increased social, economic, or cultural ties between Muslim countries, others wanted a more integrated form of unity. Their political objectives also varied. Hajj Amin al-Husaini, mufti of Jerusalem, held a congress in 1931 for the defense of Jerusalem, while Mustafa Kemal, later president of Turkey, had more ambitious objectives. In 1919 he proposed a federation of Muslim states with a permanent central organization to handle, among other things, the foreign policy of Muslim countries.

Throughout his work, Kramer gives us an account of the intellectual debates that preceded the Muslim conferences, the circumstances under which they were called, and the debates and resolutions of the assemblies. The book also contains a close analysis of the failures of each conference, including insufficient funding, personal rivalries among leaders, and interference by regional and outside powers such as Turkey, Great Britain, and France. Each chapter provides rich bibliographical source material on each conference.

Emmanuel Sivan studies the resurgence of radical—sometimes called fundamentalist—Islam in the Sunni Muslim world. He concentrates mainly on Egypt and Syria, covering Islamic radicalism from the mid 1950s to the early 1980s; one may question why the Sudan, with its strong Islamic movements, was never mentioned. Sivan analyzes the ideas of the leading radical Muslim thinkers, mainly Sayyid Qutb and Sa'id Hawwa. He also sheds light on the historical origin of at least one element in this radicalism, tracing it back to Ibn Taymiyyah the Muslim theologian and legalist of the thirteenth and fourteenth centuries, who permitted the use of force against fellow Sunni rulers in some cases. Sivan notes two important differences between the new Sunni radicalism of today and that of the traditional Muslim Brothers. First, the new Muslim radicals have abandoned the idea of the restoration of the caliphate. Second, they accept, with reluctance, the new realities in the area, that of an Arab Muslim world "divided into nation-states." Thus these movements limit their actions to the frontiers of their own countries. As a result they can influence one another, but they are not an extension of one another.

Sivan draws heavily on the writings of these Muslims in the press and publications, especially those in Syria and Egypt. However, as an Israeli, he has been limited by an inability to have personal contact or interviews with the leading contemporary Muslim thinkers and ideologues.

Sivan, on the whole, does not add a great deal to what is already known about Muslim fundamentalists; however, by focusing on Syria and Egypt, he focuses on the most active and important Sunni Muslim movements in the region.

LOUAY BAHRY
University of Tennessee
Knoxville

LaBELLE, THOMAS J. *Nonformal Education in Latin America and the Caribbean: Stability, Reform, or Revolution?* Pp. xvi, 367. New York: Praeger, 1986. $35.00.

LEVY, DANIEL C. *Higher Education and the State in Latin America: Private Challenges to Public Dominance.* Pp. xvii, 434. Chicago: University of Chicago Press, 1986. $27.50.

These two books join the sizable outpouring of materials published in recent years concerned with the general topic of education in Latin America. In both instances, these books have resulted from considerable firsthand, on-site experience and research, with major collaboration with Latin Americans familiar with the areas and topics being studied. Both books reflect these facts in their methods, scope, and tone.

LaBelle's *Nonformal Education* would have been a brief presentation except for inclusion of much background material. The introduction is followed by 11 chapters. Number one is entitled "Nonformal Education: An Introduction" and differentiates nonformal education from informal, on one side, and formal, on the other. Informal education is total life experience and the process of acquisition of knowledge; formal education is the commonplace structured procedure, with school buildings, books, degrees or certificates, and the like. Nonformal education involves deliberate, structured teaching-learning efforts, but without a structured school. It encompasses "both externally directed and self-initiated activity." Extension programs of several types, and teaching activities carried out by guerrilla groups are large-scale examples of nonformal education.

A list of chapter titles demonstrates that the book has a much broader scope than the title may imply: "Perspectives on Development as a Reflection of Political and Economic Realities"; "Education and Theories of Social Change"; "Teaching and Learning: Prescriptive and Process Approaches to Individual Change"; "Industrial Growth and Human Capital Formation"; "Human Capital and the Individual"; "Human Capital and Community Organizations"; "From Consciousness Raising to Popular Education"; "Implementation of Popular Education for Reform"; "Popular Education within Revolutionary Guerilla Warfare"; and "Rhetoric and Reality: Who Influences and Controls Nonformal Education." In addition, there are two appendixes, one of which is an extensive annotated bibliography. Each chapter is well written and informative, but it is not possible to summarize or comment here.

The Levy book consists of seven chapters, appendixes A-J, many pages of notes, an eight-page select bibliography, some 38 tables of data and information, properly interspersed in the textual material, and two full pages of abbreviations. The use of so many abbreviations on occasion is disconcerting, but the saving of space may have been necessary.

Table 1.1, in chapter 1, "Issues and Concepts," presents a wealth of data on private and total higher education enrollments for twenty Latin American nations, plus summations for total Latin America and total Spanish America—that is, the latter excludes Brazil. Other than the country names, there are 13 columns of data and dates, and, notably, only three blank spaces, indicating data not available. The table is a major achievement by itself and will be useful to many perusers of the book. Chapter 2, "Private versus Public Growth," challenges many stereotypical preconceptions. Chapters 3, 4, and 5 focus on Chile, Mexico, and Brazil, with a great detail of information and comment on historical background. The analytic structure of chapter 2, especially, is utilized to good purpose, to discuss purposes and apparent causes of changes, such as failure, exclusiveness, declining or rising elitism, modernization and dependency, Catholic reactions, and the concept of Waves I, II, and III of the private and public growth. This conception is intriguing. Chapter 6 is "Overview of Latin America," while the concluding chapter 7 is "The Consequences of Privatization: Reconceptualizing."

FLOYD B. McFARLAND
Oregon State University
Corvallis

MAOZ, MOSHE and AVNER YANIV, eds. *Syria under Assad: Domestic Constraints and Regional Risks*. Pp. 273. New York: St. Martin's Press, 1986. $35.00.

KEPEL, GILLES. *Muslim Extremism in Egypt: The Prophet and Pharaoh*. Pp.

281. Berkeley: University of California Press, 1986. $18.95.

These two books, each in its own way, help to rectify common misperceptions about Syria and about Islamic fundamentalism in Egypt, respectively.

The collection of 14 articles edited by Maoz and Yaniv is perhaps the best single volume available in English about contemporary Syria. It is comprehensive but concise; it is well written by one American and ten Israeli scholars each of whom writes with such academic objectivity that Syrian President Hafez al-Assad could find little to fault in the work. The 14 articles include a survey of modern Syrian history, politics, and economy, and relations with neighbors Turkey, Iran, Iraq, Jordan, Israel, Lebanon, the Palestinians, the United States, and the Soviet Union.

The image of Syria that emerges differs greatly from the popular perception of the country and its rulers as irrational and fanatic. All evidence here indicates that the present regime, although zealous in its ideological commitments and determined to achieve its very ambitious goals, has the capacity to make shrewd and effective domestic and foreign policies. Indeed, in both areas Syria under Assad has been rather successful, as indicated by the president's ability to retain control since 1970 despite several uprisings by dissidents, both individuals and factions, who were less skillful than he.

Even the chapter on Syrian relations with Israel demonstrates that objective situational factors, rather than calculated malice, have resulted in continued escalation of hostility. The author, Avner Yaniv, observes that whereas in the 1950s and 1960s relations were characterized by numerous small skirmishes, since then the pattern has been one of many fewer but larger encounters with extensive periods of tacit understandings. The significance of the pattern is the way it reflects how the "*power* of the US and USSR has been *refracted* into the balance of forces between Syria and Israel."

Gilles Kepel's study, *Muslim Extremism in Egypt*, is an English translation from the French of his Ph.D. thesis, greatly condensed. Although the translation is at times awkward and the style more French than American academic—vague citations, rambling philosophic discourses—the work overall is an intelligent, sympathetic, but critical survey of the more significant Muslim fundamentalist movements, leaderships, and ideologies in Egypt today. Because Cairo is the intellectual center of contemporary Arab political dynamics, events and trends there are relevant for all Middle Eastern society.

Kepel, who lived in Egypt among the subjects of his thesis for several years, selects five groups as representative of Egyptian "Islamicist" movements during the 1970s. All were much influenced by the writings of Sayyid Qutb, principal ideologue of the Muslim Brotherhood, who was executed by the Nasser regime in 1966. Since then the mother organization has become "respectable" but has spawned diverse offshoots including the faction responsible for President Anwar el-Sadat's assassination in 1981. The factions or individuals studied include those in universities and the remarkable blind Sheikh Kishk, whose sermons are tape-recorded and diffused throughout the Arab world. He emerges as today's most influential personality in Egypt, and perhaps beyond, with huge followings, not only in Cairo, but in Casablanca and Arab districts of Marseilles as well.

The survey of each faction includes a brief biography of its founder or dominant personality, a concise abstract of its ideology, and discussion of its impact on Egyptian society. Kepel observes that these movements are the expression of frustration with, hostility to, and suspicion of established institutions by the downtrodden and abysmally poor, who constitute the foundation of Egypt's societal pyramid. Through various devices, the present regime has robbed the "Islamicist movement of its role as a surrogate for all changes in the established order," but it seems unlikely that in the decade ahead the state will cope with its many dilemmas. Will "Islamicist" movements then still retain their dynamism?

DON PERETZ

State University of New York
Binghamton

MOLINEU, HAROLD. *U.S. Policy toward Latin America: From Regionalism to Globalism.* Pp. xii, 242. Boulder, CO: Westview Press, 1986. $35.00. Paperbound, $14.95.

PETRAS, JAMES et al. *Latin America: Bankers, Generals, and the Struggle for Social Justice.* Pp. xi, 187. Totowa, NJ: Rowman & Littlefield, 1986. $28.50. Paperbound, $12.50.

These days, our confusion is a very reasonable response to the complex issues that confront us, like current U.S. policy toward Nicaragua. Serious discussion that enlightens citizens is usually conspicuously absent from policy dialogue. The claims and counterclaims of this or that policymaker—or ideologue—inevitably reflect the grinding of policy axes. The test of any new book on U.S.-Latin American relations must be its ability to help us navigate this sea of confusion.

Harold Molineu's survey of U.S. policy toward Latin America is the latest in a series of works that place historical facts in an analytic perspective. In brief, the model is this: U.S. policy is shaped by the perspectives of policymakers. These perspectives are in turn shaped by ideological preferences and by the political context in the United States. Policies tend not to be shaped by either the history of past relations or by a good understanding of conditions within Latin American nations. As a result, these perspectives often turn out to be unproductive; that is, they lead to failures of policy and do not contribute to the realization of American interests in the region.

If an analytic survey is well done, an informed reader gains both a good deal of information and the intellectual tools to employ that information fruitfully. Molineu's book is well done. He examines several of these perspectives, dichotomized into "globalist" perspectives, including both a cold-war perspective and a "democratic mission" theme, and "regionalist" perspectives, including "the western hemisphere idea" and "sphere of influence" themes. Most chapters are separate historical surveys, with appropriate, if brief, case studies as illustrations of the perspectives being treated.

Molineu is critical of American intervention in Latin America, seeing it as a costly approach to achieving American goals, and his concluding chapter provides an alternative approach that is most emphatically not isolationist but realistic and pragmatic. This idea of relying on diplomacy rather than intervention is a resurgent theme in the latest literature on U.S. policy. Molineu's efforts along these lines are not as thorough or well developed as other recent efforts—for example, Blachman et al., in *Confronting Revolution*—but they are an appropriate conclusion to his book and a contribution to our understanding of the possibilities for sound alterative policy strategies.

James Petras's latest effort, produced with several coauthors contributing to separate chapters, deals with both the question of development within Latin American nations as well as the efforts of outside actors, including the U.S. government, to affect those developments. In brief, the model of the book is this: formerly, it may have been reasonable for scholars to believe that American hegemony in Latin America was a function of a global capitalist economy. But the world has become more complex, and students of Latin America need to transcend this globalist orthodoxy in order to see the possibilities of progress within those economic structures, possibilities that can be seen if we focus on power relationships as they shift with circumstances and conditions.

This is in a sense an incrementalist approach to dependence and development: Petras and his colleagues might well predict that achieving social justice in Latin America depends on revolutionary change in social structures, a common theme in the dependence literature. But here he is also stressing that in the meantime, incremental efforts have implications for the onset and timing of these major changes.

Recent developments and current policies are analyzed from within this perspective; the latest American stress on democratization, for example, is seen as a series of attempts to reduce the demands for major reforms and for social justice. International Monetary Fund activities, as another example, are assists to American bankers and Latin generals, not developmental programs leading to social justice. In general, U.S. policy is presented as attempts to maintain domination within the American sphere of influence. Nevertheless, shifts in power relationships leave room for some success in the struggle for social justice, and Petras's concluding chapter, on building democracy via socialism, includes an interesting view of the Nicaraguan revolution, worth the attention of any serious reader.

But as often happens in multi-author books, the essays in the book under review vary in quality. Some have extensive bibliographies and documentation, some little or none. Some chapters are less useful than others: the one on Guatemala, for example, is a simplistic view of past U.S. policy and adds nothing new to the current policy debate. And, in a work claiming to focus on domestic as well as international power relationships, the absence of any mention of the Church or of liberation theology is a shortcoming worth noting. On the other hand, the chapter on "resurgent democracy," coauthored by Edward S. Herman, provides interesting and valuable insights into the U.S. government's use of democratic rhetoric to mask American attempts at retarding the struggle for social justice.

In my view, U.S. policy in Latin America cannot be fully understood without using both normative and empirical benchmarks. Petras and his colleagues present factual information so that the implications can be measured against our own standards of justice and democracy. Molineu's approach, of course, is much more objective and pragmatic: the implications are couched in terms of U.S. interests. He uses many different and competing perspectives and thereby helps the reader seeking to understand different explanatory points of view. Petras, on the other hand, is not troubled by competing perspectives. His book is very useful to the reader who already shares his perspective and to the reader seeking to follow the ongoing theoretical debates within the dependence theory camp. Reading both books can certainly help alleviate our confusion in the face of the seemingly paradoxical policies of the current administration.

ROBERT H. TRUDEAU

Providence College
Rhode Island

SAVAGE, CHARLES H., Jr. and GEORGE F.F. LOMBARD. *Sons of the Machine: Case Studies of Social Change in the Workplace.* Pp. xvi, 313. Cambridge, MA: MIT Press, 1986. $25.00.

This book comprises an informative ethnographic-style series of studies of three factories in Colombia's Antioquia region. Two of the enterprises were small pottery plants in villages and the third was a garment factory in the city of Medellin. Savage and Lombard study the impact of various stages of industrialization on worker-management relations, the relationship between traditional patron systems, internal social organization of the workplace, and technological and workplace changes, including the introduction of Taylorist methods of production.

The study argues for greater management-labor understanding based on shared participation, discussion of workplace changes, greater recognition by management of workers' informal social organization at the workplace, and more concern by workers for what Savage and Lombard describe as the larger interests of the firm—as opposed to union-based economic demand-making—as the key to stability and progress.

The basic strength of this book is its detailed description of factory beginnings in a traditional setting. Savage and Lombard describe the carryover of deference patterns and reciprocal relations from preindustrial activities to the factory workplace. They show how the patron system was able to harness personal ties to industrial production in a profitable fashion with the apparent approval and support of the labor force. This rather idyllic portrayal of harmony and reconciliation in which modernity and traditionalism are fused, however, fails to reflect on a number of social costs that creep into the account: poverty, extended workdays, and child labor.

Savage and Lombard rather unreflectingly refer to the dominance of "rigid hierarchies" as having brought "the community to its present condition of relative health and stability." Their easy assimilation of "stability" and "health" provides the standards for their discussion of growing class conflict in the third firm, the El Dandy garment factory. Basing their evaluation on an organic conception of society, they view the increasing social polarization and class identification of the owners and workers as forms of irrational behavior, products of egocentric personalities and self-interested doctrines. Their failure to examine the deep structural relations and the interaction of the operations of the market and social solidarity leads them to ascribe conflictual relations to value conflicts rather than economic issues such as wages versus dividends, employers' prerogatives versus workers' rights.

It is unfortunate that Savage and Lombard fail to pursue the perspective of articulate subjects of the class-conflictual approach. The opportunity was available to explore the rationality and logic, the experiential context, that evokes these responses. On the other hand, they do provide a detailed elaboration of the context for incremental-innovative forms of leadership and authority.

There are a number of historical studies of workplace organization and growing numbers of studies of class conflict in the making of the working class that Savage and Lombard could have consulted. Instead, they claim that intellectuals view industrial workers as automatons—a claim hardly justified given the burgeoning literature on the subject. At several points, the study seems to be more concerned with providing managerial prescriptions, derived from the human relations school of management-worker relations, than with exploring the process by which labor union leaders developed a class-conflictual approach to employer-employee relations; this is the case particularly in section 3, pages 151-208.

The major strength of this study is in its attempt to describe the multidimensional roles and interests that industrial workers bring to the workplace. Savage and Lombard correctly criticize the crude wage-reductionist imagery explicit in Taylorist concepts of labor. Their efforts to locate the work site as a principal source of value change in the larger social system and their description of the interplay of workplace and community is insightful. Their effort to provide managers with strategies for labor control based on the instrumental use of informal worker networks is certainly one that will be well received by personnel managers oriented toward new shared decision-making management schemes. The larger costs of such proposals to labor in terms of worker autonomy and the insecurities resulting from the shifting movement of capital—across and within national boundaries—is not considered.

Within these limitations, there is a useful study, particularly if one is interested in understanding the stabilizing factors embedded in traditional patron-labor relations.

JAMES F. PETRAS

State University of New York
Binghamton

TAYLOR, ROBERT. *The Sino-Japanese Axis: A New Force in Asia?* Pp. viii, 127. New York: St. Martin's Press, 1985. $27.50.

AKAHA, TSUNEO. *Japan in Global Ocean Politics.* Pp. xii, 224. Honolulu: University of Hawaii Press and Law of the Sea Institute, 1985. $19.00.

Robert Taylor's brief book suggests that a Sino-Japanese partnership "could be . . . a new force in Asia and world politics at large." Taylor does little to sustain this sweeping thesis; however, he provides substantial detail with respect to Japan's role in the modernization of the Chinese economy.

Taylor emphasizes that Japan's "social cohesion" and its policy of "national integration" after the Meiji Restoration was one of the crucial factors in Japan's economic success. He suggests that China, with a similar cultural foundation, might draw on the same sort of values or traditions or at least find it possible to follow the Japanese example in its own modernization. But Taylor cautions that the free market, which Japan so readily adapted to its own needs, may face opposition in China, where Marxism has dictated the establishment of a centralized command economy. How far Beijing's recent encouragement of regional initiatives and its acceptance of a limited market economy will go is difficult to determine.

The most useful part of Taylor's book deals with Japanese economic assistance to China and the resulting increase in their mutual trade. Notable here is the 1978 bilateral trade agreement in which China promised to deliver 10 million tons of coal to Japan by 1985, a deal made possible by a Japanese loan to develop seven new mines. Equally interesting is Taylor's description of Japan's development of "compensatory trade" with the Chinese and certain joint ventures sponsored by the two powers. The real value of this study lies in its analysis of Sino-Japanese economic relations, not in the role of the two powers in international politics.

Tsuneo Akaha's *Japan in Global Ocean Politics* is a clearly organized and detailed study of Japan's response to the sweeping changes in the Law of the Seas that occurred in the mid-1970s. The book demonstrates how an apparently narrow monographic theme, when properly mounted, can provide insight on larger issues. In fact, the reader is given a substantial view of the inner workings of Japanese foreign policy and a sense of the trade-offs and compromises necessary in the formulation of policy within the bureaucracy.

Akaha explains that Japan was a vigorous supporter of freedom of the seas since its vital shipping interests and need for fishing supplies for human consumption required access to the world's seas. However, since

1945, nations have moved toward the enclosure of ocean territory. This was first true of developing nations and then became policy for the Soviet Union and the United States. By 1977, 62 states had claimed a 12-mile territorial sea and 13 had claimed a 200-mile fishing zone.

Initially, contending interests within Japan prevented Tokyo from adjusting to this reality. But, by 1977, realism prevailed. Japan extended its own coastal jurisdiction and accepted the claims of others. Akaha's comments on the implications of this face-off for Russo-Japanese relations is especially illuminating. Based on original sources and interviews with Japanese officials, this study must be regarded as the standard commentary on Japan and the Law of the Seas.

EDMUND S. WEHRLE
University of Connecticut
Storrs

WINN, PETER. *Weavers of Revolution: The Yarur Workers and Chile's Road to Socialism.* Pp. xiv, 328. New York: Oxford University Press, 1986. $19.95.

In 1971, Chilean workers forced a very reluctant president to expropriate a textile factory that had been a pillar of that nation's capitalist system. What makes this episode especially significant—and absolutely captivating—is not only the evolution of worker consciousness but the fact that the infuriated president, Salvador Allende, was himself a Socialist, the first democratically elected Marxist head of government in the Americas.

Peter Winn provides a fascinating, gripping, and novel perspective; he does so largely by providing the workers' own views. Numerous publications have now documented the macropolitics of the Allende presidential years (1970-73), but Winn's is a unique journey into micropolitics. It is a path-breaking work in a new wave of historical scholarship emphasizing the masses and listening to them. Thus *Weavers of Revolution* takes us

well beyond conventional data on worker voting patterns, coalitions with political parties, leadership background, and so forth, to a close examination of politics in a single factory, Yarur. The major source of information here is oral history, based on more than 200 interviews with workers.

The micropolitics of *Weavers* is complementary to more voluminous macropolitical studies. Indeed, Winn proves himself a competent weaver of the two. We see how, for example, Allende's presidential campaign emboldened the Yarur factory workers, his emphasis on legal avenues of change affected worker strategies, the workers' zeal for change pushed Allende away from his strategy of confronting opponents one by one, and the workers could prevail largely because of disunity within the governmental coalition. In illuminating these micro-macro links, *Weavers* does not, in my view, present new interpretations of the macro side, although it does help discredit those who have exaggerated Allende's irresponsibility and those who have underplayed the importance of divisions within Chile in explaining the demise of democracy there. Instead, it creditably relies on good secondary sources to sketch in the macro context and then provides the special intimacy of the micro approach. Consequently, Winn's book may profitably be read by those familiar with the literature on Chile's revolution and by those seeking just one interesting work on the subject.

Although this is a scholarly book, the subject it treats is ideologically charged and Winn's methodology involves close contact and mutual confidence with his subjects. Readers may well differ as to whether a desirable degree of objectivity is maintained. Winn writes of the workers, "This book is *their* [Winn's italics] story, which I have tried to tell as much as possible through their eyes and in their words." To be sure, he also says that oral history must not be treated as sacred text. Yet readers are not informed of instances in which Winn doubts the veracity of what he is told, even though worker leaders are shown to mislead their constituencies at times. Then, too, the opinions of the nonrevolutionary workers are rarely presented directly and perhaps too often are merely summarized or attributed to fear or false consciousness. Nor are examples of intimidation by revolutionary workers recounted; if they did not exist, that is worth explicit mention. At the same time, material provided—fairly—by Winn himself may cast doubt on the allegedly clear commitment of the government—which parts of it?—to democratic change. Finally, however one assesses the principals in this mighty drama, it is disappointing that fewer than fifty pages are reserved for the fascinating experiment in worker management that unfolded in the year and a half before a military coup brutally terminated the entire socialist experiment and returned the factory to private owners.

But even those who hold such reservations—and many will not—should praise this book. It is at once an adeptly told story filled with intriguing individual profiles of both workers and owners and an exploration of a crucial, yet little researched, political arena. Reflective of a poignancy found throughout the book, the epilogue reports a great irony: economic crisis has recently forced the free-market-oriented military government to assume control of the failing factory and search in vain for private buyers.

DANIEL C. LEVY

State University of New York
Albany
Yale University
New Haven
Connecticut


*EUROPE*

HANN, C. M. *A Village without Solidarity: Polish Peasants in Years of Crisis.* Pp. ix, 208. New Haven, CT: Yale University Press, 1985. $15.95.

PLOSS, SIDNEY I. *Moscow and the Polish Crisis: An Interpretation of Soviet Policies and Intentions.* Pp. x, 182. Boulder, CO: Westview Press, 1986. $29.50.

C. M. Hann, a research fellow in anthropology at Cambridge University, selected what he acknowledges is an atypical Polish village for his studies: Wislok. It is a community of a few hundred souls in the Bieszczady Mountains near the frontiers with Slovakia and the Ukraine. In 1947 the Communist authorities expelled the Ruthenian (Habsburg Ukrainian) Orthodox and Uniate Christians who had lived in the area for centuries and resettled ethnic Poles, mostly poor peasants, on their lands. These new settlers ought to have been the stuff of which a socialist peasantry was made, but in practice they quickly became alienated from the regime.

This is not the conclusion of two establishment scholars in Poland, the sociologist Henryk Jadam and the ethnographer Maria Biernacka, both of whom found the *Bieszczadzianie*—a term Hann never encountered in Wislok—fully integrated, with a strong regional consciousness, and wholly supportive of the socialist system. Hann follows Andrezj Potocki, a maverick sociologist whose work on the area has not been published in Poland, to diametrically opposite conclusions. Unlike Jadam and Biernacka, Hann and Potocki worked in the field, where they found a striking absence of economic integration and a latent hostility toward Warsaw. The Roman Catholic Church retains considerable authority, although Hann rejects the "myth" of a harmonious, church-centered "rural civilization" as a plot by Rome's emissaries to retain their power and preserve the "legitimacy of Christian doctrine."

Collectivization was a failure in Poland, where today four-fifths of the arable land belongs to more than 3 million private farmers. The case of Wislok would seem paradoxically to suggest, however, that the days of the peasantry as a sociopolitical and economic category are numbered in Poland as everywhere in industrializing societies. It is simply not possible for the family farm to compete in the modern world. What Hann calls a "peasant mentality" and the "peasant class" have survived precisely because of collectivization's failure, but new attitudes are everywhere making themselves felt among the younger generation.

Wislok was little touched by Rural Solidarity during the first couple of years of this decade, but that is not the point of Hann's title. The village has existed in its modern form only forty years and is still seeking its identity. Whether it will passively submit to dictates from Warsaw is not entirely clear, but Hann's excellent analysis provides some insights into the possibilities that lie ahead.

Sidney I. Ploss gives us little we could not get from the index of the *New York Times*. It is simply not possible to take seriously an author who calls Lenin "the only infallible Soviet leader prior to Brezhnev." One is at a loss to make any sense of the comment that "the Poles had to make concessions that were far-reaching if only rhetorical" when the author reveals in the same paragraph that "Kania and Jaruzelski acknowledged the right of the Soviet Union to intervene by force if necessary to safeguard what the Soviet leaders understood to be socialism in Poland." This study reveals nothing about Soviet intentions or policies that has not already entered the domain of common knowledge.

WOODFORD McCLELLAN
University of Virginia
Charlottesville

HOPKIRK, PETER. *Setting the East Ablaze: Lenin's Dream of an Empire in Asia.* Pp. x, 252. New York: W. W. Norton, 1985. $17.95.

The Bolshevik revolution in Russia sent shock waves around the world after October of 1917 even though it was by no means certain that the Reds could consolidate their victory. The hopes and fears engendered by this significant event were nonetheless considerably in excess of what was realistically feasible or probable. Yet, from the beginning, Lenin and his cohorts envisioned flames of their revolution spreading to both the East and West.

It was in Central Asia where much of the immediately induced dream was acted out.

Although this region had historically spawned some of the most ferocious and dominating tribes in history, it had become the backwater of Asia and subject to the shifting fortunes of its more powerful empire-building neighbors. It was here that the British sought to resist Bolshevik efforts to undermine their position in India and China. It was in this vast desert region that the White Russians made their last stand. It was also in this area that first Enver Pasha of Turkey and then the Chinese Muslim Ma Chung-yin sought to ignite the local Muslim populations into a holy war to create their own respective empires.

The Russian forces, in characteristically czarlike manner, did dominate much of the region—they are still trying in Afghanistan—but they failed to precipitate the world revolution and certainly did not ignite a Russian-dominated Asian revolution. When the empire collapsed after World War II, European powers survived without their colonies and those underdeveloped countries that underwent social revolution did so despite Russian efforts and generally separately from Russian domination.

Hopkirk's study is very readable and interesting, and it brings to light some little-known historical data. The special insights to some extremely interesting personalities make the book particularly enjoyable. The book is also a resource for providing additional perspective on the problems created between Soviet revolutionary theory and the realities of world politics. On the other hand, the title implies more than the analytical and descriptive aspects of the book can justify. The focus is more on the unique and colorful characters who sought to upset Soviet policy—and on their own special dramas—than it is on an effort to implement that policy. While that makes the story interesting, it does little to explain why there was such a gap between what the Soviets wanted to do and what they were actually able to accomplish.

ARVIN PALMER
Northland Pioneer College
Holbrook
Arizona

McNEIL, WILLIAM C. *American Money and the Weimar Republic: Economics and Politics on the Eve of the Great Depression.* Pp. x, 352. New York: Columbia University Press, 1986. $35.00.

As policymakers today confront the problems of collecting international debts from unstable democratic governments that are seeking to borrow more, they would be wise to consult the historical record. *American Money and the Weimar Republic* explains how attracting and allocating foreign loans between 1924 and 1929 became the focus of conflict between political factions within Germany and between Germany and the Allies. Because of Germany's reparation debts, governments on both sides believed that lending should be restrained and channeled, but they were reluctant to take on the responsibility.

The Dawes agreement of 1924 opened the way for German borrowing in New York and also scheduled (again) German reparation payments to the Allies. The Allies intended the Dawes loans to restore enough political and financial stability to the German government for it to pay reparations. Like the International Monetary Fund with problem debtor countries today, a reparations agent was appointed to police the agreement—to verify whether Germany was balancing its budget and to recommend whether economic conditions warranted increases or decreases in the scheduled payments. The central story of the book is how the agent's valiant efforts failed. Hope for his mission's success led the agent to tolerate temporary lapses by Germany, which then trapped the agent as the lapses became chronic.

Germans hoped that the loans, in addition to providing needed capital, would work as a lever to reduce reparations. American banks and bondholders would have reparations slashed in order to maintain prosperity in Germany and protect their investment. Because the loans mostly went for public works, unemployment relief, and investment in sectors with excess capacity already, they made no commensurate increase in Germany's ability to earn foreign exchange.

The fragility of Weimar democracy led to government deficits and demand for borrowing. When the economy slipped into depression in 1925-26 and in 1929, the borrowing needs of Weimar's new welfare state soared. Competition by American banks for the business of underwriting the loans left little restraint on the supply side of the lending process until 1929, when all the lending stopped. Being forced then to balance its budget led to maximum economic and political damage in Germany and eventually to Hitler's takeover.

The reader should not jump to conclude that American money caused the demise of the Weimar Republic. The loans were a key issue over which the parties tore apart the Republic's fragile democracy. But the readiness of the parties to do so predated the loans.

In discussing the economics of German business cycles and of reparation transfers, McNeil takes several controversial positions without adequate justification. Fortunately, this does not detract from the political analysis, because his positions are close to those of contemporaries.

McNeil gives us a useful and well-told cautionary tale. When a government turned to foreign creditors because it was politically too weak to raise resources at home, the same weaknesses led it to allocate the borrowed resources uneconomically. Being able to borrow abroad did not help democracy in Weimar Germany.

STEVEN B. WEBB

U.S. Department of State
Washington, D.C.

NARKIEWICZ, OLGA A. *Eastern Europe: 1968-1984.* Pp. ii, 273. Totowa, NJ: Barnes & Noble, 1986. $31.50.

STEVENS, JOHN NELSON. *Czechoslovakia at the Crossroads.* Pp. xiv, 349. Boulder, CO: Eastern European Monographs, 1985. Distributed by Columbia University Press, New York. $35.00.

It is often refreshing to read books on Eastern Europe written by British academics, because these authors tend to be less agitated by righteous anticommunism than their American counterparts. But what does one make of Narkiewicz's claim that "classifying the regimes [of Eastern Europe] as 'totalitarian' or 'authoritarian' in the manner of some political scientists is rather erroneous"? Granted that totalitarianism is a controversial concept; but if we are asked not to call East Germany, Romania, Bulgaria, Czechoslovakia, Poland, and—yes—Hungary authoritarian, what are they? Unfortunately, this update on political and socioeconomic developments in Eastern Europe by Olga A. Narkiewicz ventures close to becoming an apology for the regimes in power.

About the Prague Spring she writes that "many of the reforms were on the verge of collapse even before the invasion and that only the invasion saved their reputation." By contrast, John Nelson Stevens, the other author under review, quotes approvingly that "there was no evidence that Czechoslovakia's economic reform was going to fail." What another writer has called "the first authentic workers' revolution in history" (T. G. Ash, *The Polish Revolution: Solidarity* [New York: Vintage Books, 1985], p. 311) is suspected by Narkiewicz to involve an "American intervention" if not an ill-timed plot by the Central Intelligence Agency. In the end she surprises her readers with a scenario of hope that

presupposes that the two superpowers are sufficiently weakened by the mutual struggle to retain superiority, to loosen their grip on their spheres of influence. Such an event would be accompanied by a growth of dissension within the spheres of influence and by the eventual overthrow of the superpowers' dominance (p. 257).

In Iran it has happened already, she suggests, and in Poland it almost did.

The somewhat loose fit of the various parts of her argument harms the book throughout. In part it is a consequence of her reliance on long quotes from secondary sources and a change of focus—halfway through the book—from the promised analysis of Eastern Europe between 1968 and 1984 to a general discussion of the East-West conflict. Also, we learn very little about the developments in East Germany, Romania, and Bulgaria.

John Nelson Stevens's book on the CSSR's economic dilemmas is a more conventional scholarly monograph, with extensive statistical tables and graphic displays substantiating every step of the argument. Stevens leads us through Czechoslovakia's economic development, from the days before the 1948 coup up to the 1980s.

Primary attention is naturally drawn to the events surrounding the Prague Spring. Steven writes "that almost all the provisions of the [CSSR's 1967] New Economic Model have been tried at one time or another elsewhere within the Bloc" and that "any opinion that developments in the national economy *per se* triggered the Soviet intervention seems difficult to support." Workers' participation, however, introduced by the 1968 Action Program of the Communist Party, may have contributed to the basically political concerns of the Soviet Union.

While the so-called normalization after the Warsaw Pact invasion of August 1968 involved the reintroduction of the Soviet-type planning model, this was mollified by administrative decentralization and some accommodation of consumer needs. The democratization drive of the reformers, however, was stopped.

Czechoslovakia has the potential of a "Switzerland of East Europe," Stevens concludes, but in fact it is "a political and economic casualty of European and East-West conflicts."

KARL H. KAHRS
California State University
Fullerton

SCHMIDT, HELMUT. *A Grand Strategy for the West: The Anachronism of National Strategies in an Interdependent World.* Pp. xviii, 159. New Haven, CT: Yale University Press, 1985. $12.95.

CARR, JONATHAN. *Helmut Schmidt: Helmsman of Germany*. Pp. 208. New York: St. Martin's Press, 1985. $25.00.

That a person has achieved the status of a recognized international leader does not and should not endow his or her published reflections with magisterial wisdom. In the case of Helmut Schmidt, however, one encounters a statesmanlike equipoise and world-mindedness that justify incorporating his prestigious Yale University-sponsored Stimson Lectures in durable book form. What is more, his admirable rationality, his clear and concise expression, his profound appreciation of political economy as an inescapable interpenetration of politics and economics set him apart from most of his contemporaries. He appears to embody those qualities of temperance and moderation so esteemed by some of the classical political philosophers.

Helmut Schmidt is an eloquent advocate of Western—including Canada and Japan—collective security. His political realism warns him never to drop his posture of vigilance toward Soviet expansionist designs. Yet his common sense cautions against nuclear saber rattling. In particular, he dislikes the Reagan Strategic Defense Initiative because it is technologically incapable of providing an impenetrable protective umbrella. Even more, he grimly puzzles over the conceivable benefit for Germans—and Poles, too—when central Europe would become the battleground and site of frightful carnage. American leadership may be acknowledged in Western grand-strategy formulation, but certain preconditions must be met.

For its optimism, its energy, its great generosity, the United States merits respect and gratitude. Nonetheless, these qualities do not exempt the superpower from comporting itself as a true partner. Schmidt remonstrates against the American practice of repeatedly unveiling a *fait accompli*. Prior consultation with its Western allies is required, eventuating in a joint hammering out of policy and tactics. Thus Schmidt exhorts greater reliance upon conventional forces, with bold efforts exerted to lure the French back into the fold; Schmidt recommends a French commander in chief. European input toward the resolution of regional conflicts, including those in Central America and the Caribbean, should also be solicited by the United States, since the former's greater objectivity might be helpful. From a statesman's perspective, American blunders spin off repercussions impairing Western global strategy with ultimate weakening of European defense capacity.

If readers set about deliberately seeking grounds for disputation with Schmidt, they will find themselves hard put. Schmidt staunchly opposes protectionism. He advises the United States against pressuring the Japanese, favoring instead Japanese application of its surplus toward assisting developing nations. As an enlightened "conservative liberal," he urges the leading lender banks to renegotiate scheduled interest payments with the Latin American debtor nations. He also counsels the International Monetary Fund to act prudently and relax its insistence upon austerity lest the desperate poor turn toward revolutionary expedients.

To be sure, one may transgress the implicit parameters of present discourse and, while remaining within the compass of Western solidarity, apply the critique of democratic socialism. Thus Schmidt really has no solution for the chronic American adverse trade balance other than palliatives, such as a somewhat reduced defense budget. His condemning from a market-economy standpoint the European and American alleged overproduction of grain at a time when starvation is widespread evokes the Marxist clichè of "contradictions" within capitalism. However, we are dealing with a pragmatist who prefers humane corrective tinkering to the risks of radical surgery. Hence, in judging Schmidt on his own grounds, which include a constructive give-and-take with the Soviet Union and an underscoring of global interdependence, we can only hope that others of his stature attain leadership on the world scene.

The appearance of the journalist Carr's book constitutes a most opportune complement to Schmidt's lectures. For admirers of the ex-chancellor's political sagacity, what Carr offers is a quasi-biographical study of Schmidt's economic, fiscal, and foreign affairs policies and tactics. The congruence of Schmidt's prescriptions as academic lecturer with the political stands he took both within the German Social Democratic Party and as governmental officeholder becomes abundantly clear. He also sought to devise cooperative ventures with East Germany while sidestepping—not always successfully—the snares that might supply a tactical advantage to that Soviet satellite.

After sketching some of the early episodes in the family upbringing, education, military service, and character formation of his subject, Carr concentrates upon the emergence and maturation of a superb political creature. It is clear that Carr is an admirer of Schmidt, yet he is no blind devotee, unaware of his hero's limitations. Carr repeatedly calls attention to Schmidt's acerbic tongue and indicates his slippage in effectiveness during the closing phase of his chancellorship. Whatever Schmidt's failings, one gets the sense that Germany was the better because of his presence.

Carr introduces the reader to the more prominent German politicians with whom Schmidt associated, both as foils for the expression of Schmidt's personality and as ideologists prodding Schmidt into clarifying his own doctrines and positions. Thus, while opposing the sometimes reactionary policies of Franz Josef Strauss, Schmidt refused the concessions Willy Brandt advocated as a way of attracting a youthful radical constituency. And while seeking a *modus vivendi* with the Soviet Union—sometimes exasperating American critics—and urging the abatement of the superpower arms race, he incurred the wrath of pacifist elements by supporting the emplacement on German soil of the U. S. nuclear deterrent. Together with his esteemed friend Giscard d'Estaing of France, the pro-American Schmidt dared assert what

he conceived of as pro-European monetary and trade policies in defiance of U.S. preferences. Carr sees Schmidt as unmistakably his own man.

Well organized and clearly written, Carr's book is disappointing in some respects. Only with difficulty would I believe that Schmidt's marriage had no impact upon his political life, yet I was forced to that conclusion by the paucity of reference on Carr's part. The reader also discovers that the chancellor is both an accomplished pianist and a connoisseur of good painting. Again, Carr reserves scant space for the aesthetic dimension. Should one argue that, after all, this is political biography, then why the abbreviated coverage of Schmidt's attitudes toward ecological issues, the student movement, neo-Nazism, or an in-depth analysis—in view of Schmidt's Wehrmacht background—of German rearmament. Nevertheless, when all is said, Carr succeeds in making a convincing case in support of the book's subtitle: "Helmsman of Germany."

ELMER N. LEAR

Pennsylvania State University
Middletown

SPOTTS, FREDERIC and THEODOR WIESER. *Italy, a Difficult Democracy.* Pp. xi, 329. New York: Cambridge University Press, 1986. $37.50.

URBAN, JOAN BARTH. *Moscow and the Italian Communist Party: From Tagliatti to Berlinguer.* Pp. 370. Ithaca, NY: Cornell University Press, 1986. Paperbound, $14.95.

Italy appears paradoxical, and these volumes suggest some of the reasons why. The Communist Party (PCI) is still going strong, despite singular efforts by the Vatican, Washington, and sometimes Moscow to cut it down to size. About one in three Italians votes for the PCI, notwithstanding that Italy is now the world's seventh largest economy and Italians number among the most affluent people on earth. Furthermore, this transformation has occurred notwithstanding all of those indicators of excessive political conflict and governmental instability that have been Italy's steady state these last forty years.

The paradox of the democratic republic is not just its survival; it is, above all, its vigorous growth and, yes, its fundamental stability that seem to fly in the face of much of what we think we know about political systems, institutions, and behavior.

Spotts and Wieser underscore the paradox by applying to the Italian polity Galileo's comment about the earth's relationship to the sun: "And yet, it moves!" The imagery is not apt. Neither was Galileo surprised by his discovery, nor did he find it paradoxical. He meant to be sardonic regarding the obscurantist orthodoxy of his time that masqueraded as science. Similarly, Italy will look paradoxical only if we believe, deep down, that to qualify as a democracy it should be a mirror image of Great Britain or the United States.

The Spotts and Wieser survey, although it is intelligent, well informed, and often illuminating, too often reinforces many of our stereotypes of Italy. Thus, after almost 300 pages of description, some of it very lively, of Italian politics, Spotts and Wieser ask, "Why in fact does the ship, rudderless and awash, sail on instead of sinking?" A real answer would require less description and more analysis than one finds in these pages. Instead, they suggest the Italian "substructure is solid," which is a variation of the bromide, so dear to Italians, that the "legal country" is corrupt and moribund but the "real country" is sound.

Joan Barth Urban comes at this question with no such preconceptions. Her meticulous study of the relationship between the PCI and Moscow, based on both Italian and Soviet primary sources, gives us one of the more important analyses of that party to appear outside of Italy. No one who reads this study with an open mind will ever accept that picture of the PCI that its major detrac-

tors have tried to project. Urban finds that the PCI is not Marxist-Leninist, not automatically pro-Soviet or inclined to take orders from Moscow, not doctrinaire, quintessentially Italian, and genuinely committed to parliamentary democracy. We can infer from this, at a minimum, that postwar Italian democracy's successful evolution owes something to this party.

Urban also makes the point that the PCI was not automatically anti-American, either. Rather, its hostility to the United States was forced on that party by the onset of the cold war and by the United States' open support of the Christian Democratic Party. American intervention in Italy's internal politics is several times mentioned by Spotts and Wieser as well, but Urban brings us directly into the PCI, including its complex maneuvers and debates, to show how international conflict can affect national politics. When forced to make very hard choices, the PCI opted for democracy and, in a fundamental sense during the Berlinguer era, for the West. As Urban says, the PCI elected not just for autonomy within Moscow's orbit but, rather, disengagement from it.

Italians understood this, too. The nature of the PCI, and its behavior for forty years, constitute just two of many indicators that Italy's "legal country" is very sound indeed. The rest of us have to learn not to take either the Italians or the survey research teams too literally when they next tell us that Italian democracy is in crisis or in danger of falling apart.

JOSEPH LaPALOMBARA
Yale University
New Haven
Connecticut

*UNITED STATES*

GOLD, PHILIP. *Evasions: The American Way of Military Service.* Pp. xxiii, 182. New York: Paragon House, 1985. $17.95.

Can a society founded on individual liberty, fearful of central power and standing armies, and historically addicted to evading military responsibility maintain effective forces in an age of continuous national peril? Can that society ever find a morally supportable imperative for general military obligation? Yes, asserts Philip Gold of Georgetown University, but only in support of a just national strategy against a tangible danger. "Conscription," he writes,

is only necessary if it is to be the American purpose to offer this planet alternatives to either Armageddon or a communistic New Dark Age. Nothing else, nothing less, can justify its return. And if it is not to be the American purpose to provide such alternatives, then much of the currently standing military should be dismantled immediately, and the wealth and talent contained therein turned to the problem of American welfare in the world that would ensue (p. 152).

Gold makes three arguments. In a section on philosophy he examines the history of just-war theology and concludes that in a just cause the survival of the community outweighs the rights of the individual. In a section on history he examines American attitudes toward military service during the Revolutionary War and Vietnam and calls for the restoration of military idealism. In a section on policy he criticizes the course of American foreign and military strategies since World War II, raises alarming threat perceptions and contingencies, and calls for a just and morally defensible American grand purpose. Posing the existence of a simple bipolar world value structure and reasoning out of traditional just-war theory, he writes with a burst of ethnocentric Wilsonian rhetoric:

If it is to be the American purpose to offer this planet alternatives to slavery and holocaust—to practice a prudent civic virtue on a planetary scale—it will require the full participation of the American people, as well as their tacit consent. And if it does become our purpose, and we succeed, we will have become what the founding fathers always sensed we might become. The last, best hope of man (p. 155).

This lightly documented book is obviously a part of the current controversy over Ameri-

can military and foreign policy. Although they have a disarming tentative quality, Gold's arguments are confrontational and often dogmatic. The core of his contention, sometimes articulated and sometimes merely implied, is that once homogeneous values and a common definition of national policy are secured, "civic virtue" requires that individuals not only acquiesce but also help carry out the design. Military service is a unique and special condition that permits no evasion. Although he might include modifications to ensure equity and provide for an "intermediate obligation" to serve only on national territory in peacetime, he implies that once policy is established, effective resistance is unacceptable.

Half a century ago Reinhold Niebuhr addressed the same issues in *Moral Man and Immoral Society* and came to strikingly different conclusions. Like Niebuhr, many thoughtful Americans might agree with Gold pragmatically, but they would consider endowing any particular social system with objective qualities of morality and justice as dangerous to the future of the Republic as any foreign threat. Moral, just, and necessary are three quite different imperatives in a world of multiple realities. Unwilling to play out a Greek tragedy by allowing themselves to be destroyed by their own virtue, those who have learned to endure moral ambiguity might under duress impose similar policies. But they would not deceive themselves by raising the cry of justice and moral universalism. This is no mere quibble. On the crucial points of difference between moral absolutes, the political power of the community to impose conformity, and the individual's right to construct an independent moral world, rest the only important differences between us and our adversaries and, I might add, between myself and Gold.

DANIEL R. BEAVER

Center of Military History
Washington, D.C.

JACOBSOHN, GARY J. *The Supreme Court and the Decline of Constitutional Aspira-*

*tion*. Pp. ix, 182. Totowa, NJ: Rowman & Littlefield, 1986. $29.50.

This volume is another contribution to the debate over the the theoretical grounding of judicial review and the role of the Supreme Court in interpreting the Constitution. Jacobsohn joins the intellectual warfare among contesting interpretivists, noninterpretivists, activists and self-restrainers, interest-based theorists and rights-based theorists to assert that all of these modern jurisprudential approaches have lost touch with one of the essential elements in the political philosophy of the founders and framers—the natural law context of the constitutional period and of the first century thereafter.

Jacobsohn finds that each of the modern positions has its drawbacks. Interpretivism confines judicial activism and conserves constitutional purpose by tying constitutional interpretation to the specific language of the document and the intent of the framers as derivable therefrom; but it leaves the process drained of aspiration and fails to relate the exercise of judicial power to the broader purposes of the polity. The more liberal noninterpretivist theorists see the Constitution as more than a "positivistic legal document," but their theories encourage activist judges to substitute modern goals and values for those of the founders and the document itself.

Jacobsohn is convinced that to discover the underlying spirit of the Constitution and the aspirations of the framers, one must look at the Declaration of Independence, where these values are explicitly stated. The Declaration is of more than historical or rhetorical importance and the Constitution must be read in the reflected rays of its central principle, liberty. Liberty is, in Lincoln's words, " 'the apple of gold' to us. The *Union* and the *Constitution*, are the *picture* of *silver* subsequently framed around it." The Constitution protects liberty, the right of individuals to pursue their goals, but does not contain a specific vision of what society should become. The checks and balances, the governmental devices provided by the constitutional document install a political mechanism that, once set in motion, is designed to function automatically to equalize opportunity, check ambition, and secure liberty.

This meticulous reexamination of the statements on judicial review of earlier constitutional theorists—Madison, Hamilton and Lincoln, John Marshall, James Wilson and Joseph Story—scrapes away the distortions of later theorizing to emphasize an older natural rights philosophy that puts their ideas in context. Traditional thought, if correctly interpreted, supplies a moral underpinning for the process of constitutional choice. The discussion in this tightly reasoned presentation supplies some critical distinctions that will enhance the quality of the ongoing constitutional debate.

EVA R. RUBIN

North Carolina State University
Raleigh

KAHIN, GEORGE McT. *Intervention: How America Became Involved in Vietnam*. Pp. xii, 550. New York: Knopf, 1986. $24.95.

DIETZ, TERRY. *Republicans and Vietnam, 1961-1968*. Pp. xv, 1984. Westport, CT: Greenwood Press, 1986. $29.95.

Marking a pivotal event in American foreign policy, the stream of literature concerning Vietnam is unabated, but the quality varies. Here, however, are two volumes of solid caliber. Kahin has intensively studied Southeast Asia. His work is well written, documented, and, despite length, interesting. The story, to the "polarization" in the spring of 1966, is melancholy, utilizing newly declassified documents to show U.S. involvement in a culturally alien area, of military rather than of political-social perspectives. Dietz looks at Republican domestic politics and the war, clearly showing the leaders' ambivalence until the crucial 1968 election, when bipartisanship ended.

To someone immersed in Vietiana, the Kahin outlines are familiar. President Kennedy said America was prepared to meet any challenge, and when these mounted, the country raised resources inordinately. President Johnson, a domestic master, was on unfamiliar foreign ground. In his administration he was the last dove, but influenced by his advisers.

American figures in Washington and Vietnam and their judgments are chronicled. Deputy Ambassador Johnson showed moral courage when later assessing a 1964 policy action: "I don't feel" we presented "the President, in a clear cut fashion, the alternatives . . . I don't think we served the President well." Two other foreign service officers—shades of pre-Communist China—gave pessimistic appraisals in meetings with the president. The tide of views, however, was otherwise.

As escalation continued, Saigon proved predictable. Americans shouldered its forces aside, and Saigon willingly gave them more responsibilities and casualties. When a regime proved incompetent and sensed the United States wanted a change, it made private overtures to Hanoi for a neutralist settlement. Kahin describes "the fixed polarization," when the weary Vietnamese, typified by the Buddhist-led Struggle Movement, sought negotiations and a neutralist, foreign-independent government. This last non-Communist political force was eliminated and the stark, prolonged struggle against the National Liberation Front and Hanoi was poised.

At home the unique nature of the war, its duration and incremental warmaking, created complications for the Republicans and added to the dilemma of conventionally expected bipartisanship. Dietz clearly follows the Republicans from unquestioning support to dawning understanding that the Democrats were mishandling the war.

Remarkably, the Republicans gave support and muted criticisms over a long stretch. Dietz attributes this to certain key figures. Senator Dirksen and Congressman Halleck kept support for President Kennedy. That these three shared a genuine liking reinforced this support. As minority Senate leader, Dirksen was close to President Johnson and

cooperated by stressing unity and by calming his party's swelling restiveness and critical chorus.

House Republicans, led by Gerald Ford, showed a "greater innovative spirit" and sought credibility. Melvin Laird and Senator Goodell offered "intelligent criticism" of the administration. Republican support, despite strains, held until the 1968 election. Then Richard Nixon, imitating Eisenhower's go-to-Korea gambit in 1952, succeeded to the presidency by announcing he had a "secret" plan to end the war.

Either-or can prove the bane of American diplomacy. The simple alternatives, to win or to lose, so typical of American culture, confronted a world of confusing, gray alternatives in Vietnam. Compounding this were priorities and limits.

General Marshall in World War II believed an American trait required planning for a conflict lasting no more than four years. He calculated that American democracy would not engage longer without significant dissension. Thus important Vietnam problems may have been partially overshadowed by a crucial fact: it was America's longest war.

ROY M. MELBOURNE
Chapel Hill
North Carolina


MORALES, JULIO. *Puerto Rican Poverty and Migration*. Pp. xvii, 253. New York: Praeger, 1986. $33.95.

At its heart, this work is a polemic. That fact, however, does not detract from its potential value for scholars. Morales's emphasis upon the colonial nature of Puerto Rico's relationship to the United States is used more as a device for assigning blame for the current plight of poor Puerto Ricans, both on the island and on the mainland, than as a source of variables for a migration model. An open-minded scholar from the mainland will probably admit that the acceptance of some degree of guilt is appropriate. It would appear to be Morales's hope that such acceptance might lead to policy changes that would enhance the well-being of Puerto Ricans who migrate and those who do not. He does go a bit far, however, when he occasionally substitutes the island's pre-Hispanic name "Borinquen" for "Puerto Rico." For example, his usage of the ancient name in the statement that "they were pushed out of Borinquen while being pulled to New York City" is as ludicrous as would be the substitution of the Aztec name "Tenochtitlán" for present-day "Mexico City."

Morales builds his case with data from the U.S. census and secondary sources and with personal interviews with persons at the source and destination of the migratory flows. While the interview technique has a number of well-known shortcomings, they here serve to establish points that could never be divined from census data. For example, farmers and public officials in New England as well as Puerto Ricans in New England and Puerto Rico make it clear that farm labor was actively recruited from the island during and after World War II. The perspective at that time was one of a movement of labor reacting largely to pull factors. This recruitment established a base camp to which later migrants would move. The more recent migration has been "push" in nature, being related to failed economic policies on the island. Morales sees the industrialization program known as "operation bootstrap" as a U.S. government program imposed upon Puerto Rico. Operation bootstrap and an earlier "colonial" policy that transformed Puerto Rico's agriculture from its family-farm status into plantations are seen by Morales as the principal causes of present-day poverty on the island. The agricultural transformation pushed many more people from the land than could be absorbed by the allegedly ill-conceived industrialization program. It then follows that most of the out-migration of recent decades is to be blamed on the failure of those policies.

There has been another villain at work, however, and one that receives very little attention in this work. The average annual rate of natural increase in population in Puerto Rico has approached 2 percent during the past few decades. It is interesting, therefore, and probably instructive that one does not find an index reference to population or population growth. For any given development strategy for Puerto Rico, the push forces would have been less, the less rapid had been population growth. Indeed, if one takes population growth as given, the fact that Puerto Ricans are U.S. citizens can be seen as a safety valve not available to other Caribbean peoples. The reluctance to admit population growth as a factor shows up over and over in the discussion of unemployment, which is invariably seen as resulting from a shortage of demand for labor and never as an excess of supply. Whereas Morales helps us to remove our blinders with regard to the impact of colonial behavior on the Puerto Rican economy, he persists in wearing his blinders with regard to the impact of population growth.

Morales builds the implied case that citizens of Borinquen would be better off if they had never encountered the Spaniards or the North Americans. That is something that we can never know. Puerto Ricans, like other peoples of the Caribbean and Latin America, must live with the fact of a colonial history. Each of the independent neighbors has had to deal with the problems of population growth, agricultural stagnation, inadequate industrialization, and urban migration. Whether an independent Puerto Rico would respond to these problems more in the manner of Haiti or possibly the Dominican Republic we cannot know. What we do know is that none of the others have had the safety valve of legal migration to the United States nor the welfare programs provided by the United States.

Other important points emphasized in the work include the cuing system for migrants, historic and current competition among migrant groups, the ethnic nature of the political system and that system's historic and current use by various groups, the inferior status of Puerto Ricans relative to other Hispanics, and, especially, the inability of Puerto Ricans and blacks to form a coalition of the poor.

WILLIAM E. COLE
University of Tennessee
Knoxville

O'BRIEN, GAIL WILLIAMS. *The Legal Fraternity and the Making of a New South Community, 1848-1882.* Pp. xi, 231. Athens: University of Georgia Press, 1986. $23.50.

This thoughtful monograph casts new light upon a continuing historical debate: did the Civil War enable aggressive, middle-class entrepreneurs to replace precapitalistic planters in leadership roles in the postwar South? By focusing upon those who participated significantly in public affairs in Guilford County, a representative Piedmont community in North Carolina, O'Brien moves beyond previous large-scale studies, which made no effort to relate power holders to the social setting in which they operated. She also employs a more sophisticated quantitative methodology than her predecessors used in identifying and evaluating power holders. Drawing upon manuscript census records, local newspapers, government documents, and private papers, she constructs a numerical power index for more than 1800 community leaders, based upon their involvement in political institutions, economic and social organizations, civic rituals, and extra-institutional crisis management. Through a sampling of four five-year periods surrounding the census years of 1850, 1860, 1870, and 1880, she tracks her notables through time and assesses the impact of the wartime experience upon their careers.

Community leaders, as a group, remained remarkably stable throughout the period, she concludes. Although the Civil War witnessed the deaths of some "high power holders" and encouraged the rise of younger, nonresident leaders, the postwar power structure continued to draw from the same families and occupational categories that had domi-

nated the antebellum establishment. Wealthy farmers, who had promoted banks, mills, and railroads before the war, supported the industrial development of the county with equal enthusiasm in the late nineteenth century. Only merchants and other businessmen, who suffered crippling financial losses during the war, declined somewhat in influence, as attorneys replaced them at the top levels of community leadership. Economic diversification and the rise of a vigorous two-party politics contributed to the growing power of lawyers, who functioned as a strategic and stabilizing elite. Harmonizing rural and industrial interests, Guilford's legal fraternity guided the community down the paths of economic progressivism and social conservatism.

On its own terms, this is an admirable study of community development that should interest any serious student of Southern history. As an analysis of legal change and professional mores, however, it is disappointingly thin. O'Brien seems unfamiliar with any recent important works on nineteenth-century legal history, and her generalizations about lawyers are bland and predictable. The significance of the bar's increasing influence in Guilford County is yet to be explored and will require an intensive scrutiny of courthouse records and other legal materials that do not lend themselves readily to quantification.

MAXWELL BLOOMFIELD
Catholic University of America
Washington, D.C.

NOBLE, DAVID W. *The End of American History: Democracy and Capitalism, and the Metaphor of Two Worlds in Anglo-American Historical Writing, 1880-1980.* Pp. ix, 166. Minneapolis: University of Minnesota Press, 1985. $25.00. Paperbound, $14.95.

In *The End of American History* Noble makes another effort to demythologize American history. For Noble neither God's providence nor humanity's fulfillment depends on the United States. According to him the United States is neither the new Israel nor the republic of a new humanity.

An iconoclastic goal fits Noble well. Born an American Protestant, Noble saw his father lose his farm in the 1930s. Later Noble converted to Catholicism.

Describing his own inheritance as a young historian, who came to maturity in the 1940s, Noble contends that professional historians of the first order were driven during the period from 1890 to 1940 to abandon those religious and political myths, metaphors, and paradigms of a radically unique America. Noble makes his argument in reference to four major professional historians: Frederick Jackson Turner (1861-1932), Charles Beard (1874-1948), Richard Hofstadter (1916-70), William Appleman Williams (1921 to the present), and Protestant theologian and political philosopher Reinhold Niebuhr (1892-1971).

For Noble, Turner's guiding historiographical myth of the frontier rested on an insoluble paradox: as America spread west it consumed the very frontier, the abundant resources and open space, that made America singularly unique. Inevitably Turner's America destroyed itself as a republic as it exhausted the frontier and the very source of its virtue: its small and independent farming class.

Beard, who forms the axis of Noble's work, heroically but futilely, even bizarrely, struggled to define a unique America. Before World War I, Beard contended that the dynamics and rationalism of American industrialism would carry it beyond injustice and divisions of capitalism and assure a model democracy. Renouncing his pacifism, as so many of his generation did, Beard greeted his nation's entrance into World War I as a chance to create international democracy for the world. In the 1920s he abandoned his hope in international peace and world democracy, while yet more fervently contending that America had a unique destiny to play in the fulfillment of democracy. He first welcomed Franklin Delano Roosevelt as "a new Moses who would lead Americans into the new world of industrial democracy," only later to depict him as an evil conspirator who placed the United States on the destructive path of internationalism. On the eve of World War II, Beard had come to see all internationalisms, Catholicism as well as Marxism, as a threat to America's unique Jeffersonian tradition.

After World War II, Richard Hofstadter carried the demythologization of American history a step further. What he cherished about the American experience was what was empirical and pragmatic about it. His enemies became the Populists and Progressives and those like them who idealized an America of virtue; his hero was Franklin D. Roosevelt of the New Deal, who led society pragmatically in reference to specific needs, possibilities, and circumstances.

Going beyond Hofstadter in abandoning the myth of the virtuous republican America, William Appleman Williams contended that American myths of uniqueness were not merely distorted and fanatic abstractions, but instead were among the ideological tools of aggressive, international capitalism. For Williams, America's greatest, highest myths, like those of a free market and open covenants, were rationalizations for expanding national, commercial, and industrial interests.

It is altogether clear that Noble associates himself with this devolution of American myth from Turner to Williams, and it is Noble's equal intent to invite us to write a new American history. Like so many critical twentieth-century thinkers, Noble tells us that the myths and metaphors we have inherited do not work. Indeed, they endanger us. Freeing ourselves from these myths may be a matter of survival.

However, questions remain that Noble should directly confront in a future work. Is there a history of nations, peoples, and classes without myths? Will the myths of other nations not compel America to form or maintain its own myths? Will the power of the United States not invariably invite myths of uniqueness—indeed, demand myths, paradigms, and symbols, which distinguish its past, present, and future from those of other nations? Will the state and its interests, the people and their need for identity, not compel mythic stories of the history of the United States regardless of the critical qualms of professional historians? Perhaps it takes one set of myths to beat another set of myths.

In his next volume, Noble should help teach us about the paradigms and myths we need in order to write our history and our American history for our times. Noble's work is worth waiting for.

JOSEPH A. AMATO
Southwest State University
Marshall
Minnesota

RANELAGH, JOHN. *The Agency: The Rise and Decline of the CIA: From Wild Bill Donavan to William Casey.* Pp. 847. New York: Simon & Schuster, 1986. $22.95.

*The Agency* is without a doubt the finest, best-documented, and most entertainingly written study of the Central Intelligence Agency (CIA) of which I know. It traces the agency from its first gleam in the eye of Wild Bill Donavan through the first term of William Casey on behalf of President Reagan. The first third of this massive volume deals with the years when I was a foreign service officer in the Department of State. Although I never had any connection whatsoever, official or otherwise, with the CIA, the nature of my various assignments made me very much aware of its activities in some detail. John Ranelagh does use an occasional adjective that still makes me squirm after all these years, but I find nothing of substance with which to disagree.

The average citizen has a highly distorted image of what the CIA does and what it is. Its cloak-and-dagger work wins it publicity and makes the best, if inaccurate, movies, but it really is not a band of masked Lone Rangers, with Douglas Fairbanks thrown in for good measure, yahooing through the swamps and over the hills. But this is by no means to say that from its very beginnings with Donavan, who was fascinated with the underworld, it

has not right up to this very day indulged in a variety of covert activities that, to me anyway, have seemed thoroughly reprehensible. I am mindful of the justification by Dean Rusk, as secretary of state, that "there is a lot of dirty fighting in the back alleys of this world, and we have to respond in kind." I have to disagree. Covert action, almost by definition, implies violence. Inviting and easy as that violence sometimes seems, I doubt that what is gained from it is worth the price, if for no better reason than that the consequences of violence are usually unpredictable. I know involved people who now bitterly regret the decision to remove President Arbenz from office in Guatemala; Ranelagh himself suggests how much misery could have been avoided by the sudden removal of Idi Amin from the scene, but then he fails to point out that the return to power of Milton Obote, although he was much less colorful than Amin, showed him to be just as skillful a butcher of rival tribes. It may be a kind of gallows humor that I cannot resist a certain relief over the high number of known failures.

The truly great contribution of the CIA, however, from its very beginning has been superb research from its Research and Analysis Branch. The research has a unique emphasis on analysis, namely, on what the facts mean. The key to its success has been the systematic application of human logic and intuition to a large body of factual material. General Walter Bedell Smith deserves the lion's share of the credit for this success in setting up the research during his time as director and assuring its continuance. Eighty percent of the personnel, time, energy, and imagination, if not the budget, of the CIA goes into research and analysis, and almost all its data come from published, not clandestine, sources. Its phenomenal record of accuracy is due to interpretation of facts. There is nothing else quite like it, as every other intelligence agency recognizes. Since the CIA is accountable only to the U.S. president, the pity is how many presidents have elected to trust their own judgment over that of the CIA—and then usually have been wrong, even if they would not admit it.

The personality sketches throughout this book and the insights and judgments make the whole thing breathe with life for both heroes and villains, and there are plenty of both. I found much of the fun in the footnotes Ranelagh has chosen to place at the bottom of each page. Many of them contain some rather startling revelations, such as the probable role of Kim Philby in the Chinese entry into the Korean War, to say nothing of the abortive coup in Albania. And he dispels any lingering doubts I had about Alger Hiss and the Rosenbergs.

The revelations are unquestionably fascinating, but the implied lessons and their implications should not be taken lightly or lost in admiration for what seems to me a genuine literary and stylistic accomplishment.

JOHN F. MELBY

University of Guelph
Ontario
Canada

REDFORD, EMMETTE S. and RICHARD T. McCULLEY. *White House Operations: The Johnson Presidency.* Pp. xii, 246. Austin: University of Texas Press, 1986. $30.00.

This book is the fifth in a projected series of ten to twelve special studies that, together with an overall volume, will form a comprehensive administrative history of the Johnson presidency. The materials in the Lyndon B. Johnson Presidential Library, supplemented by interviews with many of those who assisted Johnson, provide the principal sources for these studies. The aim is to present the historical record "from a social science perspective that will amplify knowledge of administrative processes and of the task and problems of the presidency." Emmette S. Redford, Ashbel Smith Professor of Public Affairs at the University of Texas, serves as project director for the series. *White House Operations: The Johnson Presidency* reflects both the advantages and the disadvantages of

being part of this series.

On the plus side, Redford and McCulley provide considerable detail about President Johnson's organization of the White House Office and his use of the 48 individuals they identify as the top aides that served during his presidency. Compared to his successors Johnson retained a lean staff that varied from 250 to 263. Of these, 60 or so were directly involved with policymaking and related political activities, and only about 15 served as top aides at any one time. Johnson favored a hub-of-a-wheel form of organization among his top aides. Such a form avoided an explicit hierarchy, and at the same time it facilitated his maintaining personal contacts that allowed him to make ad hoc, and sometimes overlapping, assignments.

Redford and McCulley point out that Johnson did not ceaselessly change his staff, as some critics have alleged. Tenure among those he appointed after his election in 1964 averaged 38 months, and even those who had worked for Kennedy stayed on with Johnson for an average of 24 months. The length of tenure, however, was not uniform across the various areas of responsibility. As befitted a president who had made his name as a legislative leader, congressional liaison had the most stability. And as betokened a president who craved public affection, the tenure of aides involved with media contact shortened as public criticism of Johnson and his Vietnam war policies grew.

Redford and McCulley go on to describe relations between Johnson and his aides in developing the president's legislative program, in dealing with presidential responsibilities like national security, economic planning, science and technology, and direction of the executive branch. As once-familiar figures like Joseph A. Califano, George E. Reedy, Walt W. Rostow, Abe Fortas, and Walter W. Jennings enter the narrative, Redford and McCulley detail who did what and when, often drawing upon White House Office memorandums and interviews with the principals that give readers some sense of the personalities involved. Here is information aplenty for scholars or aficionados who want to know as much as possible about Johnson's staff operations.

On the negative side, *White House Operations* is clearly written as part of a series of interest to specialists. It contains so much detail with such a narrow focus that general readers will find completing it a tedious trudge. Moreover, Redford and McCulley exacerbate the general readers' problems by including insufficient social science theory to place the history in context. Presumably, the overall volume will contain such theory, but for now the conclusion reads more like a prolegomenon for that future volume.

Finally, there is a matter of style. Redford and McCulley write with such dispassion that much of the colorfulness of Lyndon B. Johnson and his associates is lost. Notwithstanding the supposed richness of the materials used, the narrative lacks intimacy. Perhaps this style reflects the discreetness of the library that safeguards Johnson's personal papers under seal—unavailable for inspection until 2023.

MICHAEL MARGOLIS
University of Pittsburgh
Pennslyvania

REMINI, ROBERT V. *Andrew Jackson and the Course of American Democracy, 1833-1845.* Vol. 3. Pp. xxiii, 638. New York: Harper & Row, 1984. No price.

Once upon a time there was a president who had to answer the question, What shall we do with the national surplus? This president restored a gold coinage after eliminating a strongly entrenched national bank and its paper instruments. He savored the triumph of his principles when he ordered the resumption of minting eagles and double eagles. One memento to his achievement is his own portrait on the present-day twenty-dollar paper bill issued by the Federal Reserve. Ask any coin dealer how many of these paper bills you must pay today to get just one of Andrew Jackson's twenty-dollar gold pieces.

This same president played such a strong role in both domestic and foreign affairs that he can more properly be considered the first imperial president than Thomas Jefferson. Remini shows clearly how Jackson's role in the Nullification controversy set the stage for Lincoln's response to the secession crisis.

Remini, with this work, concludes his three-volume biography of Andrew Jackson and adds one more solid building block to the literary monument he has erected to his hero.

The amount of detailed research into the last 12 years of Old Hickory's life, which included his second term in the White House, is breathtaking. The prose used is clear and keeps moving. It never rises to the impassioned level of Thomas Carlyle writing about Frederick the Great, although it belongs to the same filiopietistic school of historical biography. Remini might read Plutarch with benefit.

Does Remini find anything to criticize in Jackson? *Mirabile dictu*, yes but he presents his criticisms in the most apologetic manner possible; for example, the Spoils System expanded work opportunities for larger numbers. However, Remini does always present the arguments against Jackson made by his contemporary opponents and by critical historians since.

Outraged that his son had used a promissory note—paper—to buy a slave girl and her child, Jackson wrote him a strong letter against buying anything "on credit when you have the cash." Did the slave girl also feel outraged because she and her offspring had been purchased on credit instead of with cash? Remini does not consider this question. He does point out that by bringing some of his own slaves with him to the White House the president "helped cut costs."

In his last annual message to Congress the president pointed with pride to his relocation of practically all the Indians to the areas west of the Mississippi and that this could only benefit "civilized society."

Remini does admit that Jackson was a failure with most of his appointments. He consistently made poor and even disastrous appointments to important posts. Thus Jackson failed Machiavelli's key test for a ruler, since the Florentine emphasized that one can quickly judge the ability of a prince by the type of men with whom he has surrounded himself. Jackson seems to have succeeded in spite of his appointments.

Remini uses the microscope much more than the telescope. At times he supplements his microscopic research on day-by-day and even hour-by-hour happenings with conjecture. How does he know that Henry Clay, during his Senate speech attacking Jackson for removing the federal deposits from the Bank of the United States, was shouting and "the anger of his words animated his face," or that Clay had "glanced quickly around the room before beginning his speech"? The book is filled with such unknowable points, although they do heighten the effect of the presentation.

When Remini occasionally uses the telescope for the historical long view, the results are generally excellent. He then relates most effectively Jackson's life and works to the two and a half centuries of American history that preceded and produced him and to the century and a half that Jackson has influenced since.

Remini should give his microscope a rest for a while and use his telescope more frequently.

H. F. MACKENSEN
Fairleigh Dickinson University
Teaneck
New Jersey

SILBERMAN, CHARLES E. *A Certain People*. Pp. 458. New York: Summit Books, 1985. $19.95.

SACHAR, HOWARD M. *Diaspora*. Pp. xiv, 539. New York: Harper & Row. 1985. $27.50.

The contemporary Jew is a unique individual with an awesome heritage. The victim of centuries of brutal discrimination culminating in the Holocaust, the modern Jew

has in many nations throughout the world not merely survived but also achieved a measure of triumph. Ironically, this success also contains the seeds of potential diminution of Jews as a people with a unique cultural and religious heritage; for success has brought intermarriage of Jew and non-Jew combined with a turning away from the past and concentration on a multicultural present.

The status of the modern Jew is competently, at times brilliantly, examined in these two fine volumes. Howard Sachar, perhaps the most distinguished historian of the Jewish people, explores the Third World, the Jew outside of North America and Israel. Charles Silberman, author of several outstanding volumes on American social phenomena, explores the Jew in America.

Both books have in large measure a theme of dreams realized. Silberman writes convincingly that Jews have indeed entered the American mainstream; he presents stories and statistics of Jewish success in education, politics, business, always contrasting these tales with the problems and difficulties of the past. Unlike many other writers, he is not unduly concerned that Jews are turning from their heritage. He credits, to a large degree, the military victory of Israel in the Six-Day War of 1967 with transforming the way in which American Jews felt not only about Israel but about their own cultural identity and the future of their children.

Sachar also cites the significance of the Six-Day War, as well as the constant vigilance of Israel, in maintaining the awareness of Jews around the world about their heritage. He cites the lack of civil liberties in Russian-dominated nations and in several South American countries as still plaguing Jews; but these are problems they share with other ethnic and religious groups in totalitarian states. He believes that if there is a present threat to Jews, it is less political or economic than demographic. There were approximately 16.5 million Jews worldwide in 1939. Some 5 million were killed in the Holocaust, and today there are barely 13 million Jews, approximately 6 million of whom live in the

United States and Canada.

FRED ROTONDARO
National Italian American
    Foundation
Washington, D.C.

WATERFIELD, LARRY W. *Conflict and Crisis in Rural America*. Pp. iv, 235. New York: Greenwood Press, Praeger, 1985. $36.95.

Whether he intended it or not, Waterfield has written a consciousness-raising book. As he points out, although many people have rural roots, from two-thirds to three-fourths of Americans are urban dwellers. Most of us are out of touch with these roots and out of touch with the realities of rural life. Waterfield seeks to remedy this in the first part of the book by giving us a picture of rural America's people and its new economic, political, and social features.

What constitutes rural is not an easy thing to specify. Most of us have the idea that living in rural areas and living on the farm are pretty much the same thing. Not so. In 1980, 2.5 percent of Americans—6.6 million people—lived on farms, but this is only a small portion of the 84 million people that Waterfield includes in his tally of rural Americans. An additional 9 percent—24.0 million—live in metropolitan—statistical—areas, 35.0 million reside in unincorporated rural areas, and 17.4 million people live in towns with populations from 2500 to 25,000 inhabitants. By these figures, 31 percent of our population is rural. This book attempts to look at what is happening in these rural areas and to the people there, and to project what the future might hold.

There are several themes that run through the book, and perhaps its message can best be illustrated by discussing them. A major theme is rural America as a resource. Ultimately, the basic resource is the land, and it is from the land that food, fiber, fuel, and forests come. Another resource is the people. From them come presidents, poets, scientists,

industrialists, statesmen, and entertainers. Finally, there is a moral resource, a reminder of the virtues of God, home, motherhood, and apple pie.

A second theme that runs through the book is rural America as victim. The victimizers are a diversified lot: politicians, government bureaucrats, agribusiness and industrial corporations, bankers, urban dwellers, and the mass media, to mention just a few. The reason for the victimization is a loss of fate control by farmers and other rural dwellers. Part of this loss is due to the Supreme Court's one-person-one-vote ruling on representation in state legislatures, which passed political control of states into the hands of the urban majority in many states where power had been vested in rural politicians. Another loss of fate control is due to policies of the federal government, such as the cheap food policy that encourages overproduction and the use of farm exports as a foreign policy weapon. These policies come from Washington without the advice or consent of the ones whose pocketbooks are affected. Absentee ownership of rural industry and agribusiness corporations also minimize the input of local interests in the formation of corporate policies.

Many conflicts between rural residents and others grow out of the attempts to regain some fate control, or out of frustration due to its loss. The Moral Majority represents one of the dimensions of conflict: urban sin and Godlessness versus rural virtue. The family farmer versus the banker and/or the bureaucrat is another rural-urban battlefront. Still another conflict arises over land usage in the areas where country and city meet, and yet another concerns priorities for building and maintaining a rural infrastructure versus spending for urban needs.

A third theme is that rural America is worth saving, and that something has to be done about this immediately, before Eden is lost. Actually, this is more than a theme; it is the point of the book.

I found the book interesting, informative, and persuasive. Waterfield is correct in saying that the mass media, for the most part, ignore or do not do justice to rural America. This book serves as a partial corrective for that injustice. He develops his themes well, and he effectively marshals evidence to support his contentions. I felt that the chapters on the role of the rural areas in nuclear disaster and the composite portrait of a mid-Missouri town were somewhat out of phase with the rest of the book. In any case, one is almost sure to come away from reading this book with a new and sympathetic perspective on rural America in the 1980s.

JERRY L.L. MILLER

University of Arizona
Tucson

## SOCIOLOGY

ELAZAR, DANIEL, J. with ROZANN ROTHMAN, STEPHEN L. SCHECTER, MAREN ALLAN STEIN, and JOSEPH ZIKMUND II. *Cities of the Prairie Revisited: The Closing of the Metropolitan Frontier.* Pp. xiii, 288. Lincoln: University of Nebraska Press, 1986. $25.00.

Medium-sized cities, those with a population from 40,000 to 250,000, may not be academically fashionable to study, but one-third of all Americans reside in such cities. Looking particularly at how federal intervention has affected local government and politics, Daniel J. Elazar and his coauthors revisit a number of medium-sized, Midwestern cities in the book under review to update, a half-generation later, Elazar's 1970 book, *Cities of the Prairie*. Their book thus examines change and continuity in a way not possible in the typical snapshot account of American cities.

*Revisited* consists of two not entirely congruous parts. The first, an overview by Elazar consuming almost two-thirds of the book, sets forth a framework of analysis that centers on his concept of the "civil community." In addition, Elazar presents a typology of political culture, drawn from his earlier work, that relates the political culture of local communities to their distinctive ethnic mix. Building on this framework, the argument of the book concerns the role of political culture: it is claimed that the political culture of communities is relatively abiding and that understanding that culture provides the best handle on what local governments do.

The second part of the book consists of case studies, written by Elazar's coauthors, covering Pueblo, Colorado, and Decatur, Champaign, Urbana, and Joliet, Illinois. Although these chapters are interesting on their own terms for their treatment of change and continuity in cities of this genre, they do not succeed in extending Elazar's argument by a close analysis of how ethnicity and political culture combine to shape local decisions.

Thus one problem with the book is that we do not receive the kind of systematic study and refinement of terms that one would expect in a revisited project. The case studies do not serve this purpose; and Elazar's section gives us instead an often anecdotal commentary on his original prairie cities, combined with self-congratulatory references to his earlier text and banal statements such as, regarding school desegregation, "In each community people did what had to be done to make changes locally."

Further, the book fails to defend the importance of political cultural factors against the rival claims of authors such as Paul Peterson (*City Limits* [Chicago: University of Chicago Press, 1981]) who assert the primacy of the city's economic needs in determining local policies.

RICHARD E. FOGLESONG

Rollins College
Winter Park
Florida

FEIN, RASHI. *Medical Care, Medical Costs: The Search for a Health Insurance Policy.* Pp. viii, 240. Cambridge, MA: Harvard University Press, 1986. $20.00.

Rashi Fein combines penetrating economic analysis, an articulate moral stance, and considerable knowledge of health policy since the 1960s in the most important book on health insurance to be published in recent years. He begins by summarizing secondary sources about the history of public and private health insurance in the United States from the early twentieth century through the 1950s. In the six chapters that follow, he describes events in the 1960s and 1970s on the basis of personal experience and wide reading in primary sources. In two concluding chapters, he prescribes a program of universal health insurance to be sponsored by the federal government and administered by the states. His goal is to achieve "equitable cost control."

Both experts and general readers will learn much from Fein's exposition of health policy in the 1970s and 1980s, especially about the background of landmark events, the causes of frustration and achievement, and the merits and flaws of alternative proposals for change. Of particular importance are his analyses of the controversy about competition and regulation as tools to reduce the costs of health care and the implications of recent proposals to change the tax status of health insurance that is provided through employment. Throughout the book, Fein emphasizes that debates about health policy are struggles about competing views of equity and collective responsibility.

A few sections of the book will disappoint historians and others such as economists who study health policy. Because Fein did not take account of all the available secondary sources in the chapters on private and government health insurance before the 1960s, he ignored the connections between private and government insurance. Moreover, he occasionally substitutes logic for data. For example, he asserts that the voluntary insurance market was based on employee groups because employer-paid premiums were not subject to federal income tax. There is, however, considerable evidence that executives of insurance plans discovered in the late 1930s that they had greater losses in non-

employee groups and discouraged them from applying for coverage. Economists who advocate more competition in health care markets may accuse Fein of being too quick to dismiss their arguments on the basis of moral considerations. Despite these strictures, this book is a superb contribution to the literature on health policy.

DANIEL M. FOX
State University of New York
Stony Brook

FUCHS, VICTOR R. *The Health Economy.* Pp. viii, 401. Cambridge, MA: Harvard University Press, 1986. $25.00.

AIKEN, LINDA H. and DAVID MECHANIC, eds. *Applications of Social Science to Clinical Medicine and Health Policy.* Pp. ix, 580. New Brunswick, NJ: Rutgers University Press, 1986. $35.00. Paperbound, $14.95.

One-tenth of U.S. health care expenditures—about 1 percent of the gross national product—is spent on the care of the elderly in the last year of life. Is this an appropriate balance between care for the dying and health services for the rest of the population? This is just one of the many difficult questions that society faces in formulating health policy. *The Health Economy* and *Applications of Social Science to Clinical Medicine and Health Policy* are two books that contribute to our understanding of the ethical, clinical, and economic questions that health policy must address.

*The Health Economy* is a collection of articles written by Fuchs and previously published over the years 1967-86. The book is organized into four sections. The first section presents the case for viewing the production of health services as an economic good and thereby emphasizes the relevance of traditional economic analysis in formulating health policy. In sections 2 and 3, Fuchs presents some of the major empirical findings of his research in health economics over the past two decades. The focus of these two sections is on the physicians' services market and on the production of health. The fourth section of the book directly addresses major health policy issues. The topics in this section are national health insurance, health care for the elderly, methods of government financing of health care, and the perceived upcoming internal struggle for the control of the health care industry.

Three major points come through from reading this book. First, Fuchs makes a convincing argument concerning the necessity of establishing priorities in health policy based on effectiveness. Thus the usefulness of economic analysis is obvious. Second, the reader is impressed by the important difference between medical care—an input—and health—the output. Finally, Fuchs makes a strong case that the differences in individuals' time preferences explain a significant portion of differences in behavior affecting health. Measuring time preference effects, however, is made difficult by apparent asymmetric risk aversion.

The strong points of the Fuchs book are (1) it is easy to read regardless of the reader's technical background; (2) it provides a good introduction to issues of health economics; and (3) it is useful to advanced students who are attempting empirical research in health economics or policy. The major weaknesses are the fact that all chapters have been previously published—and are readily available in most academic libraries—and that many of the chapters are considerably out of date because the field tends to experience major changes over short periods of time. For example, physician-induced demand, the topics of chapters 4 and 6, has received considerable research attention since these chapters were originally published.

*Applications of Social Science to Clinical Medicine and Health Policy,* a collection of 24 papers by authors from many fields, provides an extensive synthesis of the literature for a broad range of topics. The book is organized into five parts. In the first part the broad issues of the relationship between science, technology, and medicine and possible causes of socioeconomic differences in

morbidity and mortality are addressed. In this section, there are also papers describing the changing medical profession and hospital industry.

In part 2, the problem of measuring health status, the role of social experiments in health policy, and our current state of knowledge about treatment and prevention of cardiovascular disease, mental illness, and cancer—the largest three disease categories contributing to mortality and morbidity—are examined. Part 3 addresses issues specific to stages in the life cycle. The topics are infant mortality, teenage childbearing, management of reproduction, and health care for the elderly. Part 4 focuses on prevention and caring. The papers point out how certain social factors can influence the vulnerability to disease and also affect the outcomes of patient-physician relationships. Part 5 discusses issues involved in the organization and delivery of health care. Topics in this section include the clinical and economic effects of policies affecting economic incentives—for example, different payment systems—the effects of the increasing supply of medical care providers, and the ethical issues of research involving human subjects, life-extending treatment, and for-profit health care enterprises.

Part 1 and the chapters on the assessment of health status and on social experiments in health—chapters 11 and 12, respectively—would be valuable reading for researchers just beginning to study the health care sector. To the economist, part 5 would be of particular interest.

The strengths of this book are (1) the broad scope of the book and the coherent organization; and (2) the timeliness of the articles—in addition to analysis of many current topics, the reader receives extensive and up-to-date bibliographies. The book has two major weaknesses. First, there is no discussion of statistical analysis in health care research despite the fact that such analysis is a major component in much of health policy research. Indeed, it can be argued that an entire section should be devoted to this topic. Second, the diversity of topics and authors coupled with the encyclopedia approach of most articles makes the book tedious reading.

KELLY EAKIN

University of Oregon
Eugene

MOORE, KRISTIN, MARGARET C. SIMMS, and CHARLES L. BETSEY. *Choice and Circumstance: Racial Differences in Adolescent Sexuality and Fertility.* Pp. xiv, 165. New Brunswick, NJ: Transaction Books, 1986. $19.95.

By the time they turn 20, 41 percent of black females and 19 percent of white females in the United States have at least one child; 86 percent of the black births and 33 percent of the white births are to unmarried mothers. Whatever one's values, the consequences are enormous, and often negative. Many of these births are concentrated in neighborhoods of poverty, crime, and disorganization. And yet some families "manage to encourage abstinence or contraceptive use as they raise their children in [this] seemingly overwhelming environment." The authors of *Choice and Circumstance* attempt to identify the factors that enable some families to succeed and to build on those factors.

Moore, Simms, and Betsey focus on differences between blacks and whites—and, secondarily, those of Spanish origin—noting that the difference in marital status and in age at first pregnancy are the most significant black-white differences. After reviewing the statistics on fertility, they devote chapters to "information and attitudes"; "contraception and abortion"; "education as a motivating factor"; "occupational plans, job training and fertility"; and "marriage and family."

Moore, Simms, and Betsey document that accurate information on conception and contraception is lacking, particularly for blacks, males, and youths from lower socioeconomic statuses; that about half of black and white teenagers at risk for pregnancy do not receive any medical family planning services despite typically delaying contraception for many months after beginning sexual activity; that programs that keep young mothers in school and provide counseling, sex education, and contraceptive services reduce the otherwise very high rate of repeat pregnancies; that lack of information and experiences with responsibility probably account for many teenagers' engaging in sexual behaviors that jeopardize their futures; and that adult blacks do not encourage early sexual activity despite the black-white differences in pregnancy.

It is argued in this book that the high "level of reliance on abortion in a modern industrial nation is appalling" and that sex education needs to include decision-making and peer- or media-resisting skills as well as information. Information about the consequences of a birth for one's future is very important and is not being provided. Hiding our heads in the sand is not working. The consequences are greatest for blacks, but are major for the entire society. Whatever one's values, "there are many pragmatic reasons to discourage early initiation of sexual activity." Moore, Simms, and Betsey provide an intelligent, objective, and well-documented book, arguing for an intelligent, pragmatic, and humane approach to a serious problem.

ABRAHAM D. LAVENDER

Florida International University
Miami

ROSENWAIKE, IRA with the assistance of BARBARA LOGUE. *The Extreme Aged in America: A Portrait of an Expanding Population.* Pp. xix, 253. Westport, CT: Greenwood Press, 1985. $35.00.

Ira Rosenwaike, with the assistance of Barbara Logue, has produced a valuable text about the demographic characteristics of the extreme aged in America. While their main purpose is to provide information about the extreme aged in America, they also provide a great deal of information about the elderly population in general. This volume should prove to be an excellent reference source for social scientists, gerontologists, public policymakers, and others interested in the extreme aged population.

As Rosenwaike and Logue point out, the elderly are not a homogeneous group and there are many differences between the elderly, in general, and subgroups of this population, like the youngest old, who are 65-69 years old, and the extreme aged, 85 years and older. Since little research has addressed the demography of the extreme aged in America, Rosenwaike and Logue proceed to provide extensive demographic information on this group. Included in the text are 14 figures and 102 tables as well as generally sound interpretations and thought-provoking implications of the data.

Rosenwaike and Logue begin by discussing the great expansion of the extreme aged population since 1940, which is primarily due to declining mortality rates among this oldest old group. They evaluate the reliability of the data on which they base their analysis, pointing out problems like the misreporting of age. Most of the chapters deal with the demographic characteristics of the population, specifically age and sex; race, ethnic group, and national origin; geographic area and geographic mobility; social and economic characteristics; living arrangements; health status; and mortality patterns. Some of these variables are cross-classified by sex, race, and marital status to provide a more complete understanding of this population.

International comparisons are offered indicating that the United States and other industrialized countries are experiencing similar demographic changes in this segment of the aged population. Projections from the Bureau of the Census and the Social Security Administration for the future expansion of the extreme aged population are compared and discussed with the inescapable conclusion that the population of the elderly, and especially the oldest subgroup, will greatly increase in the future.

The population expansion of the extreme aged and the unique characteristics of this group will have a major impact on the extreme aged themselves and their families, on national economic resources, on health care services, and on social services. In order to plan for the impact of this rapid growth, researchers, planners, and policymakers can learn much about the characteristics of the extreme aged from this useful text.

NANCY WESTLAKE VAN WINKLE
University of Kentucky
Lexington

RUBIN, EVA R. *The Supreme Court and the American Family.* Pp. 251. Westport, CT: Greenwood Press, 1986. $35.00.

Eva R. Rubin examines a substantial number of Supreme Court cases involving family-related issues. She is particularly thoughtful in revealing the implications for the American family of decisions pertaining to abortion, illegitimacy, pregnancy disability, adolescent sexuality, education, and zoning regulations. Her principal argument is that "the Court does not always scrutinize family relationships with a cool, neutral and unbiased eye, but frequently bases its decisions on stereotypical views of what the Justices think the family should be." While acknowledging that the Court, like other governmental institutions, has been uncertain regarding the direction family policy should take, more often than not, she argues, traditional family ideology rather than constitutional doctrine explains judicial outcomes.

Rubin's analysis of the policy implications of the Supreme Court's work is basically sound and occasionally quite insightful. However, the evaluation of these policies, and the discussion of their jurisprudential implications, are not always convincing in demonstrating the wisdom of the Court in embracing the author's advice that it more actively become the facilitator of social change in the area of family policy. There is considerable controversy about these policies; a more effective case needs to be made as to why the Court should join the more accountable political institutions as conscious agents of societal transformation.

For example, Rubin makes a persuasive case for viewing abortion as an equality issue. But for many in the society this is at best a peripheral issue, certainly secondary to the other moral concerns generated by the case of *Roe* v. *Wade*. It is one thing to discern traditional family ideology in the rhetoric of Supreme Court opinions—something done very well by Rubin; it is quite another to establish the legitimacy of judicial substitution of an alternative ideology.

The main weakness of this otherwise admirable study is its shallow treatment of the role of the courts in the making of social policy. Rubin's discussion of the pregnancy disability cases illustrates the problem. After an illuminating critique of the Court's work, Rubin writes, "A storm of criticism by labor and women's groups greeted the decisions, and Congress acted quickly to reverse the Court's refusal to hold that discrimination against pregnant women was sex discrimination." Why then, one wishes to know, is this not an appropriate model in other areas of family policy as well? If the Court's view of the family is so woefully out of date, does not the system supply a self-corrective mechanism that is more adept at appraising and applying social facts and that is, moreover, more consistent with the theory of popular government? It is the failure to address these sorts of questions adequately that prevents this able review of the Court's work from becoming a first-rate piece of political and constitutional analysis.

GARY J. JACOBSOHN
Williams College
Williamstown
Massachusetts

SANCTON, ANDREW. *Governing the Island of Montreal: Language Differences and Metropolitan Politics.* Pp. xxxvi, 213. Berkeley: University of California Press, 1985. $28.50.

Andrew Sancton's book details how the Montreal public service delivery system has evolved and how it has been affected by the not-so-quiet revolution in Quebec society since 1960. The work is a valuable addition to the literature on urban Canada and comparative metropolitan government. In the process, it sheds light on the English-French question in Canada and on ethnic relations more generally.

Part 1 of the book describes Montreal's ethnic composition, municipal government, and the array of separate schools and social services for the English-speaking and the French-speaking Montrealers before 1960. Part 2 focuses on the transformation of provincial politics, the growing politicization of language between 1960 and 1981, and the intimate links between local and provincial developments. Part 3 provides a carefully balanced account of the creation and operation of metropolitan government, the Montreal Urban Community; the attempted reorganization of the Montreal school boards along linguistic—English-French—rather than religious—Protestant-Catholic—lines; and the creation of new social service infrastructures. Sancton reveals how language, and other cultural and economic differences associated with language, affect efforts to reorganize public service delivery systems in metropolitan areas. A language conflict moderated by accommodation in diversity, appears, to Sancton, as a probable and desirable future. More recent developments in Quebec, the fortunes of Jean Drapeau's Montreal Civic Party notwithstanding, suggest that this scenario is not unrealistic.

Sancton's well-crafted work merits the attention not only of students of metropolitan reorganization but also of all who are concerned with peaceful settlements of human conflict. There are some weak spots, however. Sancton hints at, but does not forcefully confront, the different metropolitan reform traditions in the literature. As a result, his work seems too descriptive and confined to the Canadian experience. Sancton relies heavily on highly impressionistic accounts and outdated analyses of Montrealers of

Italian origin and ignores the wealth of available information in church and Italian community archives. At best, his analysis here is not rich. If the issue facing Montreal Jews by the 1920s was whether they could be Catholic or Protestant, the issue facing Montreal Italians, at about the same time, was whether they could be French or English. Montreal Italians also favored the creation of public—Catholic—bilingual schools—a heresy for both the French and the English. Moreover, it would have been interesting if Sancton had, in the conclusion, made explicit the theoretical generalizations embedded in his analysis. Finally, there is a problem that has nothing to do with Sancton. The book in the present form will have difficulties reaching the Canadian public. It is hoped that arrangements will be made soon for a paperback edition or some other possibility. Sancton's work deserves to reach readers in Canada.

FILIPPO SABETTI

McGill University
Montreal
Quebec
Canada

SKOLNICK, JEROME H. and DAVID H. BAYLEY. *The New Blue Line: Police Innovation in Six American Cities.* Pp. iv, 246. New York: Free Press, 1986. $17.95.

Crime embraces a peculiar metaphysics. Nothing that politicians, public administrators, or police do seems to affect its omnipresence. Whether or not the working of society is better explained through the interpretive paradigm's reality as social construction, the simple truth is that American society continues to fail controlling those whose acts it labels criminal. The central query of this book is twofold: why is business-as-usual policing not getting the job done, and what innovative policing ideas and derivative practices offer hope for improvement?

Intensive investigation of six cities—Detroit, Houston, Denver, Newark, and California's Oakland and Santa Ana—demonstrated that the tandem of technological advance and technical acumen has failed in the United States because the democratic ideal had been brushed aside by the old professionalism. The resultant, not uncommon, irony that innovation marks return to long-discarded assumptions builds upon what much contemporary political ideology would deem paradoxical: both the poorest and the most conservative of the cities embraced the key innovations early on. Flowing from these new practices and their master ideal is a "new blue line" of new professionals placing foremost the object of the hallowed twin infinitives "to serve and protect."

The people, then, come first in those innovative police organizations. Public accountability becomes more than fiscal efficiency to guard each taxpayer's dollar; it extends to seeking proactively public cooperation, assistance, and guidance. Adopting the phrase of Santa Ana's police chief, Skolnick and Bayley call the innovative framework "community-oriented policing."

Community-oriented policing involves synergistic crime prevention—a proactive neighborhood watch writ large—and comprises four elements: police-community reciprocity, areal decentralization of command, reorientation of patrol, and civilianization. The upshot is essentially participatory democracy in an expanded view of policing as at once order maintenance and value affirmation. Restoration of a sense of community with concomitant diminution of anomie may be at hand, Skolnick and Bayley suggest, though they objectively recognize dual limitation in the generalizability to all cities of their findings and the ease with which change, if possible at all, can be effected.

Because of the painstaking thoroughness and scholarly care of its highly regarded authors, this is a book not be lightly dismissed by those in police administration. It is my hope that others in public administration as well will see the value in this book: its approach to recognizing Philip Selznick's distinction between organization and institution is generalizable, indeed.

DENNIS DAILEY MURPHY
Armstrong State College
Savannah
Georgia

SONNENSTUHL, WILLIAM J. *Inside an Emotional Health Program: A Field Study of Workplace Assistance for Troubled Employees.* Pp. viii, 187. Ithaca, NY: ILR Press, 1986. $24.00. Paperbound, $10.95.

This book, which is a field study of an emotional health program for employees in a major corporation, is a contribution to the meager literature in the dramatically growing field of employee assistance, but it also suffers from severe problems. Sonnenstuhl seems as interested in making political statements on the social control function of such programs as he does in describing and thus illuminating the nature of employee assistance. Quality descriptive and analytic information is badly needed as employers continue to consider and develop various forms of dealing with employee performance problems in the workplace. Sonnenstuhl could have done a better job in making such a contribution.

Lack of clarity is a problem in this book, and it has some serious consequences. For example, Sonnenstuhl states that his interest is "in understanding how employees decide to refer themselves to the program"; however, at least one of the cases in his sample of 30 was not a self-referral at all. People in the employee assistance field generally agree that important differences exist between supervisory referrals and self-referrals; this is not an insignificant factor and should have been recognized by Sonnenstuhl. He has also been satisfied with reporting his "impressions" on some important program aspects—such as utilization rates—when it appears it would have been possible to collect data and provide answers. In addition,

his use of certain sociological concepts was more confusing than helpful. However, there are strengths and Sonnenstuhl is correct in saying that there is a dearth of field research on this topic.

The description of the concerns of employees and the reaction and assistance from the therapists will give those unfamiliar with employee assistance a sense of the field. Sonnenstuhl does a good job in identifying reasons people go for help, the concerns and constraints on the therapists, the issue of confidentiality, and the ability of therapists to achieve an accurate diagnosis and suitable treatment. The discussion of the implications of locating the service in the health department and medicalizing emotional problems is insightful and could be helpful to those setting up or evaluating a program.

The concluding chapter is weak and confusing. For example, the section on "consequences for management" does not address this topic. In the last paragraph, Sonnenstuhl suggests an alternative to "rushing employees to treatment" that comes without any prior discussion of such a finding. Such inconsistency illustrates well the problem with this book.

HELEN V. GRABER
Washington University
St. Louis
Missouri

WINNER, LANGDON. *The Whale and the Reactor: A Search for Limits in an Age of High Technology.* Pp. xiv, 200. Chicago: University of Chicago Press, 1986. $17.50.

Following the trajectory set forth by Jacques Ellul, Marshall McLuhan, and others, Langdon Winner explores "the meaning of technology for the way we live. . . . How can one look beyond the obvious facts of instrumentality to study the politics of technical objects?" Winner's aim is to develop a political philosophy of technology, noting that in the history of philosophy, technology has been either ignored or dismissed as irrelevant for understanding the nature of society. The ultimate objective, he claims, is to see "where we will draw the line, where we will be able to say, here are possibilities that wisdom suggests we avoid."

The book aspires far beyond its capacity to reach its ultimate objective. This is not to say that it is an unimportant book. It offers a compelling contrast to the view that anyone who dares to criticize technological innovation is by that virtue opposed to it. Winner, writing as a resident political scientist from Rensselaer Polytechnic Institute, is well informed about the historical forces that have led to the centralization of technological power and production. But he is also a stranger in a strange land when he meditates upon the myopia that is supposed to be so characteristic of the modern engineer.

His criticisms of modern technology are derived from specific encounters he has had with technologists who are little interested in his project of bringing philosophy to the barbarians. How ironic that he offers no counter observations about the effort to infuse the liberal arts with technology studies and to call it, of course, the new liberal arts. The two cultures produce extreme images of what each is lacking. He is far more self-critical, however, when he derides the special place that "value experts" have assumed in the discourse on technological development. His disappointment with such expertise turns on the belief that "the inquiry we need can only be a shared enterprise, a project of redemption that can and ought to include everyone."

Is this the deepest insight that can be learned from a political philosophy of technology? Unfortunately, Winner consistently defers to broad definitions of wisdom, to "general moral principles that ought to guide our action." He condemns the unchecked development of nuclear power but is also wary of the undue optimism about renewable energy sources. He hates "value talk" but cannot avoid speaking in a facsimile language, even more vague and slightly left of center in the spirit of one who can embrace Marx and Wittgenstein, though, curiously,

with no more than passing mention of Horkheimer and none whatsoever of Habermas. For that matter, what of Daniel Bell, William Leiss, Allan Mazur, and Dorothy Nelkin?

The fact that science and technology cannot answer how one ought to live, even as they increasingly determine how many must live, is not new. It is the central fact that gave life to Max Weber's ambivalence about modernity. The disenchantment of the world led now by scientists and technologists shows no signs of ending—its end would be one sign of the limits Winner seeks.

JONATHAN B. IMBER

Wellesley College
Massachusetts

## ECONOMICS

AARON, HENRY et al. *Economic Choices: 1987.* Pp. xii, 126. Washington, DC: Brookings Institution, 1986. $22.95. Paperbound, $8.95.

LAWRENCE, ROBERT Z. and ROBERT E. LITAN. *Saving Free Trade: A Pragmatic Approach.* Pp. xii, 132. Washington, DC: Brookings Institution, 1986. $22.95. Paperbound, $8.95.

AHO, C. MICHAEL and JONATHAN DAVID ARONSON. *Trade Talks; America Better Listen!* Pp. xiv, 178. New York: Council on Foreign Relations, 1985. $15.00.

*Economic Choices: 1987* is a clear, carefully argued, and well-written discussion of the likely economic consequences for 1989 of the Gramm-Rudman-Hollings Act, the Reagan administration's proposal, and a proposal by the authors for reducing the federal deficit. It is no surprise in a Brookings Institution book that the authors' proposal differs from the other two largely by recommending an increase in taxes and an adjustment in Social Security payments in order to reduce the contraction that would be required in other social programs. Several alternative methods for raising the additional revenues are included. The final chapter is a critique, with recommendations, of the entire current budgetary process.

The book is at its best—and the best is very good—when the authors dissect the first two proposals and expose their microeconomic flaws and political shortcomings. They illustrate how the Gramm-Rudman-Hollings Act is a "doomsday machine" that will result in an irrational allocation of government resources and why even this is unlikely to generate corrective congressional action. The budgetary sleight of hand of Reagan's proposed federal asset sales are nicely highlighted. The major weakness of the book is the Keynesian-economics-as-fact discussion of the macroeconomic results of the proposals, but I suppose that such an approach is to be expected from this set of authors.

*Saving Free Trade*, appropriately subtitled *A Pragmatic Approach*, argues the case for reducing the level of protection from foreign competition given to various U.S. industries and provides a program for doing so. The first of four major sections of the book asks, Why provide aid? and through a careful summary of recent economic literature really explains why one should, in most cases, not provide aid. The second section provides a history of U.S. attempts to reconcile free trade politics with efforts at reducing the effects of these movements to free trade on specific industries. This section provides an excellent concise history of U.S. legislation in the postwar era and is much recommended. The third section outlines and critiques the major proposals currently before Congress for reforming the trade adjustment process. The fourth section contains Lawrence and Litan's proposals. These proposals—which do warrant the praise "pragmatic"—are a complex of ideas that would provide fairly automatic, declining, and reasonably efficient adjustment protection for a foreign-trade-injured industry. While this book provides nothing new in the theory of trade, it is to be praised and recommended as an example of careful analysis of the issues and history of protection policy and as an example of imaginative and implementable policy proposals.

*Trade Talks* provides a well-argued analysis of the issues of the upcoming round of negotiations on the General Agreement on Tariffs and Trade (GATT). The initial section provides the history of the development of GATT. Aho and Aronson then explain why this round is likely to be much more difficult than the previous, especially from the free trade advocate's point of view. Separate sections are devoted to the likely initial concerns and bargaining positions of the United States, other industrial countries—the European Community, Japan, and Canada, mostly—and the developing nations. Since Aho and Aronson are pessimistic about the likelihood of a direct increase in free trade from this round, they offer several second-best suggestions that might satisfy some of the concerns of the participating nations and still be trade creating. The book is best in its coverage of the political issues in the negotiations and in explaining the positions of the various participants. It is weaker in the depth of the economic analysis. The recent success of the United States in the meetings at Punta del Este that set the agenda for the round of talks suggests that Aho and Aronson are a little overly pessimistic about the prospects for increasing free trade. They are, however, dead on as to the major issues.

GEORGE T. McCANDLESS, Jr.
Dartmouth College
Hanover
New Hampshire

BUCHANAN, JAMES. *Liberty, Market and State: Political Economy in the 1980's.* Pp. ix, 278. New York: Columbia University Press, 1986. $45.00.

HAYWARD, JACK. *The State and the Market Economy: Industrial Patriotism and Economic Intervention in France.* Pp. xv, 267. New York: Columbia University Press, 1986. $35.00.

James Buchanan is a major intellectual force in contemporary economics, a contractarian in the tradition of Hobbes, Rousseau, and Locke. In his collection of papers, written in the early years of the 1980s, Buchanan challenges our understanding of the principles of the market process and, more particularly, of the relationship of this process to the institutional setting within which persons make choices.

The ultimate question pursued by Buchanan in his writings is how we should organize ourselves to secure peace, freedom, and prosperity. Individuals want to be free and want to belong to a community. This implies that a balance must be struck between independence, self-reliance, and liberty, on the one hand, and community, fraternity, and dependence, on the other. Markets are basically political institutions that serve to allow people to interact voluntarily without detailed state supervision. They should never have been evaluated for their ability to maximize anything that is interpersonally comparable. Buchanan argues that prior to any meaningful discussion of the process of market interaction should come a legal-governmental order, one that contains within its allowable limits of enforceability some specification of the distribution of rights and claims among individuals. Trade and compromise must then go on to assure unanimity for any changes. This allows for a sharper conceptual separation between value-enhancing and distributional changes.

Using his contractarian approach, Buchanan examines issues such as justice and equal treatment, the ethical limits of taxation, and the political economy of debt and deficits. He describes his own transformation from a dedicated socialist to a born-again free-market advocate, as well as his struggles to sustain an institutional setting for the intellectual development of the public-choice perspective.

Buchanan is not optimistic, in any short-run context, about the prospects for academic programs to focus more on the processes within which persons make actual choices and less on the mathematical perspective—that is, on the process of maximizing within the constraints of specific wants, resources,

and technology. Classical liberalism may not dominate the contemporary scene, but Buchanan has ensured that dialogue and discussion will continue at the most fundamental level of political philosophy.

Jack Hayward's *State and the Market Economy*, in sharp contrast to Buchanan's philosophical essays, examines in great detail the specifics of intervention by government in the French economy. In the 1970s and 1980s, managers of the French state have redefined many government policies to conform to the constraints of the market. The French government, like the Japanese, organizes state-led development. Each economic policy—trade, employment, energy, and so forth—has its own particular state-society subsystem. Hayward describes the politicians, the senior civil servants, and the heads of major public and semipublic, financial, industrial, commercial, and agricultural enterprises involved in specific policies such as bankruptcy within, and the potential collapse of, the steel industry, local economic decline, and planning.

This book is not for the neophyte in French policy. For one with an appreciation of the European context, Hayward has provided an extensive review of recent French experience with state intervention in the economy.

G. S. GOLDSTEIN

Library of Parliament
Ottawa
Ontario
Canada

DiFILIPPO, ANTHONY. *Military Spending and Industrial Decline: A Study of the American Machine Tool Industry.* Pp. x, 199. Westport, CT: Greenwood Press, 1986. $35.00.

There has been unprecedented economic progress in the postwar period; we have also seen a rise in global militarization. Curiously, the two countries in the developed capitalist world that have the highest defense burden—military expenditure as a proportion of gross domestic product—the United States and Britain, have also had the worst performance in terms of economic indicators. This becomes even more stark when compared to Japan and West Germany; relatively low military burden corresponds to higher growth of aggregate output as well as of manufacturing productivity. The theoretical nexus between defense expenditure and industrial decline is a matter of considerable interest and has been well researched in recent years. The strength of DiFilippo's book lies in the specific analysis of a single, albeit major, industry; the interconnections between aggregate defense spending and the fortunes of the machine tool industry are well documented here.

After a short introduction, DiFilippo provides a succinct historical survey of the American machine tool industry and then goes on to discuss at length its structure and problems. These are then carefully related to the mechanics of U.S. defense expenditure and followed by policy prescriptions. Some comparisons with the success stories of machine tools in Japan and West Germany are welcome.

Two major reasons are given for the decline of machine tools in relation to defense. The use of military expenditure as a Keynesian fiscal stabilizer has created major problems for the machine tool industry, which is, simultaneously, vulnerable to cyclical factors as well as dependent on military demand. The difficulties are exacerbated by the exceptionally high level of defense research and development (R & D) by international standards, which seems to have starved the civilian sector of top-quality research input.

The analysis of R & D is particularly useful. There can be little doubt that for both the United States and the United Kingdom the low proportion of civilian R & D in the national total has contributed significantly to productivity decline. Japan, Germany, and the smaller European countries have done much better with government-subsidized technological progress in the non-

defense sector. It would have been useful if DiFilippo had pointed out in more detail the problems involved with military R & D in its relation to the civilian sector: low spin-off; so-called gold-plating standards, required by the defense establishment, with little use outside; competition for scarce resources such as highly skilled manpower. Overall, however, the treatment of R & D, and its deleterious effect on the machine tool industry particular and on industrialization in general, are well reached.

One major problem of analysis remains. DiFilippo's model of the cycle suggests that expansions of the defense budget have a positive effect on machine tools and that its contraction has negative feedback. It is not clear why the net effect of the fiscal stabilizer should be negative. Some questions remain: Are the slump periods greater in time than the boom periods? Are there specific asymmetries between expansion and contraction? Is the variance of military budgets having a significant effect in contrast to its mean? Are defense-induced multipliers inherently of low value compared to other forms of fiscal expansion? In the absence of adequate theoretical answers, the appeal of the book will be diminished.

DiFilippo has shown that supply-side economics coupled with high defense spending has had short-term benefits for the industry in recent years. However, the R & D burden remains; so long as Star Wars technology will absorb a high proportion of skilled resources, nondefense industries, such as machine tools, will suffer.

I believe that a fundamental structural change is about to take place with these new technologies. Their economic linkages and multipliers will be relatively small compared to the large expenditure involved. They will also be skill intensive, rather than the standard classification of (physical) capital- or labor-intensive techniques that we now have. Both these features may contribute to the technological dichotomization of economic and security considerations. It may not be possible in the future to relate the defense of the realm and the economic benefits of defense industrialization.

DiFilippo's book is a welcome contribution to a complex but important field. By concentrating on one industry and looking at governmental fiscal policy, it bridges the micro-macro gaps—a trend that will be useful in economic analysis. This book is highly recommended.

SAADET DEGER

University of London
England

DOWNS, ANTHONY. *Revolution in Real Estate Finance.* Pp. xiii, 345. Washington, DC: Brookings Institution, 1985. $31.95. Paperbound, $11.95.

Anthony Downs has written a timely and extremely interesting book about the radical changes transforming real estate financial institutions. Downs identifies and describes five important changes largely responsible for reshaping real estate: (1) shifting expectations of lenders and equity investors about the future trends of inflation; (2) the loss of housing's formerly favored position in credit markets; (3) tandem changes in fiscal and monetary policies; (4) partial deregulation of financial markets; and (5) technical improvements in the electronic transfer of funds.

The rapid increase in inflation during the late 1970s and early 1980s caused lenders to demand higher rates of return on investments and to alter fundamentally how interest charges are levied so that they could protect themselves from inflation-caused losses. The combined effects of higher inflation, the financial disintermediation suffered by savings and loans associations, and changes in the federal tax code undercut the historical preferences accorded to home ownership. Federal policies regarding taxation, interest rates, and money supply altered the relative advantages of investment alternatives, causing funds to shift from less attractive investments to those offering greater after-tax benefits.

At about the same time that lenders were repositioning themselves in an inflationary

environment, the federal government deregulated the financial services industry, freeing the market to set interest rates and allowing corporations to offer new investment products to attract savings. This more competitive market has made mortgage money for housing more expensive. Last, technological advances and shifts in institutional arrangements have accelerated the transformation of the financial marketplace.

The effects of these changes are just beginning to be recognized, and they promise to alter significantly the way families purchase housing, the way pension funds invest in real estate, and, in the long term, the way businesses and households utilize real property. In the short term, the shifts in financial conditions, practices, and technologies have created an investment bias toward real estate. This has caused considerable overbuilding in office markets across the nation. But in the longer run, especially with the recent tax reform, commercial construction will slow and buildings will become more expensive.

Perhaps the most serious implication of the revolution in real estate is that home ownership will remain expensive, as households will have to compete on equal footing with commercial, industrial, and institutional borrowers for scarce funds.

Anthony Downs has written a very good book on the changing world of real estate finance. The book will be of interest to planners, housing and economic development specialists, and social scientists.

DAVID E. DOWALL

University of California
Berkeley

HART-NIBBRIG, NAND and CLEMENT COTTINGHAM. *The Political Economy of College Sports.* Pp. xii, 126. Lexington, MA: Lexington Books, 1986. No price.

College sports in America have changed dramatically since colleges first started playing one another on a regular basis toward the end of the last century. Sports are now big business on many campuses, and there is

considerable controversy regarding the consequences of this for both student athletes and
academia and concerning whether and how
this business should be regulated. Hart-
Nibbrig and Cottingham do three things in
this book: (1) they discuss the decline of
amateurism in college sports and the sup-
planting development of a system of corporate athleticism; (2) they analyze some of
the economic and political forces influencing
corporate athleticism today; and (3) they
review some proposals for reform.

They see market forces and a "relentless
commercialism" as the driving forces transforming intercollegiate sports in the twentieth
century. They argue that the business ethic,
to some extent, has been there from the
beginning and that the commercial interests
were advanced considerably by the rationalization of football in the 1920s by the
legendary Yale coach, Walter Camp, but
that it is the introduction of television coverage in the 1960s that marks the emergence of
a strong corporate athleticism, with its prevailing ethos of winning at all costs and
generating revenue. The result is that many
college athletes are now spending their "student years" not getting an education, but,
rather, preparing to be professional athletes,
even though very few ever succeed at this.
There is still an enormous noncommercial
sector of college sports, of course, but this is
not discussed.

University presidents and faculty have
effectively relinquished control of this aspect
of higher education in the past to the National Collegiate Athletic Association
(NCAA), which was supposed to monitor
intercollegiate sports in the context of a
system of higher education. The NCAA
dates back to a time when the prevailing
ethos was amateurism, however, and it has
proved ineffective, if not totally powerless,
when faced with the market forces unleashed
by television and alumni boosters. Hart-
Nibbrig and Cottingham see the 1984 Supreme Court decision against the "monopoly
role" of the NCAA as finally heralding the
way to the "full commercialization of college
sports." Understandably, some university
presidents are now trying, rather belatedly,

to reestablish control over this aspect of
higher education.

Hart-Nibbrig and Cottingham's treatment
is fine as far as it goes. Readers interested in
the topic will find a lot of useful material
packed into this short book. I think scholars
will find it thin on original research, however.
Many authorities in the sociology or history
of sports, for example, are cited casually in
passing, but Hart-Nibbrig and Cottingham
never enter into any substantial debate on
interesting interpretative questions. Moreover, some of their analysis—for example,
their chapter on the economic base of college
sports—seems spotty and piecemeal; I felt it
needed more detail, more data, and more
rigor before I could appreciate the balance of
economic and political forces they discuss. I
would also like to have seen a fuller discussion
of proposals for reform. At the same time, I
found their combination of a systems approach with a political-economy perspective
helpful in suggesting a coherent framework
for further discussion. This book is a useful
introduction to its subject.

ADRIAN C. HAYES
State University of New York
Albany

HARVEY, DAVID. *The Urbanization of Cap-
ital: Studies in the History and Theory of
Capitalist Urbanization.* Pp. xvii, 239.
Baltimore: Johns Hopkins University
Press, 1985. $25.00.

FOGLESONG, RICHARD E. *Planning the
Capitalist City: The Colonial Era to the
1920s.* Pp. x, 286. Princeton, NJ: Princeton University Press, 1986. $25.00.

These volumes evince a common concern
with the interplay between the capitalist
economy and the built environment. Each
author seeks to show how capitalist development has shaped and been shaped by the
man-made geography of the modern city.
Each also seeks thereby to illuminate specifically urban phenomena within a generally
Marxist framework of economic analysis.

Harvey, a well-known economic geographer, offers a collection of eight essays—six published earlier and subsequently revised, two published here for the first time—in which he adds a spatial dimension to Marx's largely temporal approach to class relationships. Harvey is "primarily concerned with how capitalism creates a physical landscape of roads, houses, factories, schools, shops, and so forth in its own image and what the contradictions are that arise out of such processes of producing space." His essays are theoretical rather than descriptive, and their dense sophistication makes much of what they have to say quite difficult to fathom for anyone who is not thoroughly conversant with both Marxist economics and economic geography. What I found most instructive and worth noting in the present context was Harvey's thinking in his two chapters—numbers 5 and 6—on politics and planning. Here, and at various places elsewhere as well, he points out the ways in which the logic of the capitalist system necessitates capitalist support for an "operative geographical conception of community." In the absence of such a community, he argues, competitive individuals will fail to build and maintain the basic infrastructure without which the system as a whole cannot function and reproduce itself.

This facet of Harvey's theorizing, together with the thinking of other Marxist students of urban development—especially such Frenchmen as Manuel Castells, François Lamarche, and Edmond Preteceille—constitutes a large part of the conceptual background that lies behind Foglesong's much more accessible work in theory and history. Trained as a political scientist, Foglesong both illustrates and modifies the general ideas of his more heavily theoretical forebears and contemporaries. He does so by juxtaposing them carefully and clearly against American developments during a period of nearly three centuries, from the era of "colonial town planting" in the seventeenth century through the pursuit of technological efficiency in the early twentieth.

Foglesong shows that planners played a crucial role in helping to facilitate the smooth functioning of capitalist cities. Acting not as the direct agents of capitalist entrepreneurs but instead as semi-autonomous intellectuals, they nonetheless articulated and advanced the collective interests of the leading owners of urban property more clearly and effectively than these men could possibly have done acting on their own. At one level, they sought to overcome the property contradiction: the conflict between the self-centered impulses felt by private owners and the objective need for a greater degree of public control in order to strengthen the social and economic order on which they depended for their individual well-being. Housing reformers, planners of urban parks, leaders of the city-beautiful movement, and the more technologically oriented advocates of the city practical all succeeded in large measures owing to the ways in which—and only insofar as—their programs fitted in with the larger interests of the capitalist class properly understood.

Foglesong skillfully demonstrates that these programs functioned in a variety of ways. Improved housing and urban parks contributed to the renewal of labor power, and the movement toward more efficient transportation networks and more stringent zoning of land use fitted in quite clearly with the material requirements for both industrial production and commercial exchange. In ways that go beyond Harvey and Castells, Foglesong also focuses on the symbolic and political pursuit of middle-class hegemony. He argues that the neoclassical architecture designed by men such as Daniel Burnham and his followers was seen as helping to instill a unifying sense of civic pride and that other items on the planners' agendas also helped to maintain "social control" over the urban masses by the middle class. His remarks on the emerging solution to the "capitalist-democracy contradiction" point in the same direction. Here he argues that the emergence of public commissions of planning experts who were largely autonomous from elected officials provided an ideal way of ensuring that the socialization of urban space did not advance to the point where capitalism itself was placed in danger.

Contrary to Harvey's belief that the alliances that sustain urban capitalism are ultimately unstable, Foglesong's account of city planning thus suggests not the fragility but the great resilience of the capital order. Precisely to the extent that he demonstrates a congruence between the selfish interests of the capitalist elite and the accelerating tendency toward environmental intervention, he contradicts the expectations of anyone who would prophesy the final end of the capitalist system. It therefore comes as no surprise that despite his own Marxist bent he ends up urging his readers to work for urban reform by forging alliances within the capitalist camp as well as by building democratic opposition to capitalist exploitation. This admonition constitutes a sensible conclusion to a very well argued book, which makes a major contribution to the history of urban development and the responses it has evoked.

ANDREW LEES

Rutgers University
Camden
New Jersey

KETTL, DONALD F. *Leadership at the Fed.* Pp. xiii, 218. New Haven, CT: Yale University Press, 1986. $22.50.

A casual inspection of this book, written by a political scientist, would seem to suggest that it is yet another history of the Federal Reserve System, since it traces the evolution of that organization from its weak and uncertain beginnings in 1913 to the position of power and influence that it occupies today. A closer reading, however, reveals that it is something else. While monetary policy, the essential *raison d'être* of the Fed, is indeed reviewed here as it has developed over time, this is purely secondary to, and treated only as necessary background for,

the main purpose of the book: to evaluate the changing relations between the Fed and its various constituencies—the president, the secretary of the Treasury, Congress, and the different major sectors of the economy—to trace the sources of the growing power of the Fed, and to assess the role of the Fed's legal independence in these developments. In short, the book could more properly be described as a political history of the system.

Although this ground has been covered by others before, notably by A. J. Clifford in his 1965 book, Kettl's study differs in at least two important respects. For one thing, it draws more thoroughly than any of its predecessors on materials in all the presidential libraries, on congressional hearings and reports, on private collections of papers, and on extensive interviews with key officials. These make possible a wealth of detail never before gathered together, anecdotes that make for lively reading, and interesting vignettes of leading Fed and government officials.

Of much more importance is the great stress placed by Kettl on the leadership of the chairman of the Fed since the mid-1930s as the factor most responsible for the Fed's power, for its ability to adapt to changing circumstances, technical uncertainties, and political demands, and for the degree of its success in balancing the often conflicting interests of its different constituencies and in winning their political support for its decisions—all essential for its effectiveness, credibility, and indeed the maintenance of its legal independence. Most fundamental of all, in Kettl's judgment, are the relations between the chairman and the president; and a good deal of the book centers on the accommodating and sometimes confrontational nature of their relations since the 1930s. The analysis of these constitutes the essence and distinguishing feature of the book. Indeed, Kettl goes so far as to state, "The Fed's history is inseparable from the history of the chairmanship, which in turn is inseparable from the story of the chairman's relationship with the president."

Kettl concludes, among other things, that in the end the Fed has usually delivered policy in accord with the president's policy goals; that Congress, despite its often hostile attitude, has kept its distance from the Fed for most of the time; that Eccles, Martin, Burns, and Volcker—for all of whom Kettl clearly has enormous admiration—were "strong" chairmen who did a great deal to strengthen the Fed's power; and that the Fed's legal independence, while providing flexibility for building political support, was not itself the dominant source of the Fed's increasing power.

This interesting and well-written book, although likely to appeal mainly to political scientists, should also be of interest to economists and to students of monetary policy-making. Some may feel, however, that Kettl has unduly exaggerated the degree of importance attached to the role of the chairman, to the virtual exclusion of other Board members, the presidents of the 12 Federal Reserve banks, and the chairman's staff.

ARTHUR I. BLOOMFIELD

University of Pennsylvania
Philadelphia

SCOTT, JAMES C. *Weapons of the Weak: Everyday Forms of Peasant Resistance.* Pp. xxii, 389. New Haven, CT: Yale University Press, 1985. No price.

OHKAWA, KAZUSHI and GUSTAV RANIS, eds. *Japan and the Developing Countries.* Pp. vi, 456. New York: Basil Blackwell, 1985. $45.00.

It is a decade since James Scott published his book on peasant revolution in Southeast Asia, *The Moral Economy of the Peasant.* It became widely known in the academic world because it was chosen as the target for Samuel Popkin's eloquent if sweeping attack, in a book entitled *The Rational Peasant,* on all social science that refused to believe that peasant behavior could not be understood mainly through the economistic model of rational, self-regarding, individual behavior.

The Scott-Popkin debate, regressing as it did to primitive polarities between two radically different conceptions of humanity and the root causes of human action—socially governed and norm-governed versus individual and interest-governed behavior—did no credit to social science.

Scott has, fortunately, not abandoned his concern with norms, values, and morality as they affect peasant political behavior. Equally fortunate, he now shows more interest in the contested nature of statements of value and in the material roots of different interpretations. The major apparent shift in his orientation is away from the *problématique* of the causes of peasant revolution—a concern that, as he and others now clearly see, reflected American obsessions with the Vietnam war—toward a fascination with the daily struggles of ordinary poor peasants to mitigate and resist material and symbolic subordination and oppression. The result is a book that makes major empirical and theoretical contributions to our understanding of the role of ideas, symbols, and ideology in class struggle and that deserves to stand as a minor classic in social science.

It is noteworthy that, at a time when the social anthropological approach of intensively studying small communities is poorly regarded in most other social sciences, Scott has built this very solidly constructed intellectual edifice on a fieldwork base of a single Malaysian village of 74 households. Fortunate timing certainly played a part: Scott spent two years in this rice-growing Kedah village a few years after major economic changes associated with the introduction of double-cropping and, more important, just as combine harvesters were becoming common. Scott explains with crystal clarity, and with the assistance of data from an earlier survey conducted in the same village, how the various changes in rice production affected income distribution. Mainly because of the displacement of harvest labor by combine harvesters, the rich indeed became richer and the poor poorer—while a large middle group had on balance been little affected. This account is, however, only a prelude to the main story: the fact that the poor, who were increasingly dispensable as far as the rich were concerned, were still able to appeal to and use against the rich a set of community values to which the rich had conformed but a few years before when they had needed the labor of the poor. It is through manipulation of these values that the class struggle was largely fought, although this did not exclude more direct but covert and individual acts of resistance on the part of the poor.

For a range of reasons the ideological class struggle was especially acute in Scott's village. It may be difficult to find many similar situations in which the relations of production have changed so suddenly that the dominant class can be hoist by the petard of the value system it actively promoted but a few years before. One can, however, have every sympathy with Scott's insistence that there is neither empirical nor theoretical basis for the common assumption, sometimes these days linked with the name of Gramsci, that the poor are kept in order because they accept an ideological system propagated by the dominant class. Scott's theoretical discussion of hegemony and consciousness takes us far beyond his Malaysian village and is itself a major contribution to social science.

In contrast, Ohkawa and Ranis take us into the world of large, collective research projects, with grants from major foundations and the names of many luminaries as advisers and collaborators. Despite the title of the book, the project was concerned not with relationships between Japan and developing countries but with what lessons about economic policy can be derived for contemporary developing countries from Japan's historical growth experience. In practice, not all the 17 contributed papers actually concern themselves with this issue. More worrying, the project itself appears to have virtually ignored what should have been a central theme: how major changes in the global economic, political, military, and technological orders in the century since Japan began to become an industrial power might affect the possibility of learning any lessons from Japanese experi-

ence. Unlike Scott, this book's editors and contributors are all a long way inside all the boundaries of social science.

MICK MOORE

University of Sussex
Brighton
England

SHUBIK, MARTIN. *A Game-Theoretic Approach to Political Economy.* Pp. viii, 744. Cambridge, MA: MIT Press, 1985. $47.50.

This is the book to read for anyone interested in a survey of game theory and political economy. The book begins with a section on money, ownership, and preferences. A concern of this section and a theme that appears throughout the book is the art and practice of successful model building. The next section is about oligopolistic markets and the strategic behavior of large firms. A thesis in this section is that game theory provides an analytical framework that can unify the diverse approaches to the study of oligopoly. Part 3 is the first of two sections on general equilibrium theory—the study of an economy as a system of interrelated markets. The perspective of this section is the theory of cooperative games, the study of how the gains from cooperation are divided. In contrast, noncooperative game theory is the study of strategic interaction between players, and cooperation when it arises is seen as a product of this strategic interaction. Part 4 is devoted to general equilibrium theory from the perspective of noncooperative game theory, and in particular strategic market games. Among the issues that take center stage here are the problem of price determination, and the role of money, credit, and financial institutions. The last section of the book addresses more political parts of political economy. This section opens with analyses of externalities and public goods, issues that fall in a class of problems known as market failure. The discussion then moves to taxation, voting, government, and bureaucracy, where the focus is the relationship between political and economic questions. Shubik's ultimate interest here is the socio-political control of the economy.

This is a book that addresses many interesting questions, and almost everyone will find something of concern here. Among the issues that appear in the section on oligopoly are the strategic ramifications of production capacity and inventories, and the relationship between competitive behavior and the number and size of firms in a market. The section on strategic market games addresses an important problem that is finessed in the neoclassical approaches to general equilibrium theory: the details of price determination and market clearing mechanisms. An interesting result discussed in the final section is that in the absence of externalities and public goods, the different solution or equilibrium concepts reinforce each other. Specifically, as a market or an economy becomes larger—as the number of agents increases—the different equilibrium concepts all converge to the competitive equilibrium. This coincidence of outcomes arising from different analyses and considerations of what is important in trade and exchange provides some explanation of the power of the price system and market economies. In markets with externalities and public goods, however, convergence does not occur. This nonconvergence points to the limitations of the price system and points to the need for solutions to some classes of economic problems that lie outside of the realm of free markets, exchange, and contracting. In a discussion of voting and corporate stock, Shubik points to the role of minority shareholder protection rules in ensuring the existence of an equilibrium. The analysis of voting includes the agenda selection problem, logrolling, and vote trading. Here, Shubik points out fundamental differences between economic and political processes; "the comparison between 'spending' one's vote and one's money does not survive scrutiny." A constant theme in this book is the need to account for institutions in theoretical research. Such is not an easy matter, and among Shubik's many contributions to

game theory is his institutionally rich model building.

Readers of this book will be impressed with the breadth and depth of Martin Shubik's research. The book contains much to think about, and it is because of Shubik's insights and depth of analyses that some readers might wish that he had discussed here some recent research in game theory, such as the noncooperative approaches to cooperative behavior, incomplete information, and the issue of credible threats in oligopoly theory. Finally, the reader of this book need not be a game theorist or a theoretical economist, but should probably have some familiarity with the basic definitions and concepts of game theory.

JOHN KAMBHU

Columbia University
New York City

WRIGHT, GAVIN. *Old South, New South: Revolutions in the Southern Economy since the Civil War.* Pp. x, 321. New York: Basic Books, 1986. $19.95.

In recent years, the American South has once again become a battleground. This time the combatants are, on the one hand, those who claim the pattern of Southern industrialization as a confirmation of the inexorable workings of free market forces and, on the other, those who see in the modern South the legacy of planter values and a coercive, nonmarket system of labor relations. *Old South, New South* is Gavin Wright's intervention in this debate. For Wright, the key to the Southern experience is that "the South constituted a separate regional labor market outside the scope of national and international labor markets that were active and effective during the same era." Since it was a labor market, the tendency toward wage convergence within the South was established, although in most cases this was a convergence downward to wage levels for farm laborers. Since it was also an isolated, Southern labor market, however, reductions in regional wage differentials did not occur. Only under the external pressure of national wage and labor standards in the 1930s did these differentials begin to close. Thereafter, the South was gradually opened to the tendency to national labor market integration. As a result of this process, in the 1980s "the South as a distinct economic entity has all but disappeared."

It is impossible to do justice to *Old South, New South* in a short review. It is well written, technically and theoretically sophisticated, and historically sensitive. Its merit as an exercise in economic history is that it sees markets as social phenomena rather than as abstracted sets of economic relationships. This pays off repeatedly as Wright clarifies racial, ideological, and other dimensions of market relations. Those who still believe in the abstract logic of markets should read this book.

Wright's intelligent eclecticism does not make his analysis entirely convincing, however. It provides a better explanation of what the South used to be than of what it has become. Treating Southern development primarily in terms of the market exchange dimension of productive relations, Wright can provide only a cursory discussion of nonwage, essentially political sources of regional differentiation such as levels of unionization and of work intensity. Consequently, neither his conceptual framework nor his final chapter on the contemporary Southern economy—in which he qualifies his argument repeatedly—can rule out the possibility that there remains something distinctive about relations between capital and labor in the South.

PHILLIP J. WOOD
St. Francis Xavier University
Antigonish
Nova Scotia
Canada

## OTHER BOOKS

ABEL, THEODORE. *Why Hitler Came into Power*. Pp. xx, 323. Cambridge, MA: Harvard University Press, 1986. $35.00. Paperbound, $8.95.

ABRAMSON, ALAN J. and LESTER M. SALAMON. *The Nonprofit Sector and the New Federal Budget*. Pp. xviii, 138. Washington, DC: Urban Institute Press, 1986. Paperbound, $12.95.

ABT, CLARK, C. *A Strategy for Terminating a Nuclear War*. Pp. xiii, 253. Boulder, CO: Westview Press, 1985. Paperbound, $19.95.

ADDO, HERB et al. *Development as a Social Transformation: Reflections on the Global Problematique*. Pp. v, 281. Boulder, CO: Westview Press, 1986. Paperbound, $28.50.

AGONCILLO, TEODORO A. *The Burden of Proof: The Vargas-Laurel Collaboration Case*. Pp. xii, 453. Philippines: University of the Philippines Press, 1984. Distributed by University of Hawaii Press, Honolulu. $28.00.

ALLISON, ROY. *Finland's Relations with the Soviet Union: 1944-1984*. Pp. ix, 211. New York: St. Martin's Press, 1985. $29.95.

ARTNER, STEPHEN J. *A Change of Course: The West German Social Democrats and NATO, 1957-1961*. Pp. xviii, 242. Westport, CT: Greenwood Press, 1985. $35.00.

AXELGARD, FREDERICK W., ed. *Iraq in Transition: A Political, Economic, and Strategic Perspective*. Pp. xi, 111. Boulder, CO: Westview Press, 1986. Paperbound, $19.50.

AYOOB, MOHAMMED, ed. *Regional Security in the Third World*. Pp. 284. Boulder, CO: Westview Press, 1986. $35.00.

BARFIELD, CLAUDE E. and WILLIAM A. SCHAMBRA, eds. *The Politics of Industrial Policy*. Pp. xii, 344. Washington, DC: American Enterprise Institute for Public Policy Research, 1986. Paperbound, no price.

BARKUN, MICHAEL. *Disaster and the Millenium*. Pp. x, 246. Syracuse, NY: Syracuse University Press, 1986. Paperbound, $12.95.

BARON, SALO W. *The Contemporary Relevance of History*. Pp. viii, 158. New York: Columbia University Press, 1986. $30.00.

BAUMOL, WILLIAM J. *Microtheory: Applications and Origins*. Pp. xxvii, 286. Cambridge, MA: MIT Press, 1986. $35.00.

BAUMOL, WILLIAM J. *Superfairness: Applications and Theory*. Pp. xi, 266. Cambridge, MA: MIT Press, 1986. $20.00.

BECKFORD, JAMES A. *Cult Controversies: The Societal Response to the New Religious Movements*. Pp. viii, 327. New York: Methuen, 1985. $39.95. Paperbound, $13.95.

BENDAHMANE, DIANE B. and LEO MOSER, eds. *Toward a Better Understanding: U.S.-Japan Relations*. Pp. vii, 142. Washington, DC: Center for the Study of Foreign Affairs, 1986. Paperbound, $4.25.

BENDER, FREDERIC L., ed. *Karl Marx: The Essential Writings*. 2nd ed. Pp. xxvi, 514. Boulder, CO: Westview Press, 1986. $35.00. Paperbound, $14.85.

BENDER, LEWIS and JAMES A. STEVER, eds. *Administering the New Federalism*. Pp. ix, 369. Boulder, CO: Westview Press, 1986. Paperbound, $19.95.

BERG, ROBERT and JENNIFER SEYMOUR WHITAKER, eds. *Strategies for African Development*. Pp. xii, 603. Berkeley: University of California Press, 1986. Paperbound, $15.95.

BERGER, KATHLEEN STASSEN. *The Developing Person through Childhood and Adolescence*. 2nd ed. Pp. xviii, 627. New York: Worth, 1986. $30.95.

BJORKQVIST, KAJ. *Violent Films, Anxiety and Aggression: Experimental Studies of the Effect of Violent Films on the Level of Anxiety and Aggressiveness in Children*.

Pp. 75. Helsinki: Finnish Society of Sciences and Letters, 1985. Paperbound, no price.

BLACKWOOD, EVELYN, ed. *Anthropology and Homosexual Behavior.* Pp. xiii, 217. New York: Haworth Press, 1986. $29.95. Paperbound, $22.95.

BLÖNDAL, GÍSLI. *Fiscal Policy in the Smaller Industrial Countries, 1972-1982.* Pp. ix, 232. Washington, DC: International Monetary Fund, 1986. Paperbound, no price.

BOLES, JANET K., ed. *The Egalitarian City: Issues of Rights, Distribution, Access, and Power.* Pp. xiv, 223. New York: Praeger, 1986. $34.95.

BOLEY, G. E. SAIGBE. *Liberia: The Rise and Fall of the First Republic.* Pp. x, 225. New York: St. Martin's Press, 1985. $27.50.

BONNEY, NORMAN. *The Politics and Finance of Provincial Government in New Guinea.* Pp. ix, 81. Canberra: Australian National University, Centre for Research on Federal Financial Relations, 1986. Distributed by ANUTECH, Canberra, Australia. Paperbound, no price.

BOTTOME, EDGAR. *The Balance of Terror: Nuclear Weapons and the Illusion of Security, 1945-1985.* Revised ed. Pp. xxii, 291. Boston, MA: Beacon Press, 1986. Paperbound, $11.95.

BOYLE, KEVIN and TOM HADDEN. *Ireland: A Positive Proposal.* Pp. 127. New York: Penguin Books, 1986. Paperbound, $4.95.

BRAU, EDUARD et al. *Export Credits: Developments and Prospects.* Pp. v, 34. Washington, DC: International Monetary Fund, 1986. Paperbound, $10.00.

BRESNAN, JOHN, ed. *Crisis in the Philippines: The Marcos Era and Beyond.* Pp. xiv, 284. Princeton, NJ: Princeton University Press, 1986. $30.00. Paperbound, $10.95.

BRUNER, JEROME S., JACQUELINE J. GOODNOW, and GEORGE A. AUSTIN. *A Study of Thinking.* Pp. xx, 330. New Brunswick, NJ: Transaction Books, 1986. Paperbound, $19.95.

BURNHEIM, JOHN. *Is Democracy Possible? The Alternative to Electoral Politics.* Pp. vii, 205. Blackwood, NJ: Blackwell, 1985. No price.

CASTELLS, MANUEL. *The City and the Grassroots.* Pp. xxi, 450. Berkeley: University of California Press, 1985. $29.95. Paperbound, $14.95.

CHILD, JACK, ed. *Conflict in Central America: Approaches to Peace and Security.* Pp. xiv, 208. New York: St. Martin's Press. 1986. $27.50.

CHRISTENSEN, BENEDICTE VIBE. *Switzerland's Role as an International Financial Center.* Pp. v, 40. Washington, DC: International Monetary Fund, 1986. Paperbound, $7.50.

CLEVELAND, DIANNE. *Incest: The Story of Three Women.* Pp. xii, 112. Lexington, MA: D. C. Heath, Lexington Books, 1986. $17.00.

CLOGG, RICHARD. *Politics and the Academy: Arnold Toynbee and the Koraes Chair.* Pp. x, 117. Totowa, NJ: Frank Cass, 1986. $30.00.

CORN, JOSEPH J., ed. *Imagining Tomorrow: History, Technology, and the American Future.* Pp. vi, 237. Cambridge, MA: MIT Press, 1986. $17.50.

CREWS, KENNETH, D., ed. *Corwin's Constitution: Essays and Insights of Edward S. Corwin.* Pp. ix, 276. Westport, CT: Greenwood Press, 1986. $35.00.

DAHRENDORF, RALF and THEODORE C. SORENSON. *A Widening Atlantic: Domestic Change and Foreign Policy.* Pp. xii, 107. New York: Council on Foreign Relations, 1986. Paperbound, $5.95.

DANIELS, NORMAN. *Just Health Care.* Pp. xiii, 245. New York: Cambridge University Press, 1985. $32.50. Paperbound, $9.95.

DAVIS, KINGSLEY, ed., in association with AMYRA GROSSBARD-SCHECHTMAN. *Contemporary Marriage: Comparative Perspectives on a Changing Institution.* Pp. xiii, 432. New York: Russell Sage Foundation, 1986. Distributed by Basic Books, New York. $29.95.

DAVIS, MIKE. *Prisoners of the American Dream.* Pp. xi, 320. New York: Schocken Books, 1986. $24.95. Paperbound, $10.95.

DE JAYSAY, ANTHONY. *The State.* Pp. vii, 291. New York: Basil Blackwell, 1985. $24.95.

DE VRIES, MARGARET GARRITSEN. *The IMF in a Changing World, 1945-1985.* Pp. x, 226. Washington, DC: International Monetary Fund, 1986. Paperbound, no price.

DEBNAM, GEOFFREY *The Analysis of Power: Core Elements and Structure.* Pp. x, 112. New York: St. Martin's Press, 1984. $19.95.

DEL PRADO Y SALABARRIA, WIFREDO. *Cuba: Destiny as Choice.* Pp. 191. Miami, FL: Ediciones universal, 1985. Paperbound, no price.

DIETZE, GOTTFRIED. *Liberalism Proper and Proper Liberalism.* Pp. ix, 282. Baltimore, MD: Johns Hopkins University Press, 1984. $27.50.

DOBSON, ALAN P. *U.S. Wartime Aid to Britain, 1940-1946.* Pp. 242. New York: St. Martin's Press, 1986. $27.50.

DRUCKER, HENRY et al., eds. *Developments in British Politics.* Vol. 2. Pp. xvii, 430. New York: St. Martin's Press, 1986. $29.95. Paperbound, $12.95.

DUPREE, A. HUNTER. *Science in the Federal Government: A History of Policies and Activities.* Pp. xxi, 460. Baltimore, MD: Johns Hopkins University Press, 1986. Paperbound, no price.

ENTELIS, JOHN P. *Algeria: The Revolution Institutionalized.* Pp. xii, 239. Boulder, CO: Westview Press, 1986. $30.00.

EPSTEIN, JOSHUA M. *The 1987 Defense Budget.* Pp. viii, 61. Washington, DC: Brookings Institution, 1986. Paperbound, $7.95.

FARLEY, REYNOLDS. *Blacks and Whites: Narrowing the Gap?* Pp. xii, 235. Cambridge, MA: Harvard University Press, 1984. $19.50. Paperbound, $7.95.

FARMER, EDWARD et al. *Comparative History of Civilization in Asia.* Vol. 1, *10,000 B.C. to 1850.* Pp. xxx, 514. Boulder, CO: Westview Press, 1986. Paperbound, $24.00.

FARMER, EDWARD et al. *Comparative History of Civilization in Asia.* Vol. 2, *1350 to Present.* Pp. xxix, 433. Boulder, CO: Westview Press, 1986. Paperbound, $24.00.

*Federal-State-Local Fiscal Relations: Report to the President and Congress.* Pp. iv, 494. Washington, DC: Department of the Treasury, Office of State and Local Finance, 1985. Paperbound, no price.

FOSS, DANIEL A. and RALPH LARKIN. *Beyond Revolution: A New Theory of Social Movements.* Pp. xv, 176. South Hadley, MA: Bergin & Garvey, 1986. $34.95. Paperbound, $14.95.

FOSTER, MARY LeCRON and ROBERT A. RUBINSTEIN, eds. *Peace and War: Cross-Cultural Perspectives.* Pp. xviii, 369. New Brunswick, NJ: Transaction Books, 1986. $29.95. Paperbound, $16.95.

FRANCISCO, RONALD A. and RICHARD L. MERRITT, eds. *Berlin between Two Worlds.* Pp. xiii, 184. Boulder, CO: Westview Press, 1986. Paperbound, $18.50.

FREEMAN, J.P.G. *Britain's Nuclear Arms Control Policy in the Context of Anglo-American Relations, 1957-1968.* Pp. xvi, 317. New York: St. Martin's Press, 1986. $35.00.

FROST, MERVYN. *Towards a Normative Theory of International Relations.* Pp. x, 241. New York: Cambridge University Press, 1986. $37.50.

GARFINKLE, ADAM M. *The Politics of the Nuclear Freeze.* Pp. xviii, 258. Philadelphia: Foreign Policy Research Institute, 1984. Paperbound, $7.95.

GIDDENS, ANTHONY, ed. *Durkheim on Politics and the State.* Translated by W. D. Halls. Pp. vii, 250. Stanford, CA: Stanford University Press, 1986. $35.00.

GLENNON, JOHN P., ed. *China: Foreign Relations of the United States, 1955-1957.* Vol. 2. Pp. xxiii, 706. Washington, DC: Government Printing Office, 1986. No price.

GLENNON, JOHN P. et al., eds. *The Near*

and Middle East: Foreign Relations of the United States, 1952-1954. Vol. 9, part 1. Pp. xxxvi, 1741. Washington, DC: Government Printing Office, 1986. No price.

GONZALES, MICHAEL J. Plantation Agriculture and Social Control in Northern Peru, 1875-1933. Pp. ix, 235. Austin: University of Texas Press, 1985. $25.00.

GOULD, WILLIAM B., IV. A Primer on American Labor Law. 2nd ed. Pp. xiii, 261. Cambridge, MA: MIT Press, 1986. $25.00. Paperbound, $10.95.

GRAY, ANDREW and WILLIAM I. JENKINS. Administrative Politics in British Government. Pp. xi, 259. New York: St. Martin's Press, 1985. No price.

GÜRÜN, KAMAURAN. The Armenian File: The Myth of Innocence Exposed. Pp. xvii, 323. New York: St. Martin's Press, 1986. $29.95.

GUSFIELD, JOSEPH R. Symbolic Crusade: Status Politics and the American Temperance Movement. 2nd ed. Pp. viii, 226. Champaign: University of Illinois Press, 1986. $24.95. Paperbound, $8.95.

HAGEMAN, MARY JEANETTE. Police-Community Relations. Pp. 159. Newbury Park, CA: Sage, 1985. No price.

HAGEN, KENNETH J. and WILLIAM R. ROBERTS. Against All Enemies: Interpretations of American Military History from Colonial Times to the Present. Pp. xxi, 393. Westport, CT: Greenwood Press, 1986. $45.00. Paperbound, $18.50.

HARVEY, DAVID. Consciousness and the Urban Experience. Pp. xix, 293. Baltimore, MD: Johns Hopkins University Press, 1985. $25.00.

HAUSER, PHILIP M., DANIEL B. SUITS, and NAOHIRO OGAWA, eds. Urbanization and Migration in Asean Development. Pp. xiv, 496. Tokyo: National Institute for Research Advancement, 1985. Distributed by University of Hawaii Press, Honolulu. Paperbound, $25.00.

HEINRICH, HANS-GEORG. Hungary: Politics, Economics, and Society. Pp. xx, 198. Boulder, CO: Lynne Rienner, 1986. $25.00. Paperbound, $11.95.

HERLIHY, DAVID. Medieval Households. Pp. vii, 227. Cambridge, MA: Harvard University Press, 1985. $30.00. Paperbound, $11.95.

HODGES, GRAHAM RUSSELL. New York City Cartmen, 1667-1850. Pp. xiv, 224. New York: New York University Press, 1986. Distributed by Columbia University Press, New York. $35.00.

HOLMES, DEBORAH. Governing the Press: Media Freedom in the U.S. and Great Britain. Pp. xi, 107. Boulder, CO: Westview Press, 1986. Paperbound, $16.50.

HOPE, KEMPE RONALD. Urbanization in the Commonwealth Caribbean. Pp. xiii, 129. Boulder, CO: Westview Press, 1986. Paperbound, $18.50.

INSTITUTE OF MEDICINE OF THE NATIONAL ACADEMY OF SCIENCE. Mobilizing against AIDS: The Unfinished Story of a Virus. Pp. x, 212. Cambridge, MA: Harvard University Press, 1986. $15.00. Paperbound, $7.95.

JASANOFF, SHEILA. Risk Management and Political Culture. Pp. viii, 93. New York: Russell Sage Foundation, 1986. Distributed by Basic Books, New York. Paperbound, $5.95.

JAY, MARTIN. Marxism and Totality: The Adventures of a Concept from Lukacs to Habermas. Pp. xi, 576. Berkeley: University of California Press, 1986. Paperbound, $14.95.

JOHNSTONE, DIANA. The Politics of Euromissiles: Europe's Role in America's World. Pp. 218. London: Verso, 1984. Distributed by Schocken Books, New York. Paperbound, $6.95.

JORDAN, BOJANA VUYISILE. We Will Be Heard: A South African Exile Remembers. Pp. 172. Boston, MA: Quinlan Press, 1986. $17.95.

KIRALY, BELA and NANDOR DREISZIGER, eds. East Central European Society in World War I. Pp. xi, 623. Boulder, CO: East European Monographs, 1985. Distributed by Columbia University Press, 1985. $45.00.

KIRZNER, ISRAEL M. Discovery and the Capitalist Process. Pp. xiii, 181. Chicago: University of Chicago Press, 1985. $22.50.

KLAPP, ORRIN E. *Overload and Boredom: Essays on the Quality of Life in the Information Society.* Pp. 174. Westport, CT: Greenwood Press, 1986. $29.95.

KLINGHOFFER, ARTHUR JAY. *Israel and the Soviet Union: Alienation or Reconciliation?* Pp. x, 303. Boulder, CO: Westview Press, 1985. Paperbound, 1985.

KRAUS, SIDNEY and RICHARD M. PERLOFF. *Mass Media and Political Thought: An Information Processing Approach.* Pp. 350. Newbury Park, CA: Sage, 1985. No price.

KRUKONES, MICHAEL G. *Promises and Performance: Presidential Campaigns as Policy Predictions.* Pp. vii, 158. Lanham, MD: University Press of America, 1984. $22.75. Paperbound, $11.50.

KUZNESOF, ELIZABETH ANNE. *Household Economy and Urban Development: Sao Paolo, 1765-1836.* Pp. xvii, 216. Boulder, CO: Westview Press, 1986. Paperbound, $27.50.

*La Jurisprudence.* Pp. 444. Paris: Sirey, 1985. Paperbound, Fr380.

LACOSTE, YVES. *Ibn Khaldun: The Birth of History and the Past of the Third World.* Translated by David Macey. Pp. 214. London: Verso, 1984. Distributed by Schocken Books, New York. $30.00. Paperbound, $9.50.

LAIRD, ROBBIN F. *France, the Soviet Union, and the Nuclear Weapons Issue.* Pp. xiv, 142. Boulder, CO: Westview Press, 1985. Paperbound, $15.95.

LAL, DEEPAK and MARTIN WOLF, eds. *Stagflation, Savings, and the State: Perspectives on the Global Economy.* Pp. xii, 402. New York: Oxford University Press, 1986. No price.

LIPSET, SEYMOUR MARTIN, ed. *Unions in Transition: Entering the Second Century.* Pp. xviii, 505. San Francisco: Institute for Contemporary Studies, 1986. $29.95. Paperbound, $12.95.

LOSEV, SERGEI ANDREEVICH and YURI TYSSOVSKY. *The Middle East: Oil and Policy.* Translated by Dmitry Sventsitsky. Pp. 238. Moscow: Progress, 1985. Distributed by Imported Publications, Chicago. Paperbound, $4.95.

LOWI, THEODORE. *The Personal President: Power Invested, Promise Unfulfilled.* Pp. xiii, 221. Ithaca, NY: Cornell University Press, 1986. Paperbound, $8.95.

LUKE, TIMOTHY W. *Ideology and Soviet Industrialization.* Pp. xi, 283. Westport, CT: Greenwood Press, 1985. $35.00.

LUNN, KENNETH, ed. *Race and Labour in Twentieth-Century Britain.* Pp. vi, 186. Totowa, NJ: Frank Cass, 1986. $29.50. Paperbound, $14.95.

MacFARLANE, L. J. *The Theory and Practice of Human Rights.* Pp. 193. New York: St. Martin's Press, 1985. $25.00.

MAHARIDGE, DALE. *Journey to Nowhere: The Saga of a New Underclass.* Pp. 192. Garden City, NY: Dial Press, 1985. $24.95.

MATSON, JOHNNY L. and CYNTHIA L. FRAME. *Psychopathology among Mentally Retarded Children and Adolescents.* Pp. 119. Newbury Park, CA: Sage, 1986. Paperbound, no price.

McCLINTOCK, MICHAEL. *State Terror and Popular Resistance in El Salvador.* Pp. xi, 388. London: Zed Press, 1985. Distributed by Biblio Distribution Center, Totowa, NJ. $30.95. Paperbound, $12.95.

MICHNIK, ADAM. *Letters from Prison and Other Essays.* Translated by Maya Latynski. Pp. xiii, 354. Berkeley, CA: University of California Press, 1986. $25.00.

MIDDLEBROOK, KEVIN J. and CARLOS RICO. *The United States and Latin America in the 1980's.* Pp. xii, 648. Pittsburgh, PA: University of Pittsburgh Press, 1986. $34.95. Paperbound, $16.95.

MIKESELL, RAYMOND F. *Stockpiling Strategic Materials: An Evaluation of the National Program.* Pp. ix, 68. Washington, DC: American Enterprise Institute for Public Policy Research, 1986. Paperbound, $4.95.

MIRINGOFF, MARC L. and SANDRA OPDYCKE. *American Social Welfare*

*Policy: Reassessment and Reform.* Pp. xvi, 169. Englewood Cliffs, NJ: Prentice-Hall, 1986. No price.

MORSON, GARY SAUL, ed. *Literature and History: Theoretical Problems and Russian Case Studies.* Pp. xi, 332. Stanford, CA: Stanford University Press, 1986. $37.50.

MOSHER, FREDERICK C. *A Tale of Two Agencies: Comparative Analysis of the General Accounting Office and the Office of Management and Budget.* Pp. xxvi, 219. Baton Rouge: Louisiana State University Press, 1984. Paperbound, $8.95.

NACHT, MICHAEL. *The Age of Vulnerability: Threats to the Nuclear Stalemate.* Pp. xii, 209. Washington, DC: Brookings Institution, 1985. $26.95. Paperbound, $9.95.

NORLUND, IRENE, SVEN CEDER-ROTH, and INGELA GERDIN, eds. *Rice Societies: Asian Problems and Prospects.* Pp. x, 321. Riverdale, MD: Riverdale, 1986. Paperbound, no price.

NOVAK, MICHAEL and MICHAEL P. JACKSON, eds. *Latin America: Dependency or Interdependence?* Pp. x, 186. Washington, DC: American Enterprise Institute for Public Policy Research, 1985. Paperbound, no price.

NOVIK, NIMROD. *Encounter with Reality: Reagan and the Middle East (The First Term).* Pp. 106. Jerusalem: Jerusalem Post; Boulder, CO: Westview Press, 1986. Paperbound, $15.00.

NOVIK, NIMROD. *The United States and Israel: Domestic Determinants of a Changing U.S. Commitment.* Pp. xi, 176. Boulder, CO: Westview Press, 1986. Paperbound, $23.00.

PARK, HAN S. *Human Needs and Political Development: A Dissent to Utopian Solutions.* Pp. viii, 270. Cambridge, MA: Schenkman Books, 1984. Paperbound, no price.

PARPOLA, ASKO and BENT SMIDT HANSEN. *South Asian Religion and Society.* Riverdale, MD: Riverdale, 1986. Paperbound, no price.

PAUL, ELLEN FRANKEL, FRED D. MILLER, Jr., and JEFFREY PAUL, eds. *Human Rights.* Pp. 175. New York: Basil Blackwell, 1984.

PESEK-MAROUS, GEORGIA. *The Bull: A Religious and Secular History of Phallus Worship and Male Homosexuality.* Pp. 185. Rolling Hills, CA: Tau Press, 1984. Paperbound, $9.95.

PETERS, B. GUY. *American Public Policy: Promise and Performance.* 2nd ed. Pp. viii, 344. Chatham, NJ: Chatham House, 1986. Paperbound, $14.95.

PFIFFNER, JAMES P., ed. *The President and Economic Policy.* Pp. xii, 271. Philadelphia: Institute for the Study of Human Issues, 1986. $35.00. Paperbound, $14.95.

PIERRE, ANDREW J., ed. *The Conventional Defense of Europe: New Technologies and New Strategies.* Pp. xii, 185. New York: New York University Press, 1986. No price.

PILAT, JOSEPH, ed. *The Nonproliferation Predicament.* Pp. ix, 137. New Brunswick, NJ: Transaction Books, 1985. $19.95.

POOLE, KEITH T. and L. HARMON ZEIGLER. *Women, Public Opinion, and Politics: The Changing Political Attitudes of American Women.* Pp. xii, 196. New York: Longman, 1985. Paperbound, $12.95

POSNER, MICHAEL, ed. *Problems of International Money, 1972-85.* Pp. ix, 191. Washington, DC: International Monetary Fund, 1986. Paperbound, $8.50.

POTASH, BETTY, ed. *Widows in African Societies: Choices and Constraints.* Pp. xxii, 309. Stanford, CA: Stanford University Press, 1986. $35.00.

PRIDHAM, B. R., ed. *The Arab Gulf and the West.* Pp. xv, 251. New York: St. Martin's Press, 1985. $29.95.

PROVINE, DORIS MARIE. *Judging Credentials: Nonlawyer Judges and the Politics of Professionalism.* Pp. xvii, 248. Chicago: University of Illinois Press, 1986. $30.00. Paperbound, $13.95.

RADZINOWICZ, LEON and ROGER HOOD. *A History of English Criminal*

*Law and Its Administration.* Vol. 5, *The Emergence of Penal Policy.* Pp. xv, 1101. London: Stevens and Sons, 1986. Distributed by Carswell, Agincourt, Ontario. $126.50.

RANGEL, CARLOS. *Third World Ideology and Western Reality: Manufacturing Political Myth.* Pp. xiii, 180. New Brunswick, NJ: Transaction Books, 1986. No price. Paperbound, $19.95.

RAVENHILL, JOHN, ed. *Africa in Economic Crisis.* Pp. xiii, 359. New York: Columbia University Press, 1986. $35.00. Paperbound, $13.00.

REED, ADOLPH L. *The Jesse Jackson Phenomenon.* Pp. xii, 170. New Haven, CT: Yale University Press, 1986. Paperbound, no price.

REES, ALBERT. *Striking a Balance: Making National Economic Policy.* Pp. x, 118. Chicago: University of Chicago Press, 1986. Paperbound, $6.95.

REID, CHRISTOPHER. *Edmund Burke and the Practice of Political Writing.* Pp. xiii, 238. New York: St. Martin's Press, 1985. No price.

REYNOLDS, LLOYD G. *Economic Growth in the Third World: An Introduction.* Pp. viii, 149. New Haven, CT: Yale University Press, 1986. $24.00. Paperbound, $7.95.

RIKER, WILLIAM H. *The Art of Political Manipulation.* Pp. xiii, 152. New Haven, CT: Yale University Press, 1986. $18.50. Paperbound, $6.95.

ROBERTSON, CLAIRE and IRIS BERGER, eds. *Women and Class in Africa.* Pp. ix, 310. New York: Africana, 1986. $55.00.

ROMULO, CARLOS, P. *Forty Years: A Third World Soldier at the UN.* Pp. xix, 220. Westport, CT: Greenwood Press, 1986. $29.95.

SAUVANT, KARL P. *International Transactions in Services: The Politics of Transborder Data Flows.* Pp. xxiii, 372. Boulder, CO: Westview Press, 1986. Paperbound, $38.50.

SCHUCK, PETER H. and RODGERS M. SMITH. *Citizenship without Consent: Illegal Aliens in the American Polity.* Pp.

viii, 173. New Haven, CT: Yale University Press, 1985. $22.50. Paperbound, $6.95.

SCHULTZE, CHARLES L. *Other Times, Other Places: Macroeconomic Lessons from U.S. and European History.* Pp. xiii, 88. Washington, DC: Brookings Institution, 1986. $15.95. Paperbound, $7.95.

SHAIKEN, HARLEY. *Work Transformed: Automation and Labor in the Computer Age.* Pp. xiv, 306. Lexington, MA: D. C. Heath, Lexington Books, 1986. Paperbound, $10.95.

SHKLAR, JUDITH N. *Legalism: Law, Morals, and Political Trials.* Pp. xvi, 246. Cambridge, MA: Harvard University Press, 1986. Paperbound, $7.95.

SIMMS, MARGARET and JULIANNE M. MALVEAUX, eds. *Slipping through the Cracks: The Status of Black Women.* Pp. 302. New Brunswick, NJ: Transaction Books, 1986. Paperbound, $12.95.

SINGH, INDERJIT, LYN SQUIRE, and JOHN STRAUSS, eds. *Agricultural Household Models: Extensions, Applications, and Policy.* Pp. xi, 335. Baltimore, MD: Johns Hopkins University Press, 1986. No Price.

SKULLY, MICHAEL T. *ASEAN Financial Cooperation: Developments in Banking, Finance and Insurance.* Pp. xiii, 269. New York: St. Martin's Press, 1985. $29.95.

SMITH, LESLEY M. *The Making of Britain: The Age of Expansion.* Pp. xi, 194. New York: St. Martin's Press, 1986. $27.50.

SPIVEY, DONALD. *The Politics of Miseducation: The Booker Washington Institute of Liberia, 1929-1984.* Pp. xi, 177. Lexington: University Press of Kentucky, 1986. $18.00.

TAYLOR, TREVOR. *European Defence Cooperation.* Pp. viii, 97. Boston, MA: Routledge & Kegan Paul. Paperbound, $10.00.

TETREAULT, MARY ANN and CHARLES FREDERICK ABEL, eds. *Dependency Theory and the Return of High Politics.* Pp. xii, 270. Westport, CT: Greenwood Press, 1986. $39.95.

THERBORN, GÖRAN. *Why Some People*

*Are More Unemployed than Others: The Strange Paradox of Growth and Unemployment.* Pp. 181. London: Verso, 1986. Distributed by Schocken Books, New York. $24.95. Paperbound, $8.95.

THIRD WORLD FOUNDATION FOR SOCIAL AND ECONOMIC STUDIES. *Third World Affairs, 1986.* Pp. xxv, 476. Boulder, CO: Westview Press, 1986. Paperbound, $35.00.

TRAINER, F. E. *Abandon Affluence and Growth: Ecology and Capitalism in the World Today.* Pp. xii, 308. London: Zed Books, 1985. Distributed by Biblio Distribution Centre, Totowa, NJ. $30.95. Paperbound, $12.25.

TUCKER, D.F.B. *Law, Liberalism and Free Speech.* Pp. ix, 212, Totowa, NJ: Rowman and Littlefield, 1986. $32.50. Paperbound, $13.50.

TULLIS, F. LAMOND and W. LADD HOLLIST, eds. Pp. xxiii, 351. Lincoln: University of Nebraska Press, 1986. $29.95.

VELIKOV, YEVGENI, ed. *The Night After ...: Climatic and Biological Consequences of a Nuclear War.* Translated by Anatoli Rosenweig and Yuri Taube. Pp. xviii, 165. Moscow: Mir, 1986. Distributed by Imported Publications, Chicago. $8.95.

VINCENT, ANDREW and RAYMOND PLANT. *Philosophy, Politics and Citizenship: The Life and Thought of the British Idealists.* Pp. x, 222. New York: Basil Blackwell, 1984. $34.95.

WATTENBERG, MARTIN P. *The Decline of American Political Parties, 1952-1984.* Pp. xxi, 199. Cambridge, MA: Harvard University Press, 1986. $15.00. Paperbound, $7.95.

WEBER, EUGEN. *France: Fin de Siecle.* Pp. x, 294. Cambridge, MA: Harvard University Press, Belknap Press, 1986. $20.00.

# INDEX

# NEW from Sage

## DESIGNING GAMES AND SIMULATIONS
### An Illustrated Handbook
#### by CATHY STEIN GREENBLAT, *Rutgers University*.

At last! The first comprehensive, systematic, illustrated guide for both novice and experienced readers who wish to design games and simulations for use in teaching, training, policy-making and research. Greenblat covers both the sheer intellectual challenge of model development and the how-to basics that help you translate your model into a game format. Teachers, trainer, consultants—whether experienced developers of games and simulations or novices with an idea that needs to be translated into a workable reality—will find this practical, well-written handbook contains a wealth of experience, detail, and useful guidance.

**1987 (Autumn) / 160 pages (tent.) / 8½" x 11" format / 92 figures / $29.95 (c)**

## ACADEMIC MICROCOMPUTING
### A Resource Guide
#### by G. DAVID GARSON, *North Carolina State University*

As microcomputers increase in number, so does their applicability across many disciplines. Available for the first time is a lucid resource guide that integrates microcomputing into the university curricula. Practical and easy-to-use, **Academic Microcomputing** combines the how-to expertise and detailed references needed for the educator eager to keep up with this advancing technology.

**1986 / 176 pages / $29.95 (c) / $19.95 (p)**

## NEW TOOLS FOR SOCIAL SCIENTISTS
### Advances and Applications in Research Methods
#### edited by WILLIAM D. BERRY, *University of Kentucky*
#### & MICHAEL S. LEWIS-BECK, *University of Iowa*

The most important recent advances in quantitative social science methodology are reviewed in this volume. Composed of articles by distinguished scholars, the book is outstanding for its broad coverage of techniques applicable to numerous topics as well as its emphasis on method and application. Broad in scope and particularly attentive to application, **New Tools for Social Scientists** is an ideal companion to the core textbook of a quantitative methods course in sociology, political science, and psychology. Indeed, the book is an excellent investment for any social scientist eager to understand the latest developments in research methods.

**1986 / 288 pages / $35.00 (c) / $16.95 (p)**

**SAGE PUBLICATIONS, INC.**
2111 West Hillcrest Drive,
Newbury Park, California 91320

**SAGE PUBLICATIONS, INC.**
275 South Beverly Drive,
Beverly Hills, California 90212

**SAGE PUBLICATIONS LTD**
28 Banner Street,
London EC1Y 8QE, England

**SAGE PUBLICATIONS INDIA PVT LTD**
M-32 Market, Greater Kailash I,
New Delhi 110 048 India

# OF SPECIAL INTEREST ▬▬▬▬▬

## STATE AND MARKET
### The Politics of
### the Public and the Private
**edited by JAN-ERIK LANE,** *University of Umea*

The classic dilemma of the mixed economy is to strike a balance
between the public and private sectors. This book is an exploration of
the dilemma as it exists in the 1980s, and the policies available to
influence the balance. The volume poses the problem in terms of how
to optimize welfare by the use of the allocative mechanisms of public
policy and private markets.

While identifying decision criteria for the demarcation of public and
private sectors, **State and Market** sheds new light on the ways in
which the two sectors interact. The boundaries that have been drawn
between state and market receive a reassessment in the light of phenomena such as structured markets, competitive bureaucracies, and
underground economies.

An important contribution of the book is a discussion of the decision
criteria for determining the size and efficiency of the public sector.
Theories advanced to explain public sector growth are set forth and
the significance of cultural variables is explained.

The book makes a valuable contribution to the important area of
public policy and the mixed economy.

CONTENTS: **I. The Nature of the Public Sector** // Introduction: Public
Policy or Markets? The Demarcation Problem J-E. LANE / 1. Improvement of
Public Provision of Goods and Services H.J.G.A. van MIERLO / 2. A Model of a
Non-Budget-Maximizing Bureau E. JONSSON / 3. Economic Relations
Between City and Suburban Governments R.J. SORENSEN // **II. Public &
Private Interaction** // 4. Getting by in Three Economies: The Resources of the
Official, Unofficial, and Domestic Economies R. ROSE / 5. Government Inter-
vention into Local Economies Under Market Conditions: The Case of Urban
Renewal O.P. WILLIAMS / 6. Corporatism and the Public-Private Distinction
W. GRANT / 7. Taming the Housing Market M. KONUKIEWITZ // **III. The
Logic of Public Decision Making** // 8. From Order to Chaos: Recent Trends in
the Study of Public Administration L. LUNDQUIST / 9. The Logic of Public
Sector Growth A. WILDAVSKY / 10. The Post-Industrial City in Transition
from Private to Public T.R. GURR & D.S. KING / Indexes

**Sage Modern Politics Series Sponsored by the European Consortium for
Political Research/ECPR, Volume 9**
**1985 (July) / 305 pages / $40.00 (c) / $16.00 (p)**

**SAGE PUBLICATIONS, INC.**
2111 West Hillcrest Drive
Newbury Park, California 91320

**SAGE PUBLICATIONS, INC.**
275 South Beverly Drive
Beverly Hills, California 90212

**SAGE PUBLICATIONS LTD**
28 Banner Street
London EC1Y 8QE, England

**SAGE PUBLICATIONS INDIA PVT LTD**
M-32 Market, Greater Kailash I
New Delhi 110 048 India

Rhetoric of the Human Sciences
## Politics and Ambiguity
*William E. Connolly*
$25.00, cloth

Rhetoric of the Human Sciences
## Machiavelli and the History of Prudence
*Eugene Garver*
$28.50, cloth

## Democracy and Punishment
**Disciplinary Origins
of the United States**
*Thomas L. Dumm*
$40.00, cloth; $15.75, paper

## Political Education in the Southern
## Farmers' Alliance, 1887–1900
*Theodore Mitchell*
$39.50, cloth; $16.50, paper

## The Organizational State
**Social Choice in National Policy Domains**
*Edward O. Laumann and David Knoke*
$45.00, cloth; $19.95, paper

## Political Parties in the
## American Mold
*Leon D. Epstein*
$27.50, cloth

University of Wisconsin Press
114 N. Murray St., Madison, WI 53715